Bill Lambert

Bill Lambert
World War I Flying Ace

Samuel J. Wilson

McFarland & Company, Inc., Publishers
Jefferson, North Carolina

All photographs courtesy Bill Martin unless noted otherwise.

LIBRARY OF CONGRESS CATALOGUING-IN-PUBLICATION DATA

Names: Wilson, Samuel J., 1956– author.
Title: Bill Lambert : World War I flying ace / Samuel J. Wilson.
Description: Jefferson, North Carolina : McFarland & Company, Inc., Publishers, 2016. | Includes bibliographical references and index.
Identifiers: LCCN 2016031931 | ISBN 9781476664675 (softcover : acid free paper) ∞
Subjects: LCSH: Lambert, Bill, 1894–1982. | Fighter pilots—United States—Biography. | World War, 1914–1918—Aerial operations, British. | Great Britain. Royal Air Force. Squadron, 24. | Ironton (Ohio)—Biography.
Classification: LCC D602.L28 W55 2016 | DDC 940.4/4941092 [B]—dc23
LC record available at https://lccn.loc.gov/2016031931

ISBN (print) 978-1-4766-6467-5
ISBN (ebook) 978-1-4766-2612-3

BRITISH LIBRARY CATALOGUING DATA ARE AVAILABLE

© 2016 Samuel J. Wilson. All rights reserved

No part of this book may be reproduced or transmitted in any form or by any means, electronic or mechanical, including photocopying or recording, or by any information storage and retrieval system, without permission in writing from the publisher.

Front cover: Cadet William C. Lambert in original R.F.C. uniform 1917; photograph of British Distinguished Flying Cross medal © 2016 GBlakeley / iStock

Printed in the United States of America

*McFarland & Company, Inc., Publishers
Box 611, Jefferson, North Carolina 28640
www.mcfarlandpub.com*

To Jim Doubleday,
scholar, colleague, and friend

Table of Contents

Acknowledgments	viii
Preface	1
Introduction	3
One—The Birth of Aviation and the Road to War	9
Two—From Ironton to Canada	15
Three—Training	22
Four—Entering the Air War	30
Five—Spring 1918	41
Six—Summer: June 1918	58
Seven—Moving into Autumn: July 1918	83
Eight—Leave and Return	100
Nine—Return to the War	112
Ten—Leaving the War	139
Eleven—Barnstorming Days	145
Twelve—Life Between the Wars	156
Thirteen—Lambert in World War II and Afterward	164
Fourteen—Lambert and Friends: The Book Gets Published	176
Fifteen—Lambert as Artist	192
Sixteen—The Lambert They Knew	200
Seventeen—The Rediscovered Ace	207
Eighteen—The Final Years	216
Epilogue	222
Appendix: The Numbers Game	225
Chapter Notes	231
Bibliography	250
Index	259

Acknowledgments

I received the call to adventure to write this book during a conversation I had years ago with Richard Baumgartner. Rich's publishing company had recently published *Fritz: World War I Memoir of a German Lieutenant,* which I wanted to use in one of my college courses. During our conversation he told me about an obscure World War I pilot from Ironton, Ohio, by the name of Bill Lambert. Lambert's was an intriguing experience, but I initially refused the call until I met Lambert's friend Bill Martin in Ashland, Kentucky. Our meeting convinced me to accept the challenge and embark on the journey to write Lambert's biography. It was then that I agreed to cross the threshold and commit to leaving the ordinary world behind to follow Lambert's exploits in the skies over France in 1918.

However, on this journey I met only mentors and allies who quickly became friends. At the top of the list is my lovely wife Amy, who, along with my son James, traveled with me to various libraries and museums in my quest to find information on Lambert. It even included stopping at the home of a Great War enthusiast who flew a replica S.E.5a while we were traveling to visit our daughter Rose Mary. It was my intent to dedicate this book to Amy, but she insisted that it be dedicated to my colleague and dear friend Jim Doubleday. Who was I to argue? Jim played the role of mentor on this journey. He read and edited several manuscripts while giving sound advice from his home in Colorado. For Jim and his wife Sandie, Old Norse mythology and medieval literature took a temporary backseat to dogfights over the Western Front. I cannot thank him enough!

One of Jim's regrets was not ever meeting Bill Martin. That regret is easy to understand, because it is difficult to find a nicer gentleman than Bill Martin. He and his wife Phyllis have become dear friends as we met over the years to discuss their relationship with Lambert. It was Bill's association with Lambert and his foresight in saving Lambert's letters and documents that made this book possible. I am forever in his debt.

Bill was instrumental in putting me in touch with several people who knew Lambert. These include Klaus Staerker, Dick Uppstrom, and the Reverend William Thorpe. They are a few of the many individuals I interviewed over the years. I am indebted to Joe Unger, Rich Baumgartner, Doris Robinson, Bettie Frey and her daughters Stacey and Dana, Professor Emeritus Robin Highman from Kansas State University, Rita Baker, Paul Morton, Janenne Bruce, Kaye Welch, Elizabeth Wilson, Vivian White, and Robert Wiseman. They took time out of their busy schedules to tell me about their experiences with Lambert, or in the case of Paul Morton, barnstorming in the 1930s and flying the China/Burma/India Theatre in World War II. Sadly, some of these individuals have since passed away; however, I am grateful for having met them, and heartily sorry that they never got the chance to see how they helped to give Lambert's biography a more personal touch.

A special thanks goes to Josh Morrison, General Manager of the *Ironton Tribune,* WSAZ Television in West Virginia, Dawne Dewey and the staff at the Special Collections and Archives at Wright State University in Dayton, Ohio, Director Joe Jenkins and Marta Ramey of the Briggs Lawrence County Public Library in Ironton, the National Archives, Kew, the U.S. National Archives and Records Administration, the Directorate of History and Heritage, National Defence Headquarters, Ottawa, and the helpful and dedicated staff at the Research Division at the National Museum of the U.S. Air Force in Dayton, Ohio.

I wish to thank the University of Rio Grande for granting me a sabbatical to work on this book, and my colleagues Dr. Jacob White in Chemistry and Professor Jim Allen in Fine Arts for graciously allowing me the benefit of their expertise. I also want to thank Linda Haney of Chesapeake, Ohio, for doing independent research for me.

Preface

On 21 April 1918, a British communiqué announced that German Ace Manfred von Richthofen had been "shot down and killed" by Captain A. R. Brown, No. 209 Squadron. If one had continued to read the communiqué, he would have noticed that Captain George O. Johnson and Lieutenant William C. Lambert, of No. 24 Squadron, had successfully destroyed a "hostile Balloon." The historical importance of the first item of this communiqué is not questioned; the second item was forgotten.

From late March to mid–August 1918, William C. Lambert from Ironton, Ohio, flew as a fighter pilot for the Royal Air Force in World War I. Unbeknownst to anyone, when he was forced to hospital as a consequence of shell shock and burst eardrums, his twenty-two victories were the largest total among any American pilot in the war. By the Armistice, Lambert's total would be surpassed by Eddie Rickenbacker, the former race car driver from Columbus, Ohio, with twenty-six victories. These Ohio natives were the two greatest American aces of the war; however, Lambert was unwilling to take advantage of his war record to achieve the public acclaim that Rickenbacker enjoyed in his lifetime. It would not be until he was seventy-three years old that he would allow himself to be noticed for his exploits. His life was rejuvenated in the late 1960s until his death in 1982 by interest in the Great War from a new generation of aviation enthusiasts. For the remaining years of his life he was interviewed by newspapers and magazines for documentaries about his war experiences.

A surprising number of Americans went to Canada and joined the British flying services in the Great War. Several of them, like Lambert, went on to have distinguished records. Unfortunately, for the most part, their biographies have never been written. Consequently, this book comes at a propitious time when interest in the Great War has been rekindled with the centennial observations and war remembrances that began in 2014.

World War I aviation biographies tend to focus on the wartime exploits of pilots who achieved a level of fame. Alex Revell's *Brief Glory: The Life of Arthur Rhys Davids, DSO, MC and Bar*, Colin Pengelly's *Albert Ball V.C.: The Fighter Pilot Hero of World War I*, and Blaine Pardoe's *Terror of the Autumn Skies: The True Story of Frank Luke, America's Rogue Ace of World War I* are examples of this genre. Peter Kilduff's *Herman Göring Fighter Ace: The World War I Career of Germany's Most Infamous Airman* focuses exclusively on Göring's role in the Great War and his quest for glory. Still other books, like Norman Franks' *Fokker Dr I Aces of World War I*, have been written for an eclectic audience interested in aerial combat and World War I aircraft. Lambert's biography is a scholarly examination of the entire life of a distinct individual who took part in a war that destroyed individuality and served to define him for the rest of his life. It helps to explain how war can define an individual's existence. Unlike Rhys Davids, Ball, and Luke, Lambert survived the war and lived well into his eighties.

Lambert wrote two books, *Combat Report,* which describe his time in the R.A.F., and *Barnstorming and Girls,* which is a vivid memoir describing his life and sexual conquests as he barnstormed the Midwest and South in 1919. Both were written when he was well into his seventies. In the early years of flight, pilots were treated in a manner comparable to celebrities today. Lambert was used to getting attention from the opposite sex and special and immediate attention among the public. His experiences helped to shape his views of women, whom he believed were put on this earth for only one purpose. The latter book outraged many citizens and hurt his reputation.

Thanks to Bill Martin, a friend to Lambert in his later years, much of Lambert's personal correspondence was saved and given to the author. Some has already been donated to the Special Collections and Archives at Wright State University, which already possessed an extensive collection on Lambert. The remainder of Lambert's documentation has already been promised to the U.S. Air Force Museum in Dayton. Included in this collection are his personal letters and telegrams, photographs, articles, draft designs and patents, government documents, magazines, his log book, letters from pilots, and scores of letters from lawyers, admirers, and publishers, as well as video interviews. These sources, and personal interviews conducted over the past twelve years, help to capture the essence of the man and his lifetime.

In addition, documents on Lambert's time in the R.A.F. were supplied the National Archives, Kew, and the Directorate of History and Heritage, National Defence Headquarters, Ottawa. What records that exist from his time in the U.S. Air Force Reserve were supplied by the U.S. National Archives and Records. Files on Lambert, including extensive newspaper articles and his Will, were obtained from the Briggs Lawrence County Public Library, and the Lawrence County Museum in Ironton.

Finally, the author is indebted to Dana and Stacey Frey for allowing him to examine the personal papers and photographs of their father Royal Frey, who was Chief of the Research Division at the U.S. Air Force Museum and played an important role in Lambert's life.

Introduction

Michael Korda, in his book *Hero: The Life and Legend of Lawrence of Arabia*, describes how the concept of a hero has changed since the First World War. T.E. Lawrence was a hero in the classical sense of the word. He was a modern-day Achilles, Ajax, or Ulysses. The concept, however, has been "cheapened by the modern habit of calling everybody exposed to any kind of danger, whether voluntarily or not, 'hero.'"[1] William C. Lambert, World War I ace from Ironton, Ohio, and Distinguished Flying Cross recipient, was not Lawrence, and he did not consider himself a hero. He was someone who wanted to learn how to fly, and the Great War gave him the opportunity. Little did he know that his brief stint in the war would help to define and shape him for the rest of his life. It would help to define the essence of his existence.

When trying to qualify Lambert as a pilot, there is always the inevitable comparison with the greatest pilots of the war. It is sort of like comparing the achievements of a current sports star with the legends of the game. It is inevitable and expected. It helps to spark interest and debates. A player like Albert Pujols or Miguel Cabrera in baseball will see his career and achievements as a power hitter measured against Babe Ruth, Jimmy Foxx, and Hank Aaron. When a player begins a hitting streak that attracts the attention of the syndicated sports reporter, the name of Joe DiMaggio and his famous 56-game hitting streak will be mentioned at some point. After all, it is the yard stick by which all hitting streaks must be measured. The greatness of DiMaggio's feat can be fully comprehended when a player hits in 28 straight games, and we recognize that at that point, however, he is only halfway to DiMaggio's record. In today's sports world, 28-game hitting streaks are rare. So are American aces with over twenty victories in the First World War; however, Lambert's twenty-two victories placed him second to Eddie Rickenbacker as the American "ace of aces" in World War I. Rickenbacker became a celebrity; Lambert, who fought for the R.A.F., was almost forgotten.

World War I aces face similar scrutiny to athletes. Victories are their record. They would appear as statistics on their bubble gum cards if such things existed. In fact, after Manfred von Richthofen's fifty-second victory, the Sanke souvenir postcard firm in Germany eagerly printed thousands of copies of his photo to meet the demands of adoring fans. Their previous postcard of Richthofen had risen in popularity as his victories continued to climb.[2] Another had to be issued to meet the demand among a hero-worshiping public. Richthofen's response was that he was "only a combat pilot, but [German ace and Richthofen mentor Oswald] Boelcke ... was a hero."[3] Lambert's twenty-two victories are slightly more than a quarter of Richthofen's total of eighty. Still, Lambert's accomplishment is impressive. After all, his time in the war was quite short. There was simply never an adoring public around to shower Lambert with such accolades. In the end, he never thought much of his achievements because the British frowned upon boasting, and he believed his success paled when compared to the accomplishments of such British pilots as Edward Mannock, Billy Bishop, and Raymond Collishaw. Lambert was like the .300 hitter who realizes that there were others who hit higher and played the game better than he had. He was not a hero, just a participant in a most dangerous game.

Lambert was one of the many, the sailors, the cooks, the "who else's" of the world that Bertolt Brecht described in his poem "Questions from a Worker Who Reads." He is like last year's Super Bowl loser who is forgotten amidst the winner's celebration. Six months later, fans only remember the team that took home the trophy. All the successes achieved by the loser in reaching the game are simply forgotten like yesterday's news. Shakespeare would never have made Lambert the centerpiece of any drama. He is like Horatio, friend and companion to the hero, but not the hero himself. Outside of the Ironton area, only aviation historians are aware of Lambert's existence.

Warfare in the First World War dehumanized its participants as never before in combat. The Tomb of the Unknown Soldier was established with this war. The soldiers who made up the rank and file, who executed the failed offensive maneuvers of their commanders, were simply members of the unknown multitude, designated only by their unit and function. Lambert fought in No. 24 Squadron C Flight. Trench warfare, however, would not only change the face of the hero, but accelerate the development of the air war. For some, air flight was even equated with spiritual powers.[4] As the Western Front digressed into a war of attrition, the lack of movement forced the armies to search for alternatives to break the stalemate. The war in the air became a new front to be developed and exploited. It also gave the world new heroes.

The war also taxed its leadership. Heroes would be hard to find. It should not be surprising that the hero moniker was still awarded to conquerors, field marshals, and generals, or that some history books would attempt to romanticize their accomplishments and forgive their shortcomings. Before the First World War, five generals, George Washington, Andrew Jackson, William Henry Harrison, Zachary Taylor, and Ulysses S. Grant, became President of the United States. Afterward, only Dwight D. Eisenhower, the Supreme Commander of the Allied Expeditionary Force in World War II, would be elected to that position. No other major commander, including John J. "Black Jack" Pershing, who was promoted to the highest rank possible, General of the Armies of the United States, in 1919, would serve in the Oval Office. Heroes among the generals would be more difficult to find. It was simply the nature of the war that resulted in the wanton slaughter of millions of human beings.

Lambert, both as individual and pilot, symbolically represented the new face of war in the 20th century. He was modern, mechanical, and technocratic. He applied the principles of the material sciences and physics to his planes and his approach to the air war. In this regard, he differed from Richthofen. As a young boy in Ironton, Lambert had dreamt of flying when planes were in their infancy. He lived in a town known for its iron production where his father and uncle owned a machine shop. He was raised around guns and machines. Richthofen's reaction to the sight of airplanes flying over the Western Front in 1914 was that he "hadn't the slightest idea what our flyers did…. I considered every flyer an enormous fraud."[5] Erwin Böhme, a German ace with twenty-four victories, wrote, "Hunting is

Richthofen's whole passion and for him the ultimate.... As for flying itself, I believe he does not care very much for it. Most likely, he has never made a loop out of the sheer joy of sport, only for his own pleasure, and above all he has strictly forbidden his *Staffel* to do any 'acrobatic tricks,' as he calls them."[6] In fact, the *Jagdstaffel*, developed by Oswald Boelcke and the German equivalent of the British squadron, literally means "hunting section."[7] Richthofen, the former cavalry officer, had exchanged his horse for a plane. He was still interested only in the hunt. He wrote that he favored leading his *Staffel* "like hunting on horseback across a field."[8] He kept trophies from his air victories as he did from his hunts in the Silesian forests. In July 1916, during the German Offensive on the Eastern Front, Richthofen wrote in his memoirs how disappointed he was that he did not add "a single Russian" to his collection.[9] During the initial stages of the Michael Spring Offensive of the Germans in 1918, Richthofen was disappointed that the army moved too fast to enable him to retrieve souvenirs from his victories. He especially enjoyed displaying the strip of fabric that contained the serial number from the planes he shot down.[10] Richthofen may have been the war's ace of aces, but he was at heart a 19th century aristocrat fighting in a 20th century war with modern weapons. He had equestrian and athletic abilities. The anomaly was not unusual. It was an issue of continuity and change. Prewar pictures exists, along with early versions of cinematic newsreels, that show members of the German General Staff wearing decorative uniforms that resembled something out of the medieval age, but riding in modern automobiles. Lambert, however, was not encumbered by tradition; he worked in modern industry and wanted to master its inventions.

The technological innovation continued in the 20th century and was aided by the necessities inherent in military conflict. The individual in the air, however, continued to be the focus of attention. The early aces were more significant in the public eyes than the machines they flew. Aces were far more notable in this war than in the conflicts to follow. It may have been a result of the nature of a hero worshiping society or a fascination with the early aircrafts they flew. In the same way that Nelson is associated with Trafalgar more than his ship *Victory* or any other ship of the fleet, the aces of the Great War were more known for their victories than the planes they flew.[11] Their planes, however, also helped to define them. Richthofen was popularly associated with his red Fokker triplane, and Lambert spent his life telling anyone who cared to listen the advantages of an S.E.5a over a Sopwith Camel. It was the technological advances in the air war that allowed these individuals to achieve their fame. The Great War also saw the tank emerge as a modern weapon; however, those who drove these machines never achieved the acclaim or the celebrity status of the pilot.

Today Lambert is one of the least known figures in aviation to come out of the state of Ohio, a state that takes great pride in its citizens' contribution to the development of modern aviation. In fact, the most visible state license plate proclaims Ohio to be the "Birthplace of Aviation," and even features a replica of the Wright airplane. It is impressive how many individuals from Ohio have played major roles in the development of modern aviation. The list includes some of aviation's great inventors, innovators, pioneers, and aviators of the 19th and 20th centuries. The National Museum of the United States Air Force includes in its Ohio Aviation Heritage teacher's resource guide the Wright Brothers from Dayton, Frank P. Lahm from Mansfield, Eddie Rickenbacker from Columbus, Don Gentile from Piqua, Curtiss LeMay from Columbus, John Glenn of Cambridge, William Pitsenbarger from Piqua, and Neil Armstrong of Wapakoneta. The contributions and accomplishments of most of those are well-documented and celebrated, particularly in their home state. Others, however, are relatively unknown. Only those individuals with a keen interest in the history of aerial warfare might have heard of the two men from Piqua: Pitsenbarger and Gentile. Airman William Pitsenbarger, a rescue and survival specialist on a U.S. Air Force HH-43 Huskie helicopter, was awarded the Medal of Honor for his actions outside of Saigon on 11 July 1966. He was killed in action.[12] Twenty-five years earlier, Don Gentile was rejected for the American Army Air Corps even though he had 300 hours of flying time, because he lacked the two years of college required by the service. Consequently, he enlisted in the Royal Air Force, and by the time Pearl Harbor was attacked in December 1941, he was already a Pilot Officer and would eventually fly the Supermarine Spitfire for No. 133 Eagle Squadron in the European theater in World War II. In September 1942, three Eagle squadrons were transferred to the American Air Force. Gentile went with them and eventually flew P-47 Thunderbolts and then P-51 Mustangs. By April 1944, he was the leading American ace of the war and was eventually credited with 21.88 victories.[13] However, even with this impressive showing, his total still placed him behind Bill Lambert. Like Lambert, these two individuals from Ohio are largely forgotten.

Lambert, like Gentile, wanted to fly, and war offered him the opportunity. He would be one of approximately 300 Americans to join the Royal Flying Corps, the Royal Naval Air Service, or their successor, the Royal Air Force, during the war. A surprising number of Americans went to Canada and joined the British flying services in the Great War. Several of them, like Lambert, went on to have distinguished records. Unfortunately, for the most part, their life stories have never been told. Lambert would serve as a fighter pilot for a brief four months on the Western Front from late March to mid–August 1918. Unbeknownst to anyone at the time, when he was forced to hospital as a consequence of shell shock and burst eardrums, his twenty-two victories were the largest total among any American pilot in the war. The British, however, frowned upon pilots keeping tallies of their victories. More importantly, Lambert, who fought for the British, compared himself with the great British aces, and there were fifty-two who had had more victories. He would never have had the effrontery to compare himself with, for example, Collishaw, Bishop, and Mannock.

By the Armistice, Lambert's total would be surpassed by Eddie Rickenbacker, the former race car driver from Columbus, Ohio, with twenty-six. These Ohio natives were the two greatest American aces of the war; however, Lambert was unwilling to take advantage of his war record to achieve the public acclaim that Rickenbacker, and later Charles Lindbergh and other pilots, would enjoy in their lifetimes. While Rickenbacker went on to start his own motor car company and later purchased Eastern Airlines from General Motors, Lambert lived in relative obscurity in Ironton. Although he lived in the past, it would not be until he was 73 years old that Lambert would allow himself to be noticed for his exploits. His desire for privacy was another reason he was able to escape the public's attention until late in life.

There was, however, another reason that prevented Lambert from capitalizing on his war record: his caustic personality. He was independent, determined, and self-centered for the rest of his life. When interviewed about Lambert, his friend Klaus Staerker stated, "To put it straightforward, he was an O.C.D., stubborn, selfish, son-of-a-bitch." Klaus felt the image of the Great War pilot did not match Lambert's persona. He was "almost antisocial. He would have been more famous had he been social." Sraerker saw Lambert as living in the past. "He adjusted and survived … [but he] would not change." Staerker believed it was a lesson he had learned from the war.[14] How much of Lambert's behavior was a result of his experiences on the Western Front is a matter of conjecture, but the war continued to be the most central part of his existence.

Lambert wrote two books, *Combat Report,* which describe his time in the R.A.F., and *Barnstorming and Girls,* which is a vivid memoir describing his life and sexual conquests as he barnstormed the Midwest and South in 1919. Both were written when he was well into his seventies. In the early years of flight, pilots were treated in a manner comparable to celebrities today. Lambert was used to getting attention from the opposite sex and special and immediate attention among the public during his brief period in the war and while he barnstormed. His experiences helped to shape his views of women, whom he believed were put on this earth for only one purpose. The latter book outraged many and hurt his reputation.

After barnstorming, Lambert returned to Ironton to live and fell into anonymity, but his accomplishments were still impressive. He sold cars while at the same time designing and receiving a patent for a new metal wing for planes, which unfortunately became obsolete even before it was finished. He opened an appliance store during the Depression and continued to design devices and take out patents for inventions. In the late 1930s and early 1940s, as a result of the economic effects of the day and possibly going through a mid-life crisis, he attempted to reenlist, this time in the Royal Canadian Air Force, and used his connections in hopes of getting a Captain's commission as a pilot in the U.S. Marines. He was fortunate enough to get a job as an Industrial Designer for a local operation in Ironton just before the attack on Pearl Harbor. Afterward, he was able to enlist in the U.S. Army Air Corps and became an Engineering Officer. He served on the East Coast at Grenier Field in New Hampshire, then Holton, Maine, and later Presque Isle, Maine. He joined the U.S. Air Force Reserve after the war, retiring at the rank of Lieutenant Colonel in 1954. His life was rejuvenated from the late 1960s until his death in 1982 by interest in the Great War from a new generation of aviation enthusiasts. For the remaining fourteen years of his life, he was interviewed by newspapers and magazines for documentaries about his war experiences. He became a valuable source on planes, pilots, strategy and tactics of the air war. He was a person in demand.

This book is a detailed biography of a World War I pilot who "lived at the edge of greatness, but could never get there."[15] It helps to explain how war can define an individual's existence. But it will also be discovered that there is more to Bill Lambert's experience than four months on the Western Front. This book is an examination of the entire life of a distinct individual who took part in a war that destroyed individuality but served to define him for the rest of his life. Lambert is seen not only an individual, but also as a representative figure showing what war—especially the war from a pilot's perspective—can do to a person's life thereafter. His biography worth sharing and worth remembering.

ONE

The Birth of Aviation and the Road to War

We tend to forget how new and exciting aviation would be to someone in Bill Lambert's generation. The invention of the airplane was a 20th century one, and an Ohio one; it was the work of Wilbur and Orville Wright of Dayton. Dayton was full of inventors; by 1900 the residents of Dayton had filed, per capita, more patents than those in any other city in the country.[1] But the invention of the airplane was by long odds the most important one to come out of the city.

Wilbur and Orville Wright owned the Wright Cycle Company. The brothers had moved their shop six times and even changed its name as their business continued to grow and prosper. The Wright brothers, however, were not content simply to be prosperous businessmen. They had a great deal of the inventive spirit of their community, and they were particularly interested in designing a flying machine capable of carrying human beings. They would gradually make the transition to building airplanes, particularly after they learned of the unfortunate death of the aviation pioneer Otto Lilienthal in a glider accident in 1896.

On 30 May 1899, Wilbur wrote to the Smithsonian Institution in Washington and stated that he believed "simple flight ... is possible to man and that the experiments and investigations ... will result in the accumulation of information and knowledge and skill which will finally lead to accomplished flight."[2] Wilbur informed the Institute that he had access to a few books and various magazine and cyclopaedic articles, and that he was requesting that they send him a list of English language works on the subject. He wanted to avail himself of "all that is already known and then if possible add my mite to help on the future workers who will attain success."[3] He also assured the Smithsonian that his request was legitimate—that he was not some quack.

Wilbur had written the Smithsonian because the year before, 1898, the Secretary of the Smithsonian, Samuel Pierpont Langley, had received a $50,000 grant (a fortune in those days) from the U.S. Army Board of Ordnance and Fortifications for the construction of a flying machine. Richard Rathbun, assistant to Langley, replied to Wilbur.[4] To his credit, he treated Wilbur's request with respect. Rathbun suggested some additional books, as well as including some pamphlets and reprints of articles that where originally published in the *Smithsonian Annual Report*. The list included virtually every significant text then existing on flight,[5] especially Octave Chanute's *Progress in Flying Machines*; James Means' three *Aeronautical Annuals* for 1895, 1896, and 1897; Langley's *Story of Experiments in Mechanical Flight and Experiments in Aerodynamics*; E. C. Huffaker's *On Soaring Flight*; Louis-Pierre Mouillard's *Empire of the Air*; and Lilienthal's *The Problem of Flying* and *Practical Experiments in Soaring*. Armed with these texts, the Wrights could now attack the problem of manned flight with confidence.[6]

The key to the Wright Brother's success would be engineering. As Tim Crouch, Chairman of the Department of Aeronautics at the National Air and Space Museum of the Smithsonian, wrote of them, they "functioned as engineers, not scientists." They had a "genius for visualizing mechanical solutions to theoretical problems."[7] They were methodical and skilled in their work, who had "a tremendous work ethic and the ability to focus on problems virtually to the exclusion of all else,"[8] and they realized that "actual experience must accompany theory."[9] The Wrights understood that their invention had three main requirements: wings that would lift their craft into the air; a power plant that would be small, light and powerful; and a way to control the plane once it was in the air.[10] The brother's work with bicycles helped to unlock the secret of control. Wilbur Wright stated that Lilienthal was "the first man who really comprehended that balancing was the first instead of the last of the great problems in connection with human flight."[11] However, Lilienthal had attempted to achieve control and balance in his gliders by shifting the pilot's body weight. Wilbur was determined to find a better solution.

Lilienthal's death had been a consequence of his failure to control his glider. As a result of his death, the Wright brothers focused first on the problem of control. They realized that the body shifting to control an airplane (a method used by Chanute and others, as well as Lilienthal) was not practical. They pioneered the idea of controlling climbing and descending flight by using an elevator, a moveable wing that the pilot controlled. The also developed a viable rudder to control yawing, the right and left directional control. Finally, they solved banking, the up-and-down lateral movement of the plane. The method they used in their flyer was wing-warping. (Wing-warping did work, but it was not the best method, and it has been replaced by ailerons or spoilers as plane design continued to progress and evolve.)[12]

Because of family and business commitments, the brothers were only able to work on their invention part-time. In fact, initially it was more of a hobby than a vocation. They were still owners of a bicycle shop in Dayton, which meant that they were actively engaged in the business throughout the spring and summer until August. When Chanute offered to write Andrew Carnegie to get them a grant for $10,000 a year to work full time on their airplane, Wilbur politely responded by refusing the offer.[13] No matter how long it took, the brothers were going to build their plane on their own terms. They would use Chanute as a way to sharpen their own thinking on a variety of issues that arose during this period of trial and error.[14]

Armed with the *Monthly Weather Review* from the U.S. Weather Bureau in Washington, Wilbur selected Kitty Hawk, North Carolina, as the ideal location to test their experiment. Kitty Hawk had the sixth-highest average wind in the country at 13.4 miles per hour.[15] Wilbur would arrive there and begin testing his ideas in mid–September 1900; Orville would join him later.

The brothers initially flew their glider as a kite, and the results were quite encouraging. Wind permitting, they would take several rides in the kite. On 14 October, Orville wrote his sister to inform her that the winds were too strong to "attempt an ascent in it," so they flew it like a kite and experimented by attaching heavy chains in order to take "measurements of the 'drifts' in pounds."[16] First they flew the kite empty, then with twenty-five and fifty pounds of chains, and finally they allowed the son of a friend to take a ride in it. The boy was lighter than either of the brothers, and from the experience they were able to record that the young man had the same surface-area-to-air resistance as an adult.[17] They were also surprised that they had longitudinal control of the machine. They demonstrated lateral control, which "constituted the most critical of all controllability challenges."[18] Their kite also exhibited the basic handling and landing qualities, and they were able to use it to make some rudimentary measurements of lift and drag characteristics. In a letter to Chanute, Wilbur wrote, "The distance glided was between three and four hundred feet at an angle of one in six [i.e., one foot in descent for every six feet forward]."[19] Their tests were positive because they were able to control the "fore-and-aft balance" of the machine.[20] They returned to Dayton more than satisfied with what they had accomplished at Kitty Hawk.

But the encouraging results achieved during their first stay at Kitty Hawk would not be duplicated the following year. The brothers returned to Kitty Hawk with a new machine that included the adjustments they made from what they had learned from the previous year's experiments. Completed in mid–May, the new machine was the largest glider ever flown at that time, with a total surface area of 315 feet, two and a half times larger than the 1900 glider.[21] Unfortunately, this new glider performed worse than the one they had. Problems with the new glider's ability to lift caused the brothers to question the reliability of Lilienthal's data, along with the Smeaton coefficient for air pressure, both of which the brothers used as the basis for their experiments. On 30 July 1901, Wilbur wrote in his diary, "The lift is not much over one third that indicated by the Lilienthal tables."[22] The brothers stopped testing the new machine and began remodeling it to correct these defects, including adjusting the wing's camber (designed to create the maximum lift coefficient), from 1 in 12 to about 1 in 19, or closer to the 1900s glider airfoil shape.[23] They were able to solve the longitudinal control problems, but then confronted some additional problems with their wing warping device. Problems seemed to have plagued them throughout their stay, but by the time they left for Dayton in late August, they had learned that both their longitudinal control and front elevator worked.[24] However, they had not progressed as far as they had hoped to. Orville recalled that on the train ride home, Wilbur's frustration was evident in his statement on how long it would take for that human beings to learn to fly—a thousand years by one account, fifty years by another.[25] The next two years would show both these estimates were far too pessimistic.

Though others might have given up at this point, the Wrights continued their work with renewed energy. They proceeded to work the problems they had discovered and find solutions. First they addressed Lilienthal's data by a method that borrowed from their work with bicycles. They used a bicycle wheel attached horizontally in front of the handlebars of a bike, "with a cambered Lilienthal airfoil of the correct dimension fixed to the front of the rim."[26] Their resulting experiments showed an error with Lilienthal's data. The bothers then began to gather their own data by constructing a wind tunnel in order to "study a wide range of shapes and sizes, searching for the most efficient lifting surface."[27] This research showed that Lilienthal's figures were inaccurate for larger angles, but in fact accurate for the ranges of angles that they would be flying. However, they discovered that Lilienthal's wings were very inefficient. They also found an error in Smeaton's coefficient which resulted in the poor performances of the past year.[28] The result of their experiments was the "most reliable compilation of air foil data assembled to that point in aviation history."[29]

Now relying on their own data, the brothers returned to Kitty Hawk with renewed purpose. The 1902 glider would require more testing and adjustments, but by early October they were averaging twenty-five flights a day and on occasion achieved distances in excess of 500 feet. During one six-day period, they flew 375 flights and glided as far as 622 feet.[30] They continued to make adjustments to their machine based on these flights. They changed the fixed vertical tail into a movable rudder, and linked it to the wing-warping controls so the pilot could move both at the same time.[31] Unlike the year before, Wilbur could write his father, "We now believe that the flying problem is really nearing its solution."[32]

After the brothers had mastered the basic problems of flight, they were still faced with building an engine for powered flight. In this work, their experience with bicycles gave them no help. Fortunately for them, the internal combustion engine had already been invented and was available for their use, and they employed Charlie Taylor, a talented mechanic, in their bicycle shop. In 1896, Taylor had moved his family to Dayton and set up a machine shop there. He later subcontracted for the Wrights and then agreed to work full-time as they pursued their aviation experiments. Taylor was able to create the four-cylinder aluminum cast engine. It was a "flywheel-driven, ignition-sustaining magneto installed" engine weighing 179 pounds.[33] To offset the weight of the engine, four additional inches were added to the right wing span.[34] The engine would drive a two propeller system designed specifically by the Wrights.

As with their research into the building of their plane, nothing was left to chance about the propellers. According to Orville, "A propeller [is] simply an aeroplane [wing] traveling in a spiral course."[35] The propellers needed to be aerodynamic. The Wrights would eventually settle on propellers with a diameter of eight-and-a-half feet with a maximum blade width of eight inches. They used two contra-rotating propellers that were designed to cancel out each other's torque. The one on the right rotated clockwise while the left propeller rotated counterclockwise. Building on both current developments in the automotive industry and their knowledge and experience in building bicycles, they decided to use a chain-driven system to run the propellers.[36] With the work finally finished, the Wrights left for Kitty Hawk in late September.

The time had finally arrived, but the weather was against them. The brothers were faced with 75-mile-per-hour winds and were not able to begin testing their machine until 5 November. They faced problems involving both the propeller and the propulsion system. A fractured steel-tubing propeller shaft had to be sent back with Orville to Dayton for repairs.

They were still preparing their machine for flight when they learned that they might well be forestalled. In 1896, Langley had flown two *unmanned* flying machines over the Potomac River, a feat witnessed by Alexander Graham Bell, among others. The beginning of the war with Spain provided Langley with the opportunity to get the support and funds he needed to hopefully create a machine that was capable of both reconnaissance and "dropping high explosives into a camp of fortification."[37] In 1899, both President McKinley and Governor Theodore Roosevelt of New York helped to procure generous funding for Langley to design and construct a flying machine capable of carrying human beings. On 8 December 1903, the well-advertised and well-financed venture of Langley was to take place in the late afternoon. Unfortunately for Langley, his machine crashed into the Potomac River, and the pilot and a workman had to be rescued from the ice-cold river. Langley's failure was a gain for the Wrights. They now had the skies to themselves.

A few days after Langley's crash, the Wright brothers prepared to make history. Orville returned to Kitty Hawk. On 14 December, two days after they had installed a new shaft, Wilbur was chosen, by virtue of a coin flip, to make their first attempt to fly. Unfortunately, the flight lasted only four seconds and the plane traveled only about sixty feet. It took two days to make repairs before they could make a second attempt. On Thursday, 17 December, it was Orville's turn to conquer the air. Facing a wind gusts of twenty-seven miles per hour, Orville took his place in the plane, with his left hand on the vertical control lever and his right hand ready to start the engine. At the same time, Wilbur was in place to swing both propellers and start the plane. It was 10:35 a.m. when Orville released the plane from its mooring and began descending down the launching rail and into the wind. In a few seconds, the Wright Flyer reached a height of around ten feet and flew for fifty-nine seconds. It traveled only 852 feet, but it flew, and the event was captured by John T. Daniels on a large box camera on a tripod.[38] Later, a gust of wind would turn the machine over and damage it so it would never fly again. Even so, the birds lost a little of their wonder, and humanity would never again be the same.

Besides the excitement and adventure of flying for its own sake, something that had been a dream of human beings for centuries, the Wright brothers envisioned a number of uses for the airplane, particularly transportation (for human beings, mail, and packages) and mapping from the air. They did not at first envision any military use for the airplane. In fact, at first they believed that it would make war obsolete. In Orville's words, "A fast flying machine will render the enemy's disposition of forces so easy of observation, and its directing minds so exposed to destruction, that nations may incline more and more to universal peace."[39]

Within eleven years, this statement would prove to be naïve as the imperial powers blundered into the world's first industrialized war. During the war, Orville would recognize his mistake and see the airplane as an integral part of 20th century warfare. In a letter to the Aircraft Production Board he gave his opinion that the war's stalemate was a result of "neither side [being] able to win on account of the part the aeroplane has played ... to end the war quickly and cheaply, the supremacy in the air must be so complete as to entirely blind the enemy." Otherwise, Wright believed, the war would continue for years.[40]

War fever had been building for a long time in Europe. The imperial powers of Europe—England, France, and Germany—saw themselves as engaged in a struggle for domination. The coming war was not only foreseen but even welcomed. H.G. Wells' *Tono-Bungay* (1909), a representative book from the years directly before the war, ends with the protagonist riding down the Thames in a modern warship and dreaming of the time that it might be used in actual combat.[41] It was recognized that this war would be different from any earlier war, in that it would be an industrialized war, of technological, sophistication and industrial mobilization. But a terribly wrong conclusion was drawn from this premise: that this war, unlike earlier ones, would be a very short one, a few months at most, instead of years. And after the war, the English believed, England would once again reign supreme; the French felt that France would again dominate Europe; the Germans expected that Germany would take its rightful place in the sun.

This pre-war mood cannot be over-emphasized when we consider why the Great War occurred. If the world had been in another mood, the death of the Archduke Franz Ferdinand might well have been only a ripple in history. As it was, that death was the spark that set off the whole powder keg.

In the United States, the Great War was at first seen as a disaster characteristic of the Old World, something that the United State should stay out of at all costs. A poem by Vachel Lindsay, "Abraham Lincoln Walks at Midnight," expresses this feeling. In the poem, Lincoln cannot rest in his grave because of "the bitterness, the folly, and the pain" of the war. It ends with the question, "And who will bring white peace, / That he may sleep upon his hill again?"[42]

Later, of course, the American viewpoint would decidedly change, and at one point the United States would decide to enter the war. But long before that happened, a number of young Americans would decide to join the war and fight on the English side. (There were some who flew for the French, too, but far fewer than those who flew for the English.) Some of these young Americans were impelled by a strong attachment to the English or by the pervasive British propaganda machine, but most were not. They saw the war as a great adventure and, above all, as an opportunity to fly.

In the same way that in the 17th century the sea had beckoned such adventurers as Sir Francis Drake and Sir Walter Raleigh, in the 20th century flying would be the siren seducing young men with the allure of adventure, escape, and fame. They saw the war primarily as a chance to fly. This was not the first time that the airplane was first used in war. In 1911, in the Italian war against the Ottoman Empire, Captain Carlos Piazza carried out the first air reconnaissance flight for an hour on 23 October in a Blériot monoplane.[43] But the First World War would be the first time that airplanes were used in combat in large numbers.

The first use of the airplane in the Great War would be in reconnaissance. Captain Piazza's exploits had already shown the way, and in 1912 military maneuvers in Connecticut and by U.S. Army and by the French overseas further attested to the airplane's value in reconnaissance and artillery spotting.[44] The dogfights in the air would come later, and strafing of ground troops from the air considerably later. Whatever it was that planes were doing, war would provide a demand for pilots.

For American pilots like Edward "Eddie" Rickenbacker, "we were caught up in a great adventure, with the emphasis on thrills and excitement."[45] This call to adventure remained strong. William C. Lambert of Ironton, Ohio, was one of the many who answered this call. The call came from the British Empire and not from America. Lambert would serve overseas, and his duty would be to fly for the Royal Flying Corps in the Great War during the days of the great German offensive of 1918. His motive was neither patriotism nor hatred of the Germans nor even an overwhelming belief in the cause he served. Like many others, Lambert went to war for adventure and the chance to fly.

Two

From Ironton to Canada

William ("Bill") Lambert lived most of his life in Ironton, leaving it only to serve in two world wars and to barnstorm for a couple of years. He was born in Ironton on Saturday, 18 August 1894. The city remained his home, and he never really considered leaving it permanently. Ironton molded him. So it is important for us to understand the character and atmosphere of the place at the time he was growing up.

In the earlier 19th century, Ironton was an industrial city that boasted an abundance of resources and the potential for substantial growth in iron ore, mining, timber, and clay. As its name implies, the iron industry was particularly important. During the Civil War, pig iron from Ironton and the region around it was largely used in the manufacture of ordinance, especially heavy cannon for the artillery.[1] After the Civil War, the pig iron industry continued to flourish in Ironton. By 1887 there were 98,254 tons of metal made in Lawrence County, of which Ironton was the county seat.[2]

Unfortunately, in spite of its seemingly promising future, Ironton would become a peripheral town, serving the economic interests and requirements of larger communities.[3] During the business crisis of the 1890s, pig iron production began to decline in the Ironton region; however, the city still measured its success by the amount of pig iron it produced. Ironton became a backward-looking city, remembering the glory days of its past.[4]

The fortunes of Lambert's family, like his city's, first rose and then declined. After the Civil War, his grandfather, also called William, worked in a machine shop. One of his sons, also named William, joined his brother Reuben and Ms. Elizabeth Fisher in becoming proprietors of Lambert Brothers and Company that operated the Olive Foundry and Machine Shops located at 107 North Second Avenue. Bill Lambert, this William Lambert's son, took pride in the achievements of his family. He would later in life tell interviewers that his father and uncle owned the biggest foundry and machine shop on the Ohio between Pittsburgh and Cincinnati. However, he would add that this was "back in the days of the Civil War and after."[5] And in fact, by the second decade of the 20th century, the family machine company was no longer in operation, and Bill Lambert's father was a mechanic for the Alpha Portland Cement Company, where he worked as a master mechanic for thirty-five years.[6]

Bill Lambert partly credited his success as a pilot to being raised among motors and guns. It is probable, though we have no direct evidence of that fact, that Lambert sometimes assisted his father and uncle in their machine shop. It is certain that he had strong spatial and logical/mathematical intelligence that served him well as a pilot, designer, and painter. This ability may well have been further developed by his early experiences.

In contrast to Lambert's pride in his family's achievements, there is very little mention in his interviews or writings of his immediate family; it is as if they did not exist for him. He does mention his mother in his second book, *Barnstorming and Girls,* comparing her to a "very gracious lady" in Kentucky,[7] but there is little or no mention of anyone else in his family. For example, his brother Carl, who became a pilot after his brother, enlisting in the U.S. Army Air Service on 26 August 1918 as a member of the 42nd Aero Squadron, may well have been influenced by his brother, but there is no indication of that influence in anything Bill Lambert said or wrote. In only one interview does he even mention that he had a younger brother.

What Bill Lambert did recall of his childhood, even seventy years later, was the things he did that showed his fascination with flight, even at a very early age. In his inter-

Lambert's baby picture.

view with Robert Smith of the Air Force Logistics Command Oral History project, Lambert said he was around eight or nine years old when he built little monoplanes from umbrella ribs and sailed them off a barn.[8] He would later tell his friend Bill Martin that these experiments were carried out at his great-great grandmother's farm across the river in Greenup, Kentucky. Lambert told Martin and Smith that he had never seen a plane, so he used birds as the model.[9] The umbrella provided "the steel ribs for making the framework and the silk covering it."[10] After flying the model from a nearby barn, he realized that the plane was too heavy so he switched materials and used kite wood and paper; however, that experiment also failed because of his wing design. When he finally had a chance to study pictures of actual planes—he estimated, about a year after Kitty Hawk—Lambert made a plane with "curved wing surface." He "fashioned a cambered wing with thin copper wire and covered the surface with kite paper." This time, the model flew about 100 feet when launched from the barn roof.[11] Also about this time, Lambert began drawing pictures of airplanes, as he would for the rest of his life.

Lambert recalled also that a couple of the local Fourth of July celebrations in Ironton fed his love of flying. One year, the annual Independence Day celebration featured a hot air balloon attraction. He, and many of the other boys, did not leave until the event was over. Later in the week, they decided to build their own balloon. The smallest boy amongst them had the opportunity to take a ride in the balloon. However, even though the balloon did fly, the flight almost ended in disaster for the lone passenger.[12] This near-accident, however, by no means cooled Lambert's fascination with flying.

Later, in the summer of either 1909 or 1910, at another Fourth of July celebration in Ironton, Lambert saw his first airplane, a Wright Brothers-built Model B. By then he "was already crazy about airplanes" and figured he wanted to fly.[13] In *Combat Report*, Lambert described his excitement when he learned about the plane's arrival at the local amusement park, known as Beechwood Park. The plane arrived around noon and put on an exhibition for the crowd. "The people, never having seen anything larger than a bird flying in the air, went crazy."[14] Lambert and a few boys stayed with the pilot the rest of the day, long after the crowds dispersed. At six the next morning, he rushed to the site and brought the pilot some breakfast. When the flyer was prepared to leave on the 5th, he offered Lambert a short ride in his plane. Lambert climbed into the plane and experienced the most exciting fifteen minutes of his life up to that point. He remembered vividly that the pilot "let me handle the controls, so I really did fly that machine."[15] He wrote in the rough-draft of *Combat Report*, that even though the "episode happened almost sixty years ago … the facts remain in my memory."[16] He recalled the moment for Smith in his interview saying that he "was already crazy about airplanes and interested in them. So, naturally I figured I wanted to fly."[17]

Lambert's fascination with flying was only an extreme case of his whole generation's excitement with flying and airplanes. This excitement was fueled by print sources, aviation, and even air war, had already made a splash in literature when in 1908 H. G. Wells published his novel *The War in the Air*, which described a German air attack on Great Britain. Magazines and newspapers also played a significant role in promoting aviation. Aviation articles appeared regularly in daily papers such as the *New York Times* and *Philadelphia Inquirer*. In 1909 the

Lambert as a teenager. Lambert is in the second row, second from right.

Philadelphia Inquirer went so far as to spice up the annual Founder's Day parade by sponsoring an airship to fly over it.[18] From March 1910 until August 1914 *Collier's: The National Weekly* published around twenty-five aviation related topics every six months. One article discussed the potential dangers of aerial bombardment while another, written by Arthur Ruhl, entitled "The Aeroplane: The Annals of Aviation in the Attempt to Fly Lengthwise Rather than Downward," outlined the progress of the Wright brothers over a five year period.[19] *Century Magazine* published sixteen such articles between 1906 through 1914, including an article by the Wright Brothers describing their plane and another on August Post's record balloon flight that won him the 1911 Bennett trophy.[20] *Scientific American*, a technical magazine with much smaller circulations, but important because so many of its readers were scientists and engineers, employed an aviation editor who "actively reported aviation progress and experimentation."[21] These publications both told the nation of the progress being made in aviation and alerted the people to the failure of the U.S. to keep pace with Europeans, particularly, the French, in aviation development.

For Lambert, and for many others of his generation, along with the love of flight came a passion for engineering and design. General George P. Scriven, the Chief Signal Officer in the U.S. Army, wrote in his *Report to the Secretary of War, 1913*, "It is to be remembered that the science of the air requires the best efforts of the most highly trained men … trained and experienced men in … the development of the science of aeronautics of the future…. [T]he pilot of the airplane … is the man behind the gun."[22] As the war continued and aviation became more complex, particularly as both sides came to realize that their concept of aerial combat had been altered by the single-seat scout plane, the need for the "highly trained men" that Scrivens described became more apparent. We will see later that while in the R.F.C., Lambert was constantly with his mechanics when he was not flying, not only repairing his plane, but also trying to improve his chances of success, to give himself an edge in combat.[23] This practice was one of the most important reasons that Lambert stayed alive through his part of the war, a war in which for every 100 pilots who managed to make it to the Western Front, thirty-three were killed.[24]

When the war began, Lambert was working as an assistant chemist in the blast furnace laboratories for the Hanging Rock Iron Company located near Ironton. In his 1980 interview with Robert Smith, Lambert stated that he worked at the blast furnace as a chemist during summer vacations. He was learning the trade in hopes of someday becoming a metallurgical engineer, getting on-the-job training at the blast furnaces. In doing so, he seems to have followed the lead of a friend who had done the same thing.[25] When he left school in 1913, he simply continued full-time at his job.

Two years later, in 1915, he moved to Buffalo, New York, to work as an assistant chemist in the laboratory of the Lackawanna Steel Company located in the nearby suburb of West Seneca.[26] In articles on and interviews with Lambert, he repeatedly stated that his reasons for going to Lackawanna was to work as a chemist, but that seems unlikely. His first job at Lackawanna—and perhaps his only job, since he stayed there only a year—was as first helper on the open hearth furnace and not as a chemist.[27] He told Royal Frey that he was making twice the money and working fewer hours as a chemist in Canada.[28] If this is true, then it seems highly unlikely that he was working as a chemist while employed at Lackawanna. There were other reasons for going to Lackawanna, however, that would have weighed heavily with him. One was that airplane designer and manufacturer Glenn Curtiss had a flying field on

Two. From Ironton to Canada

the outskirts of the city. Another was that it was a little over a hundred miles from Toronto, Canada, if he wanted to enlist.

When it became apparent that the war was not going to end by Christmas 1914, as almost everyone had thought it would, Lambert decided that he wanted to get involved in it. He was not alone in this desire; approximately 15,000 Americans went to war before the United States got involved. Many crossed the Canadian border to enlist in the Canadian Expeditionary Force, and hundreds went to join the Royal Flying Corps. When Smith asked Lambert his reason for wanting to enlist, Lambert answered that he "just had the desire and wanted to get in it…. Democracy [as a reason to get into the war] didn't enter my mind."[29] This response is characteristic of many, in fact most, of these young Americans.

Lambert wanted to get into the war, but he also wanted to survive it. Lambert told Smith that he read the newspapers and everything else he could find about the war, and he knew of the slaughter going on in the trenches. "I didn't want to be a plain ordinary old foot soldier being shot up and killed."[30] At first, he thought he liked to be in the artillery. "I did have enough sense to realize that the artillery was back of the lines. I was thinking, I'd like to shoot those big guns. And that's the reason I tried for artillery."[31] For some reason, however—perhaps because he was in fact more interested in flying than in shooting big guns—he did not join the artillery. Instead, he at first worked supporting the war effort behind the lines in Canada.

According to file cards in the Directorate of History and Heritage at the National Defence Headquarters in Ottawa, Canada, Lambert worked as a "chemist and factory supervisor, Nobel plant for Canadian Explosives, Ltd., Montreal, 1914–16."[32] This information is probably correct except for the dates. It seems fairly certain that Lambert was *not* working there in 1914 and most of 1915.

Since we have so little evidence about this period of Lambert's life, we are forced to rely on his "A Very Strange Story" for some information about Lambert's activities in this period. "A Very Strange Story" is confessedly fiction, but it takes off—as do so many fictional stories—from a base of fact, and here the facts are what Lambert did and why, during this period of his life. As the story tells it, in September 1915 a young, naïve Lambert goes with an older friend to enlist in the artillery. His friend is accepted, but Lambert is rejected, supposedly because he is told that Canadians could not take Americans into their army. Even though the Lambert in this story is naïve, he knows that this explanation is nonsense. The Canadians finally confess that they really need him to work as a chemist rather than an artillery-man, because chemists are so desperately needed for the war effort. So Lambert says good-bye to his friend, leaves for Nobel to do gun-cotton analysis, and eventually becomes a supervisor, just as the file card in the Directorate of History and Heritage had said.[33]

We have Lambert's Canadian Explosives, LTD, identification papers for 1917. These papers allowed Lambert to be admitted to the factory; they are also further proof that Lambert was indeed a chemist and supervisor at the company. Lambert was an organized individual who paper-clipped his identification papers together with a card; he was also obsessed with keeping all papers that had ever been important for him. There are six papers that were issued for 1917, one for each of the first six months of the year. Next to the title "Position" is "Supervisor" or "G.C. Supervisor" on all six papers. "G.C" means the "Guncotton & Club" department. (Guncotton is another name for Nitrocellulose, which is "a pulpy or cotton like polymer derived from cellulose treated with sulfuric and nitric acids and used in the manufacture of explosives."[34]) The last identification paper issued gave Lambert admission to Canadian

Explosives from 1 June to 30 June 1917, but before this paper expired Lambert had already joined the R.F.C.[35]

We have a notebook of Lambert's, and at first it seems to be from this time in his life, since both the cover and inside have stickers from the company. However, when we look more closely at it, it seems like a general metallurgical notebook,[36] which Lambert may well have started writing during his days at the Hanging Rock Company in Ironton and continued later at Lackawanna and Canadian Explosives. In fact, he probably continued it a good deal longer, since the end pages have detailed mechanical drawings of airplanes and their controls, with comments on details in the drawing.[37] The notebook shows Lambert teaching himself about subjects he needs to know, and it is valuable for that aspect of his life, but it tells us nothing about his Canadian Explosives experience.

While Lambert worked as a chemist, he still read newspaper and magazine articles, especially about the war. One item he read was that the R.F.C. was going to establish a training center near Toronto. On 22 January 1917, the advance party of the R.F.C. Canada arrived in Toronto.[38] Even after Lambert enlisted in the R.F.C., he was told by the recruiter that "we are not yet ready to start training; we will write to you when you are to report back here."[39] In the Smith interview, Lambert puts it more vividly. He says that he was told by a recruiter, "We don't have an airplane in this country, and we don't have any flying fields … but we're getting ready…. I'll write each of you and tell you when to report back to Toronto."[40] In the rough-draft copy of *Combat Report,* Lambert wrote that he "caught the train next morning and headed north to Parry Sound and to help make high explosives for a few more months."[41] After he got a letter in May 1917, Lambert reported back to Toronto for training 10 June, joining "quite a crowd." The new recruits eventually separated into groups, and he found himself with twenty-seven others.[42]

Lambert became Cadet 70442. On 18 June 1917, he swore allegiance to King George V. He soon developed a friendship with David Pratt, who had studied French at the University of Toronto. The cadets were billeted in Burwash Hall at the University, Pratt was right at home. According to Lambert, he and his friend were known as "Pratt and Lambert, Paint and Varnish, St. Louis, Missouri."[43] Later, Lambert found it typical of the military that Pratt, even though he was proficient in French, would eventually be sent to Italy to fly Bristol fighters.

In his rough-draft manuscript, Lambert spends additional time discussing the daily mundane details of training life: the ill-fitting uniforms that had to be "spic and span, neatly pressed, and with buttons shining like gold," the "fundamentals of foot-soldier drill," physical training, the 5:00 a.m. reveille, mess-orderly duty, parade ground inspections, with someone always ready to throw the book at him. Enduring the clothing alone was enough to understand why "the poor Germans gave up—they did not have a chance."[44]

Like all military basic training, Lambert's training in Cadet Course No. 8 was designed to make him adjust to the military way of thinking and doing. Lambert had to endure sacrifices, learn self-discipline, obedience, and loyalty as he became a proud, physically fit member of the Royal Flying Corps. Although the training was supposed to last six to eight weeks, Lambert recalled that it lasted only four. That may have been a consequence of the demands for pilots after heavy causalities suffered by the R.F.C. in the skies over Arras in April 1917. However, the training stayed with him for the rest of his life, and the camaraderie were to last a lifetime. Surviving the initial stage together helped to build an *esprit de corps*. A picture of the cadets in their new uniforms was taken in front of Burwash Hall on 7 December 1917.

Lambert remembered many names later, even after almost fifty-one years and the fact that those that survived the training went on to serve in different squadrons during the war. In the rough-draft, he appeals to "the survivors of this group to be lenient with me if I am wrong with names."[45]

After ten or fourteen days, Lambert returned to the University of Toronto for more detailed training in "communications from ground to aeroplane, such as wireless, light signals and ground strips; next, artillery observation and reporting back to the batteries, both lectures and practice."[46] From the Cadet Wing the students progressed to the School of Aeronautics. As before, this school involved both lectures and practice, but the courses were more demanding and detailed. Cadets learned map reading, navigation, cross-country course plotting, artillery observation, machine gun and bomb operations, and instruments. Where Lambert excelled was in the mechanical and technical areas. He said that the study of engines, airplane rigging and machine-guns was "the most interesting part of this phase of training."[47] This comment is consistent with his upbringing in Ironton, where he grew up with guns and motors.

Cadet William C. Lambert in original R.F.C. uniform 1917. Lambert kept the swagger stick pictured here for the rest of his life.

Partly because of crowded conditions at the University, the cadets moved to Long Branch on the outskirts of Toronto to finish their training and to begin flying. Appropriately, it was the site of a flying field that had been used by the Curtiss Flying School. The government commandeered this field because it was already operational and also purchased from Curtiss all the airplanes that were being used for lessons at the school. As Lambert remembered, they stayed at that field for about ten days.[48] Of course, accommodations had not yet been built, so they were forced to move into tents to complete the final activities and lessons in the School of Aeronautics.[49] Once these activities and lessons were completed, the final step—and, of course, the one that most interested Lambert—was actually learning how to fly.

Three

Training

As Bill Lambert trained for flight and combat in Canada, he had one invaluable resource that could not be given by training. That was his trust and confidence in himself and his fate. He said that "something told me that I would survive, and this was to be my thinking all through my fighting period."[1] Even before he left Nobel for Toronto, he had felt that "there was never a German bullet made that would draw [his] blood."[2] Although later on in life Lambert would frequently debate the existence of Divine Providence with Bill Martin, there are several instances where Lambert credits God with his luck and survival as a pilot. In his manuscript "A Very Strange Story," Lambert writes, "The 'Old Gentleman' up above sure was with me that morning," during his first confrontation with the enemy.[3] In the rough-draft copy of *Combat Report,* Lambert described a scene where he was trying to take off in an Avro on his way back to Chattis Hill in England; Lambert wrote that he "trusted to the old Gentlemen [sic] up above to pull me out of that field ... [and that] the Lord helped me out of that mess."[4] Apparently the old adage that "there are no atheists in foxholes" also applied to Lambert flying over France in the Great War.

Back to Long Branch. After several additional days of lectures, physical training, and drill, Lambert finally got the chance to fly. On 16 July 1917, Lambert flew in a Curtiss "Jenny" J.N. 4 No. C.209 for 35 minutes around the aerodrome at a height of 2000 feet with Second Lieutenant H. Neville Compton as his instructor. Compton was the "Officer Commanding No. 80 C.R.S., R.F.C., Long Branch."[5] Compton congratulated Lambert after his first flight by telling him that he had done "fair." Lambert, however, felt he had done quite well.[6] But, as indicated by his *Pilot's Flying Log Book,* this would be his last chance to fly at Long Branch. The unit was broken up into smaller units, and Lambert was posted for four weeks to the R.F.C. training camp at Camp Rathbun, which was located over 140 miles east of Toronto in Deseronto.

The *Log Book* referred to in the preceding paragraph was one Lambert kept up to date throughout his time in the War, and kept afterward through the rest of his life. He refers to it often in *Combat Report.* Of course, Lambert was writing his book fifty years after his war, and after fifty years days blur together. The log book helped to revive his memory. We can always trust the log book as to what happened, though sometimes there is some conflict with the official record as to the date something happened.

At Rathbun, Lambert was kept busy with lecturers, physical training, and demonstrations. But he admitted that he wanted as much flying as possible, so he would skip classes to get additional flying time.[7] An examination of his log book shows that he got his wish. On

Three. Training

19 and 20 July, he made two "dual" flights for about thirty-five minutes. He lists "nihl" for the amount of time he flew solo, and his log was signed by Lieutenant J. A. Stewart.[8] The next week at Rathbun, Lambert liked to say that he "really earned [his] $100.00 per month pay."[9] For the week of 23–28 July 1917, Lambert flew the Jenny around the aerodrome, making right and left turns, and take-offs and landings, a total of fifty-eight times. He logged 235 minutes of dual flying and flew solo for the first time, for ten minutes, on 27 July.[10] In both the rough-draft and final version of *Combat Report*, Lambert admits he was frightened: "Yes, you can just bet, I was scared...."[11] Perhaps because he was scared, he crashed his Jenny on his solo fight while attempting to land. In *Combat Report*, he describes a landing that was near perfect except for being "ten feet too high."[12] In both the rough-draft and the final version of *Combat Report*, Lambert says that the instructor told him to immediately take another plane up and "bring her back with a three-point landing."[13] He followed orders and made a perfect landing on his second solo, restoring his confidence and faith in his abilities. His log book, however, has him soloing at 5:10 a.m. for five minutes on 28 July, the morning of the next day.[14] Either way, he "got back on his horse" and felt renewed confidence.

Lambert continued to fly at Rathbun for an additional five hours and twenty minutes of solo flying from 31 July till 6 August 1917. A solo flight on 31 July at 6:00 a.m. lists two landings, one crash, and a control wire breaking.[15] (He does not state whether the crash was a result or cause of the wire breaking.) He flew solo on 5 and 6 August in C607, the same machine that he cracked up on his first solo attempt. Now, he flew successfully for ninety minutes and landed the plane eight times over the two-day period.[16] Lambert was certainly taking advantage of his opportunity to fly. More time in the air improved Lambert's skill as a pilot and improved his chances of survival. Many of the earlier British pilots in the war, such as those over Arras in April 1917, had not had the flying time before they were in the war that Lambert had already had.

Lambert's training at Rathbun ended on 6 August 1917. He was then transferred to Camp Borden, which he described as being "approximately seventy miles north of Toronto."[17] It had been selected by the R.F.C. partly because it had previously been a training center for about 35,000 troops of the Canadian Expeditionary Force. Lambert described it as "one huge tent city. All utilities, water, sewers, electric and branch railway lines were already installed."[18]

At Camp Borden, Lambert got the opportunity to fly longer flights than he had at Rathbun. His first entry in his log book for Borden is a 45-minute flight to familiarize himself with the area, on 11 August, with an officer named Taylor. On 13 August he flew again with another officer, this time with the name of Birks.[19] In *Combat Report*, Lambert describes flying over to the city of Barrie in southern Ontario, located on the western shore of Lake Simcoe, and being able to see the city of Beaverton on the eastern shore of the lake. On several occasions in his writings, Lambert described the beautiful countryside and scenery and his desire to explore the area when he had the chance. It would become a habit of Lambert's to observe the area below him carefully, to be attentive to details. It is one of the things that helped him to be a better pilot. Often, in his unpublished manuscript, he would compare the parts of Canada he visited with the area around Ironton and the Ohio River. Lambert wrote that Birks allowed him "to explore the countryside during that flight so [he] picked out many good landmarks for future use."[20]

By the end of August, he had flown thirty-five hours and fifty minutes, of which twenty-eight hours and forty minutes were solo.[21] He had also begun to practice formation flying—

a necessity for a war pilot—and exhibited his sureness in the cockpit by attempting altitude tests. On 4 September he reached a height of 11,300 feet, the limit for a Jenny.[22] Finally, he did "dead stick landings from 5,000 feet into a circle of 100 feet diameter." This feat was a difficulty one. It took Lambert three attempts to achieve success, and some of the cadets were never successful. In a letter home, Lambert's friend and Great War ace Alvin Andrew Callender described the difficulties of cutting off the motor at fifty feet in the air and rolling the plane into a fifty foot circle. Callender found it incredibly difficult to judge his speed and said it "usually took 20 attempts before you do it right."[23] It was apparent that Lambert was honing his skills and becoming more confident and accomplished in the cockpit.

Lambert at Camp Borden. Lettering on the side of this Canuck reads, "Battle of Lundy's Lane, July 25th 1814."

In addition to his growth as a pilot while at Borden, Lambert was also progressing in his training to become a war pilot. There is a difference. In addition to learning and practicing observation and flying, he had to learn how to identify aircraft, spot them, and shoot them down. A fighter pilot had to be self-confident and aggressive and knowledgeable about gunnery. In *Combat Report*, Lambert describes how he spent periods between flights and during inclement weather studying airframes and training on machine-guns.[24] The R.F.C. had begun to improve its training methods with the inclusion of materials on aerial gunnery—for example, the 1917 release of a *Text Book on Aerial Gunnery*. As Richthofen preached, being a successful and agile pilot was of no use if one could not hit the target when in the proper position.[25] Overall, however, the standard of gunnery for pilots in the war was very poor. Lambert's standard would be considerably higher.

Lambert wrote about his machine-gun training with his usual aplomb. He had an advantage over most of the other cadets in this training, since, as previously stated, he had been raised among motors and guns. He described how he grew up on the Ohio where he shot floating targets and "birds flying overhead," so when it came to shooting he played "second fiddle" to no one at Borden.[26] Cadets had to "learn every part of those guns ... where it fit and what was it's [sic] function? We had to strip them from A to Z and then reassemble the complete gun.... We even had to do this blindfolded."[27] Here, again Lambert had an edge up on his companions, since he had stripped his motorcycle engine many times as a youngster in Ironton. Consequently, for him stripping the guns "was not too hard," and in fact he "liked the work." Cadets lacking his previous experience "had a tough time with those guns."[28]

Lambert was disappointed when it came to firing the machine guns, since cadets were given only twenty rounds to practice on the firing range. He "surprised" himself, however, when he fired his ten rounds from the Vickers gun, for he shot "those ten bullets in a circle less than two feet in diameter and six feet ahead of the areoplane." He was told he "would have hit the cockpit" of an enemy plane. Greatly encouraged by this result, Lambert would "spend as much time as possible on the range" shooting at targets, as he did later at all the training facilities he visited.[29]

Unfortunately, Lambert would get very little shooting in the air. He would only get to fire a hundred rounds from a Lewis gun at towed targets, and it would not be until he joined No. 24 Squadron that he would again get the chance to fire in the air.[30] Time pressure may well have been the reason why Lambert and the other cadets did not spend a great deal of time target-practicing in the air. Instructors were probably pressured to get pilots to Europe as quickly as possible to meet the need for them at the front.

Besides his training as a fighter pilot, Lambert received other kinds of training: as a spotter for artillery units, and as a bomber pilot. His role in the war was yet to be determined, and the R.F.C. wanted him trained for whatever he might ultimately do. In September 1917, he received training in artillery spotting. He was assigned to plot artillery bursts on a map

Lambert at machine-gun practice.

and send back the coordinates, probably using wireless, in the standard artillery code.[31] He learned how to read "Panneau signals" (signs displayed on the ground). His log book states that on 11 September he spent forty minutes identifying strips and Panneau signals.[32] The 11th of September was a busy day for him. In addition to reading Panneau signals and identifying strips that would be used in battle to mark troop movements during an offensive, he did artillery spotting by looking for and mapping "Puffs" (smoke that represented artillery shots) and relaying their locations. He also went on bombing raids using sacks of flour to represent bombs. On the next day, 12 September, he spent forty minutes on aerial photography and later used a camera gun that resembled a machine-gun where "one learned to shoot an aircraft flying at any altitude, deflection shots, head-on and from the tail."[33]

During this period, Lambert went back home to Ironton for a brief visit to see his family and friends before going overseas. *The Ironton News* from 13 September 1942 reprinted an article from "25 Years Ago" (13 September 1917), which stated that "Lambert ... arrived home last night for a brief visit with homefolks and to attend the apple show. Will has made application for a transfer to the American flying corps and believes that he will be successful in securing it within a reasonably short time."[34] The date is probably wrong—it does not seem as if he could have made it home that fast—but the visit did happen. However, it seems highly doubtful that he was in earnest about switching services. He had already given up his citizenship and sworn allegiance to King George. He told Smith in his interview that the reason he did not join the U.S. Air Service was because "I didn't want to. I was already in the RFC in Canada."[35]

After finishing his artillery spotting and bomber pilot training, Lambert would join No. 81 Squadron for three days and go back to Borden for aerial gunnery school. According to his log book, the course was to end on 11 October.[36] Finally on 13 October 1917, Lambert, along with twenty-seven other members of Course No. 8, was sent to Toronto for graduation. He became a 2nd Lieutenant and received his "Sam Browne" belt and Pilot Certificate NO. 9367.[37] Lambert was now an officer and a pilot.

Camp Borden would now be shut down for the winter. Several of the new pilots head for Texas, but Lambert found that he was to be sent to Camp Mohawk at Deseronto to be an instructor with No. 78 Squadron until 31 October. (In 1916, it was decided that *eight hours* of solo time was sufficient for a pilot to become an instructor![38]) He was not happy about this decision, but followed orders. It was a testament to his performance and abilities that he was chosen for the position, and it gave him additional flying experience, which would help him in the war.

In his rough-draft version of *Combat Report,* Lambert describes a "Hallowe'en Dinner," probably a farewell party, since his short period at Mohawk was over and he was soon to leave for England. (Describing delicious dinners is a habit that he would repeat in this manuscript and his book, *Barnstorming and Girls.*) Lambert gave a vivid description of this impressive dinner that included oysters, roast stuffed turkey, celery mayonnaise, roast sweet potatoes, string beans, and pumpkin pie. (He wrote of this dinner on 28 October 1968, almost fifty-one years to the day later.[39])

Now Lambert reported to Montreal to board the S. S. *Megantic* and join the convoy of twenty ships that would sail out of Halifax for Liverpool, England. (Convoys assembling at Halifax became standard procedure for the Royal Navy.) On the way, he remarked that the St. Lawrence valley "certainly offered scenery that is not seen on our Ohio River at home."[40]

He wrote very little about the trip to England. He did remark that he did not get seasick because he drank about "two gallons of Mother-Sill Sea Sick Remedy," and he told of the enemy submarines that they ran into on the way.[41] Lambert himself did submarine duty while on ship and was impressed by how "small destroyers dart through the water after the subs." Afterward, he wondered why he did not join the Navy.[42]

Upon arriving in London, Lambert, after a wild night at the *Café Royale*—a place the newly arrived pilots were told was strictly "out of bounds"—was informed that he would be heading for Stockbridge, Hampshire, for additional training. The flying field was located about a mile west of the village at Chattis Hill.[43] Before Lambert left Canada, he spent sixty-eight hours and fifty minutes in the air flying dual and solo, but he had flown only two types of aircraft: Curtiss and Avro.[44] Both of these planes were slower and less maneuverable than the ones he would be introduced to in England. These planes would be the ones that were actually being flown in battle. They were faster and more maneuverable, but also—at least some of them—more dangerous, at least to the inexperienced flier. It is no wonder that Lambert wrote that it was at Chattis Hill he would "really learn to fly."[45]

Lambert had the opportunity to experience very different aircraft. He would fly Avros, Sopwith Pups and Camels, Spads and his ultimate favorite, the S.E.5 (Scott Experimental 5). Throughout his life, Lambert would give interviews in which he explained the differences between these aircraft and why he preferred the S.E.5 over all the others. He would draw and sketch pictures of the various airplanes he had flown and give them to people. Before his death, he became a valuable source on Great War aviation and tactics.

In *Combat Report,* he gave a brief description of these differences between these airplanes, with comments on each. The first plane he flew in England, on 18 December 1917, was the Avro. The Avro was also the only one of these planes that he had flown earlier in Canada. He said of the Avro that it would do anything you wanted it to do as long as you had sufficient speed. Apparently Lambert put it to the test because the Squadron C.O. asked him to be careful so he would not "drive the wings off."[46]

Lambert was thrilled when this C.O. asked him to try out the "Pup." (The Pup was officially called the Scout, but pilots regarded it as the "pup" of the 1½ Strutter.) It was the first time that Lambert flew in a single-seat airplane. With the exception of having an engine that used castor oil, Lambert thought that the Pup was "one of the nicest machines that any pilot could want."[47] (The Pup used an eighty h.p. La Rhone rotary engine, and rotary engines used castor oil. One of the drawbacks of castor oil was that it tended to splash back into the faces of pilots who undoubtedly ingested some of it, which would result in indigestion and/or frequent bowel movements.) Lambert especially liked the maneuverability of the Pup. He wrote that the Pup "was undoubtedly the easiest aircraft I have ever flown—very stable, light, quick on the controls and floated in for landings like a Canadian goose."[48]

He did not care so much for the larger Sopwith Camel. (This attitude was one he shared with many other pilots.) The Sopwith Camel was the successor of the Pup. It was the first airplane to carry twin Vickers machine-guns. The breeches of these guns were enclosed in a "hump," this giving the machine its name. According to the pilots who flew it, the Camel was either "loved or detested."[49] This tricky airplane may have killed many pilots who were inexperienced and careless, but its agility made it deadly in combat. It was fast and had the ability to perform acrobatic turns with a simple touch.[50] Victor M. Yeates, in *Winged Victory,* one of the most famous novels of the war, described the Camel as "by far the most difficult of service machines to handle. Many pilots killed themselves by crashing in a right hand spin when they were learning to fly them…. They were unlike ordinary aeroplanes, being quite unstable, immoderately tail-heavy, so light on the controls that the slightest jerk or inaccuracy would hurl them all over the sky, difficult to land, deadly to crash: a list of vices to emasculate the stoutest courage, and the first flight on a Camel was always a terrible ordeal."[51] Lambert wrote that the Camel "had to be flown every damn minute! Its torque would flip you into a spin before you knew what happened. In the hands of a good pilot, however, it proved to be a great combat plane, but I wonder how [many] pilots lost their lives trying to fly it."[52]

On the other hand, Lambert liked the Spad. (Rickenbacker was the one, however, who made the Spad famous for Americans.) The Spad carried a single synchronized Vickers machine gun and a Lewis gun mounted on the central section. It made up for its comparative lack of maneuverability with greater speed and strength. It reminded Lambert of a hawk attacking a pigeon. He remarked that "it really split the sky wide open."[53] The one thing he did not like about the Spad was that it would fall like a brick.[54]

Lambert's favorite airplane, however, and the one he flew during the War, was the S.E.5. In describing his first encounter with this plane, Lambert chronicles that on a cold January morning he asked and apparently received permission to fly a Spad, but while walking to the hanger that housed it, he cast his eyes on the S.E.5. "It had a four-blade prop, a pronounced dihedral on top and bottom wings, a long slender hood out in front with what looked like an eight-cylinder engine in it…. [It had] the sweetest sounding engine that I ever sat behind. That cockpit fitted me like a new glove. All controls, switches etc. were well within close reach for any quick action. The tick and rudder bar had been made for me. Right then and there I decided that this was the aeroplane that I was going to fly."[55]

Although Lambert fell in love with this plane, and the love affair continued throughout the war, he still would tinker with it to get it to do exactly what he wanted it to do. For example, he adjusted the dihedral to a slight degree nose heavy so it would not continue to climb and possibly end up in a spin. He was able to improve the altitude of the plane to as high as 25,000 feet with his adjustments. Naturally, he shared these innovations with other members of No. 24 Squadron, and they soon spread to other squadrons.[56]

In *Combat Report*, Lambert tells his favorite story of his time at Stockbridge. He and nine others were asked by the C.O. to take ten Avros out for some formation flying practice. It becomes a three-day adventure in which he met a variety of delightful local characters and sampled the local cuisine. He calls it "a nice three day vacation which had not cost me a penny."[57] When he finally returns to Chattis Hill, he was told that he was the only pilot in his formation to make it back by plane!

This story is one that Lambert tells well and rather comically, but what is missing in it is Lambert's ability to make calculated, improvised, and appropriate decisions. He had the mechanical intelligence and skill to deal with problems of fuel, a sputtering engine, weather, limited view, and questionable and/or truncated landing fields. This ability would serve him well in France.

His skill as a pilot was evident to others, including his commanding officer. He became so proficient at flying the S.E.5 that he was called in to put on a performance for a visiting general. He showed his agility as a pilot when he successfully landed the plane after a cross-bracing wire broke while he was coming out of a full roll. The commanding general, not realizing the danger Lambert faced in attempting to land the plane, congratulated him on a good show.[58]

Lambert did some intense flying at Stockbridge. On 18 December 1917, he had accumulated seven hours and thirty minutes of dual flying and sixty-eight hours and fifty minutes of solo. By the time he left for France, he had nine hours and thirty minutes of dual and 111 hours and ten minutes of solo.[59] Moreover, a lot of this flying was acrobatics. Lambert first performed turns, landings, spin rolls, and then moved on to formation flying, as well as loops and turns, in his first Pup solo on 22 January.[60] By the middle of February, he had spent nine hours and twenty minutes performing left and right rolls, formation flying, and altitude flying, and also practiced photography while flying. None of this flying was just stunt flying, as it would be later for barnstormers. It was all practice for flying in war, where Lambert would use all these "stunts" in taking evasive action to escape a pursuing enemy pilot.

After Stockbridge, Lambert was posted to No. 2 Auxiliary School of Aerial Gunnery at Turnberry Scotland, arriving there on 9 March. Unfortunately, during his stay at Turnberry he was confronted with four days of rain and never got the chance for gunnery practice or flying.[61] It seems as if Lambert was somehow cursed whenever it came to his turn at gunnery practice! However, with this one exception, Lambert was now proficient and able in the air.

Lambert ended his first stay in England as he began it, with a trip to the *Café Royale*. The social life of an R.F.C. officer had its advantages. Lambert wrote of the five pilots who were destined to go to France the next day that they had a "wild night … [that] ended somewhere, at some time??"[62] He goes on to explain that all five pilots made it to Southampton or some other port early in the morning to travel to France. He intimates that the ride over the channel was not very pleasant due to a hangover from the previous evening in London. As far as he knew, the channel could have been calm, but the unpleasantness "could … have been due to something other than a choppy sea."[63] Drinking, socializing, and womanizing would now become staples in Lambert's life overseas. He wrote fondly of the friendships he had, the pleasant times in French cafes with his comrades, and the women he encountered in the war. It was not only the flying that created a lasting impression on Lambert, though the flying was paramount.

Four

Entering the Air War

When Lambert enters the air war, it had changed from what it had been earlier, and was even more different from the romantic view often portrayed in post-war Hollywood movies. It was never true that the air battles were one-on-one dogfights between individual planes, and it is even less true at the time that Lambert became part of the war.

The R.F.C. had a four-part classification. The largest unit was the Brigade. The Brigade was divided into Wings, the Wings into Squadrons, and the Squadrons into Flights. (No. 24 Squadron had three Flights: "A," "B," and "C.") The basic fighting unit was the flight, not the individual plane. It is the difference between an individual game, like tennis or golf, and a team game, like football or baseball. There is still need for courage and even heroism, but now it is the courage of a team player rather than individual heroism. This is one reason that Lambert is less flamboyant and boastful than Rickenbacker. He is proud of what has been accomplished, but it is pride in his team, his flight, rather than his own individual exploits.

Early in the war, it may have been that the Germans had better pilots and better planes than their opponents, though it was never so much as the "gallant but outclassed English" myth would have us believe. But now, with the newly-trained pilots and with such planes as the S.E.5 and it successor the S.E.5a, there is very little to choose between the two sides for either pilots or equipment. However, the advantage of numbers of both pilots and planes is unquestionably with the English.

This imbalance means that the German air strategy had to change. All the time that Lambert was on active service, the Germans adopted a defensive strategy to make sure that as few of their planes and pilots as possible were lost. They only engaged the English forces on the rare occasions that they had more planes than the English, or when they were caught by surprise and had to defend themselves. Otherwise, they retreated. On the other hand, the English used their superiority in the air to be constantly on the offensive, often attacking well behind the German front.

As Lambert enters the air war, he needs not only skill and confidence in the comrades protecting his back, but also courage. Courage is not fearlessness. If you do not have fear in war, you do not understand the situation. Courage consists in doing what you are afraid of; there is no courage unless you are scared. Lambert was never hesitant about admitting he was afraid of something, but he always went ahead and did what he was afraid to do.

Courage, however, is an expendable resource. Constantly risking oneself, continual stress in combat, and prolonged exposure to the horrors of war will lead to Post-Traumatic Stress Disorder (PTSD), called in the Great War "shell shock" or "combat fatigue." In war "a man's

Four. Entering the Air War

courage is his capital and he is always spending."[1] Every time Lambert heads for the front with his flight, he is spending courage. After a time, the war will take its toll.

On 16 March 1918, Lambert was posted to C Flight of No. 24 Squadron, 5th Brigade, 22nd Wing under Flight Commander Captain George E. McElroy, who was "one of the most fearless men [he] ever met."[2] According to Lambert, McElroy was "hell-bent for election."[3] McElroy was the type of leader who would go to any length and do whatever it took to achieve his objective. Lambert wrote that he was "most considerate of all those pilots under him ... he tried to keep his pilots out of trouble."[4]

Accordingly, McElroy would not allow Lambert to take part in combat until he thought he was ready. He knew that Lambert's flying skills were excellent, but these were not all that was required of a war pilot. However, that did not mean that Lambert was left to cool his heels. Not at all.

At this time No. 24 Squadron, which was equipped with S.E.5s, was based at Matigny with No. 23 Squadron, whose pilots flew Spads and later Dolphins. When on 21 March 1918, the Germans unleashed their great offensive Operation Michael, Lambert and the other three new pilots who were not allowed as yet to fly combat missions were assigned the task of ferrying planes to locations in the rear before the rapidly advancing German onslaught overran their current location. These men flew planes from Matigny to Moreuil on the 22nd, and then to Bertangles on the 26th, and finally to Conteville (twenty-five miles northwest of Bertangles) on the 28th. No. 24 would stay at Conteville until after the Allies launched their great counter offensive at Amiens on 8 August 1918.

The first entry in Lambert's log book with No. 24 Squadron is on 26 March, when he flew from Candas to Bertangles with a new S.E.5 plane from "2 A.D.S. Hesdin," which is southeast of Montreuil at the confluence of the Canche and the Ternoise rivers.[5] Lambert recalled, "These were a nerve-shattering six days of evacuation for all of us."[6] The sight of

Planes at Conteville.

displaced families clogging up the road as they attempted to take their animals and belongings away from the advancing Germans made an indelible impression on Lambert. He and the other pilots were caught up in this tragedy that "impressed itself on [his] mind to such an extent that [he] never forgot it."[7] It was impressed on his mind equally strong that the "ground was strewn for miles with wrecked and burnt planes."[8]

After these pilots landed their planes at its new location, a tender would transport them back to the previous field where the squadron was still located to continue the process of moving planes to the new bases being established behind the shifting lines.[9] "We were busy flying extra aeroplanes back to our next field, then back to the advanced area by car or tender and help evacuate other material."[10] Lambert and the others had to fly, besides S.E.5s, Spads, Dolphins, and quite possibly other aircraft, to these new locations. It may well have been in Europe that he flew his first Spad. (His log book does not have him ever flying a Spad at Stockbridge.

Lambert's service in No. 24 Squadron probably began even earlier than 26 March. He distinctly remembered assisting Lieutenant E. B. Wilson in bombing and destroying an evacuated field at Montigny on 22 March. But if he did, he neglected to note what he was doing in his log book. The first entry in his log book in Europe, as was said, is on 26 March.

McElroy still did not allow the new pilots to engage with the enemy in dogfights. Lambert began his war by ground-strafing patrols, firing on fixed ground targets, and bombing runs. As Lambert said, McElroy "told all new pilots emphatically, not to get mixed up in any action and he meant what he said."[11] Lambert and the other new pilots had to learn to identify enemy aircraft in the air as well as targets on the ground. For example, Lambert reported difficulties in identifying objects on the ground at 7,000 feet above Bertangles. Still, he was able to identify small and large craters, uprooted trees and stumps, burned out villages, and ploughed up ground.[12] Lambert was not by any means alone in this difficulty. Rickenbacker wrote that his "sense of direction in those early days was definitely bad and [he] got lost several times, particularly if there was any fog in the air."[13] Both Lambert and Rickenbacker would have had difficulties spotting, let alone identifying, enemy aircraft on their first flights. It was part of the learning curve for all war pilots.

On the afternoon of 4 April, McElroy would take Lambert and three others on a bombing raid near Villers-Bretonneux. Lambert was in S.E.5a No. 633, loaded with four twenty-pound bombs. It had been raining during the day, and the cloud cover presented a problem. After the patrol dropped their bombs near the target, McElroy showed his prowess by spotting seven enemy aircraft and shooting one down near Warfusée. It was a busy day for the squadron, with six of their planes being shot down by ground fire, but fortunately all the pilots eventually returned safely to base.[14]

Lambert covered this period in *Combat Report* in a chapter entitled "Rain, Rain, Rain." The weather was a constant issue during early April. Following this last patrol, rain washed out all possibility of flying for the next two days. However, this rain was not the horror experienced by the foot soldiers in the wet, muddy trenches. Instead, Lambert and ten or eleven of his comrades took advantage of the enforced inactivity and went to Abbeville for a hot bath and "a wild night of wine, women and song ... back at Conteville about 4:30 a.m."[15] The next day (6 April), it was still raining and cloudy, and flying was not possible. However, for Lambert that "was a very good thing, because those of us who had been to Abbeville were having a very rough time by about 8:00 a.m. Believe me that ocean was rough and the ship was pitching like a bucking bronco with a cocklebur under his saddle. Or at least that is the way it seemed to me."[16] Lambert would give his reader a number of other such accounts of the off-duty lifestyle of a young pilot as time went on.

By the afternoon of 7 April, the weather had improved and the squadron had evidently recovered sufficiently from its excesses in Abbeville, so McElroy took C Flight out again on patrol over the Villers-Bretonneux region. (Joining C Flight was Captain W. Selwyn, who would become a Flight Commander of C Flight during the time Lambert was a member of the squadron.) On this flight, Lambert recorded his first victory.

C Flight was patrolling the front around 11,000 feet above Villers-Bretonneux when three enemy two-seaters were spotted flying below them. Immediately McElroy and two other pilots attacked, with McElroy shooting down one of these two-seaters near Marcelcave. During the combat, McElroy had fallen to between 4,000 to 5,000 feet where almost immediately he spotted five Fokker triplanes attacking three S.E.5s. McElroy was able to shoot down two of these Fokkers before they broke off the engagement and headed east.[17] McElroy was a talented and deadly ace, as these conflicts show, and it is easy to see why Lambert held him in such high regard.

After these dogfights, McElroy and most of the pilots on C Flight returned to Conteville; however, Lambert was not among them. He was lost in a layer of clouds at about 10,000 feet with no airplanes in sight. In attempting to find his squadron, Lambert made one of those mistakes that happened to inexperienced fliers. It was horrifying at the time, but it becomes rather humorous as Lambert retold it later.

Lambert spotted a flight of planes below him, and naturally he assumed that they were C Flight. Spotting this formation gave him a sense of security; he was no longer lost and could return home. He had been in a dogfight, got separated from his flight, but now he had found them. Relieved, he dived down to the middle of this formation, but shortly discovered that what he thought was C Flight was four Albatros and two Pfalz fighters, German planes equipped with black crosses. Of this experience he writes, "Scared? That was no name for it, I was paralyzed with fear."[18] The way he describes his victory shows the humor (in retrospect) of the moment. He writes that he "kicked the rudder bar right and left, shut my eyes, fired both guns and trusted to luck."[19] In an interview in 1980, he said that he did not even know that he had shot the Albatros down. Until he was congratulated by his squadron mates for the victory, once he landed. They told him he had made the "damnest maneuver" they had ever seen. In this interview, he states that his mates were about 1000 feet above him.[20]

Like almost any good story, this one has more than one version. In the one Lambert tells in his book, the flight returned to Conteville without him. However, a Bristol Fighter nearby witnessed Lambert's act and probably helped to frighten away the enemy formation. Lambert remembered them heading east after his dogfight, and did not think that he alone would have been enough to cause their departure. In both these versions, however, Lambert had shot down an Albatros, and it was seen smoking on its way down. It would not be reported as hitting the ground or destroyed, but it was seen going down on fire, and that counted as a victory. This victory gave No. 24 Squadron five enemy aircraft for the day, and it gave Lambert his first victory.[21]

Lambert had conquered his fear and survived a harrowing experience. In the rough-draft copy of *Combat Report*, he made some revealing statements about himself that were omitted from the published version. One episode involves the appearance of a mythical black bird. Somewhere in the middle of closing his eyes, shooting down the Albatros, and making his escape from the German formation, he recollects seeing perched on the plane's cowling "that little 'hell cat,' red eyed, black bird, dancing around and wings flapping and shouting in fiendish glee—'boy I sure have you now; you will never get out of this; you just cannot get out of this.' That little devil sure put the 'wind up' me. I began to believe him. But fate deemed otherwise."[22] The editors were probably wise in leaving out this passage, but it does make vivid Lambert's state of mind at the time. In the rough-draft, Lambert also referred again to "the 'OLD GENTLEMAN' up above, surely took care of me that day."[23] In combat, as we have seen, Lambert was not an agnostic.

At any rate, Lambert had returned to Conteville and had found his mates there. However, unfortunately, when attempting to land at Conteville, McElroy had hit the top of a tree and crashed into a hanger. He was not badly injured, but was sent back to England for a rest. Lambert had lost an excellent Flight Commander.[24]

It may seem surprising that the Germans would have broken away from the engagement when the odds were still in their favor—two to one—even after Lambert had sent one of their planes down, but it was not unusual. They did not have the number of planes or pilots to compete with the Allies, particularly with the Americans now entering the air war. So to the Germans, discretion was the better part of valor, and Lambert could return to Conteville and safety.

On the days following Lambert's first victory, the weather was again disagreeable for flying. On the morning of the 8th, C Flight discussed the potential candidates to replace McElroy as Flight Commander. The flight favored Captain Selwyn, whom Lambert described as a "typical Englishman; duty and honor above everything … very quiet and reserved … [and] an excellent fighter pilot."[25] When the weather improved somewhat, Selwyn took C Flight on a line patrol around Moreuil Woods at 8,000 feet. They spotted "some Albatros fighters and a couple of two-seaters in the distance," but they were far out of range.[26] (Lambert seemed to be able to recall the type of fighter aircraft he faced in the sky, but he continued to refer to all observation aircraft as "two-seaters.")

Lambert had a high opinion of the pilots who flew these "two-seaters" for the Allies, even though he thought little of the machines they flew. For example, on 13 April he comments that the weather prevented members of the fighter wing from taking to the skies, but "those poor old two-seaters had to be out on reconnaissance patrols behind the enemy lines."[27] He did not envy those pilots who had to fly the old Armstrong Whitworths or R.E.8s; he knew that these planes were not only older, but slower and less maneuverable than any fighter plane, so they were hindered when attacked by members of "Richthofen's crowd." Lambert wrote that "all of them had a tough time and very few received much credit for what they did…. Many of those two-seater boys never came back, but they certainly took a heavy toll on the Germans."[28]

Returning to Lambert's log book. On 12 April, the weather had finally cleared, and the visibility was excellent. Both sides were active on the front. No. 24 Squadron was engaged in bombing and low-altitude strafing of enemy positions. In the morning hours, all three flights successfully attacked the Rosiéres aerodrome, setting fire to sheds, hangers, and planes on the ground.[29] In the afternoon, A and C Flight conducted an offensive patrol around 13,000 feet above the Hangard-Moreuil area. Selwyn was leading C Flight with Lambert, Wilson, and Daley, accompanied by Hammersley of A Flight and E. W. Lindeburg of B Flight.[30]

Four. Entering the Air War

(According to the squadron history, Hammersley left the squadron twenty-three days before Lambert joined; however, and equally authoritative source has four of Hammersley's eight victories occurred after Lambert joined the squadron, so Lambert's log book seems correct here.[31])

The Battle of Lys, the last great German offensive, had begun on 7 April, so the German fighters were out in force. Lambert and his companions found themselves facing several formations of Albatros, Pfalz and Fokker "Tripes" in what he called a "general melee ... the first real mix-up that we encountered."[32] This engagement was a full-scale dogfight, and Lambert's first experience of the chaos pilots encountered as they attempted to protect themselves and their comrades while all the same time maneuvering to shoot down the enemy. In a very short time, as dogfights tended to do, the general melee had broken up into separate combats from six to ten thousand feet involving combats between individual pilots or struggles between two or three planes, maneuvering for position and endeavoring to get the upper hand. Airplanes were everywhere. (Lambert was impressed by the astonishing rainbow colors of the German airplanes in "very fantastic and weird designs": he often remarked on them later, as well.[33])

Probably because it was his first dogfight and impressed itself on his mind, Lambert gives an elaborate description of the experience. However, some of the details, like the combat itself, can be confusing. As the air combat broke into separate battles, Lambert realizes the odds were decidedly against them. There "were twelve S.E.5s against twice that many Albatros and Pfalz scouts."[34] To make matters worse, ten Fokker Dr. I triplanes were rapidly coming from the east to join the fracas. The battle took on a life of its own as Lambert and three comrades became separated from the rest of the squadron and engaged with six Albatros and Pfalz fighters. Lindeburg of B Flight was able to shoot down a Pfalz that had been after Lambert. Hammersley and Redler each dispatched an Albatros fighters. Redler attacked his Albatros from behind and shot it down at close range. It was seen and later reported hitting the ground and bursting into flames. Lambert recalls briefly observing Redler's dogfight even though he "was trying to overcome another Albatros."[35]

In the next few moments, Lambert shot down two Albatros fighters. The second one was dispatched when it cut in front of him, and he was able to fire into the plane's fuselage from "under and slightly behind his seat."[36] He was amazed that the German pilot was still able to turn and open fire on him. The plane was observed spinning and hitting the ground. "Prior to this," as Lambert says, he had engaged an Albatros that had dived on him from the rear. Lambert managed to out-maneuver him and was able to riddle his machine with around 150 rounds from seventy yards. He saw that he had severed the Albatros' right aileron, but after spinning a short distance the pilot was able to land in a nearby field.

The battle continued for a short period in which the squadron was joined by a Spad and a Camel, with the Spad shooting down a Pfalz in flames. Overall, it was an impressive showing. Not only were a number of enemy driven down, but No. 24 suffered no casualties for the day. All planes returned safely to base, even though they were "pretty well shot up."[37]

Lambert considered that he had one plane crashed and one driven down.[38] In his log book under 12–4–18, he writes. "Two Ds; 1 out control & 1 crashed."[39] However, in the official communiqué, Lambert is given credit for only one. It states that Lambert "fired 100 rounds into an Albatross Scout from a range of a few yards. The E.A. turned and opened fire, got into a vertical dive and crashed."[40] These discrepancies, in which a pilot is given less official credit than he deserves, are not uncommon, and it was only many years later, when he was trying to establish his record, that Lambert got concerned about them. In his opinion, he now had three victories in less than three weeks of combat.

Selwyn had done well in his little time as Flight Leader of C Flight, but he was not allowed to retain the title very long. Captain George Johnson from Woodstock, Ontario, Canada arrived to take command of the flight. During the war, Johnson became an ace with eleven total victories and was awarded the Military Cross and the French Croix de Guerre with Palm. Only five of these victories would be with No. 24, so Johnson was already an ace before joining the squadron.[41] The squadron history has Johnson taking command of C Flight on 12 April and leading it until 19 June 1918. Captain Selwyn would officially succeed Johnson as Commander on 21 June and serve in that capacity until 26 August 1918.[42] Johnson and Selwyn would be Lambert's last commanders, as he would leave C Flight on 21 August.

Almost all squadrons, German or English, had mascots. Of course, various infantry and artillery regiments had mascots too, but practically each air squadron adopted animals around their base camps. Many pictures exist with pilots holding or petting dogs. In addition to dogs, cats were also adopted, and some squadrons even adopted foxes and civet cats. But No. 24 Squadron's mascots, like most squadrons, were dogs. Lambert, a lifelong lover of dogs, was delighted with these mascots. He mentions in his rough-draft copy of *Combat Report* "a very important event" with the arrival of "Jim" to No. 24 on 15 April. Jim would join "Chips" (whom Lambert described as a "small mongrel pup") as the Squadron mascots. (Jim is even mentioned in the squadron history, but without an explanation of who or what Jim was.) After a period of adjustment, the two dogs evidently got along famously, with Chips looking on Jim as a big brother. There is a picture of Jim with Lambert and C Flight comrade T. Hellett. According to Lambert, these dogs "ruled the roost. I really had a lot of pleasure with those two dogs."[43]

The weather still continued to be a problem. Faced with low clouds, rain, hail, and strong winds, C Flight was able to do very little flying, but, along with B Flight, in the morning of the 16th they managed to do some low level bombing around LaMotte, about four miles east of Villers-Bretonneux. They did not see any enemy aircraft, but when they returned to base, they discover "plenty of bullets in our planes"—probably from ground fire.[44] The mechanics undoubtedly had their work cut out, and probably were pleased that the squadron did not fly again until the 20th.

Lambert was not so pleased. He enjoyed being a pilot, and he desired action. He is bored on the ground and comically writes that all of No. 24 Squadron "want[s] another piano player."[45] On the morning of the 20th the weather has finally improved and his log book states that he was in the vicinity of Albert when he had a "Dud" engine and was forced to return home. He writes, "This was von Richthofen's territory, north of the Somme; no evidence of him or any of his followers at this time."[46]

The next day, the 21st, Lambert convinced John Daley, a transfer to the R.F.C., to join with him in the early morning hours in a balloon-busting venture. Lambert is showing his growth and daring by going on such an individual patrol, and the squadron leader is showing his confidence in Lambert by allowing him to do so. Lambert and Daley planned to attack balloons simultaneously from different angles in order to divert the ground attack. It is Lambert's strategy, but he needs Daley to make it work. They decided to do their hunting west of Albert, but eventually found that they had been beaten to the punch by two S.E.5s and a

Camel. One balloon was already burning, and the others were in the process of being cranked down as fast as possible by the German ground crew. When three Fokkers attempted to interfere with these attacking planes, Lambert and Daley came to their assistance, and their entry into the battle resulted in the Fokkers turning east to avoid a conflict. It was the usual strategy the Germans adopted when the odds were against them. After flying for some time with these other aircraft in hopes of finding further prey, Lambert and Daley broke off to return to base in order to join C Flight for an afternoon patrol.[47]

However, Daley and Lambert had started something new with this venture. Both men took to each other and quickly became close friends. They began to work as a team whenever they went on patrols together, supporting and covering each other. This teamwork continued throughout their association and would help in their survival. Their success was eventually copied by others in C Flight, as they too broke off into pairs when conducting offensive patrols.

This pairing was particularly important when their work involved dangerous activities such as trench strafing. Lambert would closely follow Daley through the German trenches for the greatest possible carnage. However, Lambert disliked trench strafing more than any other activity he did as a pilot. In the air, it was you against one or two opponents. In trench strafing, you saw on the ground the horrible effect of rapid fire machine-guns on hundreds of men and horses. (Lambert was particularly unnerved by the whinnying of the horses.) Lambert also thought it was far more dangerous than air combat because of the low-level flying and the hundreds of guns firing at you.[48] He did the work because he could see it would bring the Allies closer to victory, but he hated it.

Next, in the afternoon, Captain Johnson led C Flight on an offensive patrol in the vicinity of Albert and Marcourt. Joining Johnson on this patrol, besides Lambert and Daley, were Hellett, Selwyn, Wilson, and James Dawe. The patrol was heading over much the same territory that Lambert and Daley had patrolled earlier in the day. This patrol too would sight Fokker D VIIs, in the distance, but this time too far away to initiate a dogfight. At first they had been patrolling at about 10,000 feet, but then they changed targets and descended to attack enemy balloons. (These balloons could very well be from the same group that Lambert and Daley had attempted to attack earlier.) Johnson and Lambert employed the same strategy that Daley and Lambert had employed earlier. They attacked by diving down to about 500 feet and forcing the ground attack to choose between them. The balloon was drawn down, but was seen by both Lambert and Johnson to be smoking while it descended. They then unsuccessfully attacked a second balloon which was pulled down before they could do any damage.[49] Lambert shared credit for one kite balloon with Johnson. He now had three and one-half victories to his credit.

This statement is in accord with Lambert's log book. However, again Lambert did not receive the official credit he should have. The official history states, "We get our first balloon, which, counted as a Hun, makes our total 100 since we started with S.E.'s in February.... It was shot down by Capt. Johnson."[50] Lambert's part is not mentioned.

Lambert wrote that their activities were conducted in "Richthofen's hunting ground, but [there was] no evidence of him, or his men."[51] The reason for that was Richthofen was already dead. He was killed at 12:45 p.m., or fifteen minutes after C Flight left for its engagement with the balloons. In a later interview, Lambert said that he believed that Richthofen was killed by taking the battle to the Allied side of the line, something he rarely did. Lambert also remarked he had been in combat with Richthofen "three or four times,"[52] but in that his memory played him false. When we look at Lambert's papers and log book, we can see that it is virtually impossible for him to have engaged personally with Richthofen at any time.

For the next several days the weather was disagreeable, with thick cloud cover. It would not be until the 23rd that Lambert would again find himself in aerial combat. He was flying an afternoon flight at 3:00 p.m. with MacDonald and A Flight on an offensive patrol in the Montdidier region. MacDonald was a skilled pilot who would claim twenty victories from November 1917 to 21 June 1918, when he was sent home for rest.[53] Lambert wrote of MacDonald, "When I knew him, he was very slender looking person, and to me, not what I would term, one of robust health…. Physically I do not see how anyone, with his delicate looking stature, could have endured eleven months of that nerve-wracking pounding…. MacDonald is a great leader and a determined fighter pilot."[54] No matter how skilled and brave a pilot was, sooner or later the daily tension would get to him. Sooner or later, all pilots begin to feel fear.[55]

Lambert says that when he joined MacDonald and A Flight to take the war to the Germans, it was his first offensive patrol. The fact that he was chosen for the patrol shows how far he has come, but some of the events on the patrol show also how far he has to go to be on par with a McElroy or a MacDonald as a pilot.

Above the Montdidier area, MacDonald maneuvered his plane to attack a formation of Pfalz scouts. (The Pfalzs had been flown by such aces as Werner Voss and Erich Löwenhardt and were widely used by the German Air Force from the autumn of 1917 through the summer of 1918; however, its maneuverability and rate of climb were poor compared to most other planes then used, and therefore the Germans tended to give the plane to beginners or "inferior" pilots. Its strength was in its ability to dive, and its construction allowed for excellent forward viewing, so it was highly recommended and used in balloon busting.[56]) MacDonald dove on the Pfalz formation; Lambert "had not seen them, but pushed [his] nose down to follow Mac."[57] Lambert had reached a stage where he could be trusted to be a wing pilot on an offensive patrol, but his inability to spot the formation shows that he was to some extent still learning his trade. Unfortunately for Lambert, his Lewis gun became unclipped from its mounting, causing a tense moment as it obstructed his view of the Aldis sight. He momentarily lost sight of the flight, but was able to recover long enough to get on the tail of a Pfalz, putting a short burst of tracer bullets into its fuselage. Almost immediately, he developed engine problems and had to break off the attack and return to base after avoiding a head-on collision with another Pfalz. He made it as far as a French base at Hornoy, where he enjoyed a cool drink with a French lieutenant as mechanics replaced two defective plugs in his engine. Afterward, he returned to Conteville to discover from his friend from A Flight, the South African J. H. Southey, who was also on his first offensive patrol, that MacDonald had shot down a Pfalz on Lambert's tail.[58] Also, upon returning to base, Lambert discovered that the rest of the flight had feared that Lambert had been shot down behind the German lines during the scrap. The squadron history records that the 23rd had seen a "good show by Capt. McDonald in scrap."[59] Lambert might well reecho that comment; MacDonald had probably saved his life.

The episode above makes exciting reading; however, there is a serious question as to *when* it happened. Lambert writes in *Combat Report* that the flight took place on the 23rd, but his log book does not bear that out. His entry in the log book is the following: "23/4/18;

Four. Entering the Air War

1:30 to 3:35 p.m.; 1082; 3000 to 10,000 feet; Roye, Albert, Villers-Bretonneaux; engine bad and guns jammed."[60] *Combat Report* expands on this entry. Lambert writes that he flew with Johnson and C Flight, including Selwyn, Daley, Wilson, and Hellett and confronted a dozen Albatros and Pfalz fighters "painted in fantastic colors and designs." Lambert recognized his opponents because of the unique painting of their aircraft, and he describes a fifteen minute dogfight in which Johnson shot down a "silver-colored E.A. scout which was seen to crash."[61] Eventually they followed Johnson back to base, with Lambert continuing to have bad luck with his engine and gun problems. But the time difficulty is obvious: If Lambert had been in the air with Johnson and C Flight and had not returned until 3:35 p.m., it would have been impossible for him to have flown with MacDonald and A Flight at 3:00 p.m.

By this time, the second German offensive was grinding to a halt. Lambert refers to the Germans making a "final concentrated attack" on Villers-Bretonneaux. However, the weather was as much against him as it was against No. 24 Squadron, and French reinforcements had arrived to help the British. To assist troops, No. 24 Squadron sent out all its flights out at 6:00 a.m. on 24 April to do ground strafing; however, heavy fog resulted in a return to Conteville until 1:00 p.m. when a very low ceiling (around 200 feet) was available for offensive action against the enemy. Each plane carried four small bombs and a full load of ammunition; however, it is here where Lambert's description of the attack in the valley of the River Luce ends. There is no listing in his log book of going on this expedition; however, the likelihood is that this is the one that he describes in *Combat Report* for 23 April.

Lambert's next listing in his log book is for 3 May. The weather was too brutal for the rest of April, and heavy cloud cover made it difficult to fly. Anxiety and boredom seemed to reign in No. 24 Squadron. Lambert felt that if this was an example of sunny April in France, then he preferred Ontario or southern Ohio. For the pilots there was "plenty of mess hall activity ... [but Lambert felt] if this [weather] keeps up all of us will have to go back to flying school to learn to fly"[62]

On 25 April, Captain Johnson alone risked the weather and is credited with "a very daring reconnaissance ... when he flew some 12 miles over above the fog and returned under it about 20 ft."[63] With the force of the German offensive the day before, information on what the Germans were doing was "badly needed." According to Lambert, Johnson "immediately volunteered" for the reconnaissance mission. Since his return was so close to the ground, he had to endure intense and heavy ground fire, with his plane suffering several hits. After hearing about Johnson's experience, Lambert wrote that he "certainly would not have wanted that mission."[64] More was expected of Flight Commanders than of the pilots under them.

By now, the war was also having an effect on Lambert. Briefly in *Combat Report,* and in greater length in the rough-draft, is Lambert's remembrances of what it was like to be a combat pilot and the courage it took to face German bullets. One of the virtues of Lambert's book is that the reader gets a vivid and honest account of what it felt like to be under fire. Lambert speaks directly to the reader "who has never experienced a low mission ... or an extensive 'dog fight.'"[65] He answered the question he would hear from those who interviewed him over the years: "Were you ever scared?" Lambert never pretended to be a fearless warrior. He admitted that he was scared, and he thought that everyone was until they actually engaged the enemy. Once that happened, the pilot had no time to be scared: it was "kill or be killed."

Lambert gives a vivid picture of what it was like to be in a dog-fight: "you fly, round and round in tight circles, you dive, you roll, you twist that aeroplane inside out, you zoom maybe into a loop and maybe you spin to get that fellow off your tail; suddenly an E.A. flashes directly in front of you."[66] A pilot never hesitates to fire when he has an enemy aircraft in his sights. "Maybe you hit him or maybe you do not.... Yes, I can say, you were scared, but once it started you had no time for thinking. Everything from then on was pure instinct for survival."[67] The supposed "agnostic" once again shows his trust in Divine Providence during battle when he writes that his "bracing wires always had two tunes they played in a dive: one, 'Nearer My God to Thee,' and the other 'Home Sweet Home.'"[68] Lambert emphasizes that survival depends on the pilot being alert and at his best at all time. "The tired pilot may under these circumstances complain of having lost some of his keenness … [he may] wonder when it will be his turn to go home."[69] To prove that he had not lost his confidence, he may "execute various maneuvers dangerously close to the ground."[70]

Lambert, however, was not yet a tired pilot. He was still in the "spring" season of his life as a pilot. James Birley, a doctor who went to the Flying Corp at the end of the Somme Offensive in 1916, was the one who equated a pilot's life to the change of seasons, since in a pilot's life there are no years, but months. The "spring" season, the first two months of active service, is the period when he learns to fly and fight. It is the time when the pilot is more likely to "become a casualty than to inflict casualties on the enemy." Here is the period when "he gains experience only too often at the cost of his life." It is this period of a pilot's career, with almost three-quarters of all casualties occurring during the first three months of active service.[71] Lambert was one of the lucky ones. He had showed himself to be a survivor during the first month of "spring." The month of May would bring more challenges that would help prepare him for an active "summer" period in June.

Five

Spring 1918

Spring continued for Lambert and No. 24 Squadron as the focus of the front was shifting south with a new offensive for the German Army. This phase of the war would be known as the Third Battle of Aisne and would take place around Soissons and Rheims from 27 May until 6 June 1918.

Lambert and his comrades in No. 24 Squadron spent the latter part of April and the first week of May assisting ground troops with low-level flying attacks, or tactical ground support that delayed the German advances and gave brief respites to the tired British troops. "All pilots knew what had to be done and they did it, even before the orders were issued."[1] However, the weather was still a problem. But it began to improve around noon on 3 May with most of the 5th Brigade in action. C Flight, led by Captain Johnson, left around 10:30 a.m. and patrolled until 12:30 p.m. with no results. They flew behind the German lines around 16,000 feet above the area near Peronne, but, as they were to discover, the Germans were around ten miles to the west.

On 4 May C Flight took to the sky in the late afternoon to patrol the Moreuil-Villers-Bretanneaux area, their old stomping grounds. The same pilots—Johnson, Selwyn, Daley, Wilson, and Lambert—patrolled together. Lambert was still flying the same plane he had been flying, S.E.5a C1082.[2] He was getting comfortable with his plane and his squadron mates in C Flight. A few miles east of Villers-Bretanneux, the flight engaged "the old crowd," around eight multi-colored Albatros, Pfalz, and a Fokker Dr. I triplane. The leader of the enemy squadron, in a "fantastically colored Albatros," could, as Lambert admitted, "certainly fly an aeroplane,"[3] but he could not get into position to get a good shot at C Flight. "After all, the five of us in those S.E.5s were not exactly amateur pilots ourselves."[4] Clearly, Lambert now looked upon himself as one of the veterans of the squadron.

During this "short and fierce" conflict, planes from both sides were scattered throughout the sky. Lambert found himself on the tail of a Pfalz D-III above the Bray-Dompierre area at 6:45 p.m. around 5,000 feet. He was on its tail for a few seconds, fired a short burst, and sent it down out of control.[5] It was Lambert's plan to get within fifty yards of an opponent (twenty yards being preferable) in a position either behind or underneath the other plane before shooting his guns. Shooting at an opponent beyond that range was simply a waste of ammunition.[6] He now had four and a half victories to his credit.

The action was heavy during this dogfight, so Lambert did not have time to watch and see if the plane crashed. Lambert writes that Johnson also sent an enemy down out of control; but Johnson's record shown no confirmed victories for that day.[7] Daley and Selwyn were on the German leader's tail, but failed to register any success against a pilot who was able to so maneuver his Albatros by climbing, turning, and diving, as to escape eastward to the German lines. Anyway, Daley and Selwyn were interrupted during this fight when two enemy aircraft came to their commander's rescue. At this point, Wilson came into the fight, firing his guns at the two enemy machines, so that they broke off the attack and headed east toward the German lines.[8] The whole fight was over in a few short minutes, and Lambert had another victory on his way to becoming an ace.

The next day, the weather was again a problem with "low clouds, mist and rain," so there was limited flying for No. 24. It was also personally a bad day for Lambert. He was "Severely censored" on 5 May. Evidently he had attempted to send "photographs of RAF service machines to his sweetheart in the U.S.A."[9] This event, and the name of his sweetheart, were never mentioned by Lambert in any of his writings or interviews. We have no idea who she was. At any rate, Lambert got caught and was censored, and he learned his lesson. He wrote a number of other letters home to friends and loved ones, but he never again sent photographs of any kind.

Lambert relaxes between patrols and writes a letter home.

This may be a good place to say something about censorship and its effect on Lambert and his comrades. Censorship in the Great War, and in its successor the Second World War, went to a ridiculous degree. The effect on the soldiers (including the pilots) was that they knew almost nothing about the general pattern of the war, on either their own side or the enemy's. Anything Lambert knew about the war, besides his personal part in it, he got from English newspapers that he could find from time to time.

The squadron spent part of the day entertaining three distinguished guests from the top echelon in the R.A.F.: William Douglas Weir, 1st Viscount Weir, a Scottish industrialist and politician, founding member of the Royal Scottish Automobile Club, member of the Privy Council, and

Five. Spring 1918

Secretary of State for the R.A.F.; Major General, later Air Vice-Marshal, Sir Frederick Hugh Sykes, who served as Chief of the Air Staff From April 1918 to early 1919; and Major General, later Marshal of the Royal Air Force, and Sir John Maitland Salmond, who was the General Officer Commanding the Royal Air Force in the Field. Even with the bad weather, the squadron put on a flying display for their visitors. These squadron members "felt quite honored by this visit."[10]

Later that day (5 May), the weather cleared long enough for C Flight to fly during the late afternoon, between 5:30 and 7:30 p.m. Lambert says that he was near Mézières between 3,000 to 13,000 feet. His log book has that with another S.E.5 pilot, whose name is not mentioned, he dived on four Pfalz around 5,000 feet and sent "one down out of control." But there is absolutely no other record of this event except his log book, so this victory is no part of his official record.[11]

Over the next several days, the weather continued to be most disagreeable for flying. There was plenty of fighting to the north and south of them, but on their front the elements still played havoc on air flights. Lambert, however, did thirty minutes of local flying at around 2,000 feet to test his engine and get some target practice. To Lambert, a flier, even if he was not in the air on a mission, had to be constantly practicing to hone his flying and combat skills.

Low clouds, rain, and heavy ground mist covered No. 24's section of the front until late in the afternoon of the 8th, when it cleared enough for Johnson to take C Flight for a patrol around Rosiéres at 6:30 p.m. After the fog lifted, the flight spent ninety minutes patrolling around 14,000 feet but met no Germans. The weather improved on the 9th, and Lambert was part of a line patrol in the late morning hours (from 10:30 a.m. to 12:10 p.m.), again with no enemy aircraft sighted. The action seemed to be on other fronts at this time.

Later in the evening, C Flight joined B Flight, under Captain Cyril N. Lowe for a late evening patrol around the Albert-Villers-Bretonneux area. Leaving at 5:30 p.m. eleven S.E.5s would patrol between 10,000 to 15,000 feet looking for enemy aircraft. B Flight was flying in formation approximately 2,500 feet lower that C Flight. For the first time in days, they spotted the enemy: a formation of Albatros heading west at around 3,000 feet.[12] Lowe spotted the formation first and moved his flight into position for an attack. Lambert spotted them almost at the same time. (His acuity as a pilot was clearly increasing.) He counted eight Albatros scouts painted in a variety of colors. However, Johnson kept his flight above the fracas, for a while, to make certain the Albatros were not decoys to lure the flight into the conflict, only to be pounced on by additional enemy aircraft hiding in the clouds.

Lowe had taken the enemy by surprise: B Flight scattered them in all directions, and a melee followed. Johnson now brought C Flight down to join the fracas. Lambert writes that the action was "fast and furious and lasted possibly 15 or 20 minutes." The Germans, however, were unaware of C Flight until they "joined in the chase,"[13] and were at a disadvantage. During the engagement, Lowe was credited with shooting down an Albatros DV over Hangard Wood around 6:45 p.m. Lambert writes that he saw Lowe's "streamer straight out behind; he was on the tail of a blue and red machine."[14] Lowe fired a short burst into the Albatros, and it was seen by someone else spinning down out of control. It was listed as "Out of Control" in the records.[15] Lambert also recalls that Lowe "pounced onto another Albatros and had time for a long burst and drove him down damaged."[16] Lowe, however, is only given credit for one victory on that day.

It may seem strange that Lambert could have witnessed Lowe's exploits in the midst of a dogfight. In fact, he had a moment in which he had worked himself free from the fight, suffering only a few bullet holes in his wings. Then he maneuvered himself into position to fire about a hundred rounds into a light-blue Albatros that was attempting to elude Lieutenant T. B. Hellett. Lambert believed Hellett's guns had jammed at an inopportune moment. Lambert arrived in time to help send that Albatros into a spin and crash in a field southeast of Corbie. Lambert and Hellett both witnessed the crash, and both pilots would share equally in this victory. As with his previous victory, the shared Albatros was listed in his log book as well as in other sources.[17] The official communiqué stated that both Hellett and Lambert had fired into the E.A., with Lambert "firing 100 rounds into it. The E.A. went down in a spin from 5,000 feet and was sent to crash in a field."[18] With this victory, Lambert's total was now five, and he qualified for the coveted title of Ace.

However, the fight was not yet over. Lambert glanced to the east and saw an S.E.5 piloted by Daley closing in on an Albatros. Daley was probably not aware that on his tail was another enemy aircraft moving in for the kill. Joining in the battle, Lambert forced the attacking pilot to rethink his tactics. That Albatros turned and headed home, leaving his comrade to his fate. Lambert watched as the Albatros Daley was attacking flattened out, went into a dive, and eventually crashed into some trees. Afterward, Daley and Lambert turned west and headed for Conteville.[19]

It was a successful action for the squadron. Since 24 March, it had lost two killed in action, four wounded and two missing. The squadron had recorded forty-five enemy aircraft (including balloons) as indecisive combats, and eleven enemy aircraft driven down damaged.[20] It had been quite a successful seventeen days in spite of the weather conditions, and Lambert had shown he could carry his share of the load, or more, in combat.

In *Combat Report*, Lambert gave his readers some idea of what it was like to prepare for a morning flight. He was frank in his dislike of early patrols, probably because of the early wake-up calls and the early morning weather. Lambert speaks of his batman getting him up before daylight.

A word about the batman. The batman was the personal servant of a commissioned officers. He would take care for the officer's personal equipment, including his uniform, wake him in the morning, bring him his tea, and otherwise perform the duties of a servant. It was a desirable position, of course, because the batman was behind the lines and not involved in combat, so was more likely to survive the war, not only more likely than a common solider, but more likely to survive than the pilot he served. The position was an anachronism in modern war. A pilot was an officer and a gentleman, and gentlemen had servants.

After getting up before daylight, Lambert would proceed to dress for flight. In order to fly in the thin cold air above 15,000 feet in an open cockpit, the pilot had to go through a ritual that was akin to preparing for deep-sea diving or Arctic exploration. It meant putting on two pairs of socks (one thin and one made of heavy wool), a pair of slacks and light weight shoes. These were followed by a light cotton undershirt, and over that a heavy wool shirt that fitted under his tunic and his Sam Brown belt. After breakfast, preparation would continue with the Sidcot flying suit, (that was a standard rain coat-type design possibly lined with a very dense wool pelt), sheep-skin boots, a knitted wool helmet with a long neck piece, leather helmet with goggles, and some triple layer silk gloves that would go under his fur gloves. The pilot would then tuck his little "split-arse" cap in one of his pockets.[21]

Five. Spring 1918

After this involved procedure, Lambert was ready to meet with the other members of his flight to get his orders before going to the hanger. Johnson would give the briefing, outline the mission, and remind the flight about the dangers of taxiing across a field in the dark.[22]

Starting the plane was a scene reminiscent of what audiences would see in theaters, in movies such as *Wings, Dawn Patrol,* or *Hell's Angels.* Lambert would climb into his S.E.5a and fasten his seatbelt. Assisting him was a non-commissioned officer. Lambert would check the controls, pull the pump-gear handle for pressure, and wait for the N.C.O to yell, "Switch off." Lambert would respond in kind and wait again for the N.C.O. to roll the propeller, to suck in some gas, and yell, "Contact." Once again, Lambert would respond in kind as the N.C.O. would check the wheel chocks and give the propeller a good swing so the engine would catch. Then Lambert would throttle forward to around 800 to 900 R.P.M. and allow the engine to warm up for a few minutes. Finally, he would throttle back and motion to his N.C.O. to remove the wheel chocks. He was now ready.

As Johnson began to taxi down the field, the flight got into position. An aviation mechanic would assist each plane at its wing tip so it would be turned properly into the wind for take-off. Once Johnson began to roll down the field with his engine full on, the others would follow, picking up speed, bumping on the ground until they were airborne. Since it was still dark, the flight would find each other via their exhaust flames and begin to form in formation to travel eastward into the emerging dawn.[23]

Over the next several days after 9 May, the action was light for C Flight. Even if they came across a flight of German aircraft, as they did on 10 May during the dawn patrol when they sighted seven Fokker Dr. I triplanes flying in the area, the enemy was unwilling to force the issue.[24] Lambert wrote rather boastfully that "some of the German leaders just would not come in unless they outnumbered us at least 2 to 1; and they seldom worked west of their lines."[25] It is not that these Fokkers were against engaging C Flight; they were under orders not to risk it, although there would have been no way for Lambert to know that at the time. Planes and pilots were too scarce for the German Air Force to risk them. A popular saying among German pilots was "to return without a fight and our work done, is the task with us."[26] Allied superiority in numbers of planes and pilots forced this defensive policy on the Germans.

With a lull in the action on his front, Lambert took advantage of the time given him to go over his engine and to improve its performance. Some pilots left the maintenance of the plane entirely to the mechanics; they saw it as their sole duty to fly the plane. Lambert, with his engineering background, was the opposite. He and his N.C.O. would go over the engine "from A to Z and [they] managed to get a few more R.P.M.s out of it."[27] After taking it for a thirty-minute spin, Lambert spent an additional half an hour checking the ammunition on both the Vickers belt and the Lewis drums. He wanted to prevent gun stoppages that could prove to be disastrous in combat. Lambert wanted to be sure that the "engine and 1082 with me at the controls were working as one.... She was a good aeroplane. I wanted to take good care of her and to keep her with me as long as possible."[28] Finally, he took C1082 out and worked it through loops, curves, dives, as well as firing practice.

For the next few days the weather was good, for a change, but there was still little action against the enemy. On 12 May Lambert saw a two-seater, but there was no dogfight as the plane retired to the east.[29] He was flying C1084 at the time, because C1082's engine was knocking, and it was not performing well enough for him to take it on a mission. While he was on a morning patrol with Johnson and C Flight, he located a couple of enemy machines below through the clouds at around 5,000 or 6,000 feet, near the town of Hangard to the north. He had a bird's eye view of a dogfight between two Camels from No. 209 Squadron and an old Albatros two-seater. Before the Camels could dispose of the enemy plane, however, a S.E.5 "came out of no-where … on the scene from below and behind the Albatros," and shot it down. Lambert saw it crash.[30]

The weather again turned bad, and Lambert and No. 24 were given a few days off from combat. It was a period to rejuvenate themselves and, for Lambert, to get some additional target practice. The heavy overcast weather turned out to be a blessing because Lambert's S.E.5a C1082 was still in the shop. He spent about thirty minutes flying C8261, concentrating on improving his aim; however, his practice did not last long because the guns on that aircraft were not sighted properly. He felt he could not "hit the side of a barn with those guns."[31] This comment shows how important Lambert's mechanical and technical knowledge was to his survival, and also why he was attached to C1082 after he had spent so many hours making sure it preformed up to his expectations.

Lambert also enjoyed his down time, playing "Bumble-Puppy" with his comrades and going jackrabbit shooting with E. G. McMurtrie of B Flight. McMurtrie was a better shot than Lambert; in fact, Lambert said that McMurtrie made him "look like an amateur."[32] McMurtrie's father was an Australian sheep rancher, and McMurtrie had assisted his father by driving away wild Australian dogs from the sheep; as a result, he became very proficient with a rifle.[33]

Finally, on 15 May, the weather improved, and there was a flurry of activity. No. 24's Flights did two patrols each without registering any victories. According to Lambert, the action was "fast and furious": the D.H.4 bombers were able to deliver forty tons of bombs while being supported by No. 24's S.E.5s. Lambert, however, did not participate in these patrols.[34] Evidently C1082 was still not working right. His log book recorded that he had taken the plane up for ten minutes to check the engine, but the check evidently revealed continuing problems.

On the 16th, the weather improved even more, and the squadron had some of its best opportunities in days. This day, Lambert was also active, but his first descriptions of the day was of the action of a mixed group of fighters from A and B Flights. He adroitly describes the exploits of MacDonald, Captain Horace D. Barton, Lieutenant E. P. Crossen, Captain Conway M. G. Farrell, Captain Lowe, and Lieutenant E. Harrison.[35] This group was escorting the D.H.4s of No. 205 Squadron on a bombing mission when they encountered eight Fokker triplanes and five Albatros D Vs attacking out of the sun. The following flurry of action lasted thirty or forty minutes and ended with three Albatros confirmed as shot down out of control, a Fokker shot down by Barton that crashed in a field near Proyart, and the bombing mission by the D.H.4s ruled a success.[36] In writing his book later, Lambert did some additional research and he notes that according to German records a Sergeant Schmutzler was killed and crashed near Proyard (he even notes the differences in spelling) and a Lieutenant Wolff, who was shot down north of LaMotte, did not return.[37]

Lambert was part of a later-morning flight of one hour and fifty-five minutes around 13,000 feet in the Moreuil-Hamel area that saw some indecisive jousting with some Pfalz fighters, but he also recorded he had a dud engine.[38] This flight ended around 11:40 a.m. In the later afternoon, Lambert worked on his engine. Even though the "revs" were acceptable

Five. Spring 1918

to him, it was flying a little rough, he thought because of a worn bearing. He and his mechanic spent about an hour working on the engine, but found nothing significantly wrong. However, the roughness seemed to disappear, so he was ready for the evening flight.[39]

In this evening flight, starting at 5:15 p.m., Lambert flew about an hour and fifty minutes. All three flights this day, Lambert wrote, encountered "many enemy aircraft: 'Tripes,' Albataros, Pfalz and a number of 2-seaters were engaged throughout the day."[40] Five Albatros D Vs and three Pfalz D-IIIs attacked C Flight during their evening patrol, but after a brief flurry the enemy aircraft headed east, and an artillery barrage was unleashed. The sky became a symphony of noise and color. Far from being frightened, Lambert found beauty in the brilliant bright colors busting in the sky around him. He wrote that it was "a scene that artists have dreamed of, but have never put on canvas."[41] In his later years, he would take up painting in order to recapture just such scenes.

Lambert proved to be right about the bearing problem in C1082. On 17 May, C Flight left for the early patrol, around 6:40 a.m. and reached a height of around 6,500 to 7,000 feet eight miles east of Conteville. They were planning to patrol the area north of the Somme. Suddenly, a connecting rod went through a cylinder, disabling Lambert's plane. At that height, experiencing severe vibrations and loud clattering noises, Lambert knew he was in trouble, but kept his head. He proceeded to return to Conteville and land the plane. He had previously found that the S.E.5 had excellent gliding abilities.[42] The only problem was that he was forced to land in a field in which the grass was eight to ten inches high, obscuring obstacles. This plane went down is one of these, a "small ditch probably one foot deep and about two feet wide." This resulted in a quick stop, with the plane's momentum carrying the tail over in front of the nacelle so that Lambert was positioned upside down.[43] However, he was not hurt, and the plane, with the exception of the propeller and a slightly damaged rudder, was in solid working condition and could be repaired.

The next day, Lambert was assigned a new plane, C1870, to fly. This plane was straight from the Depot and would require, for Lambert, special attention to get the engine and rigging to work the way to which he had become accustomed. He liked the nacelle to be a little heavy so the plane would not keep ascending, and he rigged the plane so it would fly straight and level even with his hand off the steering. He credited an adjustable horizontal stabilizer in helping him to achieve this goal.[44]

It was not until the 19th that Lambert would join C Flight in an offensive patrol, in the vicinity of Albert. That day would see heavy air-fighting and bombing raids behind enemy lines. Lambert's log book has him flying from 10:15 a.m. until noon, in C1870 for the first time. He found himself in a dogfight when C Flight was briefly attacked between 14,000 and 15,000 feet by eight or ten Pfalz fighters. When a flight of six Camels joined the fray, the enemy quickly headed east, followed closely in pursuit by the Camels. However, C Flight was low on fuel and headed back to Conteville.

Lambert was flying a new machine, but that did not mean the plane had no problems. In fact, he recorded in his log book "Engine Dud." He felt a couple of times that he might have to abandon his comrades and head back to Conteville early.[45] C1870 obviously needed further work to get it to the proficiency he required. Unfortunately, there was no time available, for the entire squadron was scheduled to do escort duty. They left at 6:00 p.m. to protect No. 49 Squadron as its D.H.9s bombed targets southeast of Bray. Before reaching the target area, Lambert observed a confrontation to the east involving three Camels from No. 209 Squadron and six Germans flying the new Fokker D VII biplane. Lambert reported that the Camels got the credit for driving down three of these new machines.[46]

It is of interest to notice the way that Lambert speaks about these conflicts. He showed little or no animosity towards the German pilots, unlike someone like Mannock, who truly hated the Hun. To Lambert, the business of war was just that, business. It was his job, what he had trained for. He wrote that he "did not have anything against those men in those black-crossed aeroplanes. I did not know any of them, nor did they know any of us. Yet here we were, pouring hot fire at each other. Killed or be killed."[47] Lambert had great respect for Mannock and thought he was "remarkable" and "fearless," but he also thought Mannock "seemed to take many dangerous chances."[48] Lambert did not let his emotions get involved in his job.

As the Camels battled with the new Fokkers, the bombing mission continued, with C Flight flying at an altitude at 14,000 feet. The D.H.9s were a thousand feet below them. A and B Flights were completing the stack at different levels, higher and slightly to the rear of C to provide cover in case of enemy attacks. As the D.H.9s dropped their bombs, fifteen Fokker triplanes and Pfalz came in to attack the bombers. The D.H.9s took tactical defensive measures, much like the circling of Conestoga wagons in an old Western, forming a circle for their mutual protection. The circular action of the bombers allowed the observer to the rear of the cockpit a clear field to use his machine gun. Simultaneously both B and C Flights dove down on the enemy planes, which had already split formation and scattered. With the odds against them, the Fokkers and Pfalz decided to turn east and avoid further confrontation. Since their bombing objective had been achieved, both squadrons turned west to head back to their bases in formation. According to Lambert, upon their return both Hammersley and E. B. Wilson of C Flight reported one Fokker "Out of Control." It had been a joint attack, driving the plane off the tail of a D.H.9. Hammersely also reported shooting a second one "down Damaged," and Lieutenant Ronald T. Mark of B Flight, reported one as "forced to land."[49]

While No. 24 Squadron was busy on the front, the Germans were conducting a major air raid on London using Gotha GV heavy bombers, the biggest and last raid on London during the war. After this raid, the Gotha squadrons would be utilized on the Western Front. The R.A.F. was now taking a leaf out of the Germans' book and took the war into Germany. On 20 May, local fighting could be found north of Albert, and the German city of Coblenz was bombed. Trenchard had decided the objectives of the R.A.F., which included railroads and blast furnaces. The Germans would find it very difficult to supply the front if the railroads were not working, and blast furnaces were essential for steel production. They also presented excellent targets for night attacks.

Night bombing raids were still experimental, but they were becoming part of the arsenal of Trenchard's Independent Air Force, a branch of the R.A.F. assigned to strategic bombing.[50] The Independent Air Force also continued to attack in daylight. The success of day raids depended on the bombers keeping in formation.[51] Enemy attacks were designed to disrupt these formations, and fighter squadrons were assigned to make sure these bombing missions proceeded according to schedule and without interruptions. Lambert's No. 24 Squadron was an important part of this strategy, then, serving as escorts and protectors for the bombers.

These bombing raids changed the traditional concept of war. The distinction between soldier and civilian was breaking down. Limited war was changing into total war. Industrial centers and much-populated cities were being attacked. There were even plans to bomb

Five. Spring 1918

Berlin. These raids were one of the most important reasons that the air war was becoming a more and more important part of the Great War.[52]

On 20 May, No. 24 was busy escorting bombers to their targets. At around 6:30 a.m. a joint flight led by Captains Lowe, Commander of B Flight, and MacDonald, Commander of A Flight, took off to escort No. 205 Squadron's D.H.4s and D.H.9s on a bombing raid. Thirteen pilots from all three flights joined in this enterprise, including Lambert. They were operating from Albert to Chaulnes between 15,000 to 16,000 feet. The D.H.4s dropped their bombs around 8:15 a.m. east of Chaulnes and had begun turning to head back to base when they were attacked by seven enemy planes. Lambert remarked that at first the No. 24 Squadron pilots did not recognize the planes. They thought they were Pfalz scouts, but in reality they were the new Fokker D. VIIs, the best planes on the German side.[53] These planes were shortly joined by six more enemy aircraft, including Fokker triplanes and Plalz scouts. In the ensuing conflict, twenty-six fighters and ten D.H.4s were involved in a melee over a two-mile radius from altitudes of 18,000 to 500 feet, a dogfight that lasted three-quarters of an hour.[54]

Lambert describes this battle in great detail. In fact, he describes the duels his comrades in the Squadron were fighting before he describes his own, and in somewhat more detail. His first description is of an intense fight involving Captain Lowe and Lieutenant Mark with an enemy aircraft. During the fight, Lowe was forced to dive to about 3000 feet to extinguish flames on his plane caused by the attacking aircraft. Meanwhile, as he was diving on another opponent, Mark's wing began to disintegrate, as he headed west, he saw Lowe going down with an E.A. on his tail. Coming to Lowe's rescue, Mark dove on the opponent, driving him off Lowe's tail by firing thirty rounds of ammunition. However, the opponent maneuvered to put himself on Mark's tail and attacked, forcing Mark into a steep dive. It was now Lowe's turn to come to Mark's aid, diving on the attacking enemy aircraft while firing around sixty rounds at what Lambert called "medium range." The attack was successful; the enemy plane was forced to land "behind a small clump of trees."[55] Afterward, both Lowe and Mark headed west, with Mark having to land at Bertangles. Upon landing, his plane burst into flames. Lowe joined Mark on the ground to make sure his comrade had survived the ordeal, and then returned to Conteville and submitted his report. Both pilots had come to each other's assistance and saved one another. Each would receive the Military Cross for his heroism.[56]

Lambert then described other individual confrontations. Lieutenant John Palmer and Captain Farrell became intertwined with one Pfalz and three other enemy aircraft, climbing, firing, and diving while chasing, eluding, and being driven off each other by astute maneuvers. No casualties resulted; Farrell's guns jammed, allowing the enemy to escape.[57] Lindeberg was hampered by an engine problem, but Hammersley, Lambert records, was involved in a "long running fight, managed 6 or 7 bursts [about 250-rounds], some of them at a very close range."[58] Hammersley was able to watch this plane fall several thousand feet out of control before he was attacked by two enemy aircraft. He was able to get on the tail of one of these attackers and fire about a hundred rounds at it, but the second plane had an experienced pilot whom Lambert described as "another 'breed.'" Hammersley and this experienced pilot fought each other as far as Warfusée before the conflict was broken off and the German headed east.[59] Afterward, Hammersley and Lieutenant Hellett became embroiled in fights with seemingly the same enemy aircraft that had been earlier attacking Hammersley alone. This confrontation also ended in a draw, as the enemy was seen to have "spun down about 3000' and cleared off east."[60]

Finally, Lambert describes his own part in this conflict. (The reader has to remember, however, that all of these conflicts were taking place simultaneously.) Lambert was fortunate enough to have a bluish-green Pfalz dart twenty-five yards in front and slightly above his position with its "belly right in front." He called it "a perfect shot."[61] The Pfalz fell several thousand feet, spinning rapidly downward; however, because of the intense action, Lambert found himself unable to see if the plane crashed, since he was under attack by another enemy aircraft from above. He does remark that some of the results were confirmed by ground forces, but he does not know if his was one of them. (In fact, Lambert did get credit for a victory, but the plane was listed as "out of control."[62] It was a Pfalz D-III shot down near Chaulnes-Albert around 8:35 a.m.)[63]

The fight was not over; Lambert was under a hail of bullets from the German aircraft diving on him. However, he was able to maneuver his plane into a position where the German aircraft bypassed him, letting him get in a relatively good shot at his opponent. He did not shoot the plane down, but he did see another S.E.5, possibly Southey, get on the tail of his opponent and continue the dogfight. Flying around 12,000 feet, Lambert focused on another enemy aircraft about a hundred feet above and in front of him. Unfortunately, he was unable to get within 150 yards of the plane before he was sighted, and his opponent went into a dive and headed east.[64]

Lieutenant Daley's weak engine made it impossible for him to keep up with a two-seater near Albert, let alone one of the new D. VIIs. Daley was, however, able to shoot down a balloon near Warfusée using incendiary rounds. The balloon was observed smoking as it was being pulled down. Daley achieved this feat fifteen minutes before Lambert's victory.

Around 8:45 a.m., or about ten minutes after Lambert's victory, he, along with Barton, Hammersley, and Hellett, went after some E.A. that were flying around 8,000 feet in a protective screen for the balloons below them. Hammersley, Hellett, and Lambert all got in a number of bullets at these planes. Hammersley shot about 200 rounds in two dives, Hellett got off 150 rounds; and Lambert shot fifty rounds at two different machines.[65] But all the Germans escaped without great damage. However, with the protecting aircraft being absent, MacDonald and Southey were able to attack a balloon 6,000 feet about Marcelcave, and Dawes attacked another one around Ignaucourt.[66] Both of these attacks failed.

Overall, it was an intense and lively dogfight, with No. 24 Squadron encountering the new Fokker D. VIIs for the first time and showing great skill in their battles. No. 24 claimed four decisive victories (of which Lambert's was one) and three indecisive, without a loss.[67] For Lambert, it was his sixth victory. He wrote that there was "little serious damage, other than the after effect on one's nervous system and the physical fatigue caused by throwing those aeroplanes all over the sky."[68]

Lambert had spent some of his courage that day. He had lessened his capital, and he would continue to spend it as these battles continued. After this battle, after submitting their reports, he and his comrades went to the mess to eat and drink, including alcoholic beverages, because, as Lambert wrote, "we all needed the latter."[69] Drinking to steady one's nerves became a recurring ritual for Lambert and the others as they returned to camp from an intense day of combat.

After a brief rest, Lambert went on another mission at 4:30 p.m. to escort some D.H.9s on a bombing attack east of Albert. That was a complete success: the bombs were successfully dropped, and the only enemy aircraft they saw were too off in the distance. For Lambert, this mission "ended a strenuous day."[70]

Five. Spring 1918

There was not much action for No. 24 on the next day, 21 May. Elsewhere, the war continued, of course, with Mannheim being bombed by the British and Paris attacked by Gotha bombers. Edward Mannock, No. 74 Squadron, shot down three Pfalz D-III and one Hannover C in the Hollebeke area. These feats gave him thirty-five victories. He would get his thirty-sixth the next day, another Pfalz D-III, over Fromelles.[71] Lambert, hearing of these feats, again expressed great admiration for Mannock.

On 21 May, Lambert was again on an early morning mixed patrol led by Johnson, leaving around 7:30 a.m., headed for the area around Moreuil, flying between 10,000 and 12,000 feet. After forty-five minutes of flying, they encountered eight Pfalz and an Albatros D V; however, just as the forces became entangled, a flight of Camels appeared, and the odds against the Germans were now too great. Following policy, they broke off the engagement and headed east, but not before McDougall, Daley, Hammersley, and Wilson aggressively forced down an opponent. But since this plane landed behind the German lines, Lambert knew that this pilot would "probably ... come back and fight another day."[72]

After returning to base around 9:25 a.m., Lambert was allowed to catch his breath before going on a second offensive patrol north of the Somme River, which now included Lieutenant James Dawe.[73] Lambert's description of this second patrol in the rough-draft copy of *Combat Report* includes a detailed description of an actual fight between dogs, in order to give his readers an understanding of why the word "dogfight" is used to describe aerial combat. (Unusually, Lambert does not give a time period for this second flight.) The patrol confronted a two-seater and its Albatros escort, both of which they fired upon, and Lambert records that hits were made by Daley, Dawe, and McDougall, with the two-seater forced to land. Each of the three pilots reported that they had hit the plane's observer.[74] Overall, however, May 21 was not a particularly active day, especially when contrasted with the intense fighting of the day before.

The following day, 22 May, was an idyllic spring day: birds singing, green fields and trees, and very warm weather.[75] The air war and bombings continued on the Western Front. The railroads at Liege and Metz and the city of Mannheim were bombed by the R.A.F. No. 22 Squadron of Bristol fighters came to the aid of the D.H.4s that helped to deliver sixty tons of bombs on the Germans in day and night attacks. These Bristols engaged ten enemy fighters, crashed two and drove one down out of control. Lambert comments, "If I could not fly S.E.5s, then I would want the Bristol. It was really a fighting aeroplane."[76] The Germans were also attempting to be active in the air. They set out to bomb Paris, but only one of their original thirty machines sent out actually reached the city.

No. 24 had a less-than-productive day. Their flights returned after seeing, but not engaging, the enemy. C Flight went on an offensive patrol around 11:15 a.m. but saw only one two-seater, which made a beeline for home after noticing the S.E.5s. Unfortunately for Lambert, he was forced to return early because C1870 developed engine problems. He landed at the squadron's old field at Bertangles and discovered that the intense knocking he heard was produced by a magneto connected by only one bolt and ready to fall off. After the magneto was reattached, the engine performed as usual, and he was able to return to Conteville by 12:30 p.m. to find his mates in the mess waiting for him.[77]

Until 27 May, there was a notable lack of activity on the German side. Ludendorff was planning on unleashing his third Spring offensive, the Blücher-Yorck Offensive, or as the Allies called it, the Third Battle of the Aisne, on that day. This offensive would shift the battle south. Ludendorff's goal was to recapture the Chemin des Dames Ridge that had been lost during the Second Battle of Aisne, and threaten Paris. He hoped that this threat would force the British to shift troops to the south, weakening the Flanders front, so that he could strike north and drive the British into the sea. The previous air attacks on Paris were a build-up to this offensive.

The week before 27 May, the fighting on the front was local and relatively unimportant. So Lambert knew there was a change in the wind. He wrote, "The Germans may have plans for something down south of our sector. If they were, we were sure to find out when the time came."[78] As No. 24 conducted patrols on 23 May, C Flight faced a greater threat from anti-aircraft fire than from enemy planes; those they did see, mostly two-seaters, would break off their observation and quickly head east. In fact, his log book shows that while he was on morning patrol he engaged a two-seater that retired east.[79] Moreover, while returning back to Conteville they flew north of Montdidier around 4,000 to 5,000 feet and in the forest areas saw tracks that "had been several days old. A lot of men and equipment had been … there." He concluded that "a movement of some sort was taking place and it was going south…. Something was brewing."[80]

The next few days the weather turned bad, and rain and low cloud cover prevented any serious activity. Some reconnaissance was done, but the fighters would have been limited in their action, even if the German planes had still been there. On the 24th, the entire squadron was grounded. A Flight went for a short patrol on the morning of the 25th, to be followed in the afternoon by B flight. Lambert used this time to test his engine and found that it had low revolutions and "very rough" flying. So instead he flew C1845, a new plane out of the depot, when C Flight went on patrol at 6:30 p.m. Lambert was not at all sure how this new plane would perform, but—perhaps fortunately for him—the weather and poor visibility forced the flight to return to Conteville within thirty minutes.[81] In spite of the weather, however, there was heavy shelling by the Germans in the Villers-Bretonneux area.

It would not be until the 27th that the weather improved sufficiently for No. 24 to begin regular operations. And visibility was still an issue, particularly around 10,000 feet. Lambert was fortunate in one respect: the delay caused by the weather enabled his mechanics to get C1870 ready for use. He would be flying a plane in which he had confidence. C Flight had the 6:30 a.m. morning flight and was assigned an offensive patrol along the Somme River, working the area around Hamel and LaMotte between 9,000 and 10,000 feet. But they patrolled for almost two hours and did not see one enemy aircraft, and B and A Flights followed them with the same results. Lambert commented, "Something [was] definitely wrong. Where are they? Our skies are not empty of German aircraft because of the weather. They must have plans for action on some other front."[82]

But Lambert did not know what this action was or when it would begin. The Aisne battle began the day before Lambert became aware of it. He wrote, "It is surprising, just how little one in our position knows about the war in general. All we know is our own activity on our own small front, plus a few bulletins on the board."[83] As previously stated, all Lambert seems to have known about the war came from reading London newspapers. For example, he was unaware that the Germans had begun a move to take Paris, let alone how close to success they were.

After the initial heavy bombardment, the Germans attacked on Aisne between Soissons and Reims, forcing the Allies backward. The Germans attacked with seventeen divisions in

Five. Spring 1918

the first wave, with thirteen in reserve, and successfully captured their objective, the Chemin des Dames Ridge. This opened up an area behind the Chemin des Dames on a nine-mile front. The bridges on the Aisne were available, since the French had failed to destroy them, so the Germans crossed the Ailette, Aisne, and Vesle rivers and were sixteen miles west-northwest of Rheims by the end of the day. They had created a twenty-five mile wide fissure in the Allied front and had penetrated twelve miles.[84]

Paris was also being bombed by huge, long-range siege guns that became known later as the "Paris Guns." These guns were mounted on railroad cars and had barrels that measured more than 100 feet. It took around three minutes for the quarter-ton shells to reach the city.[85] The original goal of this offensive was to draw British troops from the north and then renew the German attack on that region; however, with this great success on the Aisne, Ludendorff now considered pursuing this attack all the way to Paris.[86]

No. 24 Squadron would feel the effects of this new offensive. A mixed group led by Captains Johnson, Lowe, and MacDonald were joined by Lieutenants E. P. Crossen, Barton, Daley, John Palmer, Farrell, and Lambert in the morning flight that left at 4:45 a.m. for Maricourt. This group contained experienced pilots; there would be no room for novices on this patrol. Unlike in the previous week or so, the enemy was out in force today.

At around 15,000 feet, around 5:30 a.m., with the sun was coming up, the flight encountered a number of enemy planes, both Albatros D Vs and Pfalz D-IIIs. Lambert estimated that they were outnumbered two-to-one by the Germans when he, Johnson, Daley, and Palmer went after four of the Albatros and three Pfalz in what became a wild dogfight occupying considerable space and time. Lambert found himself shooting a deflection shot at a diving Pfalz that was attacking Daley. He was able to drive the Pfalz off of Daley's tail, riddling its fuselage with bullets, but not disabling the pilot.[87] Almost immediately, Daley had three enemy aircraft in front of him, so Lambert once again came to Daley's assistance. As we have seen, Lambert and Daley had often worked together. They knew and trusted each other, and they were familiar with the other person's tendencies and moves, and they looked out for each other.

Lambert fired both his Lewis and Vickers guns at the nearest attacker, but the distance was too great to make an impact. These three opponents jostled for a few minutes, then the Germans headed east.[88] Almost immediately, Lambert had another enemy diving on him. During the action, every turn seemed to bring a pilot within range of another opponent and force adjustments from one opponent to another in order to maneuver to help a friend, get a kill, or avoid becoming a victim oneself. When Palmer appeared in Lambert's range, he had a "blue gray enemy machine on his tail at a very close range."[89] Lambert was able to fire around twenty rounds to drive the enemy off of Palmer. During this conflict, they worked themselves down to around 6,000 or 7,000 feet while continuing to drift further eastward.

In the midst of his fight, Lambert recalls a brief period when the sky seemed clear. He used this period to check his instruments and look at his watch to see it was 5:45 a.m. Almost immediately, this lull was interrupted by a "fantastically colored" Albatros that suddenly appeared in front of C1870.[90] In a few seconds, this plane was positioned slightly below and around thirty to fifty yards away from Lambert. Throttling forward and down, and getting the plane into his Aldis sight, he pressed both guns, shooting a burst of about fifty rounds into the plane. He recalled the pilot looking back at him, then slumping, and the plane going into a spin, which he observed for around a thousand feet before it flattened out. Lambert felt that his burst had hit the pilot and hoped that it had killed him. Lambert was not being cruel; like Mannock and almost every other pilot, he preferred death by a bullet to the "agony of awaiting the fiery death below."[91] The ultimate fate of that pilot was unknown to Lambert, because he found himself once again being assault by a new enemy aircraft. Daley would later tell him that he watched the Albatros spin down to around 500 feet, but he did not see it crash or land.[92]

During this time, the rest of the flight was about a thousand feet over Daley, providing cover. MacDonald and the others found themselves involved with three enemy aircraft that attacked them from above. MacDonald sent one down spinning before sustaining a damaged propeller and being forced to head for home. Crossen, Barton, Lowe, and Farrell continued to fire on the enemy, but with no results. Fuel was getting low, and that ended the battle. The patrol had lasted for one hour and fifty minutes, "possibly" as far as fifteen miles behind the German lines. The flight landed at Conteville around 6:35 a.m., submitted their reports by 7:30 a.m., and finally sat down in the mess to have breakfast.[93]

Lambert claimed that he had "driven down damaged" the colorful Albatros he had engaged. His log book lists "Forced 1 to land."[94] However, he received no official credit for this plane. Officially, it was listed as "unidentified E/A—driven off only."[95] Both Lambert and Daley observed the plane spinning downwards, but neither saw it crash or land, so there was no proof that it had done either.

Johnson took C Flight out around 2:00 p.m. for another offensive patrol, but it was rather uneventful. Working around 10,000 feet, they failed to see any enemy aircraft, but were harassed by anti-aircraft fire. They returned to base about 3:40 p.m., so the patrol lasted almost as long as the one in the morning, though with a quite different result.[96]

Lambert remarks on what he did in his leisure time after breakfast and before this afternoon flight. They were things that any civilian might do; he read for an hour, played ping-pong, had lunch, and went for a walk on the beautiful spring day. He even describes the farmland and comments on the local farmer who was "rich in land and livestock."[97] He also received letters from home, but strangely enough, he never comments on who sent these letters or what was in them. Granted, the book is called *Combat Report*, not *Letters from Home*, but if he mentioned the letters at all, the reader expects to know something about who was writing to him and about what.

The closest Lambert comes to telling us about these letters is a letter he wrote in response to one that his younger brother Carl wrote him. (Carl was the brother who enlisted in the American air service and, like Lambert, trained to fly.) We do not have Carl's letter, but evidently it was asking Lambert what aerial combat was like, because Lambert's letter describes his recent combat experiences, including a couple of victories he achieved in early June. It closes with a complaint about his plane not performing well and "With love to you all and best regards to all my friends. I am, Your Brother, Bill."[98] These lines are the only reference in the whole book to his family and friends at home.

In contrast to his lack of any mention of his family and friends are Lambert's frequent comments on his comrades in No. 24 Squadron. For instance, he relates his sorrow at learning from McMurtrie that he was leaving No. 24 to join an Australian S.E.5 Squadron that was "up closer to the lines." He described McMurtrie as "my kind of people. You could have dropped him down in southern Ohio and he would have been right at home."[99] Lambert also records his sorrow at losing Lieutenant Mark. Mark had flown with the squadron from

Five. Spring 1918

10 January to 28 May 1918. On 21 May, he crash-landed, and his plane broke into flames.[100] Even though Lambert believed he was well-liked and would be missed by all, he admitted that "He needs to rest."[101]

The rest of the month of May was still active for No. 24, but 29 May was an exception. C Flight's 6:20 a.m. patrol south of Moreuil produced little beyond some ground-strafing. The flight returned to base around 8:30 a.m. and went to Abbeville after lunch, to get a bath and relax. Major Robeson told them to be back at Conteville no later than 6:00 p.m.[102]

Few others that day got a respite from the war or had time for a bath. The British bombed Metz and Thionville, but the Allies were still in retreat from the German offensive. There was a large bulge between Rheims and Soissons. The Germans captured Soissons as well as the heights south of Vesle and continued their advance to the Marne River, which they would reach the next day at Château-Thierry. In three days the Germans had advanced forty miles, the longest advance of any army on the Western Front since the advent of trench warfare. They had captured approximately 60,000 prisoners, 2,000 machine guns, and immense quantities of supplies.[103]

On the 30th, Lambert reported that the enemy was more active and that No. 24 had "very little luck" against them.[104] This comment was no doubt true for the squadron as a whole, but it does not seem to apply to Lambert or C Flight as a whole. When Johnson took C Flight for a late morning patrol around Moreuil, they did not see any airplanes, but were able to bring down three balloons. All six pilots went after these balloons, firing from different angles and heights. These three balloons were well protected, so C Flight had ample payback from the guns on the ground. When the flight returned to base, Lambert examined his plane and discovered that only the plane's fabric had had any damage, but it had received quite a few bullet holes. Afterward, he made a thorough examination of the plane to make sure that the control system and engine had not suffered any unseen damages.[105] Lambert would initially receive no official credit for the downing of these balloons, but later it was officially stated that Lambert did "share in the destruction of 3 Balloons."[106]

On 31 May, the new German offensive was directly affecting No. 24 Squadron. The Germans had finally reached the Marne from Château-Thierry and were advancing on Compiegne. The French were having a rough time in the area around Soissons, and a request was made of the 22nd Wing to give assistance to the French pilots. No. 24 was one of the squadrons selected for this task. This move required a change in tactics, as they were to concentrate their "maximum efforts around Montdidier."[107] C Flight was chosen to be the first flight, leaving at 8:35 a.m. They traveled around 7,000 to 8,000 feet over Amiens, then they turned southeast and followed the Avre River, a tributary of the Somme, to Montdidier. As they approached their target from the north, they were greeted with a barrage of surprisingly heavy antiaircraft fire, which suddenly ceased as a two-seater with a trailing enemy fighter flew toward the German lines. Lambert recognized these planes for what they were: bait. C Flight, flying around 12,000 feet, noticed either seven or eight Albatros D-IIIs flying east out of the sun and slightly above them. Lambert wrote that he was not worried about these D-IIIs, because "an S.E.5 could out fly them and out maneuver them."[108] A fight did ensue, but it lasted only three or four minutes before four French Spads appeared above in support of the flight and changed the odds greatly against the Germans. As was their practice, the Germans quickly made for their lines, and C Flight continued its patrol before they headed back to Conteville, landing around 10:35 a.m.[109]

Lambert's log book shows that C Flight went back to Montdidier in the late afternoon, around 4:45 p.m. Before arriving at their destination, they rendezvoused south of Moreuil with MacDonald and A Flight at around 12,000 feet. They entered the airspace above Mondidier around 5:30 p.m., traveling in formation with C Flight positioned below A Flight. Very shortly, the two flights came into contact with eight Albatros D Vs patrolling the sky above the front. This confrontation took place above the town of Becquigny, around sixty-five miles slightly northeast of Mondidier.[110] The Albatros were operating a protection screen for a two-seater, which Lambert thought was a Halberstadt, flying observation duty below. With A Flight protecting their upper flank, Johnson led Lambert and Daley to attack the Halberstadt. Wilson, McDougall, and Hellett stayed with MacDonald and A Flight in case the Albatros came to the Halberstadt's rescue. During the brief confrontation, Daley and Lambert attempted to attack from the sides and Johnson from below, but the two-seater held its own. After a brief exchange of fire, the Halberstadt was allowed to head east, for Johnson, Daley, and Lambert needed to rejoin the others who had become involved in a scrape with the Albatros fighters above them. MacDonald and Lieutenant Dawe each shot down an Albatros. Dawe shot his down by getting on its tail as it tried to maneuver behind MacDonald. Both these planes were seen spinning downward before crashing into the ground. Later, Southey, Wilson, McDougall, and Dawe riddled another Albatros with bullets before forcing it to land. Lambert could not understand how that German pilot survived the terrible onslaught of all those guns. The remaining German fighters had already headed east to avoid further conflict.[111] A and C Flights reassembled and continued their joint patrol, returning to Conteville around 6:50 p.m.

Both MacDonald and Dawe were given credit for their victories on that day, but Lieutenant Dawe would not have long to celebrate his triumph. He was killed a week later, at the age of nineteen, when he was shot down by Lieutenant Fritz Rumey of Jasta 5 over Rosiéres on 7 June. His last victory would be on 3 June, an LVG. C destroyed southeast of Marcelcave.[112]

May had been a productive month for No. 24 and C Flight. Lambert reckoned up that, in spite of the weather, C Flight had flown on thirty-three patrols, and the squadron as a whole had recorded nineteen enemy aircraft destroyed, with eight recorded as "indecisive." The squadron could put these successes against its losses: one machine and two pilots.[113] What Lambert does not reckon in this summary are the important contribution to the war of bombing and strafing runs, protecting reconnaissance flights, and escorting D.H.4 and D.H.9 bombers on their bombing runs. It was dangerous and nerve racking, necessary work, but was not something they wanted to remember, let alone celebrate.[114]

In between describing his flights to Montdidier, unfamiliar territory to him, Lambert told his readers of the difficulties of adjusting to new terrain from the air. Finding his way back from such territory to base could be hazardous. The dash-mounted map in the S.E.5 did not include the new terrain he was flying over, and even though he carried a folded map, it was virtually impossible to use because of the wind in an open cockpit and the layers of clothes he had to wear. Lambert, however, invented a solution to his problems. He built a rolling map, using a window shade roller he got from a local farmer and two spring clips. He attached the maps to the roller by using the clips, and then he attached it to his plane. This ingenious invention was the envy of other pilots in the squadron, but unfortunately Lambert could not build other models because he had no more window shade rollers. He said he was

Five. Spring 1918

"forced to refer to them [the maps] constantly." With a sense of pride, he let his readers know that he still had them "right in front of him" as he was writing *Combat Report* many years later.[115]

Lambert had survived his spring time as a pilot. He had lived through the first two active months, when he was most likely to be killed. This was a significant accomplishment when we consider the statistics on the life-span of Great War pilots. As had been said, three-fourths of all casualties in battle occurred among pilots with less than three months of active service. Lambert was one of those who had beaten the odds. With June 1918, he was entering the summer of his year as a pilot. This is the period of "confidence and self-assurance, of initiative and dash, of skill and wise discrimination, of success and achievement."[116] June would be Lambert's most successful month as a combat pilot. It seems that summer had arrived a little early for Lambert.

Six

Summer
June 1918

June began with the Germans continuing to bomb Paris while advancing down the Ourcq River. The Third Battle of Aisne continued, and the Allies remained on the defensive. The French had retreated between the Oise and Aisne to a line south of Noyon. Their morale was plunging. Amid this confusing situation and contradictory orders, the American 2nd Division struggled to get into line to meet the German attack.[1] French Prime Minister Georges Clemenceau considered evacuating Paris as thousands of citizens fled the city for the south of France. The Germans were now only thirty-seven miles from Paris.[2]

Lambert and his whole squadron were happily unaware of all this bad news. Lambert found the first day of June to be "ideal," with the sun shining brightly throughout the day—a good day for flying. C Flight had the first patrol of the morning at 7:30 a.m. Lambert, along with Captain Johnson, Daley, Wilson, Selwyn, and Hellett, headed towards Amiens. The flight lasted about two hours as they explored the area southeast of the city at around 10,000 feet.[3] The sky was quite empty of fighters. However, the flight spied a lone L.V.G. reconnaissance plane flying about 3,000 feet below them and proceeded to attack. They were hungry for action, and reconnaissance aircraft carried back valuable information to the enemy; it was vital to stop them whenever possible. Unfortunately, as Lambert moved into position, his guns jammed. He tried replacing the Lewis drum, but it still would not respond. The Vickers was equally unresponsive as he tried to clear it. Lambert, even though frustrated by this "first gun trouble" with his plane, was rather glad it had happened, since it meant he would not have to shoot down the brave and agile German pilot flying the L.V.G. For Lambert, the failure of his guns gave him ample opportunity to see the German pilot in action. He wrote, "It was a pleasure to watch him [the pilot] … he certainly was holding his own against our 6 S.E.5s."[4] After the L.V.G. went into a dive and headed for home, Lambert remarked that he "was glad he got out of it. He and his observer certainly were brave and fearless fighters."[5] After Lambert had landed back at Conteville, he found the rest of the flight felt the same way in their admiration for these two Germans.

The flight spent the remainder of their patrol covering the area between Moreuil and Marcelcave. They saw a locomotive heading east near Rosiéres, but everyone except Lambert lacked the ammunition for an effective assault. They headed back to Conteville around 9:00 a.m., touching down about thirty minutes later.[6]

As soon as Lambert landed, he took C1870 to the hanger to check out its guns. He eventually found a well-dented cartridge in the Vickers that had caused the blockage. The Lewis had a broken part in its ejection system that had to be replaced. After clearing the guns and fixing the damage, Lambert took the plane for some brief target practice to make sure all systems were operational. Upon landing, he turned the plane over to the mechanics so that they could give it an once-over before Lambert took it up again for a second offensive patrol. He was to join an early patrol at around 7:00 p.m. with B and C Flights on a joint patrol. Lambert showed great appreciation for the job the mechanics did on his plane. He commended them for their "pride in their work," and the comradeship that existed between all of them and Lambert. They hated losing a plane as much as any pilot did. Lambert knew, and stated, that his "life depended upon their ability and honesty. They never let me down."[7] One reason for the strength of this companionship is that Lambert, unlike some other pilots, was willing to get his hands dirty working on his plane along with these mechanics. A bond and trust developed between Lambert and these mechanics that he would remember for the rest of his life. Experience and familiarity with his plane and what it could do allowed Lambert to "trump the inherent advantages of an opposing machine."[8]

Lambert's eye for details goes beyond his describing of combat or of working on his airplane. He also describes how he spends his leisure time between flights going to the nearby town of Auxi with Daley and Palmer. For example, he tells a comical story of attempting to buy new underwear. The language barrier prevents him from getting his meaning across so that he has to partly disrobe (to the delight of everyone in the store, including himself) and show his undershirt in order to get the clerk to understand what he wants to buy.[9]

Lambert also remembers in vivid details dinners that were eaten fifty years ago, and the drinks and conversations that went along with them. For example, he tells of a time when he, Daley, and Palmer treated their old French driver to a meal. He describes the old Frenchman's horse and cart, and the dinner that they ate, in great detail. Their first course was fish, and "three beautiful little waitresses came in loaded with four large platters, each with a whole fish that must have weighed almost four pounds."[10] He also describes the bowls of fish sauce, and later in the meal the roast chicken, peas and beans, white and red wine (but no water), hard French bread and soft fresh butter, a small roast lamb, and golden brown potatoes.

The most important aspect of the trip to Auxi, however, is not either the eating or drinking, but the humor and relaxation that helped these three pilots to forget about the war, if only for a brief time. As Lambert wrote, "We were not drunk, just happy, from the wonderful time that the three of us had had during the afternoon."[11] Famously, in Proust's *Remembrance of Things Past*, the whole of a past scene and its characters rise from the taste of a madeleine, a small rum-soaked cake. Evidently, for Lambert as well, tastes triggered memories.

When they arrived back at Conteville around 6:30 p.m., the three comrades examined the orderly board to see that the combined flight was to leave at 7:45 p.m. on an offensive patrol down the Amiens-Roye road. Joining B Flight would be Lieutenant F. S. Passmore, a new pilot who had been assigned to No. 24 Squadron to make up for the loss of either Mark or McMurtrie. The offensive patrol had one flight flying slightly above and in back of the other, preferably under some cloud cover, so as not to be seen by the enemy. If the lower flight was attacked, the upper flight would attack the enemy from ambush. C Flight was flying at between 8,000 to 12,000 feet, with B Flight the one operating above and slightly behind them. As the sky began to darken in the early evening, Lambert could see the signs of battle in the distance: colored flashes, magnesium flares, and the unmistakable sounds of heavy artillery.[12] Upon reaching their desired altitude, the flights were, Lambert believed, in the vicinity of Hangard when he observed a large formation in the distance. As they got closer, they were seen to be Albatros D Vs and Pfalz D-IIIs. Lambert estimated that they were around three to four thousand feet above C Flight and about five miles away. The two groups approached each other at a high rate of speed. At one time, Lambert estimated the speed as 125 miles an hour; at another time, he wrote that of a "closing speed of 250 m.p.h."[13] Unlike in previous encounters, this time the enemy was not abandoning the field to go east. The reason why became apparent as they got closer: the Germans had the odds in their favor. Lambert estimated that there were between twenty and twenty-two German airplanes approaching them. He recalls about twelve multi-colored Albatros D Vs attacking first, to be followed within a few minutes by the rainbow-colored Pfalz D-IIIs. Evidently each Albatros was painted a different primary or mixed color, and each Pfalz was painted a variety of different colors and resembled a rainbow. Even in the fading light, he writes, "they certainly wanted to be seen."[14]

Even though Lambert and his mechanics had done a thorough check of both guns, as the combat began he started to worry about their reliability. He did not want to enter another conflict without his guns in working order, especially when his flight was outnumbered. However, he had little time to worry. A red-nosed Albatros cut across his path while chasing one of Lambert's comrades and shooting both its Spandau machine guns at the S.E.5. Reacting instinctively, Lambert swung C1870 around to the right and came to the rescue of his squadron mate, shooting both his guns from a range of around fifty yards. He hit the mark, and bullets spattered the red nose of the Albatros. Finding himself a target, the Albatros broke off the engagement and headed home, but he was accompanied by another S.E.5, probably Lowe on its tail.[15] Lambert hardly had time to register what had happened; he was now being pursued by another Albatros and a Pfalz, from above and behind him. Even though Lambert was moving rapidly and unpredictably, "zigzagging and circling," and thought the relatively large distance between them provided a cushion of safety, one of these attacking pilots got in what Lambert called "a lucky burst … between the cockpit and my tail section."[16] Moving quickly, Lambert turned his "stick forward and throttle full on" and maneuvered himself onto the tail of the attacking Pfalz D-III. He was about thirty yards away and closing as he fired twenty rounds from both guns into it. Lambert saw the "pilot jerk up rigid for a second and [he] seemed to slump forward to the left of his cock-pit."[17] The Pfalz went into a spin, and Lambert was able to watch it for a short while, until he was on the defensive once again as his lower left wing was riddled with bullets from an attacking Albatros D V. Awakened to the danger facing him, Lambert, showing his skill as a pilot, placed his nose down, kicked his left rudder, and pulled his stick back, all of which placed him both below and behind his opponent. Unfortunately, when he pressed his guns, he was only able to drive the Albatros away.[18]

There is some confusion in this story, as there is with most dogfights. It is virtually impossible to get a complete picture of events. In this story, Lambert is at first sure that he has driven down a Pfalz. But later, when the flight is back at Conteville, he was walking back to the orderly room when Palmer, who was the last to arrive, informed him that he (Palmer) had chased the Pfalz D-III off Lambert's tail, and that enabled him to shoot down the Albatros D V.[19] So then Lambert claimed the Albatros as shot down. The official report is of no help here. In a letter from the Air Ministry of 21 October 1929, Lambert is given credit for "1 driven down," but the type is "not recorded."[20]

After Lambert's victory, either the Pflaz or the Albatros, the battle is still raging. In the earlier encounters, Lambert was on the "outer fringe" of the action; however, he joined forces with another S.E.5, possibly Farrell, and moved closer to the center of action as they both dived on two Pfalzs attacking Daley below. They were able to rescue their embattled friend and drive the two D-IIIs away. Afterward, Lambert noticed four Albatros fighters making for home around 500 feet below them. He, Daley, and the other plane dived and fired on these fighters from a distance of fifty yards. But the battle was winding down, the attack was unsuccessful, and the flight did not have fuel to chase these planes further. As they turned back, the three were briefly attacked by three Pfalzes in a scrap that lasted only a few minutes, with no real damage done to either side.[21] The battle was now officially over.

Afterward, Lambert waxed philosophic. They had just driven seven enemy planes away from the field, but unfortunately, they would return to fight another day. There was "only one way to prevent this; kill them."[22] Despite the contention that pilots were "knights of the air," there was no room for chivalry in modern war. The object was to kill or disable your enemy.

With the battle over, the flight managed to find each other in the twilight and to proceed back to Conteville. Remarkably, they had suffered no casualties. The trick now was to make it home in semi-darkness. Within twenty or twenty-five minutes, they were able to see the "two rows of petrol flares to guide" them in, placed there by their crews.[23] The 1st of June had been a rather remarkable day for Lambert and his mates. The next day would bring more of the same.

Bright sunshine greeted No. 24 the following morning. What clouds Lambert could see were "high over the front."[24] He had time that morning to sleep late, shave, and wander off to breakfast. He could take in the sights and sounds of the ducks, geese, and chickens in the barnyard. Both Chips and Jim, the two squadron dogs, were playing in the spring weather. It was an enjoyable morning.

Things were not so pleasant elsewhere on the front, especially for the Germans. The Third Battle of the Aisne was continuing, but supply problems, a lack of reserves, exhaustion, and fatigue would hamper the German offensive when it seemed that Paris might be in reach. When Ludendorff made the decision to continue with this offensive instead of reverting to the original objectives, his troops were ninety miles beyond their railheads. From 28 May to 3 June, twenty-seven Allied divisions, twenty-five French, and the American 2nd and 3rd divisions were fed into the line.[25] The Germans had no answering reserves, and the German troops were by now war-weary.

Returning from breakfast, Lambert checked the flight board and saw that C Flight would be joining A Flight for a joint patrol at 10:00 a.m. C Flight had its usual members: Johnson, Wilson, Selwyn, Daley, Hellett, and Lambert. It would take to the air before MacDonald and A Flight and fly at a lower altitude, with A Flight slightly above and behind. The combined flights were to travel to the Villers-Bretonneux, LaMotte, and Wiencourt areas. It took less than thirty-minutes to reach their target area, with the flight working at around 14,000 feet. They were heading into the bright sun, which gave the advantage to the German fighters. As the flight struggled with the glaring sun, Lambert for some reason (maybe the sun's glare) turned to the southeast to see German fighters approaching from around 17,000 feet. (Of course, at the distance he saw them they were only "black dots.") Since he was flying on Johnson's right, he fired a short burst from both guns and turned to meet the enemy, alerting the rest of the flight to the danger.[26]

Lambert described sixteen to eighteen Fokker D VIIs and some Albatros D Vs approaching in the same sort of "fantastic" colors he had become accustomed to. The D VIIs had "light blue fuselages, multicolored wings and mostly red noses. Some few had white rudders. They all had those weird designs painted on the sides of their fuselages."[27] As they met, a massive air battle erupted with "the sky full of whirling aeroplanes."[28] The initial advantage in this battle belonged to No. 24 Squadron, since A Flight was posted above in attacking position while the German planes fought C Flight.

The battle was hectic and personal, with individual and group fights breaking out among the various planes. Before narrating his own role in the conflict, Lambert described a spinning and smoking D VII being sent down by a member of A Flight, and his futile attempt to warn a comrade about an approaching Fokker by yelling at the "top of his voice" at the pilot. His own role in conflict began with a Fokker D VII on his tail shooting at him and putting holes in his left-bottom wing. As he engineered evasive measures by quickly moving into a sharp left turn, this Fokker was instantly attacked by another S.E.5, possibly Southey of A Flight, twenty yards behind the Fokker.[29] As these two planes continued to joust past Lambert, another Fokker traveling fast ended up in an ideal attacking position for Lambert, twenty yards in front of him. From the look of things, Lambert imagined that the pilot of that Fokker might have "wanted to commit suicide."[30] Unfortunately for Lambert, but fortunately for other pilot, Lambert overshot the Fokker and allowed a "golden opportunity" to escape. No time to brood about that. Lambert spotted Daley's S.E.5 being hounded by three enemy aircraft: a D VII on his tail, a D V on his left, and another D V "riding hard on his tail."[31] After a sharp, tight half roll positioned Lambert "nose on" this Albatros D V, he drove it off Daley's rear by giving it a short burst from his two guns. The Albatros maneuvered inside out and fell into a spin, disappearing into the clouds below.[32]

As Lambert joined Daley, there was a lull in the action. In such a lull, the fighting suddenly stops, and the pilots look around to where everyone has gone. It is, of course, only a brief respite, but happened several times (even in Lambert's personal experience) in heated combat situations involving large number of planes, where action spreads out vertically and horizontally over several miles in the sky. Lambert had a habit of checking his watch at times like these. He noted that it was now a few minutes past 11:00 a.m., so they had about an hour of patrol left. Above the clouds, he saw a single S.E.5 chasing a Fokker to the east. The sky seemed equally barren of planes until he glanced north and saw that a furious action was taking place about two miles away and 3,000 feet below them. Immediately, both pilots increased their speed by pushing down and opening up the throttle and dived into the action below. Soon they were both once again in the center of the melee.[33]

Lambert arrived was just in time to drive a D VII off a beleaguered S.E.5, while Daley targeted a different Fokker and attacked.[34] Then Lambert spotted Johnson on the tail of a Fokker D. VII and came to his assistance as another Fokker was quickly maneuvering behind Johnson's tail. Lambert fired a few short bursts and chased the Fokker off of Johnson.

As Lambert was looking for "a better target," he realized that he had become the target. The center section of his plane was riddled with bullets as two D. VIIs attacked from about a hundred yards behind him.[35] In *Combat Report,* this attack is emphasized with italics.[36] It may have been the first time that he was truly in mortal danger. He would write in the rough-draft copy that he "had been caught sound asleep."[37] (He was not by any means the first pilot to be caught.) Lambert was rescued from this precarious situation by the timely assistance of MacDonald, attacking one of the Fokkers, and by his own agility and skill. He performed a loop, probably an Immelmann turn, which landed him on the tail of the Fokker that had been diving on him. He said that it was a move he rarely used, but it saved him this time. Now, with the assistance of MacDonald, he had gone from hunted to hunter. Slightly lifting his nose, he had the D. VII in his sight and fired a short burst into it. He described how that plane "fell off to the right with its wings almost vertical" before going into a downward spin. MacDonald shot the other Fokker down. Neither plane came out its spin; they both hit the ground and burst into flames about 300 yards apart from each other.[38]

In a later interview for General Dynamics in 1980, Lambert briefly expanded on his remark that he had been "caught sound asleep." He told the interviewer that he was "day dreaming," thinking about life back in Ohio, when the attack took place. But he added that after this experience, he never made that mistake again.[39]

The fighting continued to be spread across the sky. Lambert, looking around for more action, took off 500 yards to the east to assist Daley, who was attacking a Fokker but had another one moving in on his rear. Lambert swung his plane around and headed for the second Fokker. The distance, over a hundred yards, was too large a gap to shoot the Fokker down, but Lambert did succeed in driving it off Daley's tail. Now Daley had a clear shot at his target and sent it down in a spin. Daley and Lambert went down to see that that plane hit the ground and burst into flames where the two previous Fokkers had crashed. Lambert estimated that it could not have more than 600 yards away from the other two wrecks.[40]

The battle was winding down, with those three defeats, the Germans began to break away and head east. Fuel was beginning to run low for the squadron, and the flights reassembled for the trip back to Conteville. However, as C Flight formed around Johnson with all six planes accounted for, it was noticed that two of A Flight's were missing, including MacDonald. Fortunately, when he looked to his rear on the trip back, Lambert saw both MacDonald and the other S.E.5. Although their planes had sustained several bullet holes and torn fabric could be seen flapping in the wind, all twelve planes made it safely back to Conteville, landing at 12:10 p.m.[41] This joint flight was credited with three decisive victories; MacDonald, Daley, and Lambert could each add one to their totals.

According to Lambert, there were possibly three additional Fokkers that were shot down that day, but since they were lost in the clouds and no one could verify that they crashed, no credit was given to the squadron for shooting them down. In fact, Lambert states that he "personally had seen two D. VIIs with smoke trailing, before they went into the clouds."[42] Lambert wrote that what was important was that if they were destroyed, they "could not come back on us in the future. But it would have been nice, if we could have marked up 6-decisives instead of only three."[43]

Lambert is by now a seasoned pilot, and the numbers of victories mattered both for him personally and for the squadron. Claims such as these three additional Fokkers were made all the time, and perhaps correctly, but definitive proof was required for credit. Lambert was given credit for a decisive victory that day, since the plane was seen to crash and the crash was verified by other pilots. His victory total now stood at seven.

After this combat, the planes involved in the day's actions were all in need of serious repairs, and some required overhauls. Lambert discovered that his C1870 would require a new center section, so, after the repairs, the plane would need to be re-rigged and re-aligned. Even so, Lambert was better than most, since some planes had to go back to the depot for repairs or replacement. (At the depot, a plane could be salvaged with parts being used for other machines.) However diligent the mechanics worked on these planes, it was apparent that both A and C flights would be out of action until at least the next day.[44] Lambert, as would be expected from one with his mechanical interests and his desire to have his machine performing at its peak, stayed with his crew working on C1870 until it got dark. Showing his lack of pretension, he ate with his crew on the job as they attempted to finish the task before morning. Lambert would have stayed there all night had it not been for his N.C.O. insisting that he get a good night's sleep before the morning flight. Lambert left his three crewmen around 9:00 p.m. They would finish getting C1870 ready around 3:30 a.m., in plenty of time for Lambert to test it in the morning.[45]

Things were going well for No. 24 Squadron, and also for the Allies in the larger war. On 3 June, the French and American troops forced the Germans back over Marne northeast of Château-Thierry. The Allies were not yet aware that on this day Ludendorff had decided to call off the Blücher-Yorck Offensive, partly because of this mounting resistance of the Allied soldiers. Both sides had lost around 100,000 men in this offensive, but the Germans no longer had the ability to replace them. German troops were still in the vast spaces of revolutionary Russia, and there was a new battle zone in the Crimea. Ludendorff had no reserves left to oppose the American divisions now pouring in.[46]

On 3 June, No. 24 Squadron had good weather, but there was heavy morning cloud cover. There seemed to be little enemy activity over their front, so Lambert had the time to test C1870 and make sure that it was ready for action. He took the plane up around 7:30 a.m. and put it through a series of tests. Upon landing, he took it to the hanger satisfied with its performance and grateful to his crew. In fact, all six planes of C Flight would be ready for action that day. Lambert wrote, "We had not been damaged as much as I thought."[47] Probably that was true, but it was also that the ground crews and mechanics had done another superb job in getting these planes ready, working throughout the night repairing them.

Another mixed patrol was organized around 10:00 a.m. on the 3rd, with A and C flying together once again. B Flight had had the early morning patrol. MacDonald and Johnson took their flights on a patrol of the Marcelcave-Warfusée area. Around 11:15 a.m., Crossen, Dawe, and Southey shot down an L.V.G., and Crossen engaged an Albatros two-seater that eventually made its way to safety in the east.[48] About forty minutes later, Johnson spotted five L.V.G.s doing reconnaissance below them, under some clouds. Lambert and Dawe joined Johnson in an attack that resulted in the L.V.G. also heading east. Soon after, Johnson failed to down a straggling enemy aircraft because he was low on ammunition. He gathered all the flight and headed back to Conteville, landing at 12:10 p.m. C Flight would be back on patrol at 5:45 p.m., so Lambert had plenty of time to eat lunch and enjoy the spring sunshine with his friend Daley.[49]

The early evening flight was a C Flight operation only. They patrolled the area around Rosiéres at about 15,000 feet. When they reached the Wiencourt area, they experienced heavy anti-aircraft fire and knew that those guns were probably protecting some observation two-seaters operating below the flight. At around 8,000 feet, there were four two-seaters near Caix heading west. Johnson saw them and led the flight in an attempt to get them, but they were simply too far away. Lambert felt that it was a wasted effort to go after these reconnaissance planes; but then again, they might be protected by some enemy fighters, and the conflict with them could make the trip worth-while. Unfortunately, C1870 was running rough and losing R.P.M.s. The engine was getting hot, and it was difficult to keep pace with the other S.E.5s. He lagged behind, and when Johnson gave up the chase and decided to head for home, Daley stayed back with Lambert until they reached Conteville around 7:40 p.m.[50]

The next day was a wash due to bad weather and overcast skies. A and C Flight were grounded all day. However, the pilots were not allowed to leave base, because the Wing would not give permission to leave while they had other flights in operation. If an emergency arose, No. 24 might still be called into service. Lambert did get permission to take a morning ride around the area in a motor bike that was in the shop, to Auxi Le Château and back again. He then checked out the Vickers and Lewis guns with his aviation mechanic, and began exploring for a site with plenty of shade trees that could possibly be used for a tennis court.[51]

During this brief period of inactivity, Lambert had a longing to connect with old friends and to meet fellow Americans fighting in the R.A.F. Probably he was feeling a little homesick. After reprinting a letter to his brother Carl in his manuscript, he speaks of this desire to reconnect with old friends from Canada and to meet other fellow Americans. "I have a lot of visiting to do, if I can get permission and find the time to do so."[52] Someone told him that three Americans—John McGavock Grider, Lawrence Callahan, and Elliott White Springs—had been attached to Billy Bishop's No. 85 Squadron, and he wanted to get permission to go up north and get acquainted. Lambert especially wanted to see his friend Claxton who was with No. 41 Squadron north of Amiens. He speculates that Andy Callender had probably not yet reached France yet, but he had heard that two brothers—Paul and Thayer Iaccaci, who went through training in Canada at the same time he did—were in No. 20 Squadron near St. Omer. (As things often happen in war, Lambert never visited anyone he had known while in training in Canada.[53]) Lambert was around a good many English-speaking friends in No. 24, but Americans were scarce. MacDonald was an Englishman, Crossen and Foster were Canadians, and Barton and Southey were South Africans.

The weather cleared some-

The apple orchard at Conteville, summer 1918. The British government rented this farm to use as a flying field. Lambert said, "It was a paradise for all."

what on the 5th to allow bombing activity to begin again in earnest. There was still cloud cover over some of the front, but not enough to prevent flying. C Flight would have the early morning flight. That meant rising at 5:00 a.m., an early breakfast (usually including hard-boiled eggs) and off to the Moreuil area at around 5:30 a.m. Flying at around 8,000 feet, they experienced heavy anti-aircraft fire, which they thought meant they would have company that morning; however, they would not see any Germans until around 6:45 a.m. when they spotted three two-seaters, possibly Halberstadts, below and to the east of them.[54] The flight broke into pairs, with each pair attacking a different plane. Lambert was paired with his old friend Daley as they attacked the last of the three two-seaters. He remarked that they would have their "hands full" with this plane, which shortly "shook us off and streaked off home."[55] The flight would return home around 7:30 a.m. Wilson claiming two indecisive victories, but Lambert was convinced that they did not accomplish much against these enemy pilots. After a brief respite that included lunch, writing letters home and lounging around the hut, C Flight was called to patrol at 5:00 p.m. But this hour and fifteen minute flight was uneventful with the exception of "Archie," or anti-aircraft fire. Lambert was "very well pleased" with this undemanding flight; he evidently thought he had had enough excitement for a while.[56]

On the 6th, the weather continued to be excellent for flying, with a bright sun and few clouds in the sky. Although there would be plenty of action, Lambert would have engine trouble once again and miss most of it. A mixed flight with planes from B and C Flights left at 11:00 a.m. for an offensive patrol around 9,000 feet over Moreuil. They would come into contact with a formation of Fokker Dr. Is, some new Fokker D. VIIs, and Albatros D. V.s, when Lambert noticed that his engine was dropping R.P.M.s. He realized that he had no chance of correcting the problem until he got back to Conteville, so he immediately dropped out of combat and started to return home. However, a Dr. I was not going to let a weakened pigeon like Lambert get away so easily. It pounced on Lambert's tail and started spraying C1870 with both Spandau guns. Fortunately for Lambert, Lowe saw that he was in trouble and attacked the Fokker before it could do considerable damage to Lambert's plane. His comrade stayed on the Dr. I, firing both his Vickers and Lewis guns, to give Lambert the chance to get away to safety. On his way back, his engine power increased about a hundred R.P.M.s, which allowed him to make it all the way back to Conteville. (He had earlier decided that, if the situation did not changed, he would try to land at the closer field at Bertangles.) Once he was home, the air mechanics proceeded to take the engine apart and discovered that the fuel lines and valves were clogged because of dirty fuel. The lines, valves, and carburetor all had to be removed and cleaned. Lambert had had to miss a dogfight in which ten different combats were reported, with three decisive victories and one indecisive.[57] One of the "decisives," was shot down by Lowe, was the Fokker Dr. I that had attacked Lambert.

On 7 June, the Germans began the next offensive. It was one improvised as a consequence of the early successes of the Blücher-Yorck Offensive. Operation Gneisenau, as it was called, was intended to draw more Allied troops south, while linking the north salient around Amiens with the one to the south on the Aisne. Unfortunately for the Germans, Ludendorff had still not decided if he should press the attack on the British rear, in the upper part of the salient, or continue his drive to Paris. The other great problem he had is that the French had decrypted the German secret code, so they knew of the planned attack and its timing as soon as the German generals did. In anticipation of the attack, Marshal Foch took precautions including sending a "certain number of French army corps towards the British front … to meet a German offensive," and placed the 14th Division from the Army Detachment of the North at General Pétain's disposal.[58] The French also unleashed a massive artillery barrage ten minutes before the German artillery attack was scheduled. Operation Gneisenau was doomed before it began.[59]

The excellent weather continued on the front, with very few clouds to bother the squadron as it went on an offensive patrol in the late morning hours of 7 June; however, according to the weather reports, it would be cloudy in the afternoon.[60] The records for this day are "somewhat confusing." The official records, or as Lambert calls it, "a report from Higher Authority," did not corroborate the information listed in Lambert's log book and other squadron "notes and records." In fact, as Lambert writes, "someone there must have over-looked something."[61]

According to Lambert and the rest of his squadron, a mixed flight involving the entire squadron went on patrol, with C Flight assigned the top flight so they covered the other two from above. There were five planes from C Flight, flown by Johnson, Selwyn, Daley, Wilson, and Lambert; five from A Flight, MacDonald, Dawe, Southey, Crossen and Foster; and four from B Flight, Lowe, Palmer, Farrell, and Lindeberg. (The official lists only six S.E.5s carrying out this patrol.)[62]

On this day, unusually, Lambert would have a clear and unrestricted view of the events unfolding below him—as he called it, a "grandstand seat." It was the first time he was able to watch aerial combat uninterruptedly from above, and he remarked how it was "vastly different from the view-point of a participant of one of those engagements."[63] For people who had never seen aerial combat, Lambert suggested that if they lived in "buzzard country," they should go to the top of a hill that was about 500 feet above the valley floor and watch twenty or thirty buzzards soaring, maneuvering, and flying in search of "some half dead creature" down below. These buzzards would "give you a fair idea of how those S.E.5s and 'Tripes' looked to me that morning."[64]

The squadron was on an offensive patrol over the Rosiéres area, flying around 16,000 feet, when they spotted two formations of Fokker "Tripes" about 2,000 feet below. These two formations, one consisting of eight planes and the other seven, were separated by about a mile, so A and B Flights could attack them separately, with A Flight attacking the larger formation. Lambert saw an S.E.5 piloted by Lowe swoop down on a Fokker and explode its fuel tank with a burst from its Vickers and Lewis guns. The Fokker flamed and trailed black smoke all the way down. Then Lambert saw MacDonald come to the rescue of a comrade, Dawe, being attacked by two enemy aircraft. MacDonald fired a short burst that "seemed to disintegrate" the top wing of one "Tripe" and sent it crashing to the ground. Lambert and C Flight watched these scenes anxiously. The action was too far away for them to have an effect on the outcome of these individual combats. Lambert wrote, "All we could do was to sit there paralyzed."[65] They were circling the sky above in case another enemy flight arrived to join the fracas.

This powerlessness was never more apparent than when they watched the second Fokker D. VII continue its attack on Dawe.[66] Even though MacDonald had destroyed one of the attacking planes on Dawe's tail, the other continued the attack, following Dawe all the way down to the ground while relentlessly firing his Spandau machine guns at him. Dawe, only nineteen years old, was dead!

This sight was a rude awakening for Lambert. Up to this point, his descriptions have only recorded his squadron's victories against the German pilots. These victories had become so common place that discussions in *Combat Report* were mostly on whether a victory should be decisive or indecisive. Until now, the word "defeat" did not enter his lexicon. Rather arrogantly, he had always seen the enemy as going east to avoid a confrontation, one that would inevitably have ended with the R.A.F. being victorious had the Germans ever decided to stick it out and fight. Now he had seen for himself that he and his comrades could be defeated and even killed. His confidence was shaken. He wrote, "This almost made me sick, that was the first of our men that had ever seen shot down. Poor fellow, I hope he was dead before had hit the ground."[67] Later on, Lambert came to believe that he should have seen the signs that Dawe was likely to become a casualty. In a letter of 1969, Southey wrote that he believed Dawe was under stress and possibly suffering from combat fatigue. When asked to play a game of bumble puppy the afternoon before the combat, Dawe "refused and just sat brooding in his chair and was very quiet. He appeared to be under stress and seemed to bite his tongue as he sat there."[68] In an interview, Lambert (without mentioning Dawe's name) discusses how both he and Southey attempted to console this young boy, who only talked about being killed. Lambert commented that a fighter pilot waiting to go on patrol can be "like a battery short circuiting; he is using up his will power."[69] Another image would be that Dawe, who had been with the squadron since 17 November 1917, may have finally spent his courage.

Returning to the combat that Lambert was witnessing: C Flight got a chance to join the flight when five Albatros D. V.s appeared three miles to the east and about 2,000 feet below. The fantastic color schemes, particularly the one painted in black and white checkered squares, indicated an old opponent with whom they had tangled on several previous occasions. Since these pilots were responsible for designing and painting the look of their own planes, Lambert could not believe that there would be two Albatros with the same black and white squares in the German Air Force. C Flight caught them by surprise, diving down to meet them. Unfortunately, for C flight, the Germans were leaving the battle as the flight joined in. The Germans, as usual, when outnumbered, retreated to the east. Out of frustration, the flight fired a few shots at them even though they were out of range. But the battle was over, and the flight joined A and B Flights and journeyed back to Conteville, arriving at 12:45 p.m. The final report for the day's activities showed that the squadron had decisively destroyed three Fokkers, one each by MacDonald, Lowe, and Foster, with another driven "out of control" by Crossen, and one driven down as damaged by Southey.[70] But the cost of these victories was high: the life of Dawe.

The next day was a wash for the squadron. The weather was poor: there was a scattering of clouds which seemed to move from north to south. The sun kept trying to make its presence felt, but only appeared at rare intervals. Little or no activity took place in the air on 8 June. As Lambert pointed out, they could use the rest, particularly after losing Dawe the day before. Ten pilots and twenty air mechanics got permission to head to Abbeville for some rest and relaxation. But they were ordered to be back at the base at 11:00 p.m. Lambert was with this group as it headed for a day of wine, food, and song, as well as a trip to the public bath house.[71]

The next day, 9 June, the German offensive began in earnest. The German bombardment began at midnight, with the 18th Army attacking between Ayencourt and Thiescourt around 3:45 a.m. and nine to thirteen divisions conducting the attack between Thiescourt and Rollot. By 6:00 a.m., the Germans extended the attack up to the Oise River.[72] No. 24 had been informed of this German offensive and that the squadron would be involved in larger operations than usual. The German offensive required a staunch Allied response.

Around Conteville, the weather was good in the morning and early afternoon, but then rain started to appear and hamper flying efforts. All three flights were involved in an early morning patrol (4:00 a.m. to 6:00 a.m.) and would be flying to the Noyon area, considerably further afield than their regular operations; they would be traveling a distance of around sixty miles to meet their objective. Lambert knew that they would have to pay particular attention to their fuel usage and that any forced landings would be dangerous, since they would be traveling within German-held territory down the main Amiens-Roye-Noyon road.[73] C Flight was again assigned the top or cover flight during the operation. It flew at 2,000 feet above the other two flights, which were at a distance of 18,000 feet. The entire complement of eighteen planes made the flight.

At around 4:30 a.m., over Roye, the squadron endured heavy anti-aircraft fire. From Roye, they headed to Montdidier, where they encountered a formation of Spads and Nieuports. The French and British were in the air, but the Germans were missing. By 5:30 a.m., with the sun still rising in the east, it was already time to return to Conteville because of limited fuel. The squadron would land about 6:00 a.m. with nothing to show for their efforts. They had flown 150 miles without ever seeing an enemy airplane. When asked where the enemy were that morning, someone replied they were "still in bed" enjoying a good night's sleep.[74]

In spite of the potential for rain, duty dictated that the squadron duplicate the morning trip following lunch, at 1:00 p.m. However, when they crossed west of the Amiens-Roye-Noyon road at around 5,000 feet, Lambert's plane began to develop engine trouble and to lose R.P.M.s, so he was forced to drop out and return to Conteville. Three or four other planes in the squadron were having the same problem. Palmer's plane was losing so many R.P.M.s that he trailed the others flying home at some distance and was the last to land.[75] An examination of the planes showed that the squadron had received some dirty fuel. Not only did the squadron have to worry about German planes, anti-aircraft guns, and the weather, but now dirty fuel was sabotaging their offensive operations.

After the reports had been submitted, Lambert went to the hanger to check out how much progress was made on clearing C1870's clogged fuel lines. He found his fight sergeant in the cockpit with the engine running. It was putting out more R.P.Ms than Lambert could have hoped. He knew that one could "learn what an engine was doing by feeling the vibrations though one's body."[76] He held onto one wing tip as the plane ran full throttle. Afterward, he climbed into the cockpit and put it through the full routine at 3,000 feet. Lambert's love of machines and flying come out in his description of his pleasure over the plane's performance. The machine had a life of its own. He would write, "She was good and seemed well pleased with herself. I liked her."[77] The mechanics were bound and determined that dirty fuel would no longer be a problem. After they got the system clean, they used a fine-woven felt cloth to filter all fuel that went into the plane. "From the way that engine functioned," Lambert wrote, "I would say, the felt had done the job."[78]

Lambert was now ready for his next patrol, but it would not be on 10 June. That day, it rained most of the time. Heavy rains grounded the squadron until noon. There would be some bright intervals of sun; still, C Flight would not do any flying that day.[79] However, the rest of the front was not so quiet. The German offensive continued with their advance on

Compiegne, but they did not have anything near the successes of the day before. The only success on the ground was a small gain west of the Matz River. The Germans continued to bomb Paris, and in the center they attempted to straighten out the budge of the huge salient. However, with no railroads to supply their soldiers and the rivers flowing in the wrong directions, they could not supply their troops in the salient, resulting in weakness and low morale.[80] The Gneisenau Offensive was, at best, stalled.

Meanwhile, Lambert was living the life of Riley. Lambert and Equipment Officer, Lieutenant H. R. South, the squadron's new mess officer, assembled a new hut that had arrived by lorry the day before. After finding a lovely spot under some large trees behind the hangers, they proceeded to build their new home with the assistance of several "side walk engineers," who gave sound and useful advice, but did no work. The names suggested for these new quarters included Windsor Castle, Blenheim Castle, and Buckingham Palace. (Lambert suggestion, the White House, was not well received.) Lambert now had "all the luxuries that [he] could use." Southey and he now had a dwelling that would be the envy of the squadron, a real home. They would move in immediately after lunch.[81] It would be his home until he left the squadron.

The weather continued to be an issue on the 11th, with heavy overcast but some clearing in the afternoon. C Flight finally get on an offensive patrol alone, but it was the early morning one that left at 5:00 a.m. Johnson, Daley, Selwyn, Hellett, Wilson, and Lambert would patrol

"Buckingham Palace," as they named it, was a small hut shared by Lambert and mess officer Lt. South at Conteville.

over the Noyan area between 16,000 to 17,000 feet. They saw only one plane the whole time, a two-seater reconnaissance plane that hurriedly headed east. Otherwise, no planes, not even the French, were visible during this patrol. The flight landed back at Conteville around 6:50 a.m., in time for breakfast.

Lambert then had a discussion with his air mechanics about engine concerns with C1870. Lambert felt that the engine was not performing up to his expectations. He was a stickler for details; he wanted to make sure that the engine was always running at its highest efficiency when taking the plane on patrol. Lambert explained his compulsion about the condition of his engine and plane. Yes, he admitted, he "was very cranky about them ... [but] that machine meant life or death to me. And I certainly enjoyed life."[82]

He enjoyed his life the rest of the day, since C flight would not be on patrol. Until lunch, he wrote letters home, read old newspapers, and watched Jim and Chips frolicking around chasing birds. He was shortly joined by W. J. Miller, a new pilot who had joined B Flight on 5 June as a replacement. Like all new pilots, Miller had to learn the ropes before he would be permitted to join his flight for patrol work. So he was now free to hang out with Lambert.

In the afternoon, Lambert found time to go to a neighboring farm, along with Palmer, and persuade the farmer to allow them to take his mules for a ride. These mules became the hit of the squadron as "No. 24 cavalry" came into existence. The mules became "a three mule polo team. A few of the pilots had played polo in England."[83]

At this point in his career, Lambert's *Combat Report* describes these times off more often and more fully than before. They are periods he cherished. He has no difficulty recalling his time building his new hut; going to Abbeville for wine, women, and song; or riding a mule around the base with his friends. Flying and aerial combat was his jobs, and he did it well; but these things he did in his off-time help define him as a person. No. 24 had become Lambert's family, and his feelings for his comrades run deep.

The squadron was now informed by Higher Authority that their assistance to the French was no longer necessary, so they could return to their normal patrol areas beginning on the 12th. Lambert and the rest of C Flight went on an offensive patrol that day in the Moreuil area once again. It was not ideal flying weather, but visibility was fair, even though the sky was overcast for most of the day. C Flight left around 10:45 a.m. to patrol around 12,000 feet above Moreuil, where they were harassed by the heavy anti-aircraft fire below them. They had to take evasive action to avoid being hit by the exploding projectiles. Cloud cover was heavy around 3,000 feet above the flight, so visibility was poor in that direction. Below them, however, visibility was relatively clear and unobstructed. But they were concerned about the possibility of an attack out of this cloud from above them.

Lambert's log book showed he was flying C8261 that day. At the last moment, he had been forced to leave C1870. That fact made him nervous, as he was up in "a strange, untested aeroplane." He never liked taking a plane on a patrol until he had first run it through a test course of moves and maneuvers, and unfortunately, because of the lateness of the switch, he did not get that opportunity.[84]

About noon, C Flight spotted some D.H 4s of No. 205 Squadron traveling east over German lines to do some observations, and four Fokker D. VIIs coming out of cloud cover below the flight.[85] For the first time that day, they would have a chance at aerial combat. Johnson, Selwyn, and Lambert went down to engage the Fokkers with Wilson and Hellett providing cover from above. (With the thick cloud cover, they could not be sure that the Fokkers were not a decoy.) The Fokkers forgot about the D.H.4s and went to meet the attacking S.E.5s. As usual when a dogfight started, the formation would break up, with every pilot for himself. Possibly the only way a pilot could help his comrade was to attack any enemy immediately on his friend's tail. These fights never lasted long, but individual pilots carried on fighting until others intervened either to attack or assist.[86] Johnson immediately latched on to one D. VII and sent it down out of control. It got lost in the clouds, but a pilot of one of the D.H.4 testified that he saw it hit the ground near Hangest. Johnson had another victory to his tally, his tenth.[87]

At the same time, Selwyn was on the tail of another Fokker, and Lambert had latched onto the tail of the leader. Unfortunately, what happened next showed the danger of taking off in a new, untested plane. Lambert's guns jammed after only two shots from his Vickers. A golden opportunity was missed! Lambert had to spend a few second clearing his guns, and then discovered that the Fokker was out of range and on his way to the east. He had not the time to pull his Lewis gun down or to clear the blockage of his Vickers. The battle ended around 12:15 p.m., and the flight landed back at Conteville thirty minutes later.[88] Johnson's victory was the only one for that patrol, but the D.H.4s were also free to continue with their reconnaissance work.

C Flight would have plenty of time to prepare for the 5:30 p.m. mixed flight (with A Flight). This additional time gave Lambert the opportunity both to get in a game of bumble-puppy with Southey after lunch and to get some flying in with C8361. He had checked on C1870, but the mechanics let him know that it would not be ready for the next flight. After having the guns jam on the earlier patrol, Lambert was taking no chances, so he took the plane up and fired around fifty rounds from both guns. It was a brief flight (a quarter of an hour), but he was now ready to join the afternoon patrol with greater confidence in his machine.

This patrol covered the same area south of Hangest that they had visited in the morning, but this time C Flight was accompanied by MacDonald and Foster. They were flying between 13,000 and 14,000 feet when they encountered ten Fokker D. VIIs about 2,000 feet below them headed east. The distance between them and the speed at which the Fokkers flew made it virtually impossible for the flight to get close enough to get a reliable shot off at them. Abandoning the chase, they continued their patrol and came across a two-seater (they thought, either a Halberstadt or L.V.G.) flying somewhere around 12,000 to 13,000 feet below them. Practically the entire flight—Johnson, MacDonald, Foster, Wilson, and Lambert—attacked this plane from every conceivable angle. Even under this tremendous fire, the pilot and observer continued to battle for what Lambert said was ten minutes, an eternity in air combat. Though the two-seater seemed to be a "sitting duck," as the flight ascended to regroup for a second run at their target, it attacked the flight, shooting at each of the British planes as they came into view and hitting all of them. It was an incredibly audacious ploy that won the enemy a reprieve, as the plane went into a steep dive and evaded its attackers. It also won the pilot his enemy's respect.

After returning to Conteville, the flight unanimously believed that the plane must have had metal armor, heavy steel plating, in order to avoid not being shot down from the fury of bullets they had put into it.[89] If that was the case, as seems almost certain, the plane was neither a Halberstadt nor a L.V.G., but possibly the Junkers J-I, the first all-metal aircraft that carried three machine guns. That would explain why the plane could avoid being shot down while successfully defending itself. It would also explain why the seasoned veterans of the flight were uncertain about the make of the plane, for the Junker J-I would be something new to them.

Lambert got a day's rest on 13 June, for the weather was most uncooperative, so the entire squadron being grounded for the day. Visibility was near zero; there was no possibility of flying. The squadron had a well-deserved and appreciated day of rest.

Although the day does not seem memorable, one of Lambert's comments on this day is important, not for what it tells of Lambert at the time, but for what it reveals of him in his later life. (This passage is only in the rough-draft version of *Combat Report*; it was excised from the published version.) Lambert first recalls that his batman woke him around 7:00 a.m. with a pot of tea to inform him that the day's activities were cancelled because of the weather. Relieved, Lambert went back to sleep till about 10:00 a.m. He then wrote, "Back in those days, I had no trouble going back to sleep after being wakened. But after all that affair was ended and I was back home in Ohio, I just could not go back to sleep unless I layed in bed and read for two or three hours; and if wakened by dreams etc. I had to repeat the performance. I just could not sleep."[90] This comment is the first indication we have that Lambert will take more out of this war than memories: that his experience in war, and his reaction to them, would shape his actions and personality for the rest of his life.

A day of rest was all very well, but sitting around all day could be unhealthy. It might lead to brooding like Dawe's. After Major Robeson, the Squadron Commander, gave the order that the day was a washout for flying, he suggested that they all enjoy a binge in Abbeville. Robeson knew and cared for his men, and he knew that they needed a way to let off steam. So, after going to the Field Cashier's office to cash checks, the pilots loaded up two tenders and Robeson's Crossley car and set off around 2:00 p.m., singing at the top of their voices on their way to a hot bath followed by wine, women, and food, along with more singing. The way Lambert described it was that "we had a 'binge' and I mean a 'binge.'"[91] By 10:00 p.m., the money was gone, and they were on their way back to base by 11:00 p.m.; however, the party did not end, for they continued the binge in the mess until dawn, with Robeson in attendance. By then, the place was trashed, and Lambert went to bed.

On the 14th, the weather was even worse than on the previous day. Except for a little flying in the north, there would be no flying on the front that day; it was too windy. The planes remained in their hangers. It was a good thing for No. 24, for some of these pilots did not get out of bed until supper-time. After the previous evening's binge, they were in no shape to fly. (Robeson must have known from the weather report that it was safe to allow the men to blow off steam the previous day.) Even the mascots Chips and Jim seemed to need the day to recover, as they lounged around all day. Lambert, however, showed his resilience by going on a mid-afternoon motor bike ride with Daley to "Auxie" and back. The supposed agnostic wrote, "The 'Old Gentleman' up stairs, must have planed [sic] this weather, especially for No. 24."[92]

The weather had improved on 15 June, and the squadron was finally over its hangover. They went back on offensive patrols. B Flight had the early morning duties this time, with C Flight taking off later at mid-morning, 11:05 a.m. Initially, they were over the British balloon lines, looking for attacking enemy aircraft. They had patrolled around 13,000 feet for fifteen minutes when they spotted three Albatros D.V.s around 3,000 feet below, attempting to attack the balloon line. These Albatros were old foes with whom No. 24 had often battled in the past. Lambert, flying C1870 once again, dived down with Johnson and Daley to attack the unsuspecting D.V.s. Hellett, Wilson, and Selwyn provided cover. Lambert was in the rear position of the attacking S.E.5s, resulting in Johnson and Daley attacking the two rear Albatross so that Lambert was left with the leader. Although he was able to stay above and behind the leader, it was clear that the leader was a quality pilot prepared to joust with Lambert, matching him move for move. It was a battle of maneuver between two skilled pilots, neither being able to get an initial advantage. Lambert maintained that the ultimate difference was the superiority of the S.E.5 over the Albatros. Of course, it might have been modesty, but oftentimes the machine *did* make the difference in aerial combat. Lambert was able to maneuver to get in "a perfect position for firing." He was looking through the center of his Aldis sight and determined that he was within twenty yards of his foe when he fired a short burst of about fifteen rounds that seemed to have hit the pilot.[93] (Lambert relied heavily on the Aldis sight to judge "his leads," or where to place the bullets in front of the target so that they would hit the opposing plane.[94] In this case, he was right on the mark.)

As the fight continued, Lambert knew his foe was still alive because he was moving in the cockpit. (An experienced pilot could almost judge if he had killed his adversary by the subsequent direction and reaction of the other's plane.) Lambert knew that the Albatros' engine had been badly damaged by the way the machine vibrated and fell. The pilot took the plane into a steep dive; Lambert continued to hug closely to its tail, hoping to get the opportunity to fire another short burst and finish it off. This opportunity would not avail itself, but Lambert saw the pilot struggle in the cockpit before he leveled off at 5,000 feet and watched the Albatros tear its undercarriage as it hit the ground.[95] Lambert had his eighth victory.

Or maybe not. The final call on this battle records the plane as indecisive, "driven down damaged."[96] Lambert had seen the plane crash land, but no one else had. He was certain in his own mind that the plane had been destroyed, but that certainty was not enough for the official record, in this case as in many others.

After this battle, Lambert located Johnson and Daley at between 7,000 and 8,000 feet and ascended to meet them. Hellett, Wilson, and Selwyn arrived about the same time as Lambert, so the flight was together again. Since no further prospects were in sight, they headed back to Conteville. C Flight went out a second time, accompanied by Southey from A Flight, for a two-hour evening patrol beginning at 5:00 p.m. This patrol was uneventful.

The rain would continue to battle with the sun for supremacy as C Flight took off at 7:15 a.m. on the 16th to patrol a railroad line from out of Villers-Bretonneux to a junction near Chaulnes. While patrolling between 8,000 and 10,000 feet, the flight spotted two two-seaters below them in an area near Rosiéres, but they faced heavy antiaircraft fire as they attempted to engage these aircraft. Unfortunately for Lambert, his plane C1870 was once again experiencing engine trouble. His frustration increased to the point he decided to request a new engine if the problems continued.[97] The flight continued to patrol the railway line for two hours without any activity to report except for the two-seaters returning to base.

Because of the uncertain weather, C Flight did not go out again that day. Lambert spent some of his time in a mule race, and then took C1870 up for a workout after tea time. (As we have seen, Lambert was a stickler for having his machine operate at peak performance.) It was a longer flight than normal for a workout. Lambert followed the trail of the Somme up to the Channel where he observed the ships on the salt water. They made him long for leave and London.[98] He knew he needed a break from the front. He was physically exhausted, and exhaustion was a way to drain courage. A pilot could become careless, and that might spell his doom. A couple of weeks in London would give him the time off he needed to recuperate. His leave, however, would have to wait until later in the summer. July was not far off on the calendar, but it was a lifetime in the air over the Western Front.

The weather seemed to improve on the morning of the 17th. It was fine in the morning when, at 11:15 a.m., thirteen planes from No. 24's three flights went on a squadron patrol in the Villers-Bretonneux area. On this flight from C Flight were Johnson, Selwyn, Daley, Hellett, and Lambert. This time, C Flight would take the bottom level of the patrol instead of the top. A and B Flights were providing cover this time. The squadron was over Moreuil heading east between 14,000 to 15,000 feet when it sighted ten Fokker D. VIIs about 2,000 to 3,000 feet below them, just east of Villers-Bretonneux. Lambert described the "rainbow and fantastic designs on the sides of their fuselages" as A and C Flights maneuvered to meet them.[99] Once these two forces were engaged, the joust began, with planes scattering all over the sky. From this point on, Lambert wrote, it was a "question of 'dog eat dog.'"[100]

Almost immediately, a blue-tailed Fokker blazed past Lambert to a position about twenty yards ahead of his plane. Lambert attempted to get his opponent in his sights to get a shot off. The Fokker was traveling at high speed, so he was about fifty yards off before Lambert could finally fire. Lambert called it "a very lucky shot." He saw "a burst of flame mixed with black smoke" come out of the Fokker as it dived straight down into the clouds below.[101]

What happened next can be construed as beginning evidence that Lambert really did need a break from the rigors of combat. He admitted that he was careless. Lambert spent so much time watching the Fokker dive down that he temporarily lost sight of the larger battle around him. Another Fokker took the opportunity to attach himself onto Lambert's tail and fire both guns into C1870. Had it not been for another plane from his flight coming in from above to drive the attacking Fokker off, it would have been tragic for Lambert.

Lambert, now awakened to the immediate dangers around him, quickly turned left and moved on a red and green Fokker that was fastened to the tail of a different S.E.5. It was about 200 to 300 yards below and slightly in front of Lambert. Going full throttle in his dive, he maneuvered his plane into a position where he sent around 150 to 200 rounds of ammunition into the trailing Fokker. At first, Lambert thought he had missed the plane entirely, but as he watched the plane's brief evasive maneuvers, he noticed it "quiver and shake." A few seconds later, the top left wing of the Fokker broke loose, to be followed directly by its lower wing.[102]

It was noon, and Lambert already had two victories to his credit. His total now stood at ten, but what followed was an incident that first puzzled and then sickened him. With the loss of both left wings, the Fokker was doomed, and without a parachute, so was the pilot. The opponents were down to 5,000 or 6,000 feet when the deadly burst was fired. The German pilot, realizing the hopelessness of his situation, decided to abandon ship. Lambert described what he first thought resembled a "sack of feed" falling out of the plane until he recognized it as the pilot. "That sight almost made me vomit. Believe me, I sure needed a strong drink right then."[103]

Lambert ascended to a place where he was surrounded by the action taking place above and below him. About 200 feet above, he saw Southey engaged in a battle with two Fokkers; one had a blue nose and white tail, with a large white skull and crossbones painted on the side of the fuselage. As Lambert watched Southey use a deflection shot to send this Fokker to the east, a D. VII dived under him in pursuit of another S.E.5. Lambert pushed his plane left and circled under this attacking Fokker in hopes of assisting his comrade. The S.E.5 was spinning downward and heading into the clouds with the attacking D. VII still firing its guns at it. Lambert turned to fire his guns at the attacker, at too great a distance to be effective, but hoping to distract the attacker from pursuing his prey.[104] Lambert lost sight of this battle as it moved into the clouds, but the cloud cover would give the S.E.5 the opportunity to rid himself of the attacker.

The fight was not yet over. Lambert's attempt to assist his comrade had brought him down to the lower level of combat, where the action was "fast and furious."[105] Lambert spotted a lone Fokker below and positioned himself on its tail, only this time he took a moment to check what was going on at the upper level; he was not going to get caught napping again. He fired both guns in the direction of the Fokker, but the enemy was able to successfully extradite himself from the combat by diving away.

Almost immediately, three S.E.5s had come down from the upper level to assist their comrades. The battle above was over, and they had come looking for more action. Unfortunately, the battle was all but spent, and the enemy was going east out of harm's way. The flights reassembled for their trip back to Conteville, where they landed around 12:40 p.m. and made their reports.

One combat that Lambert was not part of, and did not even see, was one in which MacDonald, Barton, and Johnson had forced a Fokker to land behind the French lines near Cachy. (Southey later claimed that his deflection shot had burst into this planes right side, and it went down immediately in a series of half rolls and was followed down by MacDonald, Johnson, and Barton.[106] However, officially Southey did not share in this victory.) It was later known that this pilot was Lieutenant Kurt Wüsthoff, an ace with twenty-seven victories and the second youngest recipient of the *Pour le Mérite*. He was such a celebrity that Major Robeson visited him while in hospital. Besides Wüsthoff, the record showed that the squadron had two other decisive victories, one that broke up in the air and another in flames, both by Lambert, and two indecisive combats recorded by Hellett. They had had a successful hunt this day.

The feat of shooting down two planes in a single day is certainly not unparalleled, but it is rare. Lambert accomplished it, officially, at least three times, 17 June being the first time. On 4 August, he would once again destroy two planes in a single day's combat. On 10 August, he would shoot down two planes and share a third with Selwyn, Harries, and Bair of C Flight. His log book also had him shooting down two planes on 12 April, but these are officially listed as "not recorded." Even so, to accomplish this task three times in his short career as a combat pilot shows that Lambert was indeed a superb pilot and tactician, an airman worthy of being called an ace.

On 18 June, the weather was fair in the morning and overcast in the afternoon. A and C Flights conducted a joint patrol over the Somme River beginning at 8:00 a.m., but Lambert had to return almost immediately because of renewed engine trouble. His flight lasted twenty-five minutes before he returned to Conteville, determined that something had to be done about C1870's continual engine problems. The flight continued on, but returned at 10:00 a.m. without sighting a single aircraft. In the early evening, around 5:00 p.m., C went on a second patrol with parts of A Flight. Lambert must have temporarily solved his difficulties, because his log book lists him as flying C1870 on this patrol.[107] Again, however, the patrol was a disappointment. They only saw two two-seaters, and those were too far away to do

Kurt Wüsthoff's colorful Fokker D. VII was shot down by No. 24 Squadron member J. H. Southey as Lambert observed from above.

anything but watch them fly off. The weather also became a problem; the flight had to return by 6:30 p.m., a half-hour early, because the rain became too intense to continue.[108] The whole day had been a wash.

The weather was still bad on the 19th, and flying was quite impossible. To pass the time, some pilots gave the three local mules a workout. Lambert tried to take a motor bike ride around the neighborhood, but the heavy mud put a stop to that attempt. The one noteworthy event that day was the transfer of C Flight Commander George Johnson. He would be followed two days later by Captain Ian MacDonald, Commander of A Flight. These two were not only good commanders, but friends to Lambert, people he could depend upon and trust. He would miss them. It was decided that Selwyn would be promoted to replace Johnson as Fight Commander of C Flight, and Hazell would replace MacDonald in that capacity for A Flight. C Flight made Selwyn buy all the drinks in the mess that night to celebrate his promotion.[109]

The rain, winds, cloud cover, mist, and overcast continued for the next few days, and the squadron was inactive. Lambert remarked that the pilots were getting bored and restless with this idleness: "This life of inactivity is not quite as nice as one might think."[110] Flights were attempted, but they usually had to return early because of high winds or ominous weather conditions. This condition continued for almost a week, until the 25th. That day was not exactly ideal for flying—the sky was overcast and the visibility poor—but it was good enough to get in some flying. Lambert would have to fly without Johnson or C1870. It was finally decided to replace the engine in his old machine, so he was given a new one, C1084. He hated to lose his old friend and hoped for the best with his new one. As it turned out, C1084 would serve him well and truly; he would fly it until early August.[111]

C Flight went on a joint patrol with members of A and B flights. Joining Captain Selwyn from C Flight that day were Wilson, Daley, and Lambert. All told, there were ten planes on this patrol leaving Conteville around 9:45 a.m. with C Flight in the lead to explore over the Somme area from a height of 15,000 to 17,000 feet. Around 11:15 a.m., they were over the town of Roye when they spotted a formation of Fokker D. VIIs and a second made up of Fokker Dr. Is about 3,000 feet below. Almost immediately, C Flight attacked, with B in support and A performing cover duty. (Once A Flight was convinced that this enemy formation was not a decoy, they joined the battle and evened the odds.) The battle came on fast and furious, with Southey and Wilson driving a Dr. I down and out of control. Lowe fired on two Fokkers and then engaged a third, a D. VII, that he sent down in flames. Wilson was attacked by a Fokker on his tail. Southey managed to drive the plane off, but not before the damage was done: Wilson's S.E.5 had caught fire and he was forced to land. Fortunately, he landed behind the Allied lines; however, he suffered serious damage to his plane and a badly burned foot. (Afterward, he was sent to a hospital and repatriated back to England. The war was over for him.) It was the first causality that C Flight had suffered since March, and Lambert noted that it was also the last casualty the flight would suffer during his term with No. 24. He said that C Flight was either lucky or good; he was inclined to believe it was more luck.[112] We might disagree.

The battle continued to rage in all directions. With all military conflicts, "confusion is an essential element of battle."[113] In the midst of this confusion, Foster dived on a "tripe" firing around a hundred rounds into it at close range. That caused the enemy aircraft to fall off in a spin while parts of the plane broke off.

Leaving one encounter, Lambert inadvertently entered a more personal and frightening one. Coming directly at him from about 150 yards away was a Fokker D. VII firing both Spandau guns. Lambert was convinced that the pilot was intent on ramming him. He reacted by firing both his Lewis and Vickers guns directly into the center of the Fokker. He aimed for the radiator in the front nacelle. Lambert's description of this encounter is, unusually for him, tinctured with fear. What the German pilot was doing was reckless and dangerous both for himself and for Lambert. He seemed to be playing a deadly game of "chicken." Time seemed to have slowed down for Lambert to a point that he could recall minute details of the combat. They closed in on each other with great speed. When there were less than fifty yards to go, Lambert could see the German pilot pulling "his goggles up with his left hand," and then trying "to rip open his flying suit with his right hand." Lambert remembered seeing "a terrible look of pain and fear" in his adversary's eyes.[114] By this time, he believed, they were only separated by about fifteen yards, then the Fokker fell off on the left wing, going nose down, as Lambert pulled his stick back and turned his plane to the right. He estimated that the two missed each other by only about a foot. The last time he saw the plane, it was spinning straight down to the ground below.

This experience left an indelible impression on Lambert. He described himself as "shaking like a leaf in a high wind."[115] He drew a sketch of the scene in 1922, "while it was still fresh in [his] mind."[116] During an interview in 1980, he showed the interviewer a picture he had made of this scene. He told Smith about it as if it had just happened: the German pilot "just reached up and pushed his goggles up—I saw him do it—they're off his eyes."[117] He continued to have dreams about this encounter. He never forgot the look of terror in that other's eyes, and speculated that he might have hit him in the chest. He continued to maintain that the German pilot was attempting to ram him, and that he had nearly succeeded.[118] It was the closest brush with death he ever had.

Before Lambert had sufficient time to recover, he was accosted from behind by a Fokker Dr. I shooting bullets through his right bottom wing. Fortunately, it was driven off by an S.E.5, and this reprieve gave Lambert enough time to avoid yet another "Tripe" by doing a half roll. He was soon joined by Selwyn and Daley, and wrote in his memoirs that he was glad to see them, because he "had not recovered from the terror of that first D. VII."[119] The three attempted to chase down a two-seater, but the distance was too great and the plane made its escape to the east. After what Lambert thought was a thirty-minute engagement, they were all ready to return to Conteville, landing shortly after noon.

The following day, the 26th, the weather was again bad for flying, with very little sun and sporadic cloud cover. German air raids continued to bother Paris, but on its front the squadron had little activity. C Flight had the early morning patrol from 5:30 to 7:45 a.m., but they engaged only a single two-seater that got away, retiring to the east, as usual.[120] It might have been that the Germans needed some time to recover from the previous day's battle. Lambert ended his comments on this day by asking, "Where are all our German fighter friends?"[121]

On 27 June, the weather improved substantially, but at first the Germans were no more present than they had been on the previous day. C Flight had the early afternoon flight, leaving at 1:00 p.m. to patrol the Somme near Bray, but they returned at 3:00 p.m. without any encounter with the enemy. After supper, in which they toasted King George V and spent the "King's Shilling" (a tradition where an amount was removed from the officer's account to pay for the daily port wine toast to the king's health), Major Robeson informed the squadron that a mixed flight of eight to ten planes would go on patrol at 7:30 p.m. Selwyn, Daley, and Lambert would be going from C Flight.[122]

The patrol was ordered to cover the Chippily-Maricourt area at around 12,000 feet. While sweeping east of Maricourt in a wide arc, the patrol spotted a mixed flight of between ten and twelve planes that included Fokker Dr. Is, some Fokker D. VIIs, and several Albatros D.V.s. The enemy was coming from the east and were approaching approximately 3,000 to 5,000 feet below where No. 24 was flying, and evidently they were unaware of the S.E.5s above them. They were after three two-seaters from No. 8 Squadron that were flying reconnaissance over the German lines below, but No. 24 did not realize this until they glided down to around 9,000 to 10,000 feet. With this German flight only 3,000 feet below them, the patrol had those Germans in a trap. Going full throttle, eight planes from the mixed flight dived on the unsuspecting Germans below; as Lambert wrote, "in a short time, we joined in the fun."[123] The leaders in this attack were Barton, Farrell, and Passmore of B Flight. By this time, a few of the rear Germans had spotted the approaching S.E.5s and quickly began to scatter. However, the remaining members of the German flight, especially three Fokker D. VIIs and two Albatros D.V.s, were unaware of the approaching British planes and continued their attack on the three reconnaissance planes.

Barton, Farrell, and Passmore were on top of those five planes, firing all of their guns at them, before these German pilots knew what hit them. The rest of No. 24 quickly engaged the balance of the enemy aircraft still around, which Lambert numbered as seven. As the planes scattered into individual dogfights, Lambert found himself about fifty yards behind a blue Albatros D.V. and maneuvered his S.E.5 slightly downward as he replicated the moves of his adversary. Lambert was able to center this Albatros in his Aldis sight and fired about seventy-five rounds from his Vickers machine gun into it. He saw the pilot slump forward and watched the Albatros fall off and spin downward, trailing smoke as it descended. As usual, he had no time to watch what happened as this airplane fell, because a Fokker D. VII was on his tail firing at him.[124]

In a later interview, Lambert discussed how he adjusted the firing mechanisms of his Lewis and Vickers guns so they could be fired simultaneously. He was still able to fire each one separately if needed, but being able to fire both at once gave him a distinct advantage in an attack.[125] Often when below an opponent, he would simply position his S.E.5 upward and fire both guns into his opponent's underbelly. His fight with the blue Albatros, however, was one of the occasions when he used only one gun. He said that the Lewis gun had a greater propensity to jam than the Vickers, so he put more trust into the stationary Vickers gun located in front of the plane. He remembered running out of ammunition once and using a pistol to fire at an opponent, but he did not hit either the airplane or the pilot. Once, when out of ammunition, he threw the plane's fire extinguisher at an opponent's plane and actually hit it. He told the interviewer that if he had hit that plane's propeller, he would have been the only pilot in the war to shoot down an enemy using a fire extinguisher.[126]

The attacking Fokker on Lambert's tail was pounced on by another S.E.5, and that allowed Lambert to do a partial loop, followed by a half roll, that together landed him on the tail of another Albatros D.V. that was now only thirty yards in front of him. This time, however, he failed to sight his opponent properly, so that plane escaped from harm. This escape, Lambert said, happened because he was "too frightened to think straight"; the Fokker had "scared the daylights out of me." He had not known that it was behind him until he "heard his guns firing at my tail end."[127] Lambert recognized how close he had come to going down smoking; he felt his own mortality, he knew that the next flight could be his last. In the past, there had been other times that Lambert had been in danger and rescued only at the last moment by one of his comrades, but this time he could not brush it off; it had hit him too hard. He wrote that he could not "be too careful in this sort of game. Those boys played for keeps."[128] Lambert was beginning to think too much about what could happen in the air. His confidence in his own invulnerability had been shaken.

The battle continued to rage. Lambert met another German face to face. This time a Fokker D. VII, with what Lambert described as "a red nose with some green paint," was less than a hundred yards directly in front of him. Quickly he fired his both his guns and watched as it "fell off and spun down slowly."[129] He did not know what ultimately happened to this pilot or his plane because a Fokker D. VII and Albatros D.V. were immediately behind him on his tail. It seemed to be Lambert's day to be the enemy's center of attention. He remarked that those Germans "would not leave me alone." They drove him down to less than 1,000 feet before he was able to "shake them off" his tail.[130]

The appearance of three Camels from No. 4 Squadron Royal Australian Air Force, played a part in convincing the Fokker and the Albatros to give up the fight. Lambert had noticed earlier that two of these Camels had attacked a Dr. I at around 6,500 feet and sent it down smoking. Then they came to Lambert's rescue and "saved his neck."[131] Following this timely

Six. Summer

rescue, Lambert joined the Camels as he looked for the balance of his squadron, which was spread all over the sky and currently out of sight. Knowing there was strength in numbers, Lambert went with the Camels as they slowly climbed to around 4,000 or 5,000 feet where the visibility improved.

It was now getting dark, and Lambert knew he was also getting low on fuel and a good distance from Conteville. He bade farewell to his Australian comrades and headed to the northwest in hopes of running into his squadron mates as he headed for home. Since it was late June, the extended daylight enabled him to reach Conteville before it became too dark. He landed at 9:30 p.m., and discovered that he had arrived before any other members of the flight, so he stayed around the hanger waiting for the rest of them to return.[132]

It had been another productive day for the squadron. Lambert had contributed to one of the decisive victories and was given credit at the time for one of the indecisive ones. In the official records, however, he was only given credit for shooting down the Albatros D. V. out of control. Apparently there was not enough evidence to substantiate the second claim. However, his total now stood at an impressive twelve victories.

The weather was quite nice on the 28th, so patrols would be possible. Lambert began the day looking over the activities board and seeing that planes from No. 4 Squadron had shot down and crashed a fighter and two two-seaters. He also saw that Captain McElroy, now of No. 40 Squadron, had shot down a balloon in flames. (No. 40 also flew S.E.5s.) Rather sadly, Lambert remarked that he wished they had McElroy back in No. 24 again.[133]

Lambert's log book lists two patrols for the day. The first one was a morning patrol from 8:45 a.m. to 10:50 a.m. at around 12,000 feet, in which C Flight engaged some Albatros D.V.s. They fired a few rounds at these fighters, but the enemy eluded them and retired to the east. The second flight was an evening one, from 6:00 p.m. to 8:05 p.m., at about 17,000 feet, in which they observed no aircraft. The log book does not say whether either of these patrols were taking place.[134]

On the next day, 29 June, the weather was very good, but the visibility was only fair. C Flight's only flight of the day would be an evening patrol, so the members of the flight had plenty of time to relax and enjoy the morning and afternoon. Lambert and his good friend Daley went on a mule ride and chased two rabbits across a field before returning to base and resting in the sun. After supper, they went on patrol. (There is some discrepancy about the time of the flight: in one place, it is listed as 5:15 p.m. to 7:25 p.m.; in another place, as between 6:00 p.m. and 8:00 p.m.[135]) On this patrol, Selwyn, Daley, and Lambert were accompanied by Foster of A Flight. They were to patrol the Rosiéres area at an altitude of 16,000 to 17,000 feet.

The two previous patrols had reported no enemy activity (with the exception of some active anti-aircraft fire as A Flight attempted to attack some enemy balloons), and at first it looked as if this inactivity would continue. But when they came in form the northeast to circle over Hangest around 6:30 p.m., they spotted eight enemy planes, some Albatros D.V.s, and Fokker D. VIIs, as well as Fokker Dr. I. These planes were three or four miles away and well below the flight's altitude, and the flight believed that they had not been seen.[136] Selwyn led the flight into attacking position as he swung around to the right in a wide circle to get behind the enemy formation. Still positioned above, the four S.E.5s dived full throttle on the enemy below. Selwyn fired first, missing a D. VII, before maneuvering on the tail of another one that he sent spinning down into the mist. The enemy pilot had lost control over his machine as it headed downward.[137]

Lambert found himself busy with two enemy planes, one a Fokker D. VII and the other an Albatros D. V., which appeared close together about 200 yards in front of him. Being still above them, he immediately went nose down, shifting his rudder from right to left while firing both guns at both enemy aircraft. These planes quickly dived straight down and were seen heading northeast at a high rate of speed. Lambert remarked that he must have "scared the daylights out of them."[138] He then saw an Albatros D.V. lagging behind and pounced on it. He was still above and about 200 yards behind the D.V., but traveling at a greater rate of speed, he was able to narrow the gap to fifty yards before firing his guns. He estimated that he shot about a hundred rounds into the Albatros before the pilot even knew that he had someone on his tail. He watched as the Albatros fell off into a "loose, jerky spin … [and] crashed into a field north of what I assumed to be Le Quesnal."[139]

Afterward, Lambert took time to judge the situation, finding that two additional S.E.5s had joined his flight. One was on the tail of the Fokker Dr. I, and Daley had just sent another enemy aircraft down in flames. The battle continued, with Daley maneuvering behind and underneath another D. VII in hopes of attacking it from below, as Foster flew under Lambert's tail firing at a light-colored Albatros. Within a few moments, however, the battle was over, for the low fuel supply meant it was time to head back to Conteville.

On the way back to join the rest of the flight, Lambert spotted three enemy aircraft in the distance and fired at a Fokker D. VII that seemed to be lagging behind. It was a futile gesture from almost 200 yards away, and Lambert knew it. The flight as a whole, however, was a success. Upon returning to Conteville, the flight realized that this patrol of only four S.E.5s had accounted for three decisive victories, one being Lambert's Albatros, and one each given to Daley and Selwyn. The flight was also credited with four indecisive victories, with each pilot on the flight being credited with one victory. Officially, however, Lambert would only be given credit for one decisive victory, the plane that was seen to crash. There was not enough evidence to give him credit for the indecisive. However, his total at the end of June had reached thirteen.

The final day of June was not a busy one for No. 24, even though the weather was good, visibility was excellent, and there was a lot of sunshine. C Flight was grounded for the day. Lambert found time to read a posting on Lieutenant William Claxton of No. 41 Squadron, who was a former member, along with Lambert, of Cadet Course No. 8 in Canada. Claxton was credited with shooting down six enemy planes on 30 June. (This remarkable feat was from a pilot who shot down thirteen enemy planes from 27 June to 30 June and would eventually shoot down thirty-seven opponents in his career.) Lambert had a sense of pride in Claxton's accomplishments because it showed that those pilots trained in Canada had received quality training. He remarked, "Cadet Course No. 8 certainly did turn out at least one outstanding fighter pilot."[140]

Lambert also had time this day to check out C1084 after a punishing day of combat. Meeting with his mechanic after breakfast, he was satisfied enough to take the plane up for a quiet flight to St. Omer and the Channel. During the afternoon, he took a ride on one of the squadron's motorbikes. He reflected that it had been a busy and productive month in spite of the weather. The squadron had been credited with twenty-four decisive combats and fifteen indecisive.[141] Lambert had been in the thick of it all.

Seven

Moving into Autumn
July 1918

July arrived. The war seemed to be continuing as usual, for the soldiers on the ground and the pilots in the air. For the high command on the Allied side, however, there was reason for optimism. The bombings behind the German lines were continuing, with the British day and night bombers delivering about forty tons of bombs to places like Mannheim, Coblenz, Trèves, and even at Thionville on the left bank of the Moselle. (Lambert sarcastically remarked that the Germans for some reason "did not appreciate our generosity."[1]) These bombs were doing great damage. Even the normally cautious General Henri Pétain had said, "If at the end of June we have held firm, our position is excellent. In July we can resume the upper hand. Then victory is ours."[2] And they had held the line in June, but Ludendorff was not yet done. He had one more card to play.

Lambert was now in the summer of his career. He exhibited confidence and self-assurance, "initiative, skill, and determination."[3] He was now a seasoned pilot. His flight could depend on him, and he trusted them to protect his rear. There had been a couple of incidents that had frightened him, and he was beginning to feel the pressure of the daily raids and to long for leave. But he was a long way yet from losing his nerve.

On the first day of July, the weather was warm with bright sun and a clear blue sky—good flying weather. Lambert's batman, following routine, came into "Buckingham Palace" (one of the names given to Lambert's hut) with a pot of tea and hot shaving water at 5:30 a.m. It was time to awaken him in order to get ready for the mixed patrol that was to leave at 7:00 a.m. Lambert was in the mess tent at 6:00 a.m. for breakfast and then went off to the hangers to join members of all three flights for an offensive patrol that would take them from near Amiens to as far as Chaulnes. Ten S.E.5s, including Selwyn, Hellett, and Lambert of C Flight, were joined by nineteen-year-old Second Lieutenant A. Wren, a novice who had joined on 20 June and had been assigned to C Flight. For this diminutive young man (Lambert wrote that he was "even smaller than Southey") it was his first patrol, so Lambert knew they "would have to watch over that lad."[4]

If Wren was looking for action on his first patrol, he would not be disappointed. Flying between 15,000 and 16,000 feet in the area around Caix, the patrol spotted what turned out to be between fifteen and twenty Albatros D.V.s and Fokker D. VIIs in the distance. The enemy was around 2,000 feet below the flight and at least two or three miles away. Realizing there were no enemy planes waiting above to ambush them, Selwyn led C Flight in a wide circle to place the bright sun behind them as they began to maneuver down to attack the top flight of Fokkers.[5] As always, they were taking the war to the enemy.

By now, the German pilots were aware they were under attack and began to scatter. In front of Lambert, about 200 yards away, was a Fokker painted a dirty gray-green. Lambert was able to narrow the gap to about seventy-five yards before he fired, but his Vickers gun had jammed. He was forced to break off the fight and clear his gun, and the enemy got away.[6]

As we have seen, Lambert always tried to get as close as possible before firing on an enemy. He felt that he needed to be within at least fifty yards to be effective; twenty was far more preferable. To Lambert, firing on an enemy beyond a hundred yards was simply wasting ammunition.[7] Attacking from seventy-five yards was beyond his comfort zone, but within the 100-yard limit he had set for himself. In this particular case, the additional distance might have given him the extra time he needed to clear his Vickers gun of its blockage without immediately facing another opponent. Wren immediately went "hell bent for election" on the tail of the same Fokker. He showed tenacity and skill in attacking this enemy, but the Fokker was able to get away from him as well.[8] Still, from this first impression, it seemed as if Wren would fit in nicely with C Flight.

After clearing his guns, Lambert worked his way down to a mix of Fokkers and Albatros fighters. He joined S.E.5s from both A and B Flight who were already engaged in what Lambert described as a "very good 'dog fight.'"[9] After entering the fray, Lambert turned to the left to outmaneuver a fancy-colored Albatros that was about to attack him. Several times, he credited his plane C1084 for its remarkable performance on that day. He wrote that she "could just about act on her own without help from me."[10] But although the plane was at peak performance and doing what he wanted, the usually reliable Vickers gun had given him trouble. Showing his skill as a pilot, Lambert was able to maneuver his plane by kicking the rudder and lifting its nose to position himself about fifty yards behind this Albatros. He fired both guns, but only the Vickers continued to fire. Apparently, he had already emptied his Lewis gun, but the previously-jammed Vickers still had ammunition remaining. The Albatros, however, was able to escape from Lambert by diving several thousand feet straight down before it leveled off and headed east.[11] If both of Lambert's guns had been available, it might have been another story.

Lambert's mishaps continued. Finding himself in a brief lull, Lambert tried to change the drum in his Lewis gun, but the wind caught the drum broadside, and Lambert lost his grip as it flew over the side of the plane. Trying to retrieve the drum, Lambert suffered a deep bruise on his arm and feared that it might have been broken; but he gathered himself together and finally locked a new ammunition drum into place in the Lewis gun. Apparently, even though the odds were in their favor, the Germans were not very aggressive during this encounter, or Lambert would not have had the time to do this.

It was almost 8:30 a.m. With only enough fuel to make it home, it was time to reassemble the flight and head back to Conteville. On the way back home, flying between 5,000 and 6,000 feet, three of the S.E.5s, including Daley, spotted three enemy observation balloons to the west. They immediately dived on these balloons and Daley sent one down in flames. Unfortunately, the other two balloons were winched down to safety before any damage could be afflicted. After landing at Conteville, about 9:30 a.m., the flight submitted its report in which they stated they had sent only one enemy aircraft down out of control, and Daley was given credit for the balloon he shot down.[12] It was not a remarkably successful patrol, but at least none of them had been shot down, and Wren had shown he would be a valuable member of the team.

As the squadron had lunch, Major Robeson informed them that Wing Command wanted the squadron to focus on tactical ground support. They were to observe the enemy's activities, including troop movement, transport, artillery, and especially any unusual movements by the German forces. Balloons were also to be given greater priority. The squadron was to focus on low-level flights until further notice. They would continue to do offensive patrols from time to time, but at longer intervals than before. Trench strafing and low-level reconnaissance were highly dangerous and not glamorous, so the new assignment was not greeted with any degree of satisfaction or excitement.[13] But it was important, in fact necessary, work. Not only did the enemy need to be observed and harassed at all possible moments, the R.A.F. needed to provide air cover and ground support for their side.

During this same lunch, Lambert began to reflect on the good life he enjoyed with his squadron mates. He appreciated their good-natured jocularity and cheer around the mess. The friendly ribbing of a friend as the two ate lunch was a memory to be cherished. However, he also wondered how many of his comrades would still be sitting around the mess at supper time. Lambert wrote, "There was always an element of fear deep down in every man seated there, but very few allowed this feeling to come to the surface. Most men in the business faced the fact: 'that what is to be, will be.'"[14] Although he still had great confidence in his flying abilities, and was far from showing a change in his behavior such as acting morose, concerns about impending doom or death were increasingly becoming part of Lambert's consciousness. Death was, perhaps, as close as the next flight. How long would his luck continue? Lambert remembered what happened to Dawe. He had been seen biting his lip and acting rather disorientated before he was shot down and killed. Lambert was now more keenly observant of his comrades' behavior than he had ever been. And he knew that C Flight was to go out at 5:00 p.m. for a second flight on a dangerous ground support mission; a return flight home was not guaranteed.

Joining Lambert on this evening patrol were some new additions to C Flight. Wren would once again be on the flight, and Second Lieutenant Thomas M. Harries as well. Harries had joined the squadron on 24 June. But he was no novice, having been posted to the squadron after serving with No. 45 Squadron for six months, during which he had claimed six victories, three of them on the same day.[15] He, Wren, Lambert, Hellett, Daley, and Selwyn went on an offensive patrol over the Mericout area, working around 15,000 feet. If the enemy did not appear, they were to continue with tactical ground support over the main east-west road leading out of LaMotte. After 6:00 p.m. they spotted some enemy aircraft to the northeast. Lambert assumed that they were operating out of Cappy, around twenty miles east of Amiens. But they were too far away for any activity to take place. Then twelve more S.E.5s, possibly from No. 41 Squadron, came in from the north, and the enemy decided that discretion was the better part of valor and headed east.

With the additional S.E.5s acting as cover, Selwyn took the flight down to support the Allied soldiers below by harassing the enemy on the east-west highway. Almost immediately, they received an assault from the antiaircraft batteries hidden in some small wooded area, until they were able to work their way down underneath their firing range. Afterward, machine-gun and ground fire presented the greatest challenge.[16]

Lambert, Daley, and possibly Harries went after some antiaircraft emplacements located in the small wood. After these have been spotted, each pilot fired both guns into the area to silence their attackers. They succeeded for the time being, but Lambert realized that their failure to carry bombs had limited their effectiveness. However, they had been forced to leave bombs back at base, not knowing if they would be engaged in aerial combat. Had they been involved in a dogfight, the extra weight of the bombs would have greatly hampered them.

While these three pilots were attacking the antiaircraft emplacements, Selwyn, Wren, and Hellett were attacking machine-gun emplacements and motor transports from around 1,000 feet over the main highway east of LaMotte. They later received a report which stated the flight had put four machine-gun emplacements out of action. They had also set one vehicle on fire and sent several others into the ditch alongside the road.[17] After this action, with ammunition running low, the flight headed back to Conteville. Even though there had been no enemy aircraft shot down, the operation had been a success.

On 2 July, the tide started turning against the Germans. They may have recaptured territory northwest of Albert, but the Allies were holding the line and even taking the offensive. Also, over a million U.S. troops had already embarked for France, and the Germans had no reserves left to answer such a force.

One of the things Lambert needed to do this day was to tinker with his plane. The previous day, he had discovered that the plane had less stability on a steep turn. As usual, he worked with his mechanic to increase the plane's efficiency. He also reduced his dihedral by half in order to increase C1084's speed and ability to climb. (A *dihedral* is the angle at which the wings of an airplane are vertically inclined.) Afterward, he pitted it against his friend Daley's machine and was able to outperform it both in level flight and on a steep climb. Lambert was willing to sacrifice some stability on a steep turn if the plane could fly and climb faster.[18]

Throughout his review of his time in the war, Lambert peppers his account with remembrances of making adjustments to his plane. It is something that is rare in pilots' memoirs. He would write, "I always felt that I should know and feel every whim, mood and temperament of the whole aeroplane.... Yes the man and the machine must blend and combine to become one living unit.... She understood me and I understood her. We were one."[19]

Lambert and the rest of C Flight would join A Flight for an early morning offensive patrol this beautiful July day, starting at 5:30 a.m. They would patrol between 12,000 and 14,000 feet along the railroad line eat of Villers-Bretonneux. As on the previous day, the mission was to engage enemy aircraft, if any, and then to assist in tactical ground support. The German Air Force seem to be absent today, so a few miles east of Rosières the flights began their descent to around 1,000 feet to initiate ground-strafing. Once again they had to contend with heavy antiaircraft, machine-gun, and rifle fire. C Flight went down to around 500 feet in hopes of locating the machine-gun nests, which were discovered hidden at fifty yard intervals by "a line of torn up bushes."[20] The flight located six machine-guns supporting troops living and hiding in a mud-and-water-trench. Flying at about a hundred feet, the flight was able to eliminate all but one of these guns. Lambert's description of this action is not one of pleasure, but of sorrow and empathy for what those German ground troops had to endure.[21]

Afterward, the flight began its search for A Flight, which they located two miles north above a railroad line at about 1,000 feet. Lambert identified the heavy black smoke of a train coming west and immediately got Selwyn's attention so that the whole group could assault the onrushing train. All twelve S.E.5s were attacking the train from all angles and eventually disabled it. Lambert believed they had killed the crew in the locomotive and derailed two cars, one of which was carrying troops who scattered for shelter on the side, into ditches, or wherever they could.

This experience caused Lambert to lament how he much "preferred to face enemy in the air, rather than those on the ground."[22] Flying could give a pilot the feeling of not being in a war, but above it. Seeing the realities of the ground war did not appeal to Lambert or any other pilot. Killing horses especially bothered many, like Lambert, who had animals of their own at home. Some writer-pilots were even more graphic and disturbing than Lambert. Mannock, in his diary entry of 20 July 1917, describes his "nauseating" journey through the trenches with "dead men's legs sticking through the sides with puttees and boots still on.... This sort of thing, together with the strong grave-yard stench ... can ... upset me for days."[23] That was the war up close and personal, not from thousands of feet up in the air.

By the time the flight had finished its assault on the train, it was almost out of ammunition and fuel. It was now time to return to Conteville. They landed at 7:35 a.m. in time for breakfast.[24] It was after breakfast that Lambert tells his readers something about himself and his childhood—the details that are missing from the beginning part of his book, where we would supposed they would be found.

Lambert tell us that after breakfast, everyone left the mess except Daley and himself. Finding themselves alone, the two begin to talk about their lives back home before the war. Daley goes first, describing his childhood in Kingston, Jamaica. It must have been an idyllic description, from Lambert's conclusion Daley's home was the place of the original "Garden of Eden," but we get no details besides his spending time on the water around the islands.[25] Lambert uses this story as an introduction to his own story of *his* idyllic life, as he now sees it back on the Ohio. He talks of himself and his younger brother going to their great-grandmother's farm in Greenup, Kentucky, for the summer when school was out. In town, he describes life on the public square before the advent of automobiles, shade trees, the colors of autumn, the new green of spring, Saturday gatherings in the area around the court house, steamboats passing on the river, and other events of a peaceful and enjoyable boyhood on the banks of the Ohio. Lambert remarks that it seems strange that "living under the stress and strain of war [a person] could during moments of relaxation, have day-dreams such as these?"[26] It seems to us quite natural. Both Daley and Lambert have been exposed to the horrors of modern war vividly and close; in their off-time, they take refuge in thoughts of an earlier peaceful time—in memory, an almost idyllic time.

On this day, Lambert enjoyed a brief respite from combat. C Flight today would take the late evening patrol at 6:30 p.m. He had plenty of time to enjoy the day and relax in the hot weather. He played a game of bumble-puppy with Hazell. This time, Hazell defeated him, ending Lambert's long winning streak. Throughout the afternoon, the pilots discussed the absence of the German fighters and speculated about the prospects of another German push in the near future. They all believed that the absence was caused by German squadrons being relocated on other fronts in anticipation of the next stage of Ludendorff's offensive. Life at home and the war were always the central topics of conversation between flights.

The German fighters continued to be absent from their sector. B Flight returned in the early afternoon from patrolling the area that they had in the morning and reported nothing except one stalled and abandoned train two miles west of Rosières—no doubt the one the squadron attacked earlier. The late flight, returning at 8:30 p.m., followed the Somme east to the city of Bray, at an altitude of 15,000 to 16,000 feet, but still they did not see any German planes.[27] They were more convinced than before that something big was brewing on the other side of the front.

On 2 July, Lambert briefly mentioned a "very strange and weird report"[28] that was posted while C Flight was out on patrol. The posting was an official order to stop "hedge-hopping," a dangerous habit of pilots coming home from a patrol. They would fly very low, almost at ground level, so that it seemed that the pilot was literally hopping over hedges. Some pilots enjoyed the practice and got a thrill out of it. (In the same way, Lambert would do loops over the field before he landed to show off, or as he called it, "feeling your oats."[29]) Apparently an S.E.5 pilot had recently flown himself into a balloon cable and got himself caught while hedge-hopping. He survived unhurt, and his plane sustained only slight damage, but the top brass wanted the practice stopped. It was simply too dangerous. Lambert was glad to see the posting. His close friend Daley was one man in the squadron who loved to hedge-hop. Lambert had pleaded with him to stop before he was seriously hurt, but Daley enjoyed doing it too much.[30] Lambert hoped that the bulletin would get his attention and cause him to quit.

Lambert was almost certainly right about the dangers of the practice, but Daley's hedge-hopping had once been fortunate for both him and Lambert. One of Lambert's prize souvenirs after the war was a piece of fabric from Richthofen's Fokker triplane. In an interview, Lambert said that the piece had come to him from Daley and told the story how he got it. Daley had been hedge-hopping over the Australian Group Commander's hut and was ordered to go back and apologize to the Commander. (Someone had evidently got the number off Daley's plane and complained to the squadron.) So Daley went to apologize, and he was enjoying a few drinks of whiskey with the Commander afterward when Richthofen was shot down.[31] As a result, he got a number of souvenirs from the plane.

On 3 July, the weather was fine, with white clouds between 10,000 and 12,000 feet. C Flight had the morning patrol, leaving at 7:30 a.m. for the LaMotte area at about 14,000 to 16,000 feet, so that they would have the cloud cover beneath them. Again, however, the enemy was absent from the sky.

Lambert, at this point, is in need of rest and recuperation. He complains that C Flight had never received any replacement pilots since Wilson was wounded on 25 June, so the six pilots had "flown each patrol without rest."[32] He added that since he joined the flight there had been only two pilot casualties, and they were only wounded, not killed. The two wounded pilots were replaced by Wren and Harries, so Lambert's statement is not literally correct. What he really wants to know is, when will someone be assigned to temporarily replace him so he could go on leave? He needed a break from the war and some relaxation in London. He had not been granted leave since 24 March. In fact, it was probably lucky that the enemy was not available for combat in those early July days. Lambert's being on edge could have resulted in a mishap or loss of concentration that might have been disastrous.

The Allies dominated the sky that day. C Flight came across an additional ten S.E.5s flying in the same vicinity. (Distance prohibited them from recognizing the squadron.) With both groups in the area, the S.E.5s would be a formidable force, and the enemy would not dare to make an appearance. With the lack of an opponent above the clouds, the flight went down through the brightly reflecting clouds and performed tactical ground support below, following Selwyn's lead. They began to encounter antiaircraft fire when they reached about 1,500 feet, and the fire continued until they were down below 1,000 feet and under the range of those guns. After that, the primary danger was machine-gun fire from the ground.

The strafing run was as disappointing as the earlier part of the patrol. There was nothing to attack except a machine-gun nest in some woods. Crisscrossing this area, from a height of about 200 feet, C Flight aggressively fired on the woods camouflaging these machine-guns. Lambert said that he had used two drums of his Lewis gun and half of his Vickers ammunition on this one strafing operation.[33] With all six planes attacking, it was a classic case of over-kill. With no enemy planes around over the past few days, the pilots took out their frustrations on these gun emplacements. With such a powerful bombardment, there was no return fire from the ground.

The flight, low on fuel, then began to ascend to return to Conteville. They had only this one ground attack to report for their two-hour patrol. On the other hand, there were comparatively few after-affects to report. Lambert's plane had only a few bullet holes.[34]

Filled with excessive energy and wanting to enjoy the day, Lambert and his friend Daley, at Lambert's suggestion, went on a motor-bike ride through the French countryside to Auxi for a few supplies. After they returned, Major Robeson informed the flight that they would not be on another patrol that day, so they were able to parley a trip to Abbeville for an evening of wine, women, song, and a bath. They arrived at 3:00 p.m. and, following a trip to the bath-house, made it over to a local café. It was a popular watering-hole for soldiers, where the tables were never empty and the air was thick with smoke and the smell of sweat. Lambert saw Canadians, Australians, New Zealanders, and French there, as well as, surprisingly, an American pilot from Birmingham, Alabama, named Jackson, who was invited to join their group.[35] When Lambert saw a group of Australians being entertained by a "half-dressed red-head trying to dance on a table," he was not concerned because "within a short time those R.A.F. wings started to send out their magnetic waves and we were soon covered with females.... Buy me a drink, dance with me, take me to bed, give me dinner. You name it, they all wanted it."[36] (The drinking and womanizing that were the central themes of this visit would become a recurrent feature of his description of the life of a World War I pilot, and the descriptions of sex would become even more detailed and lurid in his later book, *Barnstorming and Girls*.) In this episode, after wining and dining the flight "scattered to the four winds" with their respective females until they had to return to the café at 10:45 p.m. for one last drink and the ride back to Conteville.[37]

Over-drinking, of course, has been a problem with members of the military since the time of Alexander the Great. Rum rations were given to soldiers in the British trenches before they went "over the top" to attack the German lines. Pilot memoirs and letters are full of tales of drinking in the mess after a flight and while on leave in London and Paris. Lambert's *Combat Report* is full of such stories. He was especially proud of his "own" concoction of scotch on the rocks, which he says he made up while on leave in London.[38] During the war, a trip to Abbeville was a release for stress, and vices became virtues for these airmen. Binge drinking and promiscuous behavior were the norm, not the exception. When they took time to think they tended to think about the past, because it was not wise or healthy to worry about what might happen in the present. Drinking was another way to escape the war.

One horrible reminder of the war, even in Abbeville, was the disfigured soldiers returning home. Abbeville was a town with a "fair sized rail-head" that could have been considered a way station for all the troops passing through it. Many of the troops embarking, however, "were not even half-a-man. They had been carved, cut and literally chewed to pieces by high explosives, shrapnel and machine-gun fire. Whole or part of arms and legs, maybe one or both eyes or ears and maybe part of a face all gone."[39] These were scenes pilots did not see from the air or as they lounged around their bases. The millions of men damaged and deformed by the war would be visible in Europe for decades to come. These were the physical effects of the ground war, a continual reminder of what industrialized war does to human beings. As Lambert states, "Some might live for years in this condition but the lucky ones might be gone within a month or so."[40]

The Fourth of July 1918, brought out a sense of irony for Lambert. His direct ancestors had fought in the American Revolution against King George III, and now he was fighting as a volunteer for the King George V in the present war. As things turned out, he would have his "fire-works throughout the day," but it would not be because he was celebrating the American Fourth of July.

The weather that morning was fair, but with some very high winds out of the west. After returning from Abbeville about 1:00 a.m., Lambert was awakened by his batman at 6:00 a.m. He was still severely hung-over from the previous night. The footsteps of his batman "sounded like bombs exploding…. My head was going in circles. What in the name of heavens had we done last night?"[41] It seemed to him like the fireworks had already begun. He would try to sober himself up by flying without his helmet and goggles so that the cold wind could hit him in his face. He also swore that there would be "no more night before 'binges' for me."[42] (Famous last words!)

Lambert was on the 8:00 a.m. flight, a mixed patrol of A and C Flights. There were ten planes going on this flight: the five from C Flight were Selwyn, Daley, Hellett, Wren, and Lambert. They would patrol the area from Cerisy and Chipily near the Somme, then farther south over LaMotte and Warfusée. Unlike previous flights, on this one each plane carried four Cooper Mark II-B twenty-five-pound fragmentation bombs. Ground strafing was given a priority on this mission, and they were informed that it would continue to receive priority until further notice. They were to operate about 1,000 to 2,000 feet above the ground.[43] The American and Australian troops were active east of Amiens, trying to recapture Hamel and Vaire Wood from the Germans. With Amiens on their right, the flight headed east towards the ruins that were once Hamel, Cerisy, and Chipily to provide tactical ground support.

At 8:30 a.m., the sun was quite bright. Fortunately, it was not high enough in the sky to shield enemy aircraft, so when the flight began its bombing operations, they would not be surprised by a German attack from above. A Flight, led by Hazell, began the attack, with C coming up the rear. As usual, they faced heavy antiaircraft attacks when they hit 2,000 feet. These attacks would continue as they quickly descended to deliver their packages to the enemy. As the planes closed within 1,000 feet, the disruptive antiaircraft attack was supported by a prolonged attack from machine-gun and rifle fire. The enemy fire was so heavy that the attacking formation had to disperse in order to avoid the barrage. Lambert knew from previous experience that the Germans tended to place flak (antiaircraft guns) in camouflaged wooded areas. He alerted Selwyn and Daley to the presence of guns in the woods, whose location was further identified by short bursts of gunfire accompanied by smoke from the area in question. Lambert and the rest of the flight flew about 300 to 400 yards above and circled back in order to attack these guns from the rear. (It was virtually impossible, given the speed they were traveling, for the antiaircraft guns to be turned around in order to meet their advance.) On the flyby, they located two guns about fifty yards apart and were promptly greeted by heavy machine-gun fire from below. On their return, Lambert and (possibly) Daley were able to approach their targets at about 200 yards and release two of their Cooper bombs. Lambert aggressively circled back and crisscrossed the area, dropping his two remaining bombs. Daley, followed Lambert's lead, dropped his two bombs as well. After a brief respite, machine-gun fire was returned on the attackers, but it was viciously answered by the S.E.5s, who circled back and attacked from about a hundred feet above the ground, firing both their Vickers and Lewis guns into the trees below.[44] This attack was a portent of what was to become commonplace during the Second World War. To an audience reading Lambert's memoirs in the 1970s, these tactics were already an accepted part of modern war. But they had been established by the pilots of the First World War. Air power was changing the face of war.

After these attacks, Lambert and Daley went west to join Hazell and Selwyn, who were busy with a similar operation near Hamel. They joined the patrol at about 2,000 feet, and immediately experienced heavy antiaircraft fire from the forces below. Lambert recalled that the intensity of the barrage was enough to rock his plane. An explosion made him feel "like a cork floating on rough water."[45] While enduring this bombardment, Lambert, although somewhat blinded by the mid-morning sun, was able to locate bright flashes that indicated enemy aircraft coming in from the east under the cover of the sun. (The German ace Oswald Boelcke, mentor to Richthofen, established eight rules of aerial combat. His first rule was that pilots should use haze, clouds, the sun, or even the opponent's wings to hide an attack.) Lambert, maneuvering close to Hazell, directed his attention to the sun, where two to three miles to the east a large formation of enemy planes was approaching at about 6,000 to 8,000 feet. For the first time in days, the patrol would be engaged in aerial combat.

As they climbed eastward to meet the threat, the increased angle of their climb made the enemy aircraft more visible, particularly when they reached about 3,500 feet. Lambert thought there were about twenty to twenty five enemy planes in the enemy formation. They were led by Fokker D. VIIs, but also included Albatros D.V.s and some Pfalz D. III.s. Five Fokkers spread about fifty yards apart led the formation, and they were followed by the remaining aircraft branched out in a "fan-wise" formation that Lambert had never seen before. He was initially skeptical about how this formation would work, but he was impressed by these airplanes' "fantastic colors and fuselage designs." He was now benefitting by the new re-rigging of C1084. It was out climbing the other S.E.5s by about 200 feet as the Germans began their descent to meet the patrol.[46]

The five Fokkers leading the flight delivered a burst from their guns and then revealed their tactical intent as they pulled back, leveled off, turned, and maneuvered themselves behind the approaching S.E.5s. When the S.E.5s recovered from this impressive initial move, it was business as usual. The contest broke into dogfights, with Lambert in the thick of things. He got into a half-roll in order to attack an Albatros D.V. that was about 300 or 400 feet below him. His maneuver placed him about a hundred yards behind the D.V., but in excellent attacking position. All he needed to do was to close the gap and to keep any attacking aircraft off his own tail. However, violating one of his own rules, Lambert fired his Vickers gun too soon and allowed the Albatros to dive away from the attack. Afterward, Lambert moved against a Fokker who seemed to be unaware of Lambert coming out of the sun as he (the Fokker) headed west. With this advantage, Lambert was able to fix the Fokker in his sights and aimed a few yards ahead of its nose from a distance of possibly fifty yards. Unfortunately, he missed again, and the Fokker reacted by going nose down and spinning to the ground before leveling off and escaping. Afterward, Lambert extradited himself from what could have been a dangerous situation with two Fokkers, and then headed to rejoin members of his flight.[47]

So far, it seems as if Lambert was trying to get the rust out of his system, caused by the lack of air combat during the past few days. Within a few moments, however, he was able to focus on an Albatros D. V. that was diving on the tail of an S.E.5 and attempting to do some serious damage to it. After the two planes jostled for a few moments, Lambert was able to deliver a deflection shot from about fifty yards. Now he committed another and more serious error: he focused too much on this plane, ignoring what was happening around him. He admits that he was "thinking of nothing else … [and] as far as I was concerned, he was the only German in the sky."[48] He watched the Fokker dive down after he put a few bullets into its cockpit, but he knew such a dive could be misleading, so he watched the plane dive closer to the ground. He was "obsessed," and his mind became a "complete blank concerning anything else around" him.[49] He was around 1,500 feet when he was brought back to the battle by a light blue and silver Pflaz that was peppering his wings from a distance of seventy-five yards. He was lucky, as Hazell drove the attacking Pflaz off his tail. As he gained his senses, Lambert noticed that two Fokker D. VIIs above and to his right were also firing at him. He had gotten careless. He now questioned himself on how he could have gotten into such a mess, and he experienced a brief moment of "fear and panic"[50] as he put his plane into a dive to avoid this attack.

There is noticeable note of anxiety in Lambert's description of his attempt to evade these two attacking Fokkers. He states how he could feel his plane "quiver" as he estimates that it was traveling "close to 200-M.P.H in that dive."[51] Having his life in the balance was a rude awakening for Lambert. Once again, he had gotten complacent, and this time it almost cost him his life. He wrote that the only thing he could recall was "pulling the stick gently back into my belly."[52] He simply forgot the details of what happened in his dive up to the point that he was attacking another enemy plane. He believed that he could have blacked out. He was fortunate to have survived.

After the battle, when he was discussing his plane's performance with his crew, Lambert must have looked haggard, since they suggested he needed to get some rest. He recognized that he was still "very tense and nervous [yes and still damned scared; those 3-E.A.s had just about put the 'wind up' me]."[53] Luck, his skill as a pilot, his quick reaction time, and a finely-tuned airplane all played a part in his survival. However, the former agnostic credited the "Old Gentleman" upstairs for having the final say in his survival.

After his ordeal, Lambert found himself with a Fokker in his Aldis sight only twenty yards away. He fired around a hundred rounds from his Vickers gun, and based on the Fokker's erratic behavior, his belief was that some of the shots must have hit the pilot. Lambert did not know his altitude as he did with many of his other victories, but he knew he had shot the Fokker down since it crashed into the ground below. It was destroyed over Bayonvillers at around 9:00 a.m.[54] It was Lambert's fourteenth victory of the war.

Immediately afterward, Lambert attacked another D.VII that was slightly below and about 150 yards ahead of him. Accelerating to shorten the distance between them to about twenty yards, Lambert hit the trigger on his Vickers gun, only to have it jam after one shot. Instead of clearing the blockage, he continued to pursue the Fokker. At a height of only 700 or 800 feet, he rode the Fokker's tail and "literally drove it into the ground" where it crashed near Warfusée. He believed that the German pilot "was paralyzed with fear and could not move."[55] His total of victories now stood at fifteen.

After this victory, Lambert took a few brief moments to clear the stoppage in his Vickers gun. At the same time, he noticed that there were four planes burning on the ground. These burning planes were a testament to the intensity of the aerial combat on that day, and the "4th of July fireworks" that Lambert described in his book.

However, the battle was not yet over. Unlike in previous fights, on this day the Germans did not want to quit. In fact, the "fight had really developed into something vicious."[56] His flight attacked a yellow Albatros that Selwyn eventually destroyed, as well as a Fokker that Lambert attacked as it was moving into position to attack an S.E.5. He fired a short burst from both his guns against the Fokker, but from a distance of between seventy-five and a hundred yards, he could not claim to have shot the plane down. However, it was driven down, and eventually rolled into a shell hole after it landed. (Lambert was given credit for the earlier two Fokkers, one driven down at 9:00 a.m. and the second at 9:01 a.m., but not for this one "driven down."[57])

Next Lambert was confronted by another Fokker attacking on his right, but at too great a distance—perhaps 150 yards—to do any damage. As Lambert attempted to attack an Albatros going east, he was cut off by a "fantastically painted Fokker" twenty yards away, being pursued by Southey. After briefly glancing at his watch, he came to the realization that the dogfight, which had seemed to be going on forever, had lasted only fifteen or twenty minutes. His watch said 9:06 a.m. as the fight was beginning to break up, with the Germans scattered throughout the sky. He observed several of them heading toward the east with six S.E.5s chasing them.[58] In the moments that followed, Lambert took the time to check on his ammunition, fuel, pressure, and R.P.M.'s. Everything checked out, and Lambert was still good to go in case the fight continued. But it did not.

Around 9:15 a.m., the flight assembled to begin their return flight to Conteville, and then recognized that all ten planes that left this morning were present on the way home; so the four planes Lambert had seen burning on the ground all belonged to the enemy. He had two full drums of ammunition for his Lewis guns still in his rack, and both the Lewis and Vickers guns were still half-full. The same was evidently true of the rest of the flight. Since the prime directive had been tactical ground support, they decided not to take this ammunition home with them. Most of the flight, following Hazell's lead, leveled off at around 500 feet and began to attack some horse-drawn carriages and transports that were heading east on the main road of what might have been LaMotte. Lambert, however, did not take part in this attack because he could not bring himself to fire on the horses. "They suffered enough without any more from me. I just could not do it."[59] Instead, he and Daley saw gun flashes coming out of a wooded area close by and attacked the trees from a height of 200 to 300 feet. After a few passes, they had expended their ammunition, and the firing from the ground had ceased. The rest of the flight had likewise used up their ammunition, and it was time to head northwest and return to base. They landed at 10:00 a.m.

After turning C1084 over to the ground crew, Lambert headed to the recording officer to make his report along with the rest of the squadron. Their adrenaline was high. Lambert compared the shouting, yelling, whooping and hollering with chickens in the hen house when the fox arrives. (Rural analogies and comparisons were always the norm for Lambert. He was not alone. Many, or even most, of the pilots on both sides saw themselves as hunters and their activities as hunting. Of all the units in the military, only the fighter pilots "hunted."[60])

On that day, it was a tough and vicious fight in the air as well as on the ground. Lambert considered that "the ground action was terrible…. We survived the ordeal only by the will of the 'Lord Almighty.'"[61] On the air action, he said, "I can truthfully say that this one had been the worst [combats] that I had ever been through."[62] Remarkably enough, in a fierce battle with at least twenty enemy aircraft, No. 24 had suffered no major damage. Lambert's plane had about two dozen bullet holes, but only in the fabric. The engine was untouched.

After lunch, which included some stiff drinks that relaxed the squadron and put them in a better mood, the morning's flight was relived and rehashed in the mess. The tales was already reaching a legendary level. Lambert remarked that it would seem from these stories that the flight had shot down *all* of the enemy aircraft. The noise and conversation and boasting were good tonics for those who had been involved in the battle. Lambert wrote that the camaraderie "takes one's thoughts off the dangers encountered during a patrol…. Brooding does no one [especially in this business of war], any good."[63] During lunch, A and C Flights were told that they would be on another mixed flight at 2:00 p.m. east of Villers-Bretonneux. After a good lunch and a brief respite, their war would continue.

Before going on the afternoon flight, Lambert and Daley relaxed together in the sun. They continued to discuss the day's activities, but they also, at Daley's suggestion, discussed their "team" tactics for both ground strafing and aerial combat. Daley proposed that they continue to work together as closely as possible in order to support one another, even though Lambert believed that such protection would be nearly impossible. On ground attacks, they would alternate positions as lead and rear aircraft, with the rear pilot giving support to the front one. Daily and Lambert made a good pair. Both were skilled and confident pilots, each of whom believed that he would survive the war because "a German bullet would never touch his body." And both believed that ultimate survival depended upon that "Third Party," Divine Providence, looking after them, as it had up to that time.[64]

The afternoon patrol began at 2:30 p.m. Unlike the morning flight, this one contained its full complement of six planes. Harries joined C Flight on this patrol. They were headed for the area around Villers-Bretonneux and Rosières. Since their main task was ground support, they flew in close formation at about 4,000 feet, with A Flight flying 500 feet below C. At this altitude, they were again greeted by an intensive antiaircraft barrage that forced the flight to disperse in order to become less of a target. Lambert complained about the viciousness of the antiaircraft fire. "'Hells fire and damnation' Archie is terrible. Black explosions everywhere. How is it possible for an aeroplane to get through all this?"[65] ("Archie" was a phrase used by the R.F.C. to describe antiaircraft fire. It was derived from a line from a popular musical at the time: "Archibald, certainly not!")

A Flight began the attack, as C Flight continued to search the sky for enemy activity. Finding none, Selwyn led C Flight on its assault on these antiaircraft positions. Lambert knew that at their rate of speed it would be nearly impossible for the flak crews to continue to adjust to the approaching aircraft. A diving plane traveling a few thousand feet in a matter of seconds could usually avoid these attacks, but luck sometimes worked against a pilot, and planes did receive direct hits or were victimized by shrapnel. The one advantage of these attacks was that as long as the guns continued to fire, they could be sure that there were no German planes in the sky above them.[66]

Shortly, C Flight, even though somewhat scattered by the antiaircraft fire, began their attacks on enemy positions on the ground. Daley and Lambert met up as planned and attacked

Seven. Moving into Autumn

either Caix or Rosières. (Lambert seems unsure, because he states that he was around halfway between the two cities when he saw artillery flashes from the larger one. However, since he also says that they turned east, the city is probably Rosières.) They attacked wherever they saw guns firing. They flew over the town at around a hundred feet above the ground, and at that altitude they were greeted by a flurry of machine-gun and antiaircraft fire. The two followed their previously devised tactic of flying away from the town and returning from the rear to attack the gun positions with machine-gun fire while dropping two Cooper bombs each at five or six second intervals. Daley followed Lambert on this initial run from a distance of around 200 yards. Lambert remarked that about "half the place was nothing but burnt out and shot up trees, buildings, roads, everything."[67] (These ruins were, of course, the result of previous bombing and artillery attacks on the town. Lambert and Daley were simply rooting out the nests of Germans occupying the ruins.) After the initial attack, they once again approached the area from the east, with Lambert attacking a partially camouflaged antiaircraft battery between two wrecked buildings, spraying the area with between 200 to 300 bullets and dropping his remaining Cooper bombs on the site. The location was turned into rubble, and the lack of any returning fire assured Lambert that his attack had been successful. Both he and Daley were satisfied with the results.[68]

After their bombing run, Lambert and Daley flew to rejoin C Flight. Afterward, C Flight would assemble with A Flight and return to Conteville. They found their companions from C Flight rather soon, and then, following Selwyn's lead, they climbed to between 5,000 to 6,000 feet to look for A Flight; however, they only saw a flight of Sopwith Camels coming down from the north. Not finding A Flight anywhere close, they started their flight home. They were ten miles behind German lines and so faced heavy, if sporadic, antiaircraft and machine-gun fire on their return. However, they arrived safely at Conteville twenty minutes after A Flight had landed.

Upon their arrival, they discovered that they had been scheduled for another flight that evening beginning at 8:00 p.m. Lambert thought that something was brewing. The increased numbers of patrols, being told by their commanding officer to expect one or two more weeks of tactical ground support, and the appearance of the Camels meant that No. 22 Wing "had been given orders to sweep the sky clean of enemy aircraft as well as to destroy as much ground action as possible."[69] (Unknown to Lambert, east of Amiens the Australians and Americans were in the midst of recapturing Hamel. The next day, southeast of Amiens, the Australian advance line was already northeast of Villers-Bretonneux.[70] No. 24 was supporting these advances.)

Lambert was anxious about going on another flight that day, especially at night. He had finally gotten the word that he was posted for a two-week leave in London, to begin on the morning of 6 July. The last flights before leave always caused pilots increased anxiety. Lambert certainly did not want anything to spoil his leave, such as a new Allied offensive, or renewed German offensive, that would result in his leave being cancelled. There had been several examples of accidents and deaths taking place the day or night before a pilot went on a much-anticipated leave. Besides, late patrols could be dangerous. Lambert, like other pilots, never liked landing at night with only the glow of petrol flares to guide him.[71]

The evening flight took off as schedule, with the same twelve S.E.5s from A and C Flights, taking off to explore the area over the Luce River valley east of Ignaucourt. At this late hour, they had the sun behind them, setting in the west. Lambert's trepidations about the flight could be seen in his comments on the weather and the approaching darkness. He knew where the flight was supposed to operate, but he remarked that they were to work that area "if we could find it." He felt that the darkness at ground level (there was still sufficient daylight above), and the patches of fog along the river "could be treacherous down low."[72] Tactical ground support in the dark did not appeal to him. There were only two advantages to night attacks. First, with the remaining twilight, they were still able to identify any attacking enemy aircraft. Second, as it got darker, they would not have to worry about any attack from the enemy. The technology was not yet advanced far enough for airplanes to engage in dogfights in the dark. Night bombing raids were becoming more common and more effective, but not aerial combat.

As the fight began to descend for its attack, the pilots broke out into groups of two, with Lambert and Daley pairing off together as usual. They were at about 1,000 feet and had enough visibility to recognize a wooded area along the river where two artillery flashes were seen. With Daley on Lambert's left, the two pilots cautiously settled to about 400 feet as they approached the area. Daley circled to the west as Lambert moved to the east, so that they could approach the enemy from different directions. As they began their attack, they quickly descended to a height of about 150 yards and dropped their Cooper bombs, first Daley and then Lambert. Lambert observed the explosions as he ascended to around 600 or 700 feet. However, unlike his previous attack on Rosières, he could not tell the extent of the damage; the denseness of the woods and the lack of light prevented him.

When they climbed to around 1,500 feet to join the rest of the flight, they were still being bombarded with machine-gun and some light antiaircraft fire. Daley, however, was able to locate the source of some of their trouble in a wooded area near the remains of a small village on the south bank of the Luce River. Leveling off at about 600 feet, Daley showed Lambert the outline of a trench about half a mile long, filled with 300 or 400 German soldiers attempting to avoid detection and now seeking more adequate protection from the S.E.5s. Daley quickly began his descent, with Lambert following about 200 yards behind him.

Lambert was troubled by this attack. "Those are human beings down there. Can I do it? I wish that Daley had not seen this."[73] It was not a case of kill or be killed, as it was in aerial combat. It could not be justified by self-defense or depersonalized. Lambert saw the panic in the trenches. He remarked, "Those poor devils are helpless. What a slaughter this will be."[74] Daley, however, had already begun his attack and Lambert had to follow suit. He gave his plane full-throttle and dived forward, firing both his guns at the troops gathered below. He wrote, "'Lord Almighty,' how I hated this…. I could see those slugs kicking dirt up from the sides of that trench; one poor devil trying to pull, what looked like a sheet metal, over his body. Some down flat in the bottom of that ditch, a few others with faces looking up at me."[75] It was then he dropped his two remaining Cooper bombs at point-blank range. It was slaughter, it was butchery, it was the real war on the Western Front. Daley would later inform him that both his bombs also were direct hits on the trenches. Lambert admitted that such duties, however necessary in war, "sometimes made me want to quit and get out."[76] Even after fifty years, Lambert was still disturbed by this attack.

After the attack, Lambert and Daley reunited with C Flight and landed safely at Conteville at 9:30 p.m. After satisfying his hunger, scotch and cognac helped Lambert relax from what had been an eventful Fourth of July.

Lambert said the weather for 5 July was "perfect." At breakfast some of his comrades

Seven. Moving into Autumn

wanted to know if he had had enough fireworks on the Fourth to last him until next year's Independence Day. Lambert annoyed his friends by enthusiastically blurting out that he had not yet had his Fourth of July fireworks. They were not amused after the day they just experienced. One of the pilots sarcastically suggested that Lambert join an antiaircraft battery to get his fireworks. (The reader will remember that Lambert had once considered the artillery before he joined the R.F.C.) Lambert would be the "butt of all ragging" about these fireworks for days to come.[77]

When discussion turned to the day's events, Hazell informed them that it would be a repeat of yesterday's activities, with the emphasis again being on tactical ground support. From what Lambert says, the flights did not understand the need for this continued ground support. They questioned Hazell about the need for it, but they were given no answers. Some, including Lambert, believed that a big push was in the making, but no one could be sure.

A and C Flights left at 7:30 a.m. for the Luce River valley. When they reached Marcelcave at around 8:00 a.m., they were flying at around 3,000 feet with A Flight about 500 feet below them. C Flight had the upper protecting umbrella, looking out for enemy aircraft in the distance. At such low levels, both flights were in the range of the German flak guns, particularly the larger 88 mm. self-propelled mounted guns, which had already commenced firing at them. However, the fact that these guns were firing at them probably meant that there were no enemy aircraft around.

Realizing this, Selwyn followed A Flight's lead and led C Flight down to about 1,000 feet. This altitude was below the range of many of the larger German flak guns, but within the range of the smaller caliber guns and machine-guns. Again the flight paired off into three groups of two planes, with Lambert and Daley heading further east into German territory. They were en route for a small wooded area that was quite heavy with ground fire. Using their traditional tactical approach, they were again on the hunt over a small thickly wooded area, possibly thirty or forty acres, looking for the enemy. Lambert noted that "there is small game hidden there" in the woods.[78] As they got closer to their prey, there was an increase in gun fire, giving away the enemy position. The pair then began their zigzag approach to attack the enemy from two directions, Daley to the south and Lambert to the east. Lambert began his run at around 500 feet and went nose down at full throttle to about a hundred feet to assure maximum effectiveness for his assault. With Daley coming in from the south on a similar approach, Lambert fired approximately 350 shots from both his Lewis and Vickers guns into the trees and released all four of his Cooper bombs, each at about a second interval. He remarked that on his run "the ground fire is terrific."[79]

It became apparent how heavy the machine-gun fire from the ground had been on the return to Conteville. Lambert had ascended to a thousand feet and waited for Daley to complete his own bombing run. After they met, they intended to join the rest of C Flight. They continued to search for German planes, however. As they started to climb to a height of about 3,000 feet, Lambert noticed that his plane was not climbing as well as normal, and the R.P.M.s were down. Lambert's understanding of his plane's performance immediately indicated that there was a problem with his engine. The plane almost certainly had sustained some sort of damage during his recent ground assault. After alerting Daley to his problem, he began the thirty-mile trek back to base. If need be, he could stop at Bertangles, but it happened that the plane had enough power to make it back to Conteville, if not quite to the flying field. He was, however, able to make a perfect landing across the road from the field.[80]

Working with his ground crew, Lambert discovered that an armor-piercing bullet had entered near the left side of the engine and had penetrated all the way to the inner steel core where the magneto was housed. His sergeant showed him the bullet, which became one of Lambert's prized souvenirs of the war. In fact, it was the only bullet he ever collected from his military experiences in two world wars. The bullet was displayed on his wall in his Ironton home. (In an interview with Robert Smith in 1980, Lambert showed Smith the bullet and explained how it forced him to return back to base prematurely from an offensive patrol. When Smith asked him whether it came from ground fire or from an airplane, Lambert had forgotten the circumstances under which he got the bullet. He told Smith that he had been in a fight and that it "probably came off one of the enemy's aircraft guns."[81])

Lambert also forgot the name of the sergeant who helped him with his airplane, but he felt deeply indebted to him. He wrote that he hoped that this "man of few words" was still living and that he would read the book and "see just how much he and others of his crew did to save my life."[82] The sergeant discovered that the bullet apparently also struck and bent a rod just enough to prevent the full throttle from opening. This obstruction resulted in a reduction in fuel reaching the engine and a resultant decline in R.P.M.s. "That small and seemingly insignificant bent rod, could have put both me and 1084 down in German lines for the duration."[83] It was the sort of thing that could happen to a pilot just before he went on leave. Although Lambert was able to make it back to base, in addition to changing the rod, the magneto had to be replaced before he could take the plane up for a test flight. He did have the opportunity to take the plane up for a fifteen-to-twenty-minute flight, during which it performed perfectly.

Not wanting to tempt fate any more than necessary, Lambert was very happy that he had only one more flight before he left for England in the morning. However, although he was looking forward to leave, he also wanted to make sure that no one else would fly his plane while he was on leave. It was a favor that he asked of Selwyn, who agreed that (barring an emergency) C1084 would be grounded until Lambert returned.[84]

After landing from his test flight, Lambert met with Captain E. A. C. Lawson, who had recently been appointed Recording Officer. Lawson introduced him to Lieutenant Hilbert L. Bair, an officer from the American Air Service who had been assigned to 24 Squadron and C Flight to gain some flying experience. Bair and Lawson had been admiring what Lambert was able to do with his plane on his recent test flight and the overall condition and performance of the plane. Bair had had little experience with flying S.E.5s, but Lambert assured him that he would gain that experience soon enough, since S.E.5s were all the squadron flew. The young American novice was also curious about Lambert's communication with his mechanics after Lambert had landed his plane. He asked if Lambert communicated regularly with his crew in this manner. Apparently Bair had not been aware of the need for pilots to develop a close working relationship with their support staff. Lambert gave Bair some sound advice. He told him to make sure that he worked on his own plane between patrols and get to know it from "stem to stern"; his life depended on his machine and its weapons. He added a few words of caution. He told Bair not to be "too anxious and try to shoot down every enemy in the sky. There are plenty of them out there. Be damned careful all the time."[85] He told Bair he wanted to make sure Bair would still be there when he returned from leave. Then he and Lawson took the time to introduce Bair to the rest of the flight. Lambert was happy to see Bair join their group. They now had their relief pilot that would allow him to get an occasional day off even after he returned from leave.[86]

Seven. Moving into Autumn

Selwyn took Bair on a tour of the facilities while Lambert, Daley, and Southey headed back to the hut for some relaxation. They managed to get a little sleep in before tea-time, and then headed for the operational board to check out their evening assignment. Another mixed flight was planned for A and C Flights for 6:30 p.m. However, Selwyn informed Lambert that he would not be joining them. They were not willing to tempt fate, so Lambert would have the evening off to prepare for his leave, which would start the next day at 7:00 a.m. and last until 22 July. Lambert greatly appreciated Selwyn's gesture, which he described as "typically English." While at dinner, Lambert was able to enjoy a few extra drinks though the rest of the flight had to abstain in order to be prepared for the upcoming operation. It was an enjoyable meal and a good welcome party for Bair. Major Robeson introduced Bair to the rest of the squadron. Joining them for dinner was the Railway Transportation Officer, an elderly gentleman who had fought in the Boer War, who had brought Lambert's leave and transportation papers from Wing headquarters.

Lambert now had time to relax as his comrades prepared for their evening flight. After watching them leave, he retreated to his Nissen hut to begin packing for his trip to England. His train was due to leave at 9:00 a.m. from Abbeville, so Lambert wanted his batman to get him up at 6:30 a.m. in order to be on time.

On the next day, however, Lambert was so excited about going on leave that he beat his batman to the punch, being already dressed and shaved by the time his batman entered his hut with his tea. Before he left, however, Lambert made sure his sergeant knew about his conversation with Selwyn: no one was to touch C1084 while he was on leave unless they had specific orders from Selwyn or Robeson. It was like he was asking a good friend to watch over his best girl while he was away from home. Before the tender left for Abbeville, Lambert saw that C Flight was scheduled to leave at 10:30 a.m. for another round of tactical ground support.[87] It was a good day to leave the war behind.

Eight

Leave and Return

The weather on 7 July made it an ideal day for flying, but Lambert was not going to do any flying that day. Since both A Flight and C Flight would be doing tactical ground support again that day, he was just glad to miss it.

While having breakfast, Lambert received advice from his comrades about where to go and what to do while he was in London. Once again he was told to stay clear of the *Café Royale*. Commenting on their recommendations, Lambert said that if that was all the excitement he could expect, he might as well forget London and simply go to Abbeville. Before he left, he had his orderly give the Royal Automobile Club as his London address, and then went on one last stroll to the hanger to check on C1084. Afterward, he gathered his bags from the office to put them on the tender bound for Abbeville. It would be a short trip (eight miles) to catch the train for the coast. First, however, a bath was in order before he would board the train that was scheduled to arrive at 9:45 a.m. to take him to Boulogne.[1]

Lambert soon discovered that around 200 people were waiting at the Abbeville station to board trains bound for Boulogne. These included a few female nurses as well as forty or fifty injured soldiers recently released from various hospitals in France. Lambert was going on leave; these were going home for good. Initially, Lambert was worried about finding a seat for the ride to Boulogne, but that worry was resolved when several trains arrived to take passengers to the coast. While waiting for the trains to arrive, the Red Cross was doing very well, selling refreshments to the large crowd gathered.

British and French soldiers could be seen everywhere, but there were also soldiers from all the Dominions and the United States. Looking for comfort and familiarity, Lambert spotted a group of soldiers in R.F.C. uniforms and gravitated toward them. There were ten to twelve men from both Britain and Canada in this group, and though they were strangers to him, they shared a common service bond. Feeling gregarious, Lambert immediately struck up a conversation with a Captain from Toronto. They were able to make a connection when Lambert mentioned that he had lived in Nobel and Parry Sound. The Captain then asked if Lambert knew Ernest. T. Morrow, who was flying Bristols for No. 62 Squadron in the Captain's flight. Morrow had worked with Lambert at the Canadian Explosives plant in Nobel; he had also enlisted as a pilot in 1917. They had discovered a mutual acquaintance.

Afterward, Lambert and the Captain were then joined by another Canadian pilot from No. 41 Squadron. Recognizing the squadron number, Lambert asked about another friend of his, William Claxton, who was currently serving in that squadron. (As we have seen, Lambert tried to keep tabs on friends and Americans he knew serving in the R.A.F.) He was

Eight. Leave and Return

happy to discover that Claxton had gone on leave the day before, and that the chances were good that they would run into each other in London, since Claxton was also staying at the Royal Automobile Club. Lambert was glad to hear that his new acquaintance considered Claxton "one of the most fearless pilots I have ever known."[2] When Lambert informed his new friends that he was an American from Ohio, another pilot who had joined their small party said in a rather exasperated tone, "Americans everywhere; we have one from New Orleans, wherever that is." Lambert immediately knew that this Canadian was from No. 32 Squadron and the American pilot from New Orleans was his old friend from Borden, Andrew Callender. He was pleasantly surprised to find out that he had found out about these two friends while waiting for the train to Boulogne and remarked that this chance meeting was quickly becoming an "old home week reunion."[3] The news was good; his friends were still alive and still flying.

At this point, the reader needs to know one problem with Lambert's whole account of his period on leave. Unlike with his training in Canada and England and his tour with No. 24 during the war, Lambert kept no record of his period on leave. As he wrote, "Time was too precious to waste on recording my actions at that time."[4] So we have to rely solely on Lambert's memory of the events that occurred. As we have already seen, Lambert's memory was a good one, but he was sometimes wrong or confused about some details of the past. Lambert said that he was only giving the reader the "high-lights of that leave,"[5] and he is probably correct as to the highlights; but he also gives the reader a number of details, and sometimes the reader needs to take these with a grain of salt, particularly when the memory involves a highly unlikely coincidence. Such coincidences do happen, but they are rarer in most lives than they are in Lambert's memory.

As was said, several trains were used to take the troops to the Boulogne. Those wearing R.F.C. uniforms boarded the rear of a train that had just added five extra coaches to handle the large crowd. Lambert found himself a window seat and was joined by a Canadian pilot serving in No. 20 Squadron. This pilot was from British Columbia and flew Bristols. Like Lambert, he had gone through No. 8 Cadet Course and was at Borden at the same time as Lambert. It was proving to be a small world.

The train slowly made its way to the coast at a speed of fifteen to twenty miles an hour. It was 10:00 a.m., and to pass the time soldiers played cards and shot dice. A pool was started on guessing the time the train would arrive in Boulogne. Ten francs each was required to enter the game. Lambert figured they would reach the coast in about six hours, 4:00 p.m. When the train arrived fifteen minutes earlier, he had to split the 150 francs with the soldier who guessed 3:30 p.m. Afterward, the drinks would be on them.[6]

In the meantime, he discussed with the Canadian pilot sitting next to him the Iaccaci brothers, Paul and August, who were from New York and were also serving in No. 20, and he mentioned another New Yorker, Harry Bruno. Lambert remembered the Iaccaci brothers were two of the four Americans who flew at either Mohawk or Rathbun with him. He was pleased to learn that both Iaccaci brothers were doing a wonderful job for their squadron.[7] However, the Canadian pilot did not seem to know anything of Bruno.

It was a slow, hot train ride in the July, but with several stops at small towns on the way where Lambert was able to get some refreshments. He complained about the heat and was only able to get a few minutes of sleep, but his overall tone is one of excitement and adventure. He was glad to leave the war behind and was looking forward to a splendid time in London.

After arriving at Boulogne and washing the train dirt and soot off their faces, the fifteen soldiers who had taken part in the travel pool retreated to a café to spend the 150 francs that had been wagered. They were joined by several officers from different branches of the service, including the navy, until the funds were used up. Lambert described the "liquid flowing and the seas becoming rough."[8]

It was now 6:00 p.m., and Lambert and six others had decided to take the 6:30 p.m. boat across the Channel. By the time they arrived, the boat was half-full. They stowed their gear, put on life preservers, and enjoyed the trip across the sea to Folkstone. The trip was a little rough, but Lambert almost never suffered from seasickness. He recalled spending part of the trip talking to a sergeant who had spent the last fourteen months serving in the Middle East. The sergeant had landed in southern France and traveled by rail to Boulogne in order to finish the journey to England.

The transport, protected by destroyers as it made the trip to England, finally landed at Folkstone around 8:30 p.m. After disembarking, Lambert got on the train near the dock and began the trip to London, which ended shortly after 10:00 p.m. He arrived tired, dirty, hungry, and horny. His state of mind is shown in his comments, "Mothers, lock up your daughters if you wish to keep them virgins."[9] Lambert and his three new friends soon discovered the Royal Automobile Club was full, so they decided to share two rooms at the Strand Palace in London. Lambert would share a room with his new friend from No. 20 Squadron whom he met on the train to Boulogne. (Lambert later forgot this soldier's name and referred to him as "No. 20 Bristol."[10])

Even though Lambert had been up since the early morning and traveling all day, he quickly bathed, changed his clothes, went with his friends for a bite to eat. Then, around midnight, the four of them headed for the *Café Royale,* a place Lambert had known was "out of bounds" for members of the R.A.F. since his first trip to England. He described the atmosphere of jammed-up men, smoke, booze, and women of all kinds: "Wild women, tame women, meek women, ferocious women and beautiful women. Some for pay and some for love. Amazons all. And all out to conquer the male."[11] Lambert would fondly recall that time, "Boy! What a place, what a night." He would not return to the Strand Palace until 9:00 a.m.

By the next afternoon, he was prepared to hit the town once again with No. 20 Bristol when his other two roommates appeared at the door with four young women and a proposal to set up house in a ground floor flat in Jermyn Court for two weeks. They would pay their bill at the Strand and then set up house at this new establishment for the affordable sum of four pounds per week, shared equally among the four. They were to provide the food and drinks and the girls, hired for a shilling a day, "were to do the rest." The girls were hired to "take care of us for the two weeks." Allegedly, one was a former first assistant to the head chef of the Savoy Hotel, another an experienced serving maid who had served the Prime Minister for several years, the third had been the housekeeper for the First Lord of the Admiralty, and the fourth had been in charge of all the chambermaids at the Palace. They would set up house at Lambert's new residence where Lambert recalled good food, plenty of liquor, and all-night parties.[12]

This kind of arrangement was the norm, rather than the exception, for a period of the Great War. Virginia Woolf would write of this period, "No age can ever have been so stridently sex conscious as our own."[13] The Great War was a powerful aphrodisiac. During the war it was believed that regular sex was necessary for a man's physical well-being. As a consequence, the army permitted licensed brothels, known as the "maisons de tolérance," with blue lights used for officers and red for enlisted men.[14] British medical officers in Le Havre "counted 171,000 visitors to the brothels in just one street in this port town in 1915 alone."[15] The reader will remember that the authorities at Lambert's base encouraged both the pilots and the mechanics to visit Abbeville on a regular basis.

The inspiration for one of Lambert's inventions may have been a consequence of trips he made to the "Blue Lamp" district. He designed a pair of boots he called the "ten-second boots." A pair of these boots were given to the U.S. Air Force Museum after his death, and they are in a display case in the World War I section. These boots were made in London, probably while he was on leave. Lambert was dissatisfied with the time it took to remove the standard-issued flying boots. The standard boots had five laces around the instep, and the remainder of the uppers was solid leather. He needed a bootjack to remove them, and even then it took time. When he discussed the difficulty removing those boots in a 1975 interview, Lambert, in his deadpan style, said, "When you are with a girl, that [the time it took to remove these boots], can be [a] handicap."[16] Lambert's new design made it possible for the boots to come off immediately. It either took two minutes or an hour to remove the standard boots, but ten seconds with his new design.[17] Speed mattered! (As an aside, "Speed" was one of Lambert's nicknames. There are several letters to friends in which he was addressed as or affectionately signed off as "Speed.") Both during war and with women, time was of the essence.

Lambert relaxes from combat on a two-week leave in London at the Jermyn Court apartment.

The war had a tremendous impact on the women in all the warring nations. It would change society's understanding of what women could accomplish and how they should live. Women were exposed to new work challenges and environments. They achieved greater economic and social freedom, with the opportunity to work and earn more money while living independently. The war necessitated that society give these freedoms to women, even if "grudgingly."[18] Women were achieving independence from society's Victorian past as they joined the labor force to fill the gaps that resulted when men answered the call to war. What resulted was a lessening of parental authority and moral constraints at home. Casual relationships between the sexes became more common.[19] According to John Dippel, "Practically overnight, a bellicose Europe became highly sexed."[20]

War gave society a dichotomy, sanctioned public mass murder and private individual love.[21] With the constant prospect of death and destruction hanging over their heads, soldiers considered themselves privileged to a degree, particularly with regard to moral issues. An increase in morale among the troops was associated with a loosening of moral codes. Spiritual and moral pleasures were being supplanted by sensual and passionate ones. The democratization caused by the Great War meant that the millions of soldiers on both sides of the front "assumed these privileges."[22] A rebellion took place in sexual morality, and Lambert was enjoying the fruits of this rebellion.

Lambert was enjoying his new domesticity in London. The girl who was self-described as an excellent cook did not disappoint; she produced wonderful meals throughout the week. Another girl played the piano and sang like an angel, and she also knew all the catchy show tunes popular at the time. And Lambert never ceased praising these women for the meals they produced and the clean house they kept. The days were full of good food, heavy drinking, piano playing, listening to the gramophone, and even some dancing. Lambert would later qualify the drinking, writing, "You, the reader, must not believe everything that you might have read about those days of fifty years ago. We did not spend every minute of our time with a glass in our hands."[23] Yes, there were times, even while on leave, that they found time to eat, sleep, and even sightsee. Money was no object, since each of these soldiers had accumulated between four and six months' pay before going on leave. With wartime austerity and rationing, soldiers on leave with plenty of money to burn naturally attracted women looking for a good time. Here were men with plenty of money who could afford to go out and purchase rare or rationed delicacies.

On one trip to acquire more alcohol, Lambert and his friends ran into three more R.A.F. pilots and their girls. They invited them back to the flat on Jermyn Court, and the celebration continued into the next day. Lambert remembered waking at noon to the smell of breakfast that also included "a few bottles of strong drink."[24]

Someone suggested that they take in a show that evening. José Collins was playing Teresa in *Maid of the Mountains* at the Daley's Theatre in London. Lambert had seen this show three or four times back in January and February before he joined No. 24 Squadron.[25] Before attending the show, however, he decided to make a trip back to the Royal Automobile Club to check on everyone's mail. It was there that he finally ran into his old friend Claxton, who had just received a telegram from his commanding officer informing him that he just had won the Distinguished Flying Cross. This was at that time a new medal, created for the R.A.F. on 3 June 1918, awarded for acts of courage, valor, and devotion to duty for those airmen flying in active service against the enemy. Claxton was one of the first to receive this award.

These two old friends were thrilled to see each other again. According to Lambert's recollection, they had not seen each other since their days at Mohawk or Rathbun in Canada. After Lambert congratulated Claxton on winning the DFC, Claxton supposedly informed Lambert that "there is one [a telegram] in there for you also."[26] (How Claxton would have known that there was a telegram for Lambert is a mystery. Claxton had gone on leave before Lambert and would have had no idea that Lambert was in London, and so no reason to inquire if there was any mail for his friend.) However, there *was* a telegram for Lambert from

Eight. Leave and Return

Major Robeson dated 7 July 1918, informing him that he had indeed won the Distinguished Flying Cross. Like Claxton, Lambert was one of the first to receive the award. Lambert initially could not believe the news. He wrote, "The two of us were floating high above London.... Yes we were well pleased with ourselves. We walked into the bar for a couple of drinks."[27]

Lambert drank and reminisced with Claxton until it was time for Claxton, who was staying outside of town with some friends, to catch the train back home. Lambert invited Claxton to visit him while he was on leave; however, as was often the case with such invitations, this visit never happened. There was simply too much to do and too little time available. Lambert was never to see Claxton again.

Lambert's pride in his achievement was understandable and immediate. After his meeting with Claxton, he took a cab to "one of the nicest military supply stores in London," to buy a DFC ribbon, with narrow horizontal-running purple and white bars, and have it sewn onto his tunic. They had the ribbon, but the proprietor told Lambert that he was only the second or third person to buy it. It was, as he said, a very new award. Lambert managed to take strips of the fabric back to Conteville with him, which came in handy, for others at the base were to receive this award. Lambert wrote that he "walked out of that store, feeling as proud as a pea-cock with full outspread tail feathers."[28]

Lambert's pride went beyond simply receiving the award. He knew that he would personally receive his medal from King George V of England. He wrote that the idea "caused him to panic." He did not know how he would "ever live through that ordeal of the investiture."[29] Of course, he knew it would take place in the future, so for the present he had no worries and could simply delight in his award. Rather humorously, he told an interviewer that the reason he did not want to get the award from the king was that one could not turn his back on the king. He simply did not want to walk backwards "about a hundred to two hundred feet down through high ranking officers from all branches of the service lined clear down to the king's throne."[30]

Throughout his leave, Lambert met several officers and took the time to record their reactions to seeing the ribbon on his tunic. For example, after a few days he went to a local airfield with his new friend, No. 20 Bristol, to do some flying. The captain at the field, who had been shot down in August 1917 and spent six months recuperating in hospitals in France and England, asked Lambert about the ribbon, and after hearing about it remarked, "You must have a few E.A.s to your credit."[31] It was a huge source of pride for Lambert.

After leaving the shop this day, Lambert decided to walk the remaining distance back to Jermyn Court. He "wanted everyone to see that new ribbon."[32] While walking, he happened to run into a Canadian general who is also on his way home. After proper salutations, the general asked Lambert about his purple and white ribbon, since he had never before seen the decoration. Lambert told him about the DFC and how he had just received notification, including the details of his meeting Claxton and that he had also just received the new award. The general knew Claxton, or is at least was familiar with his family, and asked Lambert if he can inform him of Claxton's whereabouts in London. (The general, whose name Lambert does not remember, was familiar with some of the Claxtons from Manitoba, and Lambert's friend, William Claxton, was born in Gladstone, Manitoba.) Since Lambert did not know Claxton's exact location, only that it was outside of London proper, the general asked a favor of him. The next time he and Claxton meet, the general would like Lambert to ask Claxton if he recognizes the general's name.

In the course of their conversation, they discuss the air war over the Somme, where No. 24 Squadron was actively engaged. The general was aware of the situation on the Somme since he had "just returned from there," and gives Lambert a warning about the future: "you may be receiving worse before long."[33] It was not until later that Lambert began to concern himself with the general's warning: "Several days passed before it dawned on my brain, just what he had said."[34] But after that, the warning haunted him even after he had returned to base.

Lambert's reception at Jermyn Court was animated once his friends recognize the new purple and white ribbon adorning Lambert's uniform. There were questions and congratulations, and then they decided to begin celebrating Lambert's award, a celebration that would last throughout the night. It would take all fourteen of them (the three R.A.F. pilots and their girls were still availing themselves of the hospitality of Lambert and his friends) to the Soho area in Westminster, part of the West End of London. This area was renowned for its entertainment and restaurants, an ideal place to celebrate. Lambert remembered that the Soho area never closed; there was always action taking place. After dinner and drinks, they went to the Daley Theater to see the *Maid of the Mountains.*

Afterward, Lambert needed a break from the hectic pace he had maintained over the past few days. He did some sightseeing in London with his friend No. 20 Bristol. In writing about this sightseeing, he took time to explain and take credit for introducing a new way to cool off in the July heat. He credits himself with; a new concoction, drinking Scotch with crushed ice. This practice, as he proudly noted, was continued for the rest of his life, and it caught on with others. (The reader must remember that ice in beverages was not as universal as it became in the second half of the 20th century, and that it was, and still is, more uncommon in England than in the United States.) Lambert liked drinking Scotch, but he did not like it with either of the two usual mixers, water or soda. On a hot day in London, he got the bartender to pour Scotch over ice and let it set for a spell. He even remarked that, later, Scotch on the Rocks continued to catch on in the U.S. Army Air Corps during the World War II. He clearly remembered an evening when he introduced the drink at an officers' club in Orlando, Florida. He remarked then that "the drink was concocted … in June 1918 at the bar of the Royal Automobile Club."[35] In an interview, he expanded to the interviewer on that comment saying that "very few ever saw it before World War I when I started drinking it that way. So, Scotch on the Rocks came into existence, and that's it today."[36]

Over the next few days, Lambert found time to do some flying with his new close friend No. 20 Bristol, but they had to fly as observers. They were regretfully informed by the captain at the base that only students were given permission to fly the airplanes there, so that they were permitted to go up only as observers. Lambert said of that trip, "I never realized how huge that town really was until I flew over it that day."[37] It was the first major metropolitan area he had ever flown over.

Lambert needed to fly for two reasons. One was, of course, that he loved to fly too much to get flying out of his system, even while on leave. The other was a belief at the time that if a pilot did not fly for a time, he would lose his form and only be fit for a ground assignment.[38] Lambert would not allow such a thing to happen.

Lambert next discovered there were other benefits to being a soldier on leave than the exciting nightlife, parties, and women. A grateful nation wanted to express its gratitude to those fighting on the front and sacrificing their lives for the country. When the group of fourteen went to Soho to celebrate Lambert's DFC and to have dinner before going to see the *Maid of the Mountains*, their entire bill was paid for by an old Jewish gentleman who had lost five sons in the war and had two more currently serving in France. When Lambert and No. 20 Bristol went sightseeing, while checking their mail at the Royal Automobile Club they saw a posting on the bulletin board. It stated that a family near Norwich in Norfolk County on the east coast of England, about 125 miles from London, would accept two officers on leave. They had the clerk at the desk make the arrangements and took advantage of the hospitality of William Carr of Ditchingham Hall.

The Carr family felt it was their duty to entertain officers on leave, and Lambert was given the honor of being treated like an English gentleman. Upon seeing the house, he described it as "Tudor architecture about two and a half stories high and possibly one hundred and fifty feet across the front ... there was wealth here, that neither of us had ever seen before.... Grandeur everywhere.... I found out that the balance of the house was just as magnificent as what I saw that first day."[39] For the next few days, the two officers were treated royally to the best dining, maid service, hunting expeditions, tours, and conversations, including an after dinner conversation one evening with two veterans of the Boer War. Fifty years later, Lambert still referred to the women as "ladies." A butler was there to carry their bags and attend their needs, and the family's gun collection was the most impressive he had ever seen. He got his first look at African big game guns, including an elephant gun which he believed could shoot down a Fokker D. VII.

Across from the various gun cabinets was an extensive library. Lambert liked to read; he considered books one of his many hobbies. In the Carr's extensive library, he discovered a copy of one of his favorite books, H. Rider Haggard's *King Solomon's Mines*, originally published in 1885. Lambert had read that book as a boy, and "everything else that I could find written by Haggard."[40] He called Haggard his hero, "a man that most any adventurous young boy would worship."[41] Lambert asked if William Carr if he knew Haggard, because of his desire to meet him. Although Haggard owned the estate right next to Ditchingham Hall, Carr did not know him; but, because of Lambert's wish to meet him, he did make arrangements for Haggard to be at his house for dinner the next day. It was something he wanted to do for Lambert as gratitude for his service to Britain. Lambert wrote that to the surprise of almost everyone, he recognized Haggard immediately. (Of course, he might have been familiar with Haggard's appearance as a result of seeing his picture as a frontispiece to his books.) He sat next to him at dinner, and the two discussed Haggard's adventures and stories throughout the evening.

Lambert would cherish his brief stay in Norfolk County. It was a far cry from the debauched scenes of smoke-filled club, alcohol, women, and sex in London. He enjoyed an afternoon hunting with Carr's fifteen-year-old son, and toured the city of Norwich and marveled at its Norman architecture and historic landmarks. He and No. 20 Bristol knew they could never repay the family for their hospitality; however, they were able to show their gratitude by getting twenty gallon petrol permits for Carr. Forty gallons of rationed gasoline were of value and difficult to get in wartime.

On 19 July, the two pilots said good-bye to the Carr family and took the 3:00 p.m. train back to London. It was a sad occasion. The chance reading of the Carr's hospitality note at the Royal Automobile Club led to the most memorable part of Lambert's leave. He thought about them during the three-and-one-half hour ride back to London. He wrote that "during all these fifty one years, I have never forgotten them," and he believed there was a "special place [in heaven] reserved for them and others like them."[42] When they arrived in London, the two friends decided to take up a room at the Strand Palace before calling their friends. Upon hearing Lambert's voice over the phone, the girl on the other end of the line exclaimed excitedly, "They are back." Within an hour, they were back at Jermyn Court being mobbed by four girls. Life was back to normal, but there was only one day of leave left.

After breakfast the next day, 20 July, Lambert and some of the others lounged around the Royal Automobile Club, reading magazines and newspapers. With his leave ending the next day, Lambert was concerned about the situation at the front. He remembered his previous conversation with the Canadian general on the streets of London and resolved to inform Major Robeson about it when he returned to Conteville. However, there seemed to be little activity around the area where No. 24 was operating. Lambert hoped that this lull would continue, at least for a few days after he returned from leave; but worried that the front had been too quiet for too long and that there was a "push" on the horizon. (The "push," in fact, was already in progress.)

Lambert made plans with his new friends to take the 6:00 a.m. train to the coast in the morning. Leaving that early would allow Lambert to be in Abbeville around mid-afternoon. From there, it was only a short ride back to the airfield. Lambert and his friends spent their last evening at Jermyn Court enjoying the company of the girls, who would accompany them to the train the next morning. He could not remember any of their names—in fact, all he ever knew was their first names—but the meals they cooked and the songs they played and sang stayed with Lambert for the rest of his life.

It was early Sunday morning when they arrived at the station. Parting on the platform left all of them quite sad and depressed. The eight had bonded over the past two weeks, and they knew they would never see each other again. The train had the four airmen at the Channel in time to take the 8:00 a.m. boat across the rough waters to Boulogne, where they landed by 9:30 a.m. In a half-hour, they were on the train back to Abbeville. Somewhere along the journey, Lambert and No. 20 Bristol lost their two former suitemates. The two of them eventually arrived at Abbeville about 2:30 p.m. and arranged to get transportation back to their squadrons. Lambert called his base and got through to the orderly who told him that a tender would shortly pick him up at the station. All that remained was for Lambert and No. 20 Bristol to say their good-byes. "We sure had had a good time together. He was not too far from Conteville. We arranged to get together later. I never saw him again."[43] As with Claxton, the demands of war were simply too great. The tender from No. 24 was at the station in time to get Lambert back to Conteville before 4:00 p.m.

Upon his return to base, Lambert felt a little odd and out of place. After the good times and luxuries of London and Norfolk County, his own "Buckingham Palace" now seemed quite shabby and ordinary. He would once again have to adjust to the surroundings of war. The food would not be as good, and the tea a little substandard, and the women would not be constantly around. However, he would be flying again.

As Lambert made his way to the mess after storing his gear, he was greeted enthusiastically by members of B Flight. A and C Flights were currently on a mixed patrol, and B Flight was to go out shortly. Everyone wanted to know about his leave, and asked about the new DFC ribbon on his tunic. Lambert never shied away from receiving attention or telling a good story about himself. After he explained the ribbon, he was told that he would have to

Eight. Leave and Return

"buy the drinks for dinner tonight."[44] Lambert also let the group know that he had brought back a twelve-inch strip of ribbon for others to use as well. He soon discovered that Lowe of B Flight had been awarded the DFC the same time as he had, so Lowe would receive the first cut of the ribbon Lambert had brought back from London.

Robeson later came in to tea. He also told Lambert that the drinks were on him that evening, so like it or not, Lambert would be treating the squadron at dinner to two rounds of drinks. Lambert was still concerned about the warning that the Canadian general had given him in London, so he told Robeson, as he had planned. Robeson seemed surprised by the information and thanked him for it. He told Lambert that he would inform "Wing" about the general's warning.

On 15 July, the Germans had begun their last major offensive on the Western Front, known as the Second Battle of the Marne. It would last until 7 August 1918. The Germans had planned for the renewal of their offensive on 11 July, but delayed because the influenza epidemic that was to cause so many deaths in the upcoming year was spreading among the undernourished and weakened German troops.[45] However, the Allies were aware of Ludendorff's intentions even before the assault. German deserters, French intelligence reports, and Allied reconnaissance had prepared them for what was to come. Foch wrote in his memoirs that "the Allied High Command had in its possession reliable indications of the enemy's intentions."[46] On that day, shortly *before* the Germans artillery barrage, more than 2,500 French and American guns opened fire on German gun positions, ammunition dumps, and infantry assembly points. At 4:00 a.m. on the 15th, the German army began their advance on front that was fifty miles east and west of Reims, from Château-Thierry on the west to Main de Massiges on the east. The fighting was intense; it was hand-to-hand combat with the American 42nd Division near Souain. The Germans had one breakthrough west of Rheims where French General Jean Degoutte ignored orders to pull his front line back, so his troops suffered heavy casualties from the German bombardment.

By the 17th, however, the German

Lambert back in France with his new DFC ribbon. This uniform is now displayed at the U.S. Air Force Museum near Dayton, Ohio.

advance had been stopped, with their troops advancing no farther than six miles from their jumping-off places. On the 18th, Foch launched a tentative counter-offensive along a twenty-seven-mile front against the salient between Château-Thierry and Soissons.[47] The German advance had crossed the Marne, but within three days they were forced to retreat across the river. The retreat did not stop there; they continued their withdrawal in the days that followed.

It is these events that make the Canadian general's warning a puzzle. It would be the counter-offensive which would involve extensive use of the R.A.F. including No. 24 Squadron, but the counter-offensive had not been yet launched when the general gave his warning. Perhaps the general had heard somehow of what was on the horizon. On the other hand, the Allies were already hotly involved in the counter-offensive when Lambert arrived back at Conteville, so Robeson's surprise is puzzling.

Lambert, however, had done his duty by telling Robeson. Now he was anxious to see members of his flight, so when some S.E.5s appeared about a thousand feet above the trees, he headed for the hanger to greet his comrades. A Flight landed first. Lambert noticed there were only five planes, but he was relieved to discover from Hazell that the missing plane was Southey and he had gone on leave the day before Lambert arrived in Conteville. C Flight landed shortly afterward and rolled to the hanger where Lambert was still visiting with members of A Flight. He noticed that C also had only five planes. Of course, he had been on several patrols where only five planes from the flight had participated in an offensive operation. It could have been that one of the new pilots was a greenhorn, lacking the proper seasoning to be allowed on combat patrol immediately. Lambert watched as Selwyn, Hellett, Wren, Harries, and Bair climbed out of their planes. Daley was missing. Lambert supposed that his friend Daley must have gone on leave with Southey.

Lambert was once more the center of attention. His friends were happy to see him and gathered around to welcome him back. Like the others before them, his comrades from C Flight wanted to know about the DFC ribbon. In spite of this welcome, Lambert recognized something was wrong. He noticed they all "acted queer and seemed hesitant to talk."[48] Then he asked Selwyn if Daley was on leave. Selwyn put his arm around Lambert's shoulder and walked him towards the office. "Daley is gone." He was dead. Lambert's best friend had died shortly after Lambert's leave began. According to what Selwyn told Lambert, he had a "bad accidental crash" on the 7th and died in the local hospital the following day.[49] The squadron history records Daley's death at 8 July 1918. The details of his death are not explained, only that it was an accident and not the result of enemy fire. Daley could well have died as a result of hedgehopping.

Lambert was shocked by Daley's death. It "knocked me for a loop…. The Old Gentleman upstairs must have had a special mission for Daley."[50] It would not be easy for him to get over this death. He wrote, "Other pilots had been killed during my time, but none of them had been close to me, so I never gave their death much thought. But Daley. That was different. We had been almost like brothers for three months."[51] Their friendship had given them both a sense of security in the air. They had depended on each other. They could predict each other's moves in the air. "We had worked together as a team of two. We had thought alike. He had driven the enemy off my tail many time and I had done the same for him."[52]

Lambert could not get Daley's death off his mind throughout the evening. Dinner was enjoyable and he appreciated his friends, their questions about his leave, and even Palmer

Eight. Leave and Return

beating him at bumble-puppy, but Lambert's mind was too occupied with thoughts of Daley to focus on the game or any other activity. Later in the evening, as the night began to take hold and the pilots were sitting together in groups, Selwyn told Lambert that he needed to rest up from his leave, so he gave him the next day off. Of course, Lambert also needed more time to get used to Daley's death. Who would he pair up with during the next patrol? Who would cover his tail?

Lambert wanted to get into C1084 and take her up alone for a ride. He wanted the solitude of the air, to get back to flying and to clear his head. He was assured by Selwyn that his plane had been grounded since he left, with the exception of the ground crew taking it out every other day to keep the engine in good shape. His leave was now over. It was time for Lambert to once again enter the war, which was now heating up. He would start to use up the rest of his courage.

NINE

Return to the War

Lambert, back in Conteville, periodically remembered as he walked around base and talked with his friends on the day of his return that only the day before he was in London. His leave had been of sufficient length to help him get back on his feet. Any longer, and he might have begun replaying in his mind the near misses and close calls of the war. A veteran pilot often did that after a flight, questioning the odds. But once that started, a pilot was probably finished as a combat pilot. There was a saying in the R.A.F., "A man twice burned is finished."[1] Lambert was not yet finished, by any means.

If there was anything positive about the timing of Daley's death, it was that it did not happen before Lambert's leave, nor did Lambert know about it during his leave. Moreover, Lambert did not witness it himself. It would have had an even stronger effect on him than it did, had he been present. Daley's death was not the only worry he had, although it was the worst and most immediate one. The day after he returned to Conteville, he was informed that an American who had trained with him at Chattis Hill, Lieutenant Tarbutt of No. 56 Squadron, had been missing since mid–June.[2] Lambert was deeply troubled by Daley's death and Tarbutt's disappearance, but he was still an experienced pilot in the late summer or early autumn of his career. He would still be of great value to his squadron and the war effort, and he would have more victories. But there was a question now about how long he could last.

On 22 July, the weather was fine, and enemy planes were active in the morning, though less so later in the day.[3] Lambert was given the day off, but after breakfast he ventured to check out C1084. He was happy to find that the plane was right where he left it on the day of his leave. His crew was happy to see him, and Lambert took the plane up for a spin, asking the sergeant to leave the ammunition in place in case he wanted to get in some target practice. After sixteen days, Lambert initially felt strange to be in the air, "almost like my first solo flight."[4] It took until he reached about 1,500 feet for his confidence to return and for him to feel normal in the cockpit again. He leveled off around 5,000 feet and began to put C1084 through some basic maneuvers. He observed that C1084 was "perfect," but he himself was a little rusty. His first loop was a little slow and sloppy, but the second one was perfect. After a few more moves, he climbed to 6,000 feet and headed towards Amiens, anxious to see what was happening in that area. However, fearing that he might be victimized by friendly fire, he bypassed Amiens and traveled east up the Somme River as far as Corbie, and then followed the main railway line just east of Villers-Bretonneux, where he spotted two R.E. 8 reconnaissance planes traveling east. He offered some protection by flying several wide sweeps above

Nine. Return to the War

them, but with clear visibility and no enemy aircraft in sight, he left them to their mission and headed northwest past Bertangles and on to Conteville.

B Flight had already returned from their morning flight when Lambert landed around 9:30 a.m. The buzz around base was that there must be a push from the Allies coming soon, but everyone in authority from Wing on downward played down the possibility. For his part, Lambert returned to "Buckingham Palace" and caught up with his mail and newspapers from home that had arrived during his leave.[5] After lunch, he took C1084 up for target practice and put his plane through its paces again. This time, he was doing it to impress the troops on the ground. Lambert wrote, "I suppose that at time everyone who flies an aeroplane, does something like this."[6] Lambert was settling back into his old routine.

The next day, 23 July, Lambert got an extra day's rest to recover from his leave, because high winds and rain grounded No. 24. On the 24th, he did go on an offensive patrol, even though there were still high winds and it was cloudy. However, he had to return back to Conteville in an hour with a "Dud" engine.[7] All three flights were doing tactical ground support on designated targets: bridges, railroad lines, balloons, major highways, and the like. Neither A nor C patrol saw any enemy aircraft; B Flight, that night, did observe enemy aircraft in the vicinity, but the enemy was unwilling to engage in combat.[8] Lambert saw the continued ground support and bombing activity, including night bombing, as a prelude to a big push by the Allies. "The enemy is being softened up for something. One should be able to read between the lines."[9]

When they took to the sky on the 25th, Lambert was pleased that the squadron was temporarily released from ground duty. "Thank heavens for that. That low work tends to fray one's nerves."[10] However, again the enemy was elusive. According to the official reports, the enemy was active only in the French sector, and then only in the evening hours.[11] Some squadrons were busy. Lambert saw that No. 20 Squadron had shot down four enemy aircraft in a skirmish, and wondered if his friend from leave was involved in that fracas.[12] But the enemy was not active in the area that No. 24 covered. Lambert recorded in his log book that on the morning patrol C Flight saw five enemy aircraft (probably Fokker DV IIs) that retired to the east without any engagement taking place. On the evening patrol, the flight spotted three Albatros D.V.s far off to the east that were likewise unwilling to engage.[13] The Germans seemed to be under orders to avoid engaging the enemy on this front. This uneventful day was an example of a trend that would continue until the beginning of August.

The next day, 26 July, was a cloudy day, with rainstorms being recorded on some areas of the front. It was a day forever remembered by the R.A.F. because of Mannock's death. In a little over two weeks, Britain had lost two of its greatest air aces of the Great War. (James McCudden had died on 9 July, while Lambert was on leave in London.) It seemed that everyone knew about Mannock and was shaken by the news of his death. According to Adrian Smith, "For the British, Ball was the inspiration, McCudden the pioneer and Mannock the perfectionist: he combined the best qualities of the other two, and his innovative tactics left a lasting legacy for the RAF."[14] His death as a consequence of ground fire "was a terrific blow."[15]

In spite of the bad weather, Lambert would see action this day. He accompanied Selwyn, Hellett, Wren, Harries and Bair on a two hour patrol, beginning at 4:15 p.m. that eventually took them to 12,000 feet after bombing and otherwise attacking low-level targets. They spotted three Fokker DV IIs, but once again no action was forthcoming.[16] The next day, the 27th, the weather was so bad that "No aerial activity and no combat took place."[17] The end of July was proving unsuitable for flying. (In the trenches, of course, it was much worse.)

The weather would slightly improve, especially in the morning, on 28 July, and C Flight had the early morning patrol, beginning rather late, at 9:15 a.m. Lambert, however, was left behind, plagued with engine trouble. He had hoped to fix the problem and join his flight, but it was not to be. It took an hour to correct a fuel-line problem. (Such problems would continue to plague pilots throughout the Great War. It was necessary to go through a slow process of draining fuel and cleaning the lines to solve the problem. Often, as we have already seen, the fuel had to be poured through a cloth filter to catch the impediments that could clog an engine.)

Because of increasing cloud cover, after this morning patrol, the squadron was grounded for the rest of the day.[18] The next day was still misty, and visibility was an issue, but C Flight still went out on a two-hour patrol in the late afternoon.[19] Lambert could join his patrol this time, since the fuel-line problem had been solved. They continued tactical ground support and then went on offensive patrols at about 12,000 feet, but once again they failed to see any enemy aircraft.

Unlike the time before his leave, Lambert left very few details about what happened during these ground-strafing activities. It is almost as if he is deliberately trying to forget this part of his flights. He does not tell us if he paired off with anyone (as he used to do with Daley), or describe antiaircraft fire or machine-gun attacks from the ground, or speak of the effect of the Cooper bombs dropped on enemy positions. In fact, he gives more detail on the weather than on what he was doing in the war.

Lambert had now been back for a week, and in all that week he had had no dogfights with the enemy. The last two days of July would bring much of the same. On 30 July, C Flight had a two-hour morning flight, leaving at 10:00 a.m., in which they delivered their bombs and half their ammunition on ground targets. The weather had improved slightly, but there was still little sun—probably the reason the patrol started comparatively late in the day. The Germans were active, but it was in the northern sector of the front, away from where No. 24 was operating.[20]

On the next day, the last day of July, the weather continued to improve, but visibility was still poor. Enemy aircraft were active, particularly in the evening, but No. 24 was still not able to engage the enemy. Lambert received some bad news; it was posted that George McElroy had been killed in action. Only five days after Mannock's death, McElroy, who had left No. 24 in early April to return to No. 40 Squadron, had shot down a two-seater over Laventie at a low altitude and had been subsequently hit by antiaircraft fire and killed. The Germans dropped a message informing the R.A.F. of his death the following day. He had forty-seven victories at the time of his death.[21] Lambert does not dwell on McElroy's death in *Combat Report*, but the losses of Mannock and McElroy in a single week must have weighed on him. He had returned from leave to find his friend Daley dead. McElroy had been killed by ground fire, and Lambert had been assigned tactical ground support on a daily basis. The worry was building up on him.

On 31 July, C Flight left at 6:15 a.m. for another attack on the enemy's ground position, again returning without seeing an enemy aircraft. Lambert also realized that he had not seen a single train since his return from leave.[22] It seemed as if the Germans had all but pulled out from their front. July ended with Lambert, and in fact all No. 24 Squadron, knowing that something big was on the horizon, but not when or where.

Nine. Return to the War

A captured D.F.W. forced down by members of No. 24 Squadron at Conteville. The young German pilot had been sent for food supplies and became lost on the return flight—the observer's cockpit was full of potatoes. The squadron had baked potatoes that evening and invited the young pilot to be their guest. The following day Lambert and other squadron members took turns flying the captured airplane.

Reports coming in to the squadron indicated that the R.A.F. had increased its bombing activities all the way along the front. Even with enemy activity being "fairly active" on some fronts, the R.A.F. continued its night-bombing raids along with extensive daylight activities. This bombing strategy, including the bombing on the Epinoy aerodrome, was being pursued in earnest now by the Allies. All told, forty-five and one-half tons of bombs were dropped on the enemy on 1 August.[23]

The weather on 1 August remained the same, with adequate if not good visibility, and the squadron would continue with its ground attacks during the day. C Flight left at 10:00 a.m. for a mission east of Villers-Bretonneux. They were to follow a railroad line to Wiencourt and Caix.[24] Lambert was finally giving more details about his ground-attack activities. He says that the ground fire was more intense from "several forests and from the valleys of the Luce River."[25] They attacked these areas with the utmost fervor. Lambert does not say if they attacked in pairs or if he had a new partner, which probably means he did not, but he does say that these targets received all of the flight's Cooper bombs along with a heavy dose of machine-gun fire. The flight ended the patrol at about 1,000 feet amongst heavy antiaircraft fire; Lambert called the fire "vicious." He was probably remembering that both Mannock and McElroy had been killed by such fire.

For the first time in a considerable while, Lambert reported seen a formation of eight to ten enemy aircraft east of them. Even though these planes were 3,000 feet above C Flight and so had the advantage in the event of an attack, they elected to keep flying east and avoid confrontation. In comparison with the Allies, German planes were scarce and so were trained pilots. Again, there would be no aerial combat for the flight, so they headed back to Conteville, arriving at lunch time (around noon).[26]

C Flight went back on patrol that afternoon, around 4:30 p.m. They continued with tactical ground support and faced heavy antiaircraft fire, so that it was difficult to keep in formation. But when the "Archie" suddenly ceased, Lambert recognized that enemy aircraft were present. "The six of us came alive. Company is coming in for a hand out."[27] He spotted seven Fokker D. VIIs slightly above them, at a distance he estimated to be a couple of miles to the south. He alerted Selwyn and the rest of the flight as the Fokkers approached for the attack. Although at a disadvantage, the flight climbed to meet the challenge head-on; it had been some time since they had had the opportunity to engage the enemy. At the combined speed they were traveling towards each other, it was only matter of moments before they would meet and combat would ensue. Almost immediately, however, the Fokkers abandoned the battle, made a quick right turn, and headed eastward. At first, Lambert could not make sense of their maneuver, particularly when considering that they had the initial advantage. But in a few seconds he spotted the reason for the Fokkers' quick exit. Appearing in the north was a flight of Sopwith Dolphins coming to join the fracas. The odds were too great for the Germans to stick around and fight. Leaving the Dolphins in control of the field, C Flight headed back to Conteville, landing about 6:35 p.m. Lambert wrote in his log book that he had seen the enemy, but that nothing had taken place.[28]

For the next two days, the weather washed out any activity by No. 24. Enemy activity was slight, but the R.A.F. continued bombing as best as they could under the conditions. On 4 August, it was still raining in the morning with low cloud cover, but the weather was good enough for C Flight to go on an offensive patrol around Rosiéres in the early morning at 8:30 a.m.[29] They were 8,000 feet over Rosiéres in forty-five minutes, when they spotted about a mile away six Fokkers guarding a two-seater DFW reconnaissance plane. The DFW was about 1,000 feet above and to the south of them, with the Fokkers approximately 2,000 feet above the two-seater. Unlike the previous encounter, the action would not be interrupted by the sudden appearance of additional Allied aircraft. The Germans also seemed to also be eager for an encounter. As C Flight continued to climb to meet the Fokkers, Lambert's attention was on the two-seater. As Selwyn and the others engaged the Fokkers, Lambert maneuvered C1084 underneath the DFW and fired both his Lewis and Vickers guns into the entire underbelly of the two-seater, riddling it with bullets from rudder to engine. The DFW went nosedown into a spin that Lambert watched for around 1,000 feet until his attention was diverted by a bright blue Fokker that passed about ten yards off his right wing. Lambert could not believe his luck as he sized up the plane in his Aldis sight and coolly eased off the rudder to improve the angle of his shot. In spite of his leave and recent lack of activity, he seemed to have lost none of his hunting skills. As he prepared to finish this Fokker, he was startled by bullets crashing around his cockpit and felt "a slight jerk on the right side of my suit collar."[30] He saw behind him two Spandau machine-guns firing at him from a red-nosed Fokker positioned about fifty yards behind him. He was "stunned and almost paralyzed."[31] In a later interview, the interviewer reminded him of the bullet that creased the collar of his flying suit. He said that he "didn't know about that until I got back to the airdrome and saw where the collar was burned. If that bullet had been two inches farther front, what would have happened? Boy!"[32]

By going after the reconnaissance plane, Lambert had made himself the target of the Fokkers that were sent to protect it. He knew that fighters protecting a reconnaissance plane often used this planes as a means to entice enemy fighters into a trap. Once the opponent would go after the reconnaissance plane, the fighters would pounce on the enemy plane and secure an attack from close range and behind. Lambert had fallen for this ruse and had almost died as a result.

Immediately, in order to escape the Fokker, Lambert began evasive maneuvers by putting his plane's nose down with his "right and left legs sawing back and forth on my rudder bar."[33] He knew he would be difficult to hit as long as he maintained these maneuvers. He continued to move a step ahead of the attacking Fokker until one of his comrades came to his rescue and drove the attacking Fokker off his tail. He did not know who it was, but "I was scared and thankful.... I started to shake like a leaf in a high wind. That was close."[34] Lambert was at 4,500 feet as he gained his composure and looked for the rest of his flight.

In a few seconds, Lambert spotted four of his comrades engaged with five Fokkers a short distance away. He pulled back on his stick and in a full-throttle climb quickly joined the action. He maneuvered himself to the edge of the battle, circled around, and placed C1084 behind an unsuspecting Fokker. After his latest brush with death, he was paying close attention to the rules of air combat. He was attacking his opponent from behind, firing at close range with the enemy plane squarely in his sights. From a distance of around fifty yards, Lambert fired both guns into the unsuspecting Fokker and saw the "pilot jerk in his seat ... [as] his aeroplane fell off into a spin."[35] He next added a revealing comment: that the German pilot "had been caught asleep, just as I had been a few minutes before."[36] He realized both that he was not the only one who had lapses in the air and how deadly these lapses could be, but how fortunate he was to have survived. Lambert thought he had wounded the pilot; he watched as the Fokker leveled off and lost its landing gear as it made contact with the ground. He recalled seeing the pilot climb out of the plane and sit or fall on the ground.[37]

Uncharacteristically, Lambert did not recall how the combat ended, or even whether it continued after he sent the Fokker nose down to the ground. He also does not tell of the successes of his comrades in this fight. It would be simple speculation to say why he had not done so, but it might be because of his near escape hit him so hard that he could not remember much of what happened.

Lambert located Selwyn and the rest of the flight, and they returned to Conteville, landing around 10:00 a.m. In making their reports, Lambert was given credit for shooting down the DFW. Several of his comrades had seen the plane hit the ground. The Fokker was another matter. No one else saw the plane go down, so initially no credit was given. Ultimately, however, he was given credit for one plane crashed (the DFW) and one "driven down damaged—forced to land."[38] Lambert now had his sixteenth and seventeenth victories of the war.

On 5 August, No. 24 send each flight on two ground patrols, even though it rained throughout the day and there was stormy weather. Lambert gives a general description that the three flights attacked "designated targets between the main rail line and the Luce River."[39] The official communiqué states that very few of the enemy were seen and that no combats took place on that day. The reason for the lack of details on this action was Lambert did not fly that day. He and his aviation mechanics spent the day repairing the damage done to his plane during the previous day's encounter. He says, "The dash board and some of the instruments were destroyed. How I ever finished that patrol with all that damage is a mystery to me."[40] Once again, he thanked Divine Providence for watching over him. But in spite of his successes, he was given quite a scare by the attacking red-nosed Fokker, and the damage to C1084 was substantial enough to show how close he had come to not making it back. He was thankful that none of the bullets had penetrated his fuel tank. If they had, they would certainly have caused a fire, and fire was one thing that all pilots dreaded. The longer a pilot survived the odds, the more he will realize the odds are turning against him. How long can he survive before his time is up?

Lambert got a couple of days to revive from his encounter. Rain showers with low clouds continued on 6 August, and No. 24 was washed out for the entire day. However, he was in action the next day. Even though visibility was poor and there was ground mist, the weather was good enough to take to the skies.[41] Lambert recorded that there was a heavy concentration of activity from Albert down to around Moreuil. He saw a large number of Allied aircraft working beneath them as No. 24 patrolled its sector of the front. There was an increase in the variety of aircraft, indicating that more squadrons than usual were participating. Lambert notice, in addition to other S.E.5s, Camels, Dolphins, even a few Spads and Bristols. The planes were being used to hide the noise being made by moving troops into position for the upcoming offensive.[42] Lambert knew that something was up. Soon the Allies would unleash the offensive operation.

No. 24 had sent out A and B Flights for tactical ground support and to observe enemy ground activity. They were to report enemy action: troop movements, gun locations, or "any other suspicious action."[43] C Flight, however, was spared ground activity. It went on an offensive patrol at 12:10 p.m. at 19,000. In Lambert's words, "Our orders were to sweep the sky of any E.A."[44] Once again, they were working the area around the Luce River and the main railroad line. At around 1:15 p.m., the flight was well behind the German lines and feeling the effects of the cold air at high altitude. Lambert, lifting his goggles off his eyes in order to get a better look, spotted two German two-seater reconnaissance planes heading west at about 12,000 feet. He got Selwyn's attention, and the two began their assault on these planes by attempting to separate them from each other. (From Lambert's description, it seems that he had taken on some leadership and responsibility along with Selwyn.) Lambert with two others, swung off to the right in order to hit these planes from different directions, and then patiently waited until Selwyn and his group separated the German reconnaissance planes. Afterward, each group separately attacked a different plane.[45]

Lambert's group took the plane that went to the left, with Lambert positioning himself on the plane's tail and the other two comrades flanking the German plane from different sides. It was a textbook maneuver. From Lambert's description, it seems that the observer did not recognize what had happened. They opened fire from a distance of around a hundred yards, but the distance was too great to do any damage. The Allied fire simply alerted the observer, who returned fire as the pilot began evasive maneuvers. The German plane, which they identified afterward as a Halberstadt, went into a dive and then turned to the left. Lambert was able to stay on its tail, and the S.E.5 on the right (possibly Wren) was able to maintain its position as they closed within fifty yards. At this range, Lambert, pressed both guns and apparently hit the observer. He was seen to "let go of his guns and slump down out of sight in his cockpit."[46] Knowing that the observer might be playing a ruse, Lambert would not let

Nine. Return to the War

up on his guns as he continued to fire into the plane. Unfortunately, the Halberstadt was able to evade the S.E.5s. It slowly pulled away and headed east. They chased it down to 8,000 feet where they began to encounter antiaircraft fire. Lambert wrote either they were shooting badly or the plane had some type of protective light armor-plating. (The flight had had this discussion in the past when failing to shoot down an enemy plane when the odds were overwhelmingly in their favor.) It was known that the Germans were experimenting with metal plating on aircraft. With the odds stacked so heavily against the Halberstad, Lambert and the other S.E.5 should have sent it down. Lambert's log book records that he had silenced one of the observers, and he had had the plane in his sight and had hit it several times with both his guns.[47] Both reconnaissance planes escaped their attackers in spite of the number of shots that were put into them. (Selwyn remarked that each plane in his group fired at least 400 rounds of ammunition at their Halberstadt.[48]) This would be listed as an indecisive combat, for no planes were shot down. C Flight made it back to Conteville around 2:15 p.m. without seeing any other enemy aircraft in the sky.

That evening, Major Robeson informed the squadron that the Allied Offensive was planned for the next morning. The wait was over, and the last hundred days of the war were to begin with the beginning of the Second Battle of Amiens on 8 August 1918. The day before the offensive was to be unleashed, at the German High Command at Spa, Colonel Mertz von Quirnheim noted that Ludendorff was in a "completely inert mood," and remarked that Germany had "lost the war if we cannot pull ourselves together."[49] Ludendorff rejected any talk of defense; he was preparing four minor offensives. He sent a message to the Kaiser: "I hope we shall soon have our attack on Amiens in full swing, when the troops have pulled themselves together."[50] Foch and Douglas Haig had been patiently bidding their time before unleashing their counter-offensive. The Allies would integrate all the modern technologies of the war and set them on the unsuspecting Germans. They had concentrated a large infantry force, the British 4th and French 1st Armies, on the Amiens front from Morlancourt to Montdidier, along with 530 British and seventy French tanks in front of Amiens. These forces were supported by massive fleets of aircraft. The two Canadian battalions near Kemmel were supplied with 38,000 air photographs to supplement their large-scale maps for the coming attack. Foch also utilized the large reservoir of American troops to support his offensive. World war had arrived. At 4:00 a.m. on the 8th, the Allied offensive began with an intensive artillery barrage that virtually destroyed the enemy's batteries.[51] The breech in the German lines was initially not any larger than what the Germans had suffered at Cambrai in 1917; however, "for the first time whole divisions had failed, and in many cases allowed themselves to be captured without resistance."[52] Ludendorff, in the most-quoted line from his memoirs, would call 8 August "the black day for the German Army."[53] The war would continue until November, but the end was no longer in doubt: Germany had lost.

On the 8th, the weather was fair, but there was rain and clouds in the morning. The mist and early fog aided the Allied forces in maintaining surprise and confusing the enemy. No. 24 took part with tactical ground support and offensive patrols to aid the troops. They used ground strafing and bombings to disrupt the enemy. Unlike his usual pattern in *Combat Report*, Lambert discusses A Flight, though it followed C Flight on a patrol in the late morning. Evidently, Lambert discussed A Flight first because he, like several of their pilots, would suffer the fate of being shot down that day by ground fire.

A Flight suffered a number of causalities that day as they patrolled the area between

Proyart and Chaunes. Two pilots, Watkins and Barton, were shot down by machine-gun fire from the ground. Barton helped Watkins walk back to a dressing station until they were able to find a tank that would take Watkins back for aid. Then Barton found his way back to Conteville where he was, ironically, given his leave warrant. Southey, who had just returned from leave on 6 August, was shot down between Rosiéres and Roye. He was replaced on the evening flight by Lieutenant F. E. Beauchamp, who was promptly shot down and taken prisoner by the Germans.[54] However, A Flight did have some successes. During the evening patrol, Captain Hazell was credited with three decisive and one indecisive.[55] Both the casualties and the successes show that the front had finally heated up.

C Flight took to the skies at 10:50 a.m. to do ground strafing. Before leaving, the flight agreed to stay close together and cooperate as much as possible in their assault on the German fortifications and troops in the area near Caix. But these plans were doomed not to come to fruition. As Lambert wrote, "Within minutes, we were separated and each man was on his own,"[56] so he could tell only what happened to him in the air this day. As the flight traveled through a light drizzle over their target area, Lambert noticed a couple of balloons slightly to the west around 1,500 feet. He signaled Selwyn and they both went after the balloons, each pilot taking a different one. What Lambert recalls is both the fury of the ground fire and the appearance of numerous Allied aircraft in the sky. The German air force seemed to be missing. As Selwyn and Lambert continued their approaches to the balloons, Lambert noticed the ground crews feverishly attempting to bring the balloons down before the planes begin their assault. He was between 600 to 800 feet above them when he pressed his stick forward to begin diving on the balloon. At full throttle, his plane traveling at 165 M.P.H. as he made his first pass at the balloon, while in the process firing both his guns at it. After this pass, Lambert watched as both observers, wearing parachutes, wasted no time in jumping out of the basket. The balloon was not on fire, but Lambert observed it shrinking as he turned his plane around and headed west. He had hit the balloon and it was deflating. When the day was done, he was given credit for this balloon as a decisive action.

Looking down on the enemy on the ground, Lambert observed that with the force of the allied advance, "most of the enemy seems to be panic-stricken. They seem to be going in all directions."[57] He describes the carnage he sees on the ground below, particularly the fate of horses. (The plight of horses in war had always had the strongest effect on him.) The debris covering the ground included dead horses and men. Horses could be found lying in the water-filled trenches. There were wagons and gun-limbers with some horses still attached to them. "Even above the noise of my engine, I could hear the faint scream of wounded horses below me."[58] These sight and sound played on his nerves.

Lambert realized that he was on his own. He continued his tactical ground support, lowering his plane to a height of less than 200 feet to attack a machine-gun crew near a bunch of trees. After silencing this gun, he continued to head east to look for targets to attack, trying at the same time to avoid antiaircraft fire. Near the Luce, Lambert spotted and investigated a motor transport consisting of twenty or thirty vehicles moving east. This convoy was escorted by a British Medium Mark A Whippet tank, armed with four Hotchkiss machine-guns. He had never seen a Whippet before. While investigating this convoy, he spotted what turned out to be a German antitank gun, "built like a very large rifle," which was waiting to ambush the convoy. Lambert was fascinated by the gun, but he had also puzzled by the lack of ground fire as he flew over the area. He correctly deduced that he was not fired upon because the convoy was the main objective. After several failed attempts to get the convoy's attention, Lambert flew near ground level and fired a short burst of machine-gun fire approximately fifty yards in front of the tank. The maneuvered worked; the convoy came to a halt. (Lambert had been inspired to this maneuver by analogy to the way that one ship stopped another one at sea by shooting over its bow.) After successfully alerting the convoy to the danger, Lambert was free to attack the antitank gun. He fired both guns at it, and scattered and killed members of its crew.[59] After circling back, Lambert saw the Whippet and two armored cars near the site of the antiaircraft gun. With the convoy safe, Lambert continued his lone assault on the enemy by climbing to about 1,000 feet and heading further east to investigate a forest.

Lambert admits that from the height he was flying "it was very hard to know just exactly who was below me."[60] It was a fluid front where an entrenched enemy position could suddenly become an Allied stronghold. This was the first time he had been supporting a major Allied offensive where the enemy would be in retreat. In the confusion, at times he had to go down and investigate in order to be certain that he was attacking a foe and not a friend, and that descent involved a high degree of risk,

War makes strange bedfellows. Lambert suddenly found himself joining up with a Camel that was in the area. No doubt, it was from one of those squadrons he had previously noticed flying beneath him when he and Selwyn joined together to attack the observation balloons. Both planes had been separated from the others in their flights. Knowing the advantage of numbers, Lambert got the Camel pilot's attention and assistance in attacking the forest area, which seemed to be a cover for enemy activity. As he had done with Daley in the past, Lambert and the Camel, trailing about 200 yards behind him, entered the east side of the forest at about 300 yards altitude and dropped all four of their Cooper bombs while traveling at a speed of about 160 M.P.H. As Lambert said, "We really plastered that place."[61] But their actions alerted the enemy hidden amongst the trees to their presence, and the German ground forces were now determined to shoot both planes down, as we have seen several other planes of No. 24 Squadron were shot down.

After attacking the forest area, Lambert and the Camel pilot both spotted a downed Camel about 1,000 yards to the south. The downed Camel seemed to be in good shape, but Lambert was concerned about its pilot, who was nowhere in sight. After they investigated and Lambert was attempting to climb, his plane took a direct hit in its main fuel tank. He stated that the hit "must have torn a tremendous hole through my tank."[62] He was quickly covered from chest to feet with gasoline. As he told an interviewer later, he was "ringing wet, and I had on that thin, not exactly thin, but summer flying clothes."[63] The gasoline had also soaked much of the cockpit.

Lambert responded coolly and collectively to this harrowing experience. Acting quickly, he shut off his engine to prevent a fire, and began to look for a possible landing site. He had to find one quickly, because the engine had been overheating at the time it was shut off. With any luck, the site would be in Allied hands, but because of the changing front it was difficult to judge where the front was and what separated the Allied lines from the Germans. And he had no time to spare.

A pilot's worst fear was a fiery death. The technology of the day did little to prevent planes from bursting into flames when successfully attacked by enemy aircraft or ground forces. Boelcke wrote that, "It is strange that my opponents catch fire so often—I have only to attack and then the enemy either catches fire or at least sheds his wings."[64] Later that very day, when Lambert witnessed for the first time a dogfight from the ground, what he saw corroborated Boelcke's words. Lambert "watched a Camel burn a D VII; an Albatros D V collide with a Fokker and come down locked together. I watched one Dolphin shoot the wings off a D VII and a second or two later bring another down in flames…. About the same time I watch[ed] a Camel coming down with black smoke and fire trailing behind."[65] Without parachutes, fire meant almost certain death to pilots. The Germans had already issued parachutes to their pilots, but unfortunately the Allies had yet to employ this vital safety practice.

Luckily, Lambert was able to land his plane with no difficulties and remove himself from it quickly. Even though he had shut off the engine, the propeller continued to rotate due to the overheating. A spark from an engine firing spasmodically could ignite a fire. He was now on the ground and safe for the moment. In pilots' lore, any landing you can walk away from is a good landing.

However, Lambert was not really safe yet. He now noticed about twenty-five soldiers about 300 yards away, coming towards him.[66] At first he thought they were British infantry and was relieved, but then he realized from their uniforms that they were German soldiers and that he had to act quickly if he wanted to avoid being captured. He said in an interview later, "Maybe 15 minutes before that was our line. But they'd come in and pushed again and I was inside the German's line."[67] Lambert proceeded to do what he later described as "a very foolish thing."[68] In fact, he acted quickly and courageously. He immediately switched to his emergency or gravity fuel tank and hit the ignition switch, and the plane to begin to move forward. There was about five gallons of gasoline in the center section, and with the engine already warm, it started right up. Lambert reached into the breast pocket of his "Sidcot" suit and pulled out his Webley Mk VI revolver, released the safety, and began shooting at the advancing Germans, who were now within about twenty yards of the plane.[69] "I saw one German grab his belly with both hands."[70] The remaining Germans returned fire, but Lambert pushed the throttle forward and was able to get his plane into the air at a height of between 100 and 200 feet before it sustained another hit. Luckily, he was able to gently land his plane a second time on a "fairly good spot of ground."[71] However, the plane continued to roll. It rolled into a shell crater where it crashed its landing gear, propeller, and the tip of its left bottom wing.[72] His plane had its tail in the air, but its flying days were over.

Lambert was safely on the ground again, but he had no idea where he was. However, he saw a British cavalry unit emerging from a cluster of trees about 200 yards away. He had safely made it to Allied lines. Lambert jumped out of his plane and started to run in the direction of the cavalry unit as the Germans shelled the area around the plane. For some inexplicable reason, he briefly returned to the plane to retrieve the clock on its dashboard. He could never quite explain how he got that clock out of the aircraft so quickly: it had long screws and was solidly placed through the plywood. At times, he attributed it to a moment of superhuman strength.[73] (This watch would be proudly displayed on the bedroom wall in his Ironton home until he died.)

The Germans continued their shelling as Lambert left. He turned back for one more look at his plane. He recalled the fire getting heavier and some of the shells hitting C1084. In *Combat Report*, he sadly reminisced over the loss of his favorite plane, one that he had flown since 25 June 1918: "Farewell old girl; you have been a faithful friend…. Your work is finished. You have been perfect. Farewell 1084."[74] Lambert described this event as "the narrowest escape I had" during the war.⁷⁵ Once again, the Old Gentleman upstairs was looking out for Lambert.

Once Lambert was safely in the hands of the cavalry, he reported to the captain in charge of the unit. Lambert's first concern was the convoy he had spotted before he was shot down. The captain grasped the situation and quickly dispatched men to warn the convoy and to inform the artillery about the anti-tank gun's whereabouts. (It may seem strange that Lambert would have considered the anti-tank gun still a threat, since he had already scattered its gun crew with nearly 300 rounds of machine-gun fire; but he had not destroyed the gun itself, and scattered crewmen can reunite.) The men sent to warn the convoy soon returned with word that the convoy commander had understood Lambert's warning and was in possession of the anti-tank gun. Lambert had done his duty and exceeded expectations. His actions had helped clear the forest of between 200 or 300 men and enemy machine-guns.⁷⁶

The captain also got a message to No. 22 Wing and No. 24 Squadron that Lambert was safe. He was then escorted by horse back to an artillery battery. This trip was his first view of a battlefield from ground level. The amount of destruction shocked him. "Dead horses, dead men both ours and theirs in the water and mud. Burnt out vehicles scattered about. One Fokker triplane, crashed and burned. I saw the tail and about half of the fuselage of a Camel sticking up out of the mud."⁷⁷

At the artillery battery, the noise was deafening as the guns continued firing upon German positions in the wooded area Lambert had just flown over. He was again shocked at the size of the guns, the intensity of the noise, and the amount of recoil of the guns in the battery. It was a far different experience than he was accustomed to in the air. At the battery, he met a Canadian major who had received his message about the troops hidden in the forest area, two miles ahead of their current position. The major had to pull cotton out of his ears in order to communicate with Lambert.

Grateful for Lambert's information, the major showed Lambert a map so that he could understand where the battle was raging at present. (It was one of the ironies of Lambert's position that he almost never really knew where he was during the war.) From the map, he discovered that they were about a mile south of Wiencourt with the Luce around a mile south of their position. The major also informed Lambert that No. 24 had sent a tender to pick him up that evening between 5:00 and 6:00 p.m., so he had a couple of hours before they would be there to get him.⁷⁸ In this time, Lambert had an amicable lunch and conversation with the Canadian major. (Lambert always seemed to get along well with the different soldiers he met during this war, regardless of their nationality or branch. Later in civilian life, he lost that ability.)

With some time to spare before the tender would arrive, Lambert, who had (as the reader will remember) once considered joining the artillery, spent a few moments watching the batteries in action. He was impressed by their efficiency, but he wrote, "Believe me that noise was terrible, even with cotton in my ears."⁷⁹ He told the commanding officer of one battery that he had worked in Nobel producing the cordite that was used by the artillery. In another coincidence, the officer told Lambert that his brother, who had been injured in the war, had been working at Nobel for the past year.

During this conversation, an R.E.8 dropped a message telling the battery to hold its fire. The enemy troops in the forest had surrendered. Now the German prisoners were transported to the rear, and Lambert got his first and last opportunity to see a large concentration of enemy up close. The sight left a lasting impression on him. Three or four thousand prisoners, from boys as young as fifteen to men as old as fifty, were paraded past them on their way to the rear. For Lambert, "They were the sorriest mass of humanity" he had ever seen. He wondered if he had fired on any of them earlier that day.[80] They were a beaten army, and Lambert showed compassion for them.

The tender arrived around 6:00 p.m. to take Lambert on the long trek back to Conteville. The N.C.O. and driver promptly told Lambert that Barton and Watkins of B Flight had also been shot down in their general vicinity. The Canadian major inquired concerning their whereabouts, but there was no news on either of them. Lambert thanked the major for his hospitality and began the long, tedious drive over the war torn landscape back to Amiens. Not only was it an unpleasant sight to behold, but also the damage done to the roads inhibited their progress. Once at Amiens, they briefly stopped for dinner where they were the guests of two colonels, one an Australian and another Canadian. Then they left for Conteville and finally arrived around 11:00 p.m.

On entering the office, Lambert discovered a subdued and concerned group of pilots in this small room, waiting for news on their comrades. It was a day like no other any of them had ever experienced. Lambert sat on the floor and waited with the others to hear about their missing friends. While they were waiting, they received a call from Brigade congratulating the squadron for a job well done. No. 24 was one of eleven squadrons involved in the actions of a day that saw eighteen enemy aircraft destroyed, in addition to the extensive ground support throughout the day.[81] Besides the number of conflicts that took place along the battle front, over thirty-seven and one-quarter tons of bombs were dropped on the enemy.[82] On the Somme bridges alone, there was 205 individual daylight flights that dropped twelve tons of bombs.[83]

Lambert wrote that No. 24 would face the best the Germans had to offer during this offensive. He listed Jasta 4, commanded by Ernst Udet; Jasta 10, commanded by Erich Löwenhardt; and Jasta 11, commanded by Lothar von Richthofen, patrolling within an area of eight to ten square miles in the vicinity of his squadron. (On 10 August 1918, Löwenhardt, after scoring his fifty-fourth victory over an S.E.5 near Chaulnes, would collide with Lieutenant Alfred Wenz of his own squadron and be killed when his parachute failed to open.[84])

The appearance of these German squadrons that had been brought in to reinforce the battle areas helps to explain the increase in British casualties. Overall, it had been a productive day for the Allies, but it had come at a high cost, with No. 24 losing ten planes over the day. The R.A.F. casualty list for the day had forty-five airplanes lost and fifty-two others wrecked or damaged, out of the 700 serviceable day-flying airplanes, for a loss of more than thirteen percent for the day. Fifty-seven individuals were reported missing with four killed and nineteen wounded, or approximately one casualty for every twenty hours flown on the active fronts.[85] Lambert had survived, however, and would be recognized for his efforts against the anti-tank gun that day.[86] (He would also write the details of the day's events in a letter home to his parents, published in the Ironton paper, which he had with him and used many years later when he wrote his account of that day for *Combat Report*.[87]

The Allied offensive continued on next day, the 9th, with an advance on the Franco-British front. Eventually the German forces in Montdidier were surrounded. The city was attacked from the north and south, and the Germans were forced to evacuate it by the evening of 10 August.[88] The momentum of the offensive was slowing down with the reduced number of tanks available on the second day to support the infantry, the difficulties of going over the old destroyed Somme battlefield, and the German response to the Allied offensive, but the Allied forces were still making progress. German fighter aircraft had been brought in to reinforce the area, as Lambert had seen, and Allied planes were forced to spend more time on offensive patrols to counter these new enemies, so they had to do less tactical ground support.[89]

No. 24 was busy throughout the day with both ground support and offensive patrols. On the ground support, Lambert remarked that "this low work is not good. The nerves of about every pilot in the squadron are about shot. Most of the pilots had been doing this for about three weeks."[90] Lambert himself certainly showed this strain. He says that although nobody complained about this activity, and everyone did their duty, "all any one has to do, is to look into the face of any pilot and watch his actions"[91] Of himself, he says, "Believe me, I do not like it. I would rather face five or six Germans in the air, than to do this ground strafing. You can at least see where the bullets might come from and then try to dodge them."[92] The mental strain of flying is proportional to the danger a pilot faces in combat, and ground strafing increased this danger.[93]

C Flight was due out at 4:00 p.m., with some of the pilots having to make the trip to the supply depot at 8:00 a.m. to get new planes. Lambert would not join them. Of course he had to get a new plane, but he took one of the two spare machines already on the field. His new plane, B8395, would now replace his beloved C1084. Lambert spent most of the day checking it out and putting it through its paces to make sure he understood its quirks before taking it out on patrol. He also made sure to take the plane to the air a couple of times in order to check out the range and accuracy of its guns.[94]

After a brief stop at the mess for some tea and toast, Lambert joined Selwyn, Hellett, Harries, Wren, and Bair on the field with his new plane. Each plane was carrying its full load of ammunition and four Cooper bombs for the upcoming mission. C Flight was assigned to patrol the main railway line and attack anything they found. The high command wanted pressure on the Germans and chaos behind their lines to disrupt any attempt to stall the Allied offensive. The flight proceeded to destroy areas of the track on their way to Rosiéres, which was still in German hands. They were still low enough (around 2,000 feet) to face machine-gun and light antiaircraft fire from the German held positions.[95]

Lambert was still getting used to his new plane as the flight ascended to about 8,000 feet for an offensive patrol. While making his ascent, Lambert observed enemy aircraft in the east. What he observed was a two-seater escorted by six Fokker D. VIIs. The observation plane was flying at around 6,000 feet, with the Fokkers positioned behind and above it. Since it was the late afternoon, C Flight had the advantage of having the sun at their back. Selwyn and Harries separated to attack the L.V.G. reconnaissance plane. Unlike when Lambert attacked the two-seater by himself, Selwyn attacked the L.V.G. with Harries, using a pincer tactic, with one coming in from behind and the other attacking the flank. The rest of the flight positioned themselves to protect their comrades from the attacking Fokkers. (It was this sort of organized cooperation that was missing from Lambert's assault on the DFW on 4 August.)

Even with this protective screen of S.E.5s, one of the Fokkers managed to get through and go after Selwyn. That plane was close to Lambert, so he went after it. Turning his rudder slightly left, he closed the gap between them and eventually positioned himself within fifty yards of the unsuspecting Fokker. He briefly sized up the plane in his Aldis sight and fired both guns into the tail section of the plane. Apparently B8395 was passing its initial test. Lambert briefly noticed that something became detached from the enemy plane near the cockpit and flew into the air. He then repositioned himself for another attack and fired two short bursts into the Fokker, from within twenty-five yards, hitting the pilot. He watched as the pilot slipped back into his seat, slumped in the cockpit, but continued to move. The German pilot attempted to do a loop, but eventually stalled his airplane and fell into a spin that took the Fokker to around 2,000 feet before leveling off. If the maneuver had been intentional, it would have been an adroit one. But Lambert noticed that the plane was staggering and wobbling as if the pilot was unable to control its movements. He was hit—still alive, but only partially able to maneuver his plane. The dogfight had taken place at about 4,500 feet, and Lambert was able to see the gradual descent of the plane from that height to the ground. Its landing gear was torn off, and the plane slid on its undercarriage before stopping.[96]

In this attack, Lambert showed himself to be a skilled veteran who was able to shoot down a plane with minimum firepower. He now had another victory to add to his total. With his balloon the day before, Lambert now had nineteen victories. He was the leading American ace in the war at this time, but no one, least of all Lambert, was aware of it.

After this encounter, Lambert would join up with the rest of the flight as they head back to Conteville, landing around 5:50 p.m. He and Selwyn were both credited with two indecisive that day. Selwyn was sure that he hit the observer in the back of the L.V.G., but there was apparently no independent confirmation that the plane was shot down. There was apparently the same lack of any independent testimony with Lambert.

C Flight had the early morning flight on the 10th, leaving around 6:15 a.m., to cover the main east-west road from Villers-Bretonneux to Estrees.[97] They were once again to do tactical ground support, so they loaded up with the full complement of weapons, including four Cooper bombs apiece. (Over the past month, these bombs had now become standard equipment for the S.E.5s as they made their daily patrols.) Evidently, on this day, no enemy aircraft were spotted.

On the early-morning patrol the next day, C Flight came across a German convoy near Mericourt and scattered the troops. Selwyn laid his bombs in front of the convoy, creating a series of craters that made passage of the guns and troops very difficult. The rest of the flight followed their leader, attacking the stalled convoy. It was a clever tactic that disrupted and terrorized the German troops and their convoy.

Afterward, they ascended to 8,000 to 10,000 feet for an offensive patrol. Antiaircraft fire was still heavy at that height, but they were finally out of range of the deadly machine-gun fire they faced when ground strafing. When they were coming in for a ground attack, the machine-gun fire was deadlier and more accurate than antiaircraft fire. A pilot could see the black puffs of smoke from antiaircraft fire and adjust his flight accordingly; he knew when he was being fired at by machine-guns, but was frequently unaware of the origins of the attack. Lambert returned to Conteville several times with bullet holes in his plane from these ground attacks, and the same could be said of all the other pilots in the squadron.

On their offensive patrol, C Flight was able to spot two enemy reconnaissance aircraft—either L.V.G. Cs or Halberstadts. With the advantage of the sun behind them, the flight divided up and attacked both planes simultaneously. Selwyn, Lambert, Harries, and Bair went after the machine on the right, and Hellett and Wren attacking the one on the left. Both these

German pilots were quite skilled, but with four different S.E.5s coming at one plane from different angles (Lambert attacking from underneath), the odds seemed to be against that plane. In fact, Lambert remarked, "those two boys do not have a chance."[98] However, they fought back hard and the S.E.5s were riddled with enough bullet holes that they required extra maintenance when they returned to Conteville. It seems, however, that they did not have protective metal covering, unlike the Halberstadt the flight encountered on 7 August. Lambert positioned B8395 about fifty yards underneath the reconnaissance plane and fired both guns into its underbelly, peppering it from the tail to the nacelle. While Lambert was hitting the plane from underneath, bullets from the other three pilots were hitting their marks from their different approach angles. In fact, Lambert had to fly away from his current location in order to avoid being hit by stray bullets from his comrades. He positioned himself above the reconnaissance plane and took pity on his opponent as he watched the plane getting pummeled before it abruptly nose-dived and crashed into the ground and exploded into flames. He remarked, "Poor devils, I hope they were dead before they hit. They certainly put up a game fight."[99]

Afterward, they returned to Conteville, landing in time for breakfast. For this victory, each of the four members received one-quarter credit. It seems rather silly to award a quarter to each member, but it figured in an airman's final total. When Lambert's victory total was reconfigured in 1968, Lambert would have "19½ Aircraft destroyed" as well as balloons."[100]

The flight landed at 8:20 a.m. and did not have long to wait for its next patrol. At 11:00 a.m., they took to the skies again for some ground strafing. Lambert, however, was not along. He was stuck at home with a dud engine. He barely gotten off the ground when he had to return to Conteville. His log book lists him as flying for only fifteen minutes. The rest of the flight returned by 12:45 p.m.

On the ground, Lambert was questioning once again why there were no replacements available for No. 24 Squadron. Of course, C Flight had the full complement of six pilots, but in cases of engine trouble, there was no one available to replace the pilot on a patrol. Since March, they had had two men wounded and Daley killed. Bair was their last replacement pilot, and he had arrived over a month ago, on 5 July.[101]

Lambert did not know it, and it would have made no difference if he had, but this question about replacement pilots was probably being asked in every squadron. The Allied offensive asked much of everyone. Pilots, certainly, were being pushed to their limits. Replacements were needed everywhere on the front. There was simply no pilots available at the time for any flight that had already had its full complement of members.

Lambert needed a break from ground strafing. He was disheartened, to say the least, when he realized that C Flight was to join A Flight in an offensive patrol almost immediately, at 1:15 p.m. But he was pleasantly relieved for two reasons: first, his crew had corrected the problem; second, and even better, the patrol was purely an offensive one. He would not be required to load Cooper bombs onto his plane, thus making it heavy, and he would not be required to do ground strafing. He left his crew to finish the details and went to lunch.

Over lunch, the two flights discussed tactics for the upcoming operation. C Flight would support A Flight by flying slightly above and behind them. They were to meet above Bertangles and then patrol the area around Chaulnes, from 10,000 to 12,000 feet. C Flight reached Bertangles first. Upon arriving, they were greeted by their "old friends" in the German anti-aircraft batteries. The black smoke of their barrage was evident all around them. Lambert had grown accustomed to the sight and sound of this barrage. He knew how it operated and how to identify its type and distance. What he was waiting for was the barrage to stop, because that would signal German planes were in their vicinity.

When the antiaircraft fire finally ceased, Lambert noticed that the enemy planes were about 4,000 feet above them in the north and coming at them in two layers. It was an unusual formation, both in number and variety of planes. Lambert was able to identify three Albatros D.V.s, a Pfalz D. III, eleven Fokker D. VIIs, and three reconnaissance planes. Two of these two-seaters were Hannover C.s, and one was a Halberstadt or L.V.G. C.[102] To have reconnaissance planes participate in an offensive attack was highly irregular. However, according to Lambert, the Hannover "can maneuver equal to a fighter and due to the man in the rear, they are more dangerous than a fighter plane."[103] In fact, Lambert remembered that a Bristol pilot told him that the Hannover could "outfight" a Bristol fighter.[104] The presence of the three reconnaissance planes could also have been a sign of how low the Germans were on fighter planes.

The first layer of enemy planes—seven multicolored Fokkers and one Hannover—attacked A Flight. The second layer—four Fokkers, three Albatros fighters, the Pflaz, the other Hannover, and the Halberstadt—went after C Flight. Lambert entered this fight not quite sure how his plane would perform. It was one of many times he missed his old reliable C1084. With the enemy attacking from above, theirs was the initial advantage. But as usual, it is only a matter of moments before the two groups become intertwined, rolling and surging in a dogfight, with the planes separating into individual battles. Lambert found himself embroiled with a gold-painted Fokker with a blue-green tail. As the fight unfolded, he maneuvered his plane to the right to get behind the Fokker and close the gap between them. He pushed the throttle forward and increased the plane's power in order to close the gap to within fifty yards, an acceptable distance to begin an attack. Lambert then fired both guns, hitting the Fokker and sending it "into the craziest maneuver that I have ever seen."[105] The nose of the Fokker was up, but the tail kept waving up and down. Lambert believed, but was not certain, that he may have severed the elevator shaft of that Fokker with some of his bullets. They were at around 5,000 feet and Lambert, who saw another Fokker approaching, did not have time to watch the one he had damaged hit the ground. He briefly saw the plane performing the same erratic maneuvers as it descended.

Lambert quickly made a diversionary steep-right climbing turn, and then leveled off before making a wide loop and half roll in hopes of avoiding the oncoming Fokker. As he came out of his turn, he seemed to have lost sight of the other plane and was puzzled. But then he noticed the second Fokker hit the ground and explode.[106] Undoubtedly, another Allied pilot must have killed or severely wounded the pilot, so he was unable to control his aircraft before it hit the ground. In a matter of minutes, C Flight had destroyed two of the attacking D. VIIs, and Lambert added another victory to his steadily rising total.

After this encounter, Lambert discovered that he was now 3,000 to 4,000 feet below where the action was. He climbed as fast as possible to join the intense battle. As he was ascending, he noticed the Halberstad trying to extricate itself from the fracas and head east, as well as a seeing a smoking Albatros within twenty yards flashing by him at a high rate of speed. He decided to forget both these planes and focused on a Fokker with a green nacelle, a red fuselage with wide white stripes on the side, a blue tail, and a white rudder. The colors alone made it stand out. It was maneuvering on an S.E.5's tail, so Lambert positioned himself on the Fokker's right side and fired into it from around fifty yards. He drove it left and off the tail of his comrade.[107]

Almost immediately, Lambert was hit in the rear by machine-gun fire from an Albatros around a hundred yards away. It was too far to do significant damage, but it awakened Lambert to the danger. Taking evasive action, Lambert went nose down and pulled a right-climbing move to maneuver himself both behind and above the Albatros, but the Albatros duplicated his move and still enjoyed the advantage on Lambert. He was rescued when two of his comrades joined the fight and drove the attacking Albatros off him.

It was a hellacious fight, with continuous stroke and counterstroke. Lambert's experience showed, as he was focused on the immediate task and quickly adapted to the changing reality of the air battle. Now temporarily freed, he decided to go after a Hannover that was marginally above and to his left. The Hannover was currently engaged in a heated struggle with an S.E.5 as Lambert went nose up and above him. Lambert quickly positioned himself to the right of the unsuspecting two-seater. The Hannover's attention was fully focused on the other S.E.5 as Lambert used a deflection shot from about thirty feet, placing his bullets five to six yards ahead of the advancing Hannover's path. He let go about fifty rounds from each gun and watched as he hit the observer and the plane fell into a spin until it hit the ground "with a terrific burst of fire and smoke."[108] It had been only five minutes between shooting down the Fokker over Fouquescourt and the Hannover northeast of Parvillers.[109] What seemed like an eternity had taken only seconds. Almost immediately, Lambert saw two other enemy aircraft, also spewing heavy black smoke, hit the ground and explode. The offensive patrol had already had a great deal of success. Lambert remarked, "Someone around me is doing a good job."[110] The same could be said of Lambert himself. The fight was not yet over, and Lambert now had his twenty-first victory.

After a quick encounter with another Albatros, Lambert made contact with Hazell before checking his fuel gage. Fuel was low, so it was time to head for home. It had been a strenuous and exhausting fight. Both sides realized it was now over. The enemy continued its trek eastward as all twelve S.E.5s circled around and followed Hazell back to Conteville, landing around 3:30 p.m. Once on the ground, Lambert made a quick examination of B8395 that revealed some bullet holes in sections of the wings, but overall the plane had performed admirably and initially only seemed to need some moderate repairs. In such a fight, all the planes had sustained damage from the enemy machine-guns. It was not until the flight went on patrol again that evening that he knew that his plane had sustained more damage than he had thought. He was forced to fly a new plane—S.E.5 1945—on this flight.

Before he went in for tea, Lambert said how physically exhausted he was by this recent battle. "I was tired and I believe that all the others were also. A thing like this could wear one down, both physically and mentally."[111] After tea, he went back to "Buckingham Palace" and slept until it was time for dinner. The evening flight proved to be uneventful—luckily, if everyone on the patrol was as unready as Lambert for further combat. For the day, Lambert would be given credit for driving a Fokker out of control and crashing a Hannover. He would also share in the destruction of the L.V.G. C that was shot down at 7:50 a.m. on the first patrol. No. 24 would record seven decisive combats. It was Lambert's most successful day as a combat pilot.

On 11 August, the weather was fine, with the enemy quite active on the front lines. The Fourth Army headquarters' operation orders admitted that the German resistance was becoming more effective as the British advance continued. Artillery was needed to assist the infantry, and this was to be supplemented by a new allotment of tanks.[112] The German Air Force was seen to be flying in large formations (as No. 24 had already experienced) as the Germans attempted to re-stabilize a front that had become compromised by the Allied offensive. Not only did the Allied air force respond to the enemy aggressively, but also over thirty-one tons of bombs were dropped on German positions at night, followed by an additional twenty-nine and one-half tons dropped during the day.[113] The German Air Force could not prevent the R.A.F. from doing their job; all they could hope for was to make it as difficult as possible and force them to pay an increasingly high price for their actions.[114]

No. 24 continued with ground strafing, with A Flight taking the early morning patrol at 4:45 a.m. on the 11th over the Rosiéres area. Lambert made a point of mentioning a new pilot who flew with them that morning, Second Lieutenant J. S. Haigh. Lambert had been clamoring for replacements, and one had arrived; however, he would be with them only for a very short time. Haigh would be killed four days later by antiaircraft fire. "All that had been seen, was one S.E. 5 going down with parts of the machine flying off in space. Poor fellow, he had lasted but six days."[115]

C Flight would not leave for patrol until 10:45 a.m., after B had returned from its morning flight. Unlike the two previous morning patrols that both did tactical ground support, C Flight would go on an offensive patrol around Chaulnes. However, Lambert was forced to return after only five minutes. He was losing R.P.M.s, but his log book shows him returning because of his guns. When attempting to fire his guns, he experienced blockage that he could not clear. He then approached Selwyn and signaled to him that he needed to return to Conteville. Back there, he discovered cartridges that were bent and jammed tightly into each gun. He tried to get both guns replaced quickly. He also had his crew look over the engine to correct whatever problem was causing the low R.P.M.s. Lambert had hoped to rejoin the flight before it reached Bertangles; however, it proved to be impossible. He was grounded until his comrades returned around 12:30 p.m. From what Lambert then learned, he did not miss much on this patrol. They had seen some enemy planes, but none had engaged.[116]

There two issues that gave Lambert trouble that morning—mechanical problems to the engines, and guns jamming—continued to plague Lambert's new S.E.5. The reader can perhaps better understand now Lambert's attachment to his old reliable C1084. That plane had had problems too, of course, but towards the end there were very few of them. Most planes in the Great War were plagued with the same problems that plagued Lambert's new plane; it was not that he had received a lemon. But he continued to think longingly about his old plane.

The 12th of August was a fine summer day, with good visibility. Around forty-seven tons of bombs were dropped, with about half of that total being delivered at night. The enemy air force was active all along the battle front during the morning, but particularly on the 2nd Brigade front.[117] This was the day that the Battle of Amiens ended in an Allied victory. In spite of all this activity, however, No. 24 Squadron does not seem at first to have been active. Lambert's log book records no flights.

In *Combat Report*, however, Lambert writes that C Flight went on offensive patrol from 2:00 p.m. to 4:00 p.m. over Rosiéres. He describes seeing Allied airplanes filling the sky above and below their position. They saw no enemy aircraft and "enjoyed the scenery and the bright sun."[118] It was more like a joy ride than an offensive patrol, which is probably why Lambert did not bother recording it in his log.

Lambert also found time to discuss the use of parachutes by German pilots. News had reached No. 24 that No. 29 Squadron had seen a German pilot jump out of his plane and float to earth, using a parachute. Lambert remarked that over the past couple of weeks they had heard about the Germans using parachutes, but no one had seen it yet; now there was confirmation. He was critical of the Allied High Command for not adopting this invention: "The lives of many of our men could have been saved…. U.S. air services did not accept that life saver until 1921."[119] Lambert would not see a parachute in action until he returned to Ohio in 1919; then he saw a number of parachute jumps at McCook Field in Dayton.[120]

On 13 August, the weather was good and the enemy was active, even in the air, but No. 24 was spared any difficult operations. Lambert even remarked that they had it easy. In *Combat Report* he stated that C Flight went on an offensive patrol after 1:00 p.m. over Bray and returned to Conteville around 3:00 p.m.; however, this flight is not recorded in his log book.[121] Like the other flight which was not recorded in his log book, this one was a joy ride compared to the usual offensive flight. Not only were there no enemy aircraft seen on this patrol, but Lambert, circling at 15,000 feet, only saw a few burst of antiaircraft fire.[122] B8395's engine was not performing well, so he knew that he would have to work on it after his return to base.

After the flight, Lambert talked with his crew about the engine problems he had encountered. He wanted them to take a look at the plane before taking it out for a test flight. They did fix the problem, and Lambert took the plane out for twenty-five minutes, testing his engine at 2,000 feet.[123] (This flight is recorded in his log book.)

The success of the Allied offensive finally disrupted the domestic comforts of Conteville. At dinner that evening, Robeson informed the squadron of how pleased the upper brass was with their performance and hard work over the past few weeks. The Germans were in retreat and had been driven back a significant distance by the Allied onslaught. Now, after almost six months, they would follow the moving front back to Bertangles. The reader will remember that when Lambert arrived, he was a novice pilot who was not allowed on combat patrols; consequently, he was assigned to ferry planes farther west from Bertangles before the onslaught of Operation Michael, the German Spring Offensive in March 1918. Now the tide had turned: Lambert, now a seasoned veteran, was returning to Bertangles with the Germans on the run. There they would be closer to the front and so save quantities of gas. The move would take place on the 14th.

The plan was that the flights would fly their airplanes to Bertangles in the early afternoon, with the ground crews disassembling things in the morning and reassembling them in Bertangles by the evening. Lambert, of course, wanted to make sure that "Buckingham Palace" was not left behind, so he hunted down South to make sure it would be sent to their new location. Lambert was nostalgic for Conteville as he left it: "That orchard had given us relaxation and pleasure since March. That place seemed like a second home to me."[124]

For Lambert, Bertangles had one big advantage and one major disadvantage. The advantage was that it was only ten miles away from Amiens, a large city with great possibilities. The disadvantage was that it was a prime target for German bombing raids.[125] Bertangles was a large base; No. 24 would be sharing with at least six other squadrons: two additional S.E.5 squadrons; two Camel squadrons including No. 209; a Bristol squadron, No. 48; and No. 3 Squadron, made up of Spads and Dolphins.[126] It is easy to understand why it was such an inviting target.

The 14th was another fine day, though with some haze. The bombing offensive continued with even greater intensity; over thirty-seven tons of bombs were dropped at night, with an additional twenty-two and one-half tons in daylight. The enemy was not as active in the sky as they had been over the past few days.[127] Douglas Haig, Commander-in-Chief of the British Expeditionary Force, informed Foch that over the past forty-eight hours the German artillery had increased considerably along the front of the British Fourth and French First armies. Haig wanted to delay an operation scheduled for the 16th until there was sufficient artillery support. He also wanted to change the area of attack from that south of the Somme and use an indirect approach by the British Third Army and attack north of the Andre in a southwesterly direction. After careful consideration, Foch came around to Haig's idea and changed the plan of attack. He recognized that the enemy had been able to put together and solidify a resistance, using its old (1916) defensive fortification on the Somme.[128] The Allies wanted to keep the pressure on the Germans on all fronts without giving them a respite. Foch would continue to unleash "a series of connected punches at sensitive spots" so a considerable section of the front would be in a constant state of flux.[129]

No. 24 had other ideas on its mind. Everyone was up early for the big move, but the flights would also continue to canvas the sky for the enemy. C Flight joined A Flight on a joint patrol at 7:00 a.m. Remarkably, even before they took off, the ground crews had already dismantled C and B Flights hangers and were loading them on trucks for the trip to Bertangles. The move was on schedule, and those fixtures would be set up at the new field by nightfall. Lambert had already packed his gear and given it to South so that it would be at the new base when he arrived there later in the day. For now, he had a patrol to fly.

The joint flight rendezvoused over Bertangles and then traveled to the Foucaucourt-Estrees area. The fact that they had to rendezvous over Bertangles shows why the move was being made. In the future, they would eliminate this extra time spent traveling. On this last patrol from Conteville, C flight would follow A in a protective screen as they looked for the enemy.[130] On their way past Bertangles, the joint flight was assailed with antiaircraft fire as they ventured farther into German territory. When the flak disappeared, Lambert and the others knew that enemy aircraft were near. He was not disappointed, for they spotted twenty, most of them Fokker D. VIIs along with some Albatros D.V.s, a couple of miles to the north and about 1,000 feet above their present position. Lambert noticed from the colorful exterior of the D.VIIs that they were from the same squadron that C Flight had faced a few days before. A seasoned veteran like Lambert acutely remembered these characteristics. Following Hazell's lead, the joint patrol maneuvered its planes so that they would be level with the attacking enemy when the two met for battle.

As the two forces collided in combat, Lambert remarked that he could hear some of the guns even over the roar of his engine.[131] He quickly found himself close on the tail of a Fokker when bullets hit the top right wing of his plane. Immediately turning to see where the attack came from, he saw an Albatros around 150 yards away shooting at him from behind. He immediately went into evasive maneuvers, but was saved from any further problems when he witnessed the Albatros accelerating nose down with one of his comrades on its tail, firing both his guns from a distance of about fifty yards.[132] The fight was on, and Lambert was once again in the center of things.

As he avoided the Albatros, Lambert noticed a S.E.5 being pursued by a Fokker that was closing quickly on its tail. Almost instantaneously, Lambert pushed B8395 into position and got the attacking flier in his Aldis sight. He maneuvered his plane within acceptable range and opened fire with both his guns. He believed some of the tracers may have hit the enemy plane, but at least if it did not go down, he had driven it off the tail of the S.E.5.[133] There were many times, as we have seen, when Lambert was saved during an attack by the timely arrival of a comrade to distract and drive the enemy off. The recent scrape with the Albatros was just one example. He was just returning the favor to a comrade in need.

C Flight was still fighting above A, but the momentum of these dogfights pushed the two flights closer together. Eventually, Lambert and the other members of C Flight found themselves near where Hazell and A Flight were operating. But just as the struggle was heating up, the enemy planes made an abrupt withdraw. This action made no sense until Lambert suddenly noticed that about twenty Camels had joined the fracas and were diving on the Germans from above. As we have seen, the Germans avoided battles with stronger numbers, since they would certainly suffer casualties they could not afford. With the Camels' arrival, the odds were too great for the Germans to stick around.

With the battle over, Hazell led A Flight in a northwesterly turn to begin the trip back to Conteville, with C Flight close behind them. They landed at around 9:05 a.m. The place already looked deserted, since—as has been said—the hangers had all been shipped on to Bertangles. However, Lambert's mechanics were still around to help patch up holes in his machine and replace the rudder that, unknown to him, was damaged beyond repair. Lambert had heard and felt bullets during the attack, but was unaware of the damage to his rudder until he landed. Apparently the attacking Albatros had been a better shot than Lambert had realized, and the timely arrival of the Camels had been of great though unrealized benefit to him. For this encounter, the squadron gave the joint patrol credit of one decisive and three indecisive, though Lambert remarked that they would not receive any credit from the R.A.F.'s "Higher Authority."[134]

Lambert had let his crew know that he needed the repairs done to B8395 before he left for Bertangles after lunch. Unfortunately, given the damage that had been done to the rudder, it could not be ready in time. Lambert would fly another plane, No. 4022, to Bertangles. An American, Lieutenant J. A. Rorison, recently of No. 85 Squadron, would fly Lambert's plane when the crew had finished with the repairs. He had been assigned to B Flight, which was currently on patrol. Once the flight had returned to Conteville, he would bring B8395 to the new base with the rest of his flight. "Buckingham Palace" was still assembled, so Lambert managed to grab a few toilet articles to take with him on the journey to his new base. He did not want to get caught without them in case he would be downed behind enemy lines.

While waiting around for lunch, Lambert and the rest of his comrades became nostalgic over their old home. "We all sat around, taking our last look at this paradise that had been our home since March. I believe that everyone feels as badly about this as I do."[135] In fact, Lambert called their stay at Conteville "a wonderful vacation here in this orchard."[136] "Paradise" and "a wonderful vacation" seemed to be an unusual way of referring to a place near the front in wartime, but we must remember that they were not only moving from a familiar place to an unfamiliar one, but also from a place of safety to one that might well not be so safe. Conteville had never been the target of bombing all during the time Lambert had been there. There was no certainty that Bertangles would be safe from bombing.

At 2:00 p.m., Lambert flew No. 4022 down with A and C Flights to Bertangles. It was a brief (twenty minute) flight to their new home.[137] There were so many squadrons there that they had to be shown where No. 24 was stationed, about one-half mile across the field from the other squadrons. After they arrived, South was able to take Lambert to "Buckingham Palace," now assembled. He was pleasantly surprised to find his personal effects placed where they had been the last time he was in the hut. Normalcy seemed to have been maintained. It made the transition to Bertangles that much easier. Their hangers were situated near a grove of trees, and they were appreciative of the shade these trees gave. South, the industrious mess sergeant, had outdone himself and more than fulfilled Major Robeson's orders.

Now they were all on their way to Amiens for dinner. (The kitchen and mess would not be ready until much later that evening, so only late arrivals could have dinner on base.) Before they left, Lambert wanted to take B8395 out to get a feel of the area around Bertangles. Rorison had brought it in without any difficulties, so it was ready for Lambert to put it through its paces. However, he made sure he would be back on base before the squadron left for Amiens at 7:00 p.m. After dinner and a quick tour of the city, including the famed Cathedral of Amiens, the squadron was back at Bertangles and in bed by 10:30 p.m.[138] The move had been exhausting, and there was still a war waiting to be fought in the morning.

On 15 August, the squadron was set to begin its first patrols from its new home. The weather was agreeable, and the bombing campaign against the Germans continued unabated. Almost forty-two tons of bombs were dropped throughout the day on German positions. The number of bombs dropped per day had steadily increased as the war continued. It was also reported that very few members of the German Air Force were seen in the sky on that day.[139]

According to Lambert, No. 24 was not very active, either. Most of what action there was again tactical ground support. Lambert's log has him once again dealing with a "Dud engine."[140] His B8395 was simply not yet at the level of his old reliable C1084. With the amount of activity he was faced with on the front, he did not have the time to make the adjustments that he did on C1084. He had had similar engine and gun problems in the beginning on that plane, but he had labored on it long and hard to get the plane exactly the way he wanted it. Now, he was turning his plane over to his trusted crew with greater frequency in order to get it ready for the next flight. Time, the stress of ground support missions, and the extra stress of multiple missions—all were sapping Lambert's strength. On his first day at the new base, he watched the other squadrons across the field get ready for flight. "What a pleasure it is to watch someone else work…. We watch a flight of Bristols and Camels go out together. A pleasant sight as long as we are not in it."[141]

The squadron tried to maintain as much consistency as possible with their move to Bertangles. Consistency was necessary for morale and performance. Lambert remarked that there was practically no change from Conteville, except that they were now closer to the front and could now hear the German heavy guns in the east. He knew that they would get used to the noise after a while. Moreover, No. 24 would be making visits to the site of these guns in the not—too—distant future, and these attacks should result in these guns being moved considerably farther east.[142]

At around 5:00 p.m. on 15 August, C Flight would join A Flight on an offensive patrol between Rosiéres and Chaulnes. By the time they reached the target area, however, B8395 had become too erratic to continue its mission. Lambert had noticed that he was experiencing engine problems before they reached the location: the plane was sluggish and not holding its "revs." It had had ignition troubles in the past, but now Lambert thought the problem was with the valves; one or two of the exhausts on the values might be open. The tachometer was

Nine. Return to the War

registering around 1,400 to 1,500 R.P.M.s. Lambert was frustrated. What made the situation particularly dangerous was the heavy antiaircraft fire they were experiencing at that moment. The necessary evasive movements further exposed B8395's vulnerability, so when he was at about 10,000 feet, Lambert moved next to Selwyn and notified him that he was returning to Bertangles. He landed around 6:00 p.m. and immediately had his crew examine the engine to find why it was losing power. When the flight finally returned at 7:00 p.m., Lambert learned of Haigh's death. Since they had not seen any enemy aircraft, antiaircraft fire must have scored a direct hit on the novice pilot.[143]

By this time, the German High Command already feared defeat before the year was over. Ironically, on 16 August, while American troops landed in Vladivostok, Lloyd George was preparing a memorandum for the Dominion Prime Ministers in which he established the case for delaying a decisive offensive on the Western Front until 1920.[144] Pessimism abounded on both sides in August 1918. Victory still had to be won on the battlefield. On this day, the weather continued clear over the front. The German aircraft were active over the morning hour, but outside of that time, the skies were rather quiet. However, the Allied bombing campaign continued unabated, with over eleven and one-half tons of bombs dropped at night and over twenty-one in daylight.[145]

Once again, No. 24's action was rather limited on this day. One indecisive is recorded in the early afternoon, an Albatros two-seater, by Lieutenant W. C. Stirling of A Flight. Other areas of the front saw far more action. For example, Lambert reported on a bombing raid that had taken place twenty miles behind the lines near the railroad station at the Haubourdin Aerodrome. It was a raid involving four squadrons, two from the Australian Flying Corps, and sixty-five aircraft. All told, they dropped 136 of the twenty-five-pound bombs and six of the forty-pound bombs during the raid. They destroyed three large hangers filled with airplanes and some additional ones on the field, along with a variety of huts, an officers' mess, and other ancillary buildings.

C Flight did fly an offensive patrol from 10:15 a.m. to 12:20 p.m. at around 13,000 feet in the area around Cappy, but Lambert referred to this flight as a "joy ride" with only limited interruptions by antiaircraft fire. He recorded that enemy aircraft were seen, but retired to the east without engaging.[146] For his own part, Lambert was pleased that his crew had discovered and replaced two badly burned exhaust values in B8395. The plane performed well in this late morning flight, so he was hopeful that the problems plaguing it were finally solved.

On 17 August, the weather was good in the morning, becoming overcast in the afternoon. The bombing raids continued, with twenty and one-half tons being dropped in the evening and an additional thirteen and one-half tons dropped during daylight. The raids on aerodromes continued with an attack on the Lomme Aerodrome. As with the attack on Haubourdin the day before, four squadrons, including two from the Australian Air Force, went on this raid. The defenses around Lomme were stronger than those at Haubourdin, so the raid was not nearly as successful. One plane was lost, but 104 of the twenty-five-pound bombs were dropped, along with two of the forty-pounders. As with the Haubourdin raid, machines were damaged and direct hits were made on hangers, workshops, and huts. The extent of the damage was seen by the photographs taken during the raid. Lambert remarked, "Those boys up north are really pounding the Germans."[147]

No 24, however, was having another relatively easy day. C Flight made an offensive patrol from 2:00 p.m. to 4:00 p.m. Again, they did not see any enemy aircraft, but this time they experience some heavy antiaircraft fire.[148] Lambert tells the reader nothing more about this day.

The next day, 18 August, was treated very differently. It was not be a busy day for the squadron, but it was an important one for Lambert: it was his birthday. He lists his age as twenty-three, but he was in fact twenty-four. On this day he confidently expected to live to be a hundred. In fact, he reckons that in 1918 he had seventy-seven more years to go. He made this boast—that he would live to be a hundred—numerous times when writing *Combat Report* and when giving interviews in the 1970s and 1980s. He wanted to host a birthday party at the U.S. Air Force Museum in Dayton to celebrate the event. He got close to his goal, but ultimately fell short of it.

On this birthday, the weather was bad—low clouds and high winds. There was no night bombing, and only one and one-half tons were dropped during the day. Activity was limited on both sides. According to Lambert, "every squadron at Bertangles did practically nothing today."[149] A Flight was involved in a "special mission" during which Hazell shot down a two-seater in flames. Lambert had time to enjoy his birthday. He took the opportunity to visit the other squadrons, including No. 84, around Bertangles. He once again met with Alec Matthews from Lewisburg, West Virginia, whom he had met earlier in the summer. Lambert and Matthews spent their time talking about their homes back in Ohio and West Virginia. Matthews hospitably treated Lambert to lunch at his squadron's mess.[150] They planned to meet again to talk over old times after the war, if not sooner, but unfortunately Matthews did not survive the war.

On the next day, 19 August, the weather improved to fair, if somewhat cloudy. It was enough improved for the bombing to resume, with fourteen and one-half tons being dropped at night and almost seventeen tons during the day. As had been the case before, the German Air Force was active in the morning hours, but seemingly absent from the sky later in the day.[151] The Germans were trying to halt Allied offensive activity before it got started, and they considered that the Allies were more likely to launch an attack before dawn than in the afternoon.

On this day, No. 24 Squadron would see more action than it had since arriving at Bertangles. C Flight would go on an offensive patrol at 10:15 a.m. over Fresnoy in north-central France. (Fresnoy was three miles northeast of Roye and about six miles southwest of Nesle.) They would be operating at around 18,000 feet, one of the highest altitudes Lambert had ever been on during a patrol. They had been patrolling this area for about a half an hour when they encountered five Fokker D. VIIs, painted in multifarious colors, that were slightly above them and actually willing to do battle. The Fokkers attacked in two layers; three came down to do battle, while two remained above in case of an Allied ruse. (The reader will remember that when on joint patrol, Lambert and his fellow pilots followed the same plan, with one flight below and the other above.)

For Lambert, the two members of the protective screen attracted his attention. He was going at it alone. (It was one of those times he could have used Daley.) He was trying to prevent these two from joining the fracas below at an opportune time that would off-set the odds in their favor.[152] So, while Selwyn, Bair, Hellett, Wren, and Harries busied themselves with the three remaining Fokkers, Lambert showed initiative and courage by going after these two by himself.

The three Fokkers involved in the conflict below Lambert were all destroyed. Three decisive victories were recorded in the squadron history, one each to Selwyn, Bair, and Harries, though none of the three are recognized in the official communiqué. (In reporting this combat, Lambert used the Squadron report, as he had no time to observe the action.)

While the two forces were engaged below, Lambert above saw that the two Fokkers were separated from each other by about one-half mile. This separation gave him the opportunity to focus on one of these planes without the immediate risk of being attacked by the other. So he moved slightly above and to the south of the closest Fokker. Evidently the two German pilots were focused so intently on the action below that they did not notice Lambert's presence. It was an ideal situation for Lambert. Unfortunately, Lambert committed a classic blunder: he fired at the plane from too great a distance, around a hundred yards away. He succeeded only in alerting the enemy pilots to his presence. Now, instead of having a surprise attack and perhaps an easy victory, Lambert was engaged in a ferocious struggle as the Fokker performed an evasive roll and began to come down at Lambert, firing both of its machine-guns. Reacting quickly, Lambert went down full-throttle, then into a wide loop followed by a sharp left turn. This action put him slightly above the Fokker while traveling in the same direction. He was unable to fire at the Fokker, but at the same time he was also out of the range of the Fokker's guns. The two planes maneuvered and counter-maneuver for the best striking position as they descended to around 13,000 to 14,000 feet. Luckily for Lambert, he was aided by the arrival of two Dolphins who attacked the second Fokker.[153] Comrades from another squadron had rescued him from a potentially dangerous situation. There were times that Lambert seemed to live a charmed life, and this was one of them.

Lambert was now free to concentrate on his own private battle. The Fokker was now as much as 400 yards away and making his escape to the east as Lambert throttled down to accelerate the chase. Lambert closed the gap because he had the distinct advantage of being above and behind his opponent. This position allowed him to make up distance even though the two planes were going at almost identical speeds (170 miles per hour). In his attempt to escape, the German pilot turned to see Lambert approach. Seeing that turn, Lambert knew he had the advantage. He closed to within fifty yards and then put the Fokker squarely in his Aldis sight. At this point, Lambert was able to fire only ten rounds from both guns, but they were enough to bring the Fokker down. He watched as it hit the ground west of Nesle. It was 11:59 a.m., and Lambert was at about 6,000 feet, or 12,000 feet lower than when the dogfight began.[154] It had been a well-fought battle. After his initial error, Lambert had out-maneuvered and out-attacked the Fokker. This victory was his twenty-second and would be the last one he would earn in the war.

When Lambert finally got his bearings, he finally realized he was alone, separated from all the rest of the flight, and that he was also low on fuel—low enough that he would probably not have enough to return to Bertangles. A quick check of his emergency tank revealed only a limited amount of fuel, so he had to begin his return voyage with the knowledge he would need to find a friendly field to procure the gas necessary for his return. Fortune again smiled on Lambert, for, as he headed northwest in the direction of home, he saw two Dolphins of No. 23 Squadron and a French Spad. He recognized the markings on the Dolphins and knew their origin. Knowing that there was safety in numbers, Lambert followed these three planes back to the French aerodrome to get the assistance he needed. Once he was safely on his way to land, the Dolphins turned north to head back to their base. Switching to his emergency tank, Lambert followed the French pilot down and landed behind the Spad at around 12:25 p.m.

Lambert did not understand French, but he was able to make them aware of his needs. They refueled B8395 and treat him to a delicious lunch in their officers' mess. Lambert was impressed with these officers' accommodations. "Boy! Do these Frenchmen live in luxury?"[155]

After a brief but enjoyable stay at the French aerodrome, Lambert left at around 2:25 p.m. It was a short uneventful flight back to Bertangles. He landed just before 3:00 p.m.; the rest of his flight had been there for some time. They had broken off the fight with enough fuel to make it back to base while Lambert was chasing down his Fokker. Lambert had made a second mistake by not paying attention to his fuel gage.

Now that he was safely on the ground and at his home base, Lambert gave his report to his orderly so it could be given to Captain Lawson. The last entry in his log book records the flight from the French Aerodrome lasting only twenty minutes at a height of 2,000 feet.[156] This short flight would be his last flight of the war. Lambert's world changed after this flight. He wrote, "From here on for the next couple of months, events are very fuzzy and in some cases, a complete blank. I do not know what happened to me."[157]

Ten

Leaving the War

What happened to Lambert was that he had suffered what we would now call a nervous breakdown. This breakdown was only one symptom, though the most immediately disturbing one, of his condition, which we would now call Post-Traumatic Stress Disorder (PTSD). This term was not known at the time, but the condition was known and recognized. It was called "shell shock" or "battle fatigue" (sometimes "combat fatigue"). Another symptom of PTSD, which lasted far longer than the nervous breakdown, was his inability to sleep because of nightmares in which he was back in battle and in great danger. And a third result of the condition was a complete personality change, in which Lambert went from a social, confident man, anxious to try new experiences, able to get along with almost anyone, to—in his old age—an antisocial person, fearful of trying anything new, and increasingly isolated.

We need to look, first, at Lambert's few memories from the period of the nervous breakdown. Then we need to consider why Lambert was so reluctant, all his life, to say what had happened to him. He freely discussed a physical problem that he had at the same time—a ruptured eardrum—but he was very reluctant to discuss the mental problem that he obviously had. He had good reasons for this reluctance, and we need to see what they were.

The last entry in Lambert's log book was written on 19 August. The squadron history has his last day in C Flight as 21 August. His official records show him admitted to hospital on 21 August.[1] It was evidently apparent to everyone when Lambert last landed at Bertangles both that he was disoriented and that he had blood in his ears. Even though Lambert wrote that his memory of this period was "almost a total blank" until 1 October 1918, he disputed the official date of his leaving the squadron, because he had vague memories of an attack on No. 48 Squadron at Bertangles that took place after dinner on the 24th. The attack did take place on that day, and Lambert recalled at the time of the attack he was dining with Robeson at No. 46 Squadron, and that a concert was in progress at No. 48. The concert room was one that did not sustain any damage from the bombing, but it was severely damaged by machine-gun fire. There were about fifty casualties from this attack. Lambert could very well have still been at Bertangles while waiting for the paper work to arrange his transportation to England, but no doubt Robeson, Selwyn, and the medical staff had already determined by the 21st that Lambert's flying days were over. The squadron history lists two replacements arriving to C Flight during the week of Lambert's last flight. Lambert was replaced by either Lieutenant W. G. C. Geraghty, who arrived on the 18th, or Lieutenant J. T. Menzies, who was posted to the flight on the 22nd.[2] Replacements had finally arrived to give members of C Flight a rest, but it was not the way Lambert had envisioned.

He has some memories after that, but what he was able to recall from the time he left No. 24 Squadron were bits and pieces of events that attest to his serious mental collapse. One of these memories is watching someone load his personal gear on a tender, but Lambert had no idea who this person was or where he was going. He also remembered swimming with another pilot on a beach. After he had returned from his swim, a small dog, which he described as a "French bull dog," had defecated on his towel. He recollected seeing a large building on a bluff overlooking the sandy beach. A nurse watched over them as they swam and then took them back to what had previously been a resort hotel, but had been turned into a hospital. It was only then that Lambert and his fellow pilot realized they were patients at the hospital. Lambert remembered the day as either 28 or 29 August.³

According to the records, he was already in England. Lambert, however, was certain that he was in a British Base Hospital at this time. He thought that the town where the hospital was might have been Wimereux, near Boulogne.⁴ In fact, there was a major hospital which dealt with "mental cases," at Wimereux. It was "one of the largest and busiest mental hospitals in France."⁵

Lambert's stay in France cannot be verified because of the destruction of documents, but he is probably correct. The established medical procedure at that time was to take an injured soldier just off the battlefield to the regimental medical officer, usually found at the Regimental Aid Post. The medical decision at this post dictated whether the soldier was sent to the Advanced Dressing Station, a Base Hospital or evacuated to Britain.⁶ However, the events of the war also affected where soldiers would be treated. For example, the introduction of unrestricted submarine warfare restricted the movement of transports across the Channel, so more soldiers were treated in France.⁷ It is entirely possible that Lambert was sent to Wimereux and designated for Britain later. At Wimereux, he would have been on the coast and under the care of a medical staff where nurses could have been assigned to him and even taken him to the beach for a swim.

After his swimming on the beach, Lambert's next memory is walking around the deck of a Channel boat with his fellow pilot-patient and their nurse on a bright sunny day. Afterward, he recollected, but was not sure, that he might have spent the entire month of September 1918 in a London hospital. This hospital was undoubtedly Queen Alexandra's Hospital.

Lambert had two vivid memories of his stay in this hospital. He remembered these events because they were both painful and shocking to him, and he could not forget them even after fifty years. The first memory was a procedure two doctors performed on him in order to help heal his ruptured eardrums. Today it sounds like a version of medieval torture. Lambert recalls them putting a "flexible wire looking contraption," about a foot long, which was attached to an electrical cord, through one of his nostrils to a section of his ear. When they were done, the doctors would repeat the procedure through the other nostril. Lambert emphasized the unpleasantness of this treatment, which was repeated every second or third day for a couple of weeks.⁸

The second memory was of an injured pilot whose leg was attached to pulleys and ropes, but was "bare from the hip down to about mid-way between the knee and ankle."⁹ The condition of that pilot's leg was horrendous, and it was devastating to Lambert to look at the injury. He remembered, "At one place, I could see the bare bone."¹⁰ He believed the pilot was an American, but the young man was never awake, so Lambert never spoke to him. To show the effect of this young man's injury on him, Lambert put a request in *Combat Report* to this person to contact him if he was still alive, if he had survived his injuries.[11] For the rest of his life, to Lambert this pilot was still the young man he saw in the hospital in 1918. He never got over that sight.

Ruptured eardrums were a common problem with pilots in the Great War. Like Lambert, Rickenbacker spent time in hospital recovering from the strain flying had had on his ears.[12] The eardrum is simply a tiny membrane located inside the ear canal. A ruptured eardrum is a tear or hole in this membrane. The most common cause of ruptured eardrum is sudden pressure changes, and constant changes in altitude and therefore pressure that a combat pilot experienced could cause a severe rupture.[13] For example, during his last flight, Lambert was active around 18,000 feet before he ascended to attack the two Fokkers. While he was engaged in a dogfight with a Fokker D. VII, he rapidly descended to around 13,000 to 14,000 feet. When he shot the Fokker down he was at 6,000 feet, or 12,000 feet below where he started. These maneuvers took place over a brief stretch of time; Lambert's body did not have time to adjust to the different changes in pressure.

Consider the physical effects these pressure changes had on Lambert. A person at sea level will have 20.9 percent oxygen level in the air. "At 18,000 feet ... there is 52% of the oxygen available at sea level."[14] As Lambert rose to meet the two Fokkers, he may have gone above 19,000 feet, or the equivalent of being on the summit of Mt. Kilimanjaro without an oxygen mask. The pressure on his body would have been immense. His oxygen level would have been at 10.1 percent, or less than fifty percent of the oxygen available at sea level. These were not unusual conditions for Lambert; they were conditions he might face whenever he went out on offensive patrol. Lambert had also adjusted his dihedral so his plane would have the ability to climb faster and higher. He told an interviewer that he "got up to twenty-five thousand feet before I fell off one time."[15] When climbers scale a high mountain, they will take the time to adjust to their new altitude. Great War pilots did not have that luxury.

The ruptured eardrums, then were a real and serious problem, but they were curable, and the doctors at the time knew how to cure them. The same could not be said of Lambert's other problem. In a newspaper article written in 1968, Lambert told the reporter that after returning from his last flight, he began to bleed from only one ear. After that, everything was hazy. He was sent to a hospital in France and then London, but he was "in a coma most of the time."[16] The reporter wrote that it was "the extreme changes in altitude he was constantly subjected to which caused his illness."[17] The "extreme changes in altitude" certainly caused the ruptured ear drum, and that in turn would cause the bleeding from the ear, and the lack of oxygen would make a person disorientated for a short time. But the pressure changes would not have caused a coma lasting a month. Another article, "Colonel Lambert Still Flying Legend," from 1980, gives a truer picture: "his [Lambert's] war career ended in 1918, when he was hospitalized with combat fatigue and a ruptured eardrum."[18]

Over the years, Lambert willingly discussed the physical reason he was sent to the hospital, but not the mental reason. The cause for his reluctance is not far to seek. Lambert's condition is what we would now call Post-Traumatic Stress Disorder (PTSD). There was no such term at the time. The condition was known—in fact, there were many patients with PTSD—but it had different names: "combat fatigue" at first, and later and more commonly "shell shock." Everyone could understand that being subjected to the constant pounding of shells—the hideous noise, the constant fear, the stink of death all around—could cause someone to break. It was far more difficult for most to understand how the stress associated with aerial battle—the constant presence of unexpected danger, the ever-present fear of death, and the overuse of alcohol to give the pilot some temporary relief from his tension—could lead to the same condition. Fellow war pilots would understand, but it was hard for civilians—including the medical establishment—to grasp the level of stress a pilot was under.

The popular term for Lambert's condition had by 1918 been replaced in the medical lexicon by *neurasthenia*.[19] At first glance, this term seems like the correct one. Among the symptoms of neurasthenia was chronic fatigue and sleep disturbances, usually connected to depression. The problem was that most people, including most doctors, equated neurasthenia to weakness of nerves and weakness of will. They thought it was a condition that the patients had always had; the stress of war simply brought it out, it did not cause it.

Since the condition itself was misunderstood, it followed that the treatment was usually ineffective. The inventor of this treatment was Silas Weir Mitchell. While working as a medic during the American Civil War, he had confronted with a large number of cases of what would now be considered PTSD among soldiers. The future physician considered all these cases neurasthenia and developed what became the standard cure for neurasthenia. He prescribed seclusion, massage, electricity, and immobility, along with a restricted diet. His diagnostic label and method of treatment were adopted by doctors on both sides of the Atlantic, and his treatment became the standard and inexpensive way to treat "shell shock." It usually did not work; it almost never brought about a complete cure.[20]

Early on in the war, the medical profession could hardly cope with the mental cases that came to their attention, particularly with the overwhelming number of physical casualties that they had to deal with. Consequently, many of those soldiers suffering from PTSD were simply returned to the front, because of the doctors' realization that there was nothing that could be done for them. When treatment was attempted, it was irregular, uncoordinated, and disconnected. A patient could find himself in a hospital for a couple of days or months.[21] Each stricken soldier turned out to be a separate case. The term "shell shock" began to be used because it was observed that when several soldiers came back from the front with the same condition, the only thing they seemed to have in common to explain their conditions was that they were all suffering from the after-effects of shelling. But the shelling, of course, could have been simply the last event in a long-running series of causes.

Fortunately for Lambert, by the time he entered hospital treatment had improved. It was also fortunate that he was an officer, because in such cases officers were viewed with more sympathy and less suspicion than enlisted men. Officers reporting the same effects of "shell shock" were believed; enlisted men reporting exactly the same effects were regarded as malingerers, trying to escape from their military duties. However, it is still true that the understanding of the effects of "shell shock" on soldiers was in its infancy, and the treatment, while well-intentioned, was not necessarily helpful.

We can now see why Lambert was so reluctant to talk about his "combat fatigue." He thought that most civilians would see it as weakness of will and weakness of nerve, and would pity him as someone who should never have been part of the war. Lambert knew that he had strong nerves and a strong will, and that he had done good service in war, and he did not want anyone to think otherwise.

Lambert's nervous breakdown and coma was gone in about a month. (We do not know if the treatment he got in the hospital did any good, or if simply not having the constant stress of combat was enough to cure him.) His PTSD, however, was not cured and his sufferings were genuine and long-lasting. As we will see, his barnstorming and especially the sexual encounters that went along with it were attempts to cope with his depression. Far later on in life, he was still having the nightmares that were flashbacks to battles in the air. And, as was said earlier and will be seen later on, his PTSD permanently changed his open, optimistic, social character to its opposite.

One further comment before continuing. This writer does not mean to scoff at or condemn the doctors at the time. They did as well as they could with what they knew. We need to remember that in the United States, it was not until veterans started returning from the Vietnam War that the nation as a whole was aware of PTSD. In England, it was not until 1986, four years after the Falkland Island War, that the Ministry of Defence in Great Britain recognized Post-Traumatic Stress Disorder as a legitimate medical condition.[22] And even if the condition has now been recognized, the number of homeless veterans still suffering from its effects shows us that we still do not know how to treat it.

In a little over a month, Lambert had been released from the hospital. The month-long stay was an indication that his injuries were serious, but not life-threatening. After his release, Lambert was given the standard three-month sick leave on Home Establishment and told to report to the Air Ministry for his next posting. He reported the next day and waited in line with several other pilots to be interviewed. When his turn came, Lambert was given the option of spending his sick leave in England or returning to Ohio, but told that his trip back home would come at his own expense. He chose to return to Ironton and procured the necessary papers for the journey.

Lambert was informed that he had to report back to the Air Ministry after the three months had elapsed. The war was still in progress. The Allies were now winning all along the line. The Germans continued to withdraw from the area north and south of La Bassée Canal. The British had recaptured Armentières, and the French occupied St. Quentin. Still, no one suspected that the Armistice was only a month away. Lambert was expected to return because it was thought that his service in the war would still be needed.

Lambert secured passage in the *Meleta*, a small, fast steamer that would take him to New York.[23] (The spelling of the ship's name is Lambert's, and he was probably mistaken. On 21 April 1917, the Canadian Pacific Line launched the S.S. *Melita*. Its maiden voyage was on 25 January 1918, from Liverpool to St. John, New Brunswick.[24] The correct spelling of the name is probably *Melita*.) His memory of this period of his life is uncertain, though not so bad as in his month of coma. (He wrote in *Barnstorming and Girls*, about a period even later than this one, that his "mind was still a blank, just as it had been since August, just as if I was flying through thick clouds."[25]) He may have shared a stateroom with another pilot who was wearing the new blue uniform of the service. (The R.A.F. had unified the R.F.C. and R.N.A.S. on 1 April. Now they had adopted a new blue uniform for their own separate identity from the Navy and Army.) He seemed to remember that this pilot was also from Ohio, but he could not remember his name.

It would have seemed natural to Lambert to look for a pilot to share the stateroom with. The reader will remember that while in London, he spent his time in company with other pilots, and that he had gravitated to other pilots when waiting for the train to take him to the coast and from it.

The Melita was transporting Canadian and American soldiers across the Atlantic, along with a large number of wounded and nurses to take care of them. Lambert might not be certain who he shared his stateroom with, but he clearly remembered that he and his roommate, whoever he was, took turns taking nurses to the room. According to Lambert, the ship's staterooms were always busy.[26] Sex always seemed to be on Lambert's mind, and sexual experiences were the highlights of every event and more clearly remembered than anything else.

The *Melita* was fast enough to travel the Atlantic Ocean without the protections of a convoy and escorts. The captain followed the appropriate zigzag pattern across the ocean and successfully avoided submarine contact until they were three days out of New York. At that point, a submarine and the *Melita* exchanged fire without doing damage to either vessel. Afterward, the *Melita* contacted the U.S. Navy by wireless and was escorted to Halifax or another Canadian port, probably St. John. There the ship unloaded the Canadian passengers. Once these had disembarked, it headed for New York, where it landed on either 7 or 8 of November.

Lambert was finally back in America. However, he was stopped at Customs and forced to pay an eight dollar entry duty. Since he was wearing a British uniform, he was listed as an alien. Even though he was an American, he had to pay to get back into his own country. Lambert was outraged by this incident. "That was a hell of a welcome," he wrote.[27] In fact, he would take the matter up with the U.S. Congress until he was reimbursed the $8. He did not care about the money; it was a matter of principle to him. He was in Washington, D.C., on 11 November when the Armistice was announced. The war and Lambert's combat service, were both over.

Eleven

Barnstorming Days

When Lambert came home from the war, he was, like many other veterans, at loose ends. He had spent his time being prepared for, and showing great skill and bravery in, his career as a fighter, and that career was now over. He was "nervous and very restless" from his PTSD, so he could not settle down to life in his own home town of Ironton, at least not yet. He still loved flying as long as the flying did not involve shooting, so he decided to become a barnstormer.

Barnstorming is a term with a complicated history. It first meant conducting a campaign for speaking tours in rural areas, making brief stops in many small towns. Then the word began to mean touring small towns and giving theatrical performances, often melodramas. The meaning that applies to Lambert in flying, especially stunt flying, in rural areas. Another meaning, for a professional or semi-pro athletic team, is to tour an area playing exhibition games. The likeness between all of these meanings, of course, is touring a rural area and showing that area something the people in the area would not otherwise experience.

American in 1919, the years Lambert began his barnstorming, was ripe for this experience. The overwhelming majority of Americans, particularly in rural areas, (and Ohio was still largely rural), had not even seen an airplane. Crowds of people would line up to pay for a ride. The arrival of a barnstormer became one of the most exciting events to happen in these places. For $25, Lambert and his partner "Dave" were offering them the opportunity to actually take a ride in an airplane. It was an entrepreneurial opportunity that presented itself in post-war America, and the two partners took full advantage of it before the market became saturated with other pilots undercutting them. (Lambert wrote that the marked was so saturated with barnstormers by the end of 1920 that a person could purchase a ride for as little as $5.)[1]

According to Lambert in his book *Barnstorming and Girls*, the impetus for his career in barnstorming came from another pilot, Edward "Eddie" Stinson, who later became famous as an airplane manufacturer, founder of the Stinson Aircraft Company. Shortly after Lambert's return to Ironton, Stinson, who was already famous both as a pilot and as a civilian instructor for the U.S. Air Service, was barnstorming in the Ironton area and landed a couple of JN4s at Hanging Rock. Lambert remembered seeing the plane fly over his home and hearing the OX-5 engine of the Curtiss Jenny. Someone told Stinson about Lambert, and he approached Lambert to go for a ride in one of his planes. (It was Lambert's first time flying a plane since he was sent to hospital on 18 August 1918.) Stinson wanted to see if what he had been told about Lambert being a notable war pilot was true, because he needed a new partner. He told

Lambert that his previous partner had quit on him and asked him (Lambert) to take his place. Lambert did carry a few passengers for him, but he finally turned down Stinson's offer and opted to go into barnstorming for himself.[2] He got the barnstorming bug from this brief experience, and he also saw the financial advantages of barnstorming.

The information we have on Lambert's barnstorming career comes from his book *Barnstorming and Girls*, but this book is not as reliable an account as is *Combat Report*, on his time in the Royal Air Force. Both books were written a long time after the events they describe, but in *Combat Report* Lambert had the advantage of having his log book to refresh his memory. He had no such advantage in writing *Barnstorming and Girls*, and as a consequence some of the dates and even some of the events described, are highly questionable. For example, the book supposedly ends in December 1919, but Lambert continued his barnstorming into 1920; and some of the details must come from this latter part of his barnstorming career, because he refers to both advantages and difficulties created by Prohibition, yet the law creating Prohibition, the Volstead Act, did not take effect until 16 January 1920.

Edward Stinson is one of the few people in *Barnstorming and Girls* who is given his real name. All of the women in the book, and most of the men, are given aliases. Even Lambert's partner gets the name "Dave." We know, however, what his real name was, from 1920 articles in the *Ironton Register* that give Lambert's partner's name as Lieutenant F. J. Buffington. There is also an advertisement in the paper that gives the company name, "The Rafusa Fliers" (from R.A.F. and U.S.A.), that Lambert and his partner used when they were barnstorming in 1919. The first article, "Trespassing on Pasture Land Caused Warrant," appeared on Monday, 24 May 1920. It stated that Captain Lambert of the Royal Flying Corps "was served with a warrant for arrest by Squire W. H. Neal's court Saturday afternoon."[3] Unable to find a landing plane, Lambert had landed his plane on ground rented by Henry Hall from the Lucas estate on the south side of town. Apparently, local citizens who had crowded onto the pasture to see the plane "had broken down the fence surrounding the lot and allowed several cows to wander off."[4] According to the article, Lambert had arrived on Saturday, 22 May, from Cincinnati with the "first airplane shipment of merchandise to the city." He had originally landed on the Barger field at Hanging Rock, but had to move his plane on Sunday because Clarke Barger was breaking ground to plant a crop. It was then he landed on Hall's pasture. However, "the situation was adjusted with but little difficulty by the aviator and his friends."[5] The article noted that Lambert received congratulations "on his merchandise delivery, the first accomplished by airplane."[6] Two weeks later, on Tuesday, 1 June, another article appeared in the *Register*, "New Airplane Arrives Here," that announces the arrival of Buffington from Cincinnati with a new airplane to join Lambert at the Flying Field at the County Infirmary. Apparently, Lambert had wrecked his plane on Saturday afternoon during a take-off at Beachwood Park Field.[7] Just two days later, on 3 June 1920, there is an advertisement in the paper announcing that "the Rafusa Flyers are now prepared to carry passengers for the remainder of the week."[8] Interested individuals were given a phone number to call for appointments or told to come directly to the Flying Field, because "the aviators will be here but a short time longer and you should not miss this opportunity to take a trip in the air in a new plane handled by skilled pilots."[9] It seemed certain that the "Dave" of the book is in fact Buffington. We can see from these articles what some of the dangers and misfortunes of barnstorming could be, as well as the way excited crowds welcomed the barnstormers, even toward the end of Lambert's barnstorming period.

Lambert had evidently decided on barnstorming before he ever met "Dave." He was going to Dayton because airplanes were there, and he might want to fly again. On his way to Dayton, he meets in Cincinnati a married woman he calls "Helen" and begins an affair with her. (The train from the Ironton station to Dayton would first go to Cincinnati before continuing on to Dayton.) However, he tells "Helen" he must leave her for a while and go to Dayton "about my airplane deal."[10] He meets "Dave" at a Dayton hotel. Lambert states that, after he became close friends with "Dave" in a short time, "Dave" suggests that the two of them go into business together and buy one of the surplus JN4s that the U.S government was selling.[11] Dave's log book showed that he had only had ten hours actual flying time, however, it would be Dave's father who would loan the money to purchase the JN4 and the spare parts that enabled them to go barnstorming.[12] It is doubtful that Lambert could have found the money himself to pay for a plane. The two partners were to pay Dave's father out of their barnstorming profits.

Until the weather improved in late February 1919, "Dave" and Lambert had to stay in the Cincinnati-Dayton area, giving rides to people in the local river communities. They named their venture *Rafusa Flyers,* after their service in both armies (R.A.F.–U.S.A.). At $25 for a five-minute or $75 for a half-hour flight over Cincinnati, they made plenty of money. Even though, by Lambert's account, they spent the money freely, entertaining women and having a good time, they made enough to reimburse Dave's father in a short time.

When the weather improved, Dave suggest that they travel down south following the Louisville and Nashville (L & N) Railroad, looking for fields near cities and towns to set up shop. Following the railroad was by no means the fastest way south, but it would insure that they did not get lost. This was a time before there were interstate highways, a time of unpaved roads. The railroad was the only reliable indicator of direction.

Lambert's and Dave's *modus operandi* as they traveled south was to land in the field of a local farmer and make arrangements to rent the space. Often, they were allowed to use the field free of cost. They would ingratiate themselves with the family offering them free rides in their planes. If possible, they would also negotiate meals and accommodations with the family. (Remember, these were also days before motels.) Afterward, they would go to the nearest town to purchase supplies, particularly oil and gasoline. While there, they would stop at the local newspaper office and offer staff members free rides in return for free publicity. At the field, they would take around twenty passengers a day until the market dried up, earning an average of $500 a day, excellent pay for the time. An extra-long ride could be accommodated at an additional cost. Such rides were desirable to the partners because they could use the opportunity to scope out additional landing fields as they worked their way south. They would often acquire additional funding by advertising a local bank or company on the side of the plane. At each stop, they would simply repaint the JN4 with another firm's name on it. The advertising alone generally brought in between $300 and $500.[13] Barnstorming was a lucrative enterprise for a while.

Lambert was in one way quite different from other barnstormers. He rarely did stunt flying—dangerous, death-defying aerial acts—to attract a crowd. It may have been his war experiences, where he was doing what would have been called "stunts" simply to escape from an enemy plane or to put himself in position to attack another that led him not to bother with such dangerous tricks. Lambert was a practical businessman and he realized quickly that selling rides was the best way to earn a profit from his venture. Another pilot, Roscoe

Turner, who began his barnstorming career shortly after Lambert, came to learn what Lambert already knew: stunting and dangerous tricks might attract large audiences, but it was selling rides that brought in the money.[14]

When Lambert and "Dave" got to the Lexington area, they happened to land in a field that belonged to an artillery captain who had been in France during the war and had worked on R.A.F. reconnaissance planes. His son, who Lambert called "Tom Blue Berry," became their mechanic. The son's background and qualifications for his job, according to *Barnstorming and Girls*, were that he had been a mechanic in the American Air Service, but had never made it overseas. In an interview with Robert Smith, however, Lambert said that the boy "had been out in France with a squadron, and he had mechanics training and ability. He knew that Curtiss airplane form stem to stern."[15] Lambert and "Dave" took "Tom Blue Berry" with them as they traveled south. His job was to help maintain the plane, sell tickets, and do other assigned duties. The two partners agreed to pay "Tom" ten percent of the take.[16]

Lambert, "Dave," and "Tom" went south as far as Atlanta, stopping on the way in such places as Jenkins and Ashland, Kentucky, and Athens, Tennessee. On one occasion, Lambert described visiting a local picture show in Athens and watching a Pathé newsreel that carried a story of a pilot carrying a passenger in a JN4 near Boston. Lambert immediately left the show and went to the theater manager to discuss his idea of making an advertising newsreel. He worked out a deal by which he would be paid a thousand dollars to shoot a newsreel featuring the local community and businesses of Athens, and also advertising his operation. The manager would arrange for a newsreel group from Atlanta, Georgia, to come to Athens, and Lambert would explain to them how they could take pictures from the air using a small hand camera. (His war experience in photography was an asset.) The manager and Lambert discussed ways to advertise the event so they would attract a large crowd, both at the airfield

Lambert barnstorming near Copper Hill, Tennessee, around Christmas 1919.

Eleven. Barnstorming Days 149

and downtown, to be featured in the newsreel. A local paper with a large circulation area would advertise the event, and the downtown area would have large banners. The entire community would be involved and excited over the prospect of being seen in the picture show. At first, the manager believed that Lambert's fee was "pretty steep," but he quickly realized the potential for Athens and his theater, so he agreed to Lambert's terms. The town would pay half, and the theater pay half, of Lambert's fees.[17] The selling point was that the newsreel would be shown at local area theaters, with both Athens and Lambert being the beneficiaries.

When time came to shoot the newsreel, Lambert, contrary to his habit, put on quite a show from the air both above the field and over the town. He performed loops and barrel rolls that were impressive—and dangerous for a Curtiss Jenny. Perhaps he should have used better judgment, but he was caught up in the moment. Undoubtedly, it made good film. Lambert believed that "at least 75% of the population of a ten mile radius" came out for the occasion.[18] It was another successful business venture. Lambert was able to see the film when he reached Atlanta in late November and contacted the newsreel crew about a showing.

While in Atlanta, Lambert was able to make a second newsreel featuring the Mack Sennett Bathing Beauties. (Mack Sennett was also famous for slapstick comedies starring the Keystone Kops.) The theater manager hired Lambert to have the girls throw leaflets advertising their show over Peachtree Street and downtown Atlanta. The newsreel captured the action. The girls were also pictured in their bathing suits grouped around Lambert's plane.[19] When Lambert later wrote *Barnstorming and Girls,* he featured one of these pictures on the front cover, and others were included inside the book—again showing Lambert's sense for advertising!

In Atlanta, Lambert and his team got probably their single biggest payment when a national company, Sherwin-Williams, hired them to advertise. The company wanted its name and slogan on the fuselage and lower wing of the plane, the company name on one wing and the slogan "We cover the earth" on the other. They wanted to purchase six weeks' worth of advertising. Lambert informed them that he and his team would not be in Atlanta that long, because they were returning to Dayton in late December. However, the company saw the advantage in advertising their paints all the way up to Dayton and paid accordingly.[20]

One of Lambert's experiences while barnstorming had nothing to do with barnstorming; it was completely different use of the airplane. While Lambert was in Lexington, two civil engineers hired Lambert to take pictures from the air that would help them with surveying part of the L & N Railroad from Kentucky through Tennessee. Lambert's training and experience in the war paid off again. These engineers understood the financial benefits, the savings on time and labor, in taking pictures from the air. Lambert later told Robert Smith that "they paid pretty heavy for that. I don't mean any peanuts; we got good money for that."[21] One would expect that Lambert would have followed up on this success by contacting other engineering firms to see if they wanted the same kind or other kinds of aerial photography, but as far as we know, he did not. He was evidently having too good of time barnstorming.

The second part of the title of Lambert's book, *and Girls,* explains why he was having such a good time that he called 1919 "one of the happiest years of my life."[22] When he returned to Ironton, Lambert, had what could certainly be called an unhealthy interest in sex. He was still suffering badly from PTSD, as he would to some degree for the rest of his life, and sex seemed to him to be the only respite he had from the painful memories. He wrote that he

Mack Sennett's bathing beauties. Stennett paid Lambert $500 to fly them (one at a time) down Peachtree Street past Five Points in Atlanta as a publicity stunt. This picture became the cover for Lambert's book *Barnstorming and Girls*.

felt that "home town life was wearing [him] down.... There was no freedom.... Women were my one real relaxation ... women were the only relaxation capable of taking my mind off those horrible days in France during the summer of 1918."[23] He would repeatedly state throughout the book that sex was the only thing that could let him deal with the terrible memories of the war. While barnstorming, Lambert wrote, he "did miss some of those terrible days in France, and, as I thought back on them, I found many that I dreaded to think about."[24] He went into barnstorming only partly for the money; the more important reason was that it was a way that he would meet a number of young, sexually available women.

The book was written after he had already finished *Combat Report* and the death of his wife in 1971. Her death may help to explain the heavy focus in his book on his sexual exploits during the year before he married her. It is doubtful that he would have published such a book if she were still living, particularly as he describes the two of them being in a *ménage à trois* with her best friend.[25] He warned his readers that he was not going to conceal his love affairs, so if they had problems with such details they should "lay the book aside; do not read it ... read the book at your discretion.... I could not have written it without combining girls with flying."[26] He also informed his audience that his first encounter with sex was when he was seven years old. Apparently a sixteen-year-old girl attempted to rape him. He did not know what she was attempting to do, and sexual intercourse with the young female did not take place. The most intriguing aspect of Lambert's remembrance of this attack was his questioning "What satisfaction could I have given her?"[27] His inability to perform sexually was a concern for him. This incident obviously bothered Lambert. It may have given him a feeling of sexual inadequacy, and his incessant desire for sex described in *Barnstorming and Girls* (and on leaves in *Combat Report*) might have been an attempt to overcome this feeling.

The book was published in 1980. Two of Lambert's best friends at the time, Bill Martin and Klaus Staerker, claimed, with few notable exceptions, Lambert rarely discussed his sexual exploits with them. They did not see Lambert as that kind of man, and they agreed that his personality—controlling, arrogant, and abrasive—would make him unattractive to women. Staerker thought that that part of the book was probably fictitious.[28] But, although they were certainly right about the Lambert they knew, they had not known the young Lambert, the romantic war pilot and barnstormer.

There are a number of comments by people that show us that the sexual attractiveness of barnstorming pilots was not a phenomenon confined to Lambert. Robert Higham, the publisher of *Barnstorming and Girls,* for Sunflower Press, wrote in his "Publisher's Foreword" to the book that it was a "lusty tale of a young hero, a new knight in shining armour with a D.F.C. to prove it, who returned home to a land where aeroplanes had rarely, if ever, been seen ... this book is a contribution, however lusty, to social, aviation and technological history, which tells a good deal about all three in the post-war exuberance of the summer of 1919 in rural mid–America."[29] Higham understood that "young love-starved widows and girls thought that he [Lambert] and his partner were their dreams come true.... The young men who became barnstormers were full of vim and vigour and knew that any moment might be their last, especially if they had flown in combat in France in World War I without a parachute. So they lived life to the full, as indeed did their sons in World War II, if in a more subdued way."[30] Higham had captured the allure of flying and barnstorming in the interwar period. The reviewers of *Aviation News* agreed with Higham. "The female population of the small communities they visited ... flocked to the field to see what it was all about.... The adventure and carefree attitude adopted by the barnstorming community comes through in almost every paragraph."[31] According to Martin Caidin, "The girls, the young girls with wide eyes and long lashes and bodies that were something to see beneath their thin summer cotton dresses, etched clearly in the wind ... well, they sort of took your mind off flying."[32]

In the nature of things, most of Lambert's sexual experiences were one-night stands. But there were two that were far longer affairs. One was the one with "Helen," already mentioned as someone Lambert met in Cincinnati and begun an affair with even before he went to Dayton and met "Dave" and bought a surplus Jenny to begin his barnstorming days. Later on, he flew back to Cincinnati to carry on the affair, and continued on to Dayton (with "Helen" along this time) to buy five more Jennies, along with spare parts, accessories, and spare motors.[33] No doubt he could use all of these, but it still seems that Lambert is in part manufacturing an excuse to see "Helen" again. There are times that he refers to "Helen" as "my wife," though the relationship does not stop him from shacking up with other women at every place he stops.

But then "Helen" died. Her death was unexpected, both for Lambert and the reader. Lambert never mentions any disease that she has had, or any other reason for her death. After "Helen" did not show up for a liaison in Cincinnati, Lambert gets the news of her death over the phone from a friend of hers. What we do know is his reaction: he was in shock for over a week. Of course, she may not have died. She may have decided that the relationship was going nowhere, or have heard that her husband would soon be coming home, and have broken it off for either reason or both. That might well have affected Lambert like a death, and a death would have been less of an insult to his male pride.

However, Lambert recovered from this blow. In August, he returned to Dayton with "Judie," who seems to have taken over "Helen's" place in his life. He showed "Judie" a good time in Dayton, which at the same time consolidating a business deal. As with "Helen," Lambert bestows on "Judie" the semi-official title of "my wife," even though the two are not married. But in December 1919, Lambert gave "Judie" a wedding ring. "Judie" even wing-walked, with Lambert at the controls of the JN4, during a celebration that took place at a small town twenty miles outside of Atlanta.[34] However, as with "Helen," Lambert continues to fornicate with other women at every stop he makes.

It is tempting to say that "Judie" is the name Lambert gives in the book to his actual wife-to-be, Chloe Ann, and it may be correct. However, if it is, Lambert has changed the facts in at least two important ways, perhaps to something he would have preferred to be true. The first is the matter of the wing-walking. Chloe Ann, in fact, was afraid of planes. She would never have wing-walked, or even flown with Lambert. She even made Lambert give up flying after a serious crash, and it was not until after he did that the two of them were married, in Ashland, Kentucky, on 29 December 1920.

Second, in his description of "Judie," Lambert said that she was a war widow with a son named "Danny." According to Lambert, "Danny" was given a free ride in Lambert's plane, and the two of them became instantly attached to each other. Like most young boys at the time, "Danny" was enthralled with planes and flight, as children in the 1960s would be with astronauts and space travel. The attraction of "Judie" to Lambert followed after that of "Danny" to him.

Chloe Ann did not have a son. She did have one daughter, Clyda, the daughter of her first husband Clyde Miller Forson, who had died in 1914. (She was divorced from her second husband, James Gordon Brubaker, perhaps because of the affair between herself and Lambert.) Unlike the relationship between Lambert and "Danny," Clyda and Lambert had what was at best a strained relationship. There are touches of feeling for each other in the relationship. For example, years later, soon after the death of Chloe Ann, a death that hit Lambert hard, Clyda sent him a Christmas card that read in part, "If ever I can be of help in any way I'm a phone call away—that 'Rabbit' VW goes from 0–60 in a hurry."[35] However, in a letter to Bill Martin of 15 December 1984, only three years after that card, Clyda wrote, "That part of my life I've tried very hard to forget, but being human it would be a lie to say I had truly forgiven Bill Lambert, then I think I will not be the one to sit in final judgment of him or anyone."[36]

After the marriage between Lambert and Chloe Ann, there are no accounts of extramarital affairs. Lambert seems to have settled down. But the book ends before the marriage; and in the book, every woman Lambert desires, which is practically every young and reasonably attractive woman he meets while barnstorming, is immediately and irresistibly attracted to him and wants to have sexual relations with him. There is no mention of any time that a woman refuses his advances, though there must have been some. If sex does not take place, it is because the opportunity is never there, or the woman is too young, or is the sister of a friend. In the same way, everyone Lambert socializes with is captivated by "his" famous drink, Scotch on the rocks, which he introduces at every available opportunity.

Besides barnstorming and women, there is one more aspect to Lambert's life during this year. It is the organization and supply of a bootlegging operation. The Volstead Act, or the Eighteenth Amendment, was due to take effect on 16 January 1920. It was already clear that a number of people were going to try to flaunt the Amendment, and that selling illicit liquor was going to be immensely profitable. A friend or acquaintance in Ironton had approached Lambert in Ironton, probably soon after he returned from the war, with a business proposition. Lambert, and a number of other pilots that Lambert would recruit, would fly illegal booze to various destinations. Lambert's original trip to Dayton to buy airplanes and spare parts seems to have been in furtherance of this plan. Lambert was also going to advertise in the Toronto, Canada, and Dayton areas for trained pilots to be used in this business. The future bootlegger in Ironton needed at least twelve pilots for the operation.

Of course, since the operation was an illegal one, there had to be a cover for it. It was supposed to be one of the first of the air passenger lines. Pilots would be paid sixty percent of all the passenger fees they carried and $200 a month. In addition, they were to carry "certain cargo" for which they would receive an extra $100 a trip.[37] Bootlegging presented opportunities and big cash payouts for pilots willing to get involved. For example, Floyd "Slats" Rodgers, a barnstormer from Texas, brought illicit alcohol across the border from Mexico. "Slats" received $20 for each case he delivered. His customers could easily afford this cost; they were planning to sell each fifth of whiskey for as much as $50.[38] With the annual teachers' salary at around $970, and the annual average earning of the fliers at around $1,236, flying for bootleggers was a profitable racket.

Lambert's plan may have been to barnstorm until prohibition went into effect and then begin working for the bootlegger, running a passenger operation that also supplied illegal alcohol to a growing market. He wrote that "there was an organization being formed in Ohio, Kentucky, West Virginia, and Pennsylvania that would control several million dollars. Just as soon as I could see one man in my hometown, I would return with not less than five times the cost of those five aeroplanes."[39] His job was "to find the aeroplanes, pilots to fly them and also to establish training fields for their use."[40]

Lambert also pursued the possibility of incorporating and creating a company, with stock holders each investing $100,000 in this venture. "Whoever starts first will get the business."[41] He discussed this enterprise with Dave's father and other wealthy people he met while barnstorming. They all seem to be extremely willing to invest in the airplane business; and, given the immense profits possible in bootlegging one can see why.

Given that Lambert had launched an impressive operation that seems to have been fully funded and supplied, we naturally question why he did not continue with it. Why did he go back to barnstorming, and why was he selling automobiles in the 1920s, instead of being part of the organization he himself had set up?

One reasons was that Lambert did not show as much interest in developing the corporate side of the business as he did flying. In fact, the corporate side was left up to Dave's father and other men of business. That became clear when Lambert told the pilots he was recruiting and hiring, "My part in this project will end just as soon as you get your aeroplanes flyable and get located on your respective fields and start to work."[42] Lambert was also making a great money and having too much fun flying and fornicating to see or fully understand the bigger picture and its possibilities. He never took his business operation to the next level. It may have simply required too much of a lifestyle change, one he could not fully understand.

Another reasons could be that Lambert's personality as well as the fact that he would not be in charge of the operation. The moneyed men would be giving orders, and Lambert, like the other pilots he recruited, would be working for them. This way of doing things was not in Lambert's nature. As Klaus Staerker repeated stated, Lambert had to be in control. Lambert's personality, which some people found offensive and others simply tolerated, is another consideration. Several people had difficulties getting along with Lambert. In spite of his assertion that there was considerable interest in his venture, his rough demeanor may have been an obstacle for his getting financial backing.

Besides these possibilities, there is the fact that he was a newly-wed with a step-child. It may have been Chloe Ann, at least in part, who prevented him from moving to Dayton and becoming the general manager for Consolidated Aircraft Supply and Maintenance Company. Lambert would often tell people that she grounded him after they got married. It may have been a convenient excuse, but in fact it was partially true.

Finally, the great profits in bootlegging brought with them considerable danger. The danger was not only from the Federal agents, but also—and perhaps more—from other bootleggers, angry at someone trying to muscle in on their territory. After being in constant danger for so long in the Great War, and after his breakdown from the stress of that life, Lambert did not take danger well. Barnstorming had its dangers too, but he was in control of these. He was not being shot at from ambush the moment he touched down at any place.

Barnstorming and Girls ends with Lambert and "Dave" planning an elaborate party for New Year's Eve in Dayton. Prohibition would take effect in the coming January, so they were intent on enjoying themselves. They seem to have invited practically everyone they knew or met to the event, which included the people who bought their damaged barnstorming plane in mid–December. A landing accident disabled their plane with a broken landing gear and propeller. For the first time in almost a year, Lambert was without a plane to fly. He, along with "Dave" and "Tom" and their girls, would have to make the trip north by automobile. They planned to travel the same route that had been followed on the way down, and to stay at the same hotels that had been their temporary refuges when they barnstormed the region. They would also meet with friends they had made along the way and enjoy their hospitality.

Barnstorming and Girls ends with the beginning of this trip north, so we do not know the details of the Dayton party. It was the end of a year that had proved both profitable and enjoyable to Lambert. It was as if he did not want the year to end, and we can see why. The year had been therapeutic for him. His PTSD was not completely gone, but it was greatly lessened. He had been able to slowly adjust to his life as a civilian, and he had enjoyed himself. Robin Higham said it best when he described Lambert as living the "lusty tale of a young hero."

Lambert had made the correct decision when he opted for returning to Ironton instead of going on Home Establishment. He was on the road back from his breakdown, and had gone a considerable way along the road. Lambert always considered 1919 one of the best years of his life. And his future looked promising. The war in Europe was in the past; peace had begun with the signing of the Versailles Treaty. It would be a troubled and uneasy peace, but no one knew that yet, and there was great rejoicing in Europe. In America, Warren G.

Harding would soon run for the presidency, and win, on a campaign slogan that promised "a return to normalcy." Lambert was happy and content as he traveled to Dayton to welcome 1920 in high style. He knew that the war was finally over; he thought his personal war was also over; he anticipated with a good deal of pleasure what the future would have in store for him.

Twelve

Life Between the Wars

After the bad accident with his plane, Lambert no longer worked as an aviator. (The *Ironton City Directories* for 1922–1923 still list his profession as "aviator," but of course the information in these directories comes from the previous years.)[1] He settled down in Ironton and took up different professions there, especially salesman, inventor, and designer. Towards the end of this period, and especially after World War II had broken out, Lambert tried a number of ways of getting back into aviation, but until the United States was involved in the war, he had no luck with any of his attempts.

We do not know as much about this period in Lambert's life as we do about his combat experience and his barnstorming days. This lack of information is not Lambert's fault; he was almost obsessive about record keeping. But after his death, a number of these items were simply tossed out. We know the general outline of Lambert's life in this period, partly from public records and partly from comments he made to friends and acquaintances and to reporters. About some details of this time, we know far more. But we do not have the day-to-day kind of record that we had in *Combat Report*.

It seems that, when Lambert first came back to Ironton, he had no plans to live there the rest of his life. The *Ironton City Directories* for 1922–1923 list Lambert and Chloe Ann as tenants living with Lambert's parents, along with his brother Carl, at 318 Hepler Street. In the 1924–25 *Directories,* Lambert and Chloe Ann were listed as living in another place, 2315 South 5th Street, but still as tenants.[2] It is not until the 1926–27 *Directories* that Lambert and Chloe Ann are listed as being in their permanent residence of 2506 South Tenth Street, where they would reside the rest of their lives.

One of the events we have a good deal of information about is the near-fatal accident which resulted in Lambert's giving up flying. There are still some unanswered questions about the accident, though. The story is told in detail in the *Morning Irontonian;* it was big news at the time. And Lambert discussed the event with Bill Martin later on, in the 1970s. On Sunday, 24 October 1920, Lambert, now referred to as Captain Lambert, and Howard Anson, a 19 or 20-year-old (two different articles in the paper give him two different ages), were involved in a "spectacular airplane accident which was witnessed by hundreds of spectators."[3] Lambert's plane was doing loops and stunts shortly before 2:00 p.m. "directly over the heart of the city at the height of 1500 feet." After executing a "graceful loop" the machine started a tail spin and was seen by spectators to be "out of control and was really falling." Hundreds of people rushed to the riverbank as the plane crashed "in the willows and sandy bank just under Riverview Park at the foot of Park Avenue with the pilot and passenger still in it."⁴ The paper reported that "news of the accident spread like wildfire and in a few minutes an immense crowd had assembled."⁵

Lambert's plane was wrecked, but repairable. Anson was unconscious and rushed to the Charles S. Grey Deaconess Hospital on Quincy Street where he was treated for what seemed to be a fractured skull over one eye, and a large gash in his groin. He would not regain consciousness until late in the afternoon. The doctors reported that his injuries were serious, but "not necessarily fatal." Lambert, who was seen walking up the banks of the river, was listed as not being seriously injured, but was nonetheless taken to the Marting Hospital, located at 311 S. 5th Street, with "a badly sprained left wrist, a severe flesh wound in the back, a gash across the nose and minor cuts and bruises."⁶ (There were three hospitals in Ironton at the time. The third hospital was the Roosevelt Hospital on 5th and Washington Streets.) Another article, "Anson's Chances for Recovery Grow Brighter," that was printed later in the week, reported that Lambert was still in the hospital and was recovering nicely from his injuries.⁷ Apparently his injuries were more serious than first reported.

Two pictures taken of the accident show a demolished plane that seems impossible to rebuild. In addition to these pictures, there is a picture in Bill Martin's collection which shows Lambert examining the wreck with his back to the camera and his shirt severely ripped and dirty. He is examining the damaged plane with a large number of people around him and the plane. The Tuesday news article states that a Lieutenant Buffington began repairs on the Monday following the accident. Martin also had a copy of a studio picture taken around this time that show two immaculately dressed men, Lambert in a three-piece suit and tie with a nicely trimmed mustache, and a man who seems slightly younger on his left in a suit and bow tie. What is of interest and quite telling is both men are wearing hats with goggles positioned on them. This picture may well be the only one we have of Lieutenant Buffington.

It was initially reported that on the evening of the accident, that Anson "made no statements regarding the accident except that he must have been unconscious when the plane hit." In a follow-up article that appeared in the paper a few days later, it was reported that it was two days after the accident "when he fully recovered consciousness." He told relatives that "when he felt the plane was falling he closed his eyes, grasped the sides of the airplane as firmly as he could and remembered nothing more until Tuesday."⁸ Lambert stated that "he could not account for the accident other than that Anson may have become excited and fouled the controls…. He says that he does not know that this is the case but that the controls refused to work when he attempted to come out of the spin."⁹ The article paints Lambert as a reluctant hero who showed his skill as a pilot "undoubtedly saving his own life and that of the passenger as both undoubtedly would have perished."¹⁰

A number of folklore details were later added to the story. One was that Anson had recently broken up with his girlfriend, and someone had overheard him say he was going to kill himself. Another version had Anson hanging from the side of the plane with Lambert attempting to get him back into the cockpit. The most surprising addition to the story, however, is a remark that Anson made to a neighbor, that Lambert had "tried to kill" him.¹¹ The remark may have been made partly in jest, but it still needs explanation.

That explanation may come from what Lambert said about the incident: that Anson had frozen at the controls of the plane. It was not Anson's first lesson, but Lambert had him doing loops and spins in a Curtiss Jenny with an open cockpit, and he panicked. The plane had dual controls, but Anson would not respond to Lambert's commands to release the controls so he could fly the plane as it came out of a loop. Anson panicked and grabbed the controls and would not let it go. Anson's memory was, as previously stated, that "he closed his eyes and grasped the sides of the plane as firmly as he could," but with his eyes closed he might easily have grasped the controls instead. Like other pilots training novices to fly, Lambert carried a wrench in the cockpit for just such an occasion. Other barnstormers were known to carry hammers or large tools for such a purpose and used them if necessary. It was a precautionary measure since several accidents and deaths had occurred as a consequence of novices freezing at the controls of a plane. As a last resort, pilots would hit the novice on the head with the tool, sometimes repeatedly, in order to dislodge him from the controls so they could fly and land the plane and save their lives. It is probable that the damage done to Anson's skull, which was reported as the slightly fractured outer bones over one eye, was not a result of the crash, but was caused by Lambert striking Anson repeatedly on the side of the head in order to get control of the plane. If Anson's last memory was of Lambert striking him on the side of his head, it is no wonder that he would speak of Lambert as "trying to kill" him.

After this accident, as we have seen, Chloe Ann "grounded" Lambert. He had to find work that did not involve flying. The *Ironton City Directories* for 1924–25 lists Lambert as a salesman for The Ryan and Gilfillan Company, an automobile agency that sold Marmon motor cars, but Lambert told Smith in an interview that he was selling these cars around 1922. He never said exactly why he chose this job, but it does not seem difficult to figure out. His ability at selling rides during his barnstorming days would have given him confidence in his ability as a salesman. And he had always been interested in and good with engines. The reader will remember his constant tinkering with the engines of his planes during the Great War to coax every bit of energy out of them. If he could no longer be a flyer, being around automobiles must have seemed like the next best thing.

His choice of this career, and even the make of automobile he sold, was appropriate to the period. Henry Ford had created the Model T in 1908, and had thus made an automobile within reach of the average working man. But the automobiles that were associated with the Roaring Twenties were higher-end cars: cars that were sporty, flashy, and fast; cars that satisfied the era's desire for speed, excitement, even a spice of danger. The Stutz Bearcat and the Pierce-Arrow were almost synonymous with the '20s. The Marmon was even more expensive than these cars. Lambert told Smith that the Marmon was "really some automobile. It was around six or eight thousand dollars in those days for just a plain open Marmon automobile."[12] The Marmon Wasp, driven by Ray Harroun, won the first Indianapolis 500 Race in 1911 with an average speed of 74.602 M.P.H. It took him six hours, forty-two minutes and eight seconds to finish the race.[13]

Another appeal of the Marmon to Lambert was that it had been designed by someone who had a connection to aviation. He remembered that the company was founded by two brothers, Harold and Walter Marmon, who "did some work on the Liberty engine in World War I, and later they built a 12 cylinder-V-12-for the P-51, or something, in World War II."[14] In fact, it was Howard Marmon who invented the Marmon, and he did help to design the Liberty engine. It was so much like Lambert that he would remember Marmon's connection to the Great War.

Lambert did well as a car salesman, and he seems to have enjoyed the job. He remembered selling a two passenger Marmon roadster to a butcher in his neighborhood for around

Twelve. Life Between the Wars 159

A recently married Lambert in his Ironton home.

$8,000, and going to Indianapolis with him to pick up his car. He figured he sold around fifty or sixty Marmons in Ironton, including two to a doctor. He also recalled trading a millionaire from western Ohio a Marmon for two Pierce Arrows, including an open speedster that he kept for himself for a year. He sold the seven-passenger sedan to a man who started a bus line between Portsmouth and Ironton.[15] Lambert seems to have had a flair for selling.

However, in 1929, the Ryan and Gilfillan Company went out of business. According to Lambert, the reason was the company lost its show yard. He said that "the state highway closed us up. They needed our ground for an overhead crossing on the railroad.... They just put us out of business as far as the automobile business was concerned."[16] No doubt, the loss of this property was a severe blow for the company; but they could probably have opened somewhere else in Ironton. But 1929 was also the year of Black Friday, the stock market crash that precipitated, if it did not cause, the Great Depression. The owners may have seen the handwriting on the wall and realized that the times were not propitious for a company selling high-end cars, and taken the closing of their yard as a convenient excuse to get out of business.

During this time of selling cars, there was one thing Lambert did *not* do that caused him grief later on. He did not get his pilot's license. The Air Commerce Act of 1926 required the licensing of all pilots. President Coolidge had established the Aeronautics Branch of the Commerce Department to enforce the new aviation regulations. The first person to receive a pilot's license was the Assistant Secretary of Commerce for Aeronautics, William P. MacCracken, Jr., on 2 April 1927. Lambert may have felt that to be required to get a pilot's license was somewhat of an insult to a Great War ace. But in the 1930s, when he attempted to get a job in aviation, his refusal to get this license would severely limit him. Without a license, he would not be allowed to fly commercial planes, so that companies would not even consider hiring him.[17]

During this time, also, Lambert did get one offer to use his flying skills. Howard Hughes was making *Hell's Angels,* a Great War aviation epic. Hughes had a passion for realism. He had purchased thirty-seven authentic war planes, besides converting other planes into vintage Great War planes. He also decided to hire only experienced fliers and to pay them the salary of $200.00 a week. There was an overture from Hughes to Lambert to be one of these trained pilots, but Lambert turned him down. He was settled in Ironton, he had just purchased a home, and he had a good-paying career in selling. Besides, as he said, he did not want to "get in the middle of a bunch of greenhorns doing something like that and run the risk of getting killed."[18] Based on the causalities that were incurred in making this film, Lambert was wise to refuse. Four people were killed during the filming, and Hughes himself had a plane accident that nearly killed him and affected his health all the rest of his life.[19]

Lambert bounced back from The Ryan and Gilfillan Company's going out of business. For a year, he was working for someone else. In the 1930 *Ironton Directories,* Lambert is listed as the manager of The Radio Shop.[20] But then he went into business for himself. He always wanted to be in charge. In later *Directories,* he is listed as the owner of Lambert Electric Company, an authorized agent for General Electric Company. He sold ranges, water heaters, and commercial equipment. Evidently he started with Frigidaire, but later he would sell both Frigidaire and GE products. His stationary advertised Frigidaire Sales and Service, Flowing Cold household and commercial air conditioning, and Cincinnati Butcher's Supplies.[21]

Lambert was still involved with selling and with engines. It was simply that the engines were smaller and were rapidly evolving from luxury to necessities. There was a far bigger market for these conveniences, even in the Depression, than there was for a high-end luxury automobile. Rita Baker remembered that Lambert installed a Kelvinator for the Baker family, who lived next store to Lambert on 10th Street. The remarkable thing about this sale was that it was the first refrigerator the Bakers ever owned.[22] Lambert described business as "extremely good" during the Depression. He credited his success to hardworking salesmen and the effort they put into selling these products. But he also maintained that even in the Depression, some people still had money, and a few even spent it. He was able to find these people. Lambert always prided himself on making a little money during what was a trying time for the country.[23]

One event that resonated with people living along the Ohio River during the Great Depression was the Flood of 1937. Almost everyone had a story of how they were affected by the flood, which took place in late January and early February. It was reported that the Ohio River crested at between twenty to twenty-eight feet above the flood stage. The flood caused a million dollars' worth of damage, and Ironton, like many cities on the Ohio, reacted by building flood walls in order to prevent a recurrence of this disaster.[24] Lambert told Robert Smith that his shop at 309 Vernon Street had seventeen feet of water in front of it. His store, which sold belts for appliances, radios, high-priced switch material, and large appliances, faced the prospects of a catastrophe with the destruction of his inventory. Lambert recalled that he had approximately $3,000 invested in just the belts in his store. Acting quickly, they proceeded to stack the equipment on top of the front window, which was about ten feet high.

Lambert estimated that he had between $8,000 to $10,000 worth of inventory stacked on top of those windows, but through their efforts they were able to stay in business.[25]

At the same time that he was involved with this business, Lambert was trying to develop his drafting and designing skills, and in fact received two patents. This fact is testimony not only to his ability to put his ideas on paper, but also to his dogged determination. The first patent, "Wing Structures for Airplanes," was a particularly difficult one to obtain. Not only did Lambert have to describe the wing structure exactly so it could be copied, but he also had to show in detail how this invention was different from that in earlier patent wings, of which there were a good many. Moreover, he had to describe in detail the tests he had conducted on the rib and spar section of the wings. All this work took time and money. The first letter written about this patent application was 5 December 1928; the patent was not granted until 16 December 1930. And the patent was not granted to Lambert alone, but to Lambert, his employer (at the time) Dean Gilfillan, and Elmer Stewart, a Patents, Trademarks and Copyright Attorney living in Washington, D.C. Clearly, Lambert had needed someone else to assume the costs of the patent, and Gilfillan had at first been the one to do so; as the cost escalated, Gilfillan was no longer willing to pay all of them, and Stewart assumed some of the costs in return for a share in the patent.

Unfortunately, after all this time and money and effort, Lambert's patent was not marketable, and would never be marketable. At least as far as the aviation industry was concerned, Lambert was living in the past. His invention assumed a straight wing, the kind of wing that was on the planes he flew in the Great War. But the standard for the airline industry, then and now, had become the slated (cantilevered) wing, and Lambert's invention would not work with that kind of wing. There were other problems with the design from a production point of view, but they might have been gotten over. But this fact—that Lambert's invention was designed for a straight-winged plane—meant that the wing was already antiquated even while he was working on it. The invention was a real one, but no one in the aviation industry wanted it.

Lambert's other patent, his Combined Chin Rests and Pipe Supports, was somewhat easier to get. (This invention was trademarked as the "Dry Ez Adjustable Pipe Rest.") There were fewer conflicting patents, and it was easier for Lambert to demonstrate that his invention was different from these others. For example, one conflicting patent was for a Nursing Bottle Bracket. Lambert admired the ingenuity of the inventor of this device, but it was fairly easy for him to show that his invention had essential differences. However, the application still took a considerable time, partly because one of the conflicting patents was a Swiss one, and Lambert had to wait for a copy of this patent to arrive.

The Combined Chin Rests and Pipe Supports seems to be an illustration of the old saying "Necessity is the mother of invention." When he was asked in an interview how he happened to invent the pipe rest, Lambert responded that he "just invented it; I wanted it.... I didn't have to think about it. The pain in my jaw from a heavy pipe was tremendous. It hurt my jaw! ... So, I had to get something to ease up that pain.... So, there it is."[26] No doubt the claim that he "didn't have to think about it" is overstated, and Lambert did have to do some thinking about and working out the device, but evidently not much.

Again, Lambert used the services of Elmer Stewart, the Washington attorney who had been his lawyer for the wing design. This time, Stewart's fee was only $75 (plus another $75 to register the trademark).[27] Even so, Lambert again had to have someone partner with him on the patent to pay for the costs and then share in the presumed rewards. This time, that person was Edward Rist, a member of a prominent family in Ironton. Lambert's first letter to Stewart about the pipe rest was in January of 1931; the patent was finally granted on 11 October 1932.

Well before he got the patent Lambert was networking to get his device sold, but he had tough going. One letter he received on 27 January 1932 from a friend of his from Nobel days shows what the trouble was. His correspondent thanked him for sending him a pipe-holder, saying he found it "quite a novel and interesting thing. However, I don't believe I could do much with it around these parts, as dull as everything is."[28] The Depression was not the time to try to market a new device that was something of a luxury. It was simply the wrong time to sell the product.

As the economic situation improved in the 1940s, Lambert again attempted to market his pipe rest. He contacted Dr. Armitage Whitman in New York City, who was associated in some way with the Horace Le Gris Cigar Stand at the Harvard Club. In a letter sent to Lambert on 19 September 1940, Whitman thanked Lambert for his pipe gadget, "which arrived yesterday, and which I am already using with much satisfaction."[29] Whitman showed the rest to Le Gris, "and he immediately gave me an order for a dozen, which I enclose."[30] Whitman even offered, provided Lambert gave him the prices and other business details, to place them at the Yale, Princeton, and Columbia clubs, because "they went over well to such a representative clientele."[31] On 24 September, Whitman responded to a letter he received from Lambert by asking him to send the pipe rest directly to Le Gris at the Harvard Club, and letting him know that if these sold well, he would be ordering more of them for the other university clubs unless Lambert had his "own arrangements with a distributing agent."[32] So there was certainly interest in his pipe rest. But Lambert never did make any arrangement with a distributing agent, and he was too buy himself to market the product, so the sales were limited.

However, Lambert always took great pride in his invention of the pipe rest. He printed stationary with his line-engraved portrait on it, with him wearing a hat and smoking a pipe with his invention attached to it. The stationary included his name for the item, the *Dry-Ez Pipe Rest*. His interview with General Dynamics and some newspaper photographs show Lambert smoking his pipe with an attached Dry-Ez pipe rest on the stem. He had display cards made to go with his pipe rest. It was one of the things for which he would be remembered when people reminisced about him after his death.

Lambert's last patent effort with Stewart involved a four-cycle engine which made "four strokes, each stroke being the movement of the piston in one direction only and thus requiring two completed revolutions of the crank shaft for each power stroke."[33] He made a fully designed blueprint with an explanation of how the engine functioned. This engine would have been a small one, probably for the household appliances Lambert had been involved with for the past decade. For his patent application, he contacted Stewart for the third time on 8 September 1939. Unfortunately, when Stewart searched for possibly competing patents, he discovered too many—at least seventeen different ones, the earliest being one given to Arthur Histon of Yonkers, New York, on 2 April 1889.[34] Lambert did not pursue this patent any further. Evidently, he realized that his idea was not as originally as he had thought.

In the fall of 1940, on 5 November, Lambert contacted Chrysler, General Motors, and Packard about "an automobile body design intended to accommodate an air conditioning system."[35] All three companies rejected his design; but the time he had spent making a wooden model of this car, as well as the various designs he had made for the patents he got and tried to get, prepared him for his next job, as tool designer for the Henrites Products Company.

A newspaper article in the local paper alerted people to the fact that Lambert was quitting his electrical business. It announced that after nine and one-half years the Lamberts "have decided to close their business due to Mr. Lambert being affiliated with The Henrite Products Company and Mrs. Lambert desiring to take a much needed rest from the routine of the business world."[36] The article went on to inform the public that the products and supplies formerly sold by the Lamberts would be sold at "the same location by Fred Campbell, manager, and former customers and guarantees will be taken care of as usual."[37]

An article that appeared considerably later in the Ironton papers, "Henrites Have expanded Since Spring of 1927," celebrated the history of the company and explained the type of products they produced. The article stated, "Products manufactured at the plant are graphite and metal graphite motor and generator brushes, resistors, molded carbon products, molded mechanical rubber specialties and rubber bonded-to-metal parts ... [which] are used on automotive and industrial motors and generators and on motors for appliances such as washing machines, refrigerators, etc.... The manufacture of molded mechanical rubber specialties and rubber bonded-to-metal parts was started by the Henrite Products Corporation in 1934."[38] Henrites shipped its products overseas. The war in Europe led to an increase in demand in the United States for more industrial products, and Henrites was a growing company. Its first factory building, around 5,000 square feet, was completed in Ironton in 1927. It employed around twenty-five workers. By 1947, there would be 400 people working in several buildings totaling over 100,000 square feet.[39]

While Lambert was in the business of selling appliances, he would certainly have purchased brushes and other supplies from Henrites. Evidently, he had turned this business connection into a job. He became an original custom machinery designer for Henrites, beginning in June 1941.

Lambert liked his new job. It satisfied his wish to be around engines and his sense of inventiveness, as well as his desire to be important. As he told Smith, "We had to make every bit of machinery to build it. Somebody had to design that machinery."[40] He also no longer had the stress of running his own business, and Chloe Ann could once enjoy being a housewife again. Lambert's life was going well; but as with the rest of America, it would change with the events in Hawaii on the morning of 7 December 1941.

Thirteen

Lambert in World War II and Afterward

For a good part of the last ten years, Lambert had been applying for jobs in the civilian aircraft industry, but he had no success. There were good reasons for this lack of success. Lambert still had no pilot's license; he had not kept up with advances in aviation, as shown by his wing patent; and he was settled down with Chloe Ann in Ironton and was reluctant to leave that security. This last was the probable reason that he turned down the one offer he had, from George T. Eaton of Olympia, Washington, who had designed a small military plane covered with Bakelite, to be used by the Chinese Army against the invading Japanese. Eaton had done a great deal of the design work already, but he needed now to produce the planes and to get financing, which he hoped to get from wealthy Chinese Americans. It was a gamble, but one that might produce excellent returns. The Lambert that returned from the war and went barnstorming might have leaped at the chance, but Lambert was older now and far more set in his ways and unwilling to gamble.

As the war grew, Lambert tried to get some kind of a position, not necessarily a flying position, that would allow him to be part of a military aviation unit. His first application was to the Royal Canadian Air Force (R.C.A.F), and he was in fact offered a commission in the special Reserve, R.C.A.F., in the "[Non-Flying List] Link Trainer Branch, with the rank of Temporary Flying Officer."[1] A problem arose, however, when he asked for one-half of his salary to be sent to Chloe Ann, for in the Second World War the Canadian government did not allow money to be sent out of the country. Lambert stated that this is what "killed" his joining the Canadian Air Force.[2] He also applied to Fort Hayes, but he was quickly and thoroughly rejected.[3] The application was a three-stage process, and Lambert was rejected at all three stages. He had failed to get his pilot's license, he had not kept up with his flying, and he was too old. Flying was a young man's game, still.

When the United States actually entered the war, however, Lambert tried again, pulling what strings he could. He had Major General George Richards, U.S. Marine Corps retired, write a letter to Lieutenant-General Henry H. "Hap" Arnold, Chief of the Air Corps. Evidently, it was this letter that gained him a commission. On 9 August 1942, Lambert went to the Station Hospital at Fort Hayes for a physical examination. On 2 September, he received an appointment with the rank of Captain. He was sent a form for the oath of office, which he "requested to execute and return promptly" since it will "constitute an acceptance of your appointment."[4] On 12 September, at the Fort Hayes Exchange, Lambert spent $41.50 to purchase his uniform, raincoat, clothing accessories, and footlocker for his new stint in the army. After years of failure, Lambert was finally in the U.S. Army and with the rank of Captain.

We have very little information on what Lambert did in the U.S. Army. Unlike the First World War, in the Second World War Lambert kept no log. He did write many letters home to Chloe Ann, for a while a letter a day, and she kept many of them. But these letters, which under other circumstances might have been a major source of information, were written under the strict censorship rules of the Second World War, and therefore have on the vaguest and least useful information on exactly what Lambert was doing. He did talk to his friends about his experiences in this war, at a time afterward when there would have been no reason for censorship. But at this time, Lambert was an old man and, like other old men, living in the past, and his experiences as a young man flying for the R.A.F. were both more vivid to him and more interesting than his experiences in the Second World War. We do know something from his conversations, but not enough.

There is another reason that we know so little about Lambert's life in the Army, and that reason has nothing to do with Lambert himself. On 12 July 1973, a fire in the National Personnel Records Center in St. Louis destroyed eighty percent of Army records from 1912 to 1960, and seventy-five percent of Air Force Records from 25 September 1947 to 1964 with names alphabetically after James E. Hubbard. The fire burned out of control for twenty-two hours, and it took two days before the firefighters were able to enter the building. Approximately sixteen to eighteen million Official Military Personnel Files were destroyed in the fire.[5] Unfortunately, Lambert's files were a casualty of this fire. Some of what is known is that his place of entry was Ironton, his date of service lasted from 17 September 1942 to 23 May 1946, and he was discharged at the rank of Major; but the rest of his records are not available.[6]

One thing we do know that he did *not* do; he did no combat flying. His being 48 years old meant that he was "automatically" grounded by the United States Army Air Corps. His time in the military during the Second World War, then, was very different from his time in the First World War. It was spent almost entirely state-side, with a few trips to Iceland and Greenland, and it was far safer than but definitely not as exciting as combat. However, Lambert seems to have enjoyed his job, to have done it well, and to have recognized that he was an important part of the total war effort.

The fact that he did not do any combat flying did not mean that he did not do any flying. Lambert told a friend that he flew, officially and unofficially, B-24s and B-17s after they landed at his base. "I put in pretty near 500 hours flying in World War II, unofficially,"[7] he said.

Lambert remembered in detail his experiences of flying a B-24 in foggy New England weather in 1942. The Army Air Corps had decided to develop the Ground Control Approach landing system (GCA) at their base where he was stationed. Lambert got acquainted with one of the pilots in the Officers' Mess who told Lambert what he was doing and soon asked if he (Lambert) would like to participate. Lambert jumped at the chance. He was then given permission by the C.O. to be the co-pilot on trips to test the GCA device. He co-piloted the operation until the experiments ended. With the help of the pilot, Lambert learned to fly, take off, and land the large B-24 in heavy fog. Lambert recalled that when asked to land the airplane, he told the pilot that "I'm a little afraid to land it," but he was quickly reassured by the pilot that he was quite capable of maneuvering the aircraft. Lambert followed the pilot's lead and learned how to take-off, fly, and land the plane while blind. He would begin by going around eight or ten miles away from the runway at a height between eight to ten thousand feet. He would then proceed to land the plane from directions being given to him from the ground. Ground control would talk to him throughout the flight and continued to give him the adjustments he needed to make. He told a friend, "Sure it was scary until you got used to it."[8] He also spent some time on "those old Link Trainers" that helped to familiarize him with what he needed to do in the actual airplane. These trainers "would do the same thing as an actual airplane." He worked with the pilot on this experiment for over a month. Before the pilot returned to Washington, he asked Lambert why he was not flying B-24s? Lambert's response was simply "I'm grounded, I'm not allowed to fly." The pilot subsequently informed Lambert that he was "ten times better than a lot of them," and promised to put Lambert in for a blind landing certificate or green card when he got back to Washington. It was issued to him on 10 January 1943,[9] and Lambert proudly displayed it.

There could hardly have been a greater contrast in aviation between the B-24 and the Curtiss Jenny that was the last plane Lambert had flown, many years ago. The B-24 was a heavy bomber, a mainstay in America's war against Germany. The plane originated in 1938 and received an upgrade in 1941. It first saw action with the R.A.F. Depending on the model, it required a crew of seven to ten for its missions. On a bombing run, the crew would include a pilot and co-pilot, flight engineer, navigator, bombardier/nose gunner, radio operator/dorsal gunner, two waist gunners, ball turret gunner, and tail gunner. The B-24 was slightly over 67 feet in length and had a wingspan of 110 feet. It was equipped with four Pratt & Whitney R-1830–65 Twin Wasps engines with an output of 4,800 horse power. Its top speed was 290 M.P.H. with a range of 2,100 miles. Its armaments included four turrets with two Browning 0.50 inch machine guns and two guns in its waist, and it had a maximum bomb load of 12,000 pounds.[10]

The B-24 achieved fame when the Ninth Air Force flew them in their attack on the Ploesti Oil Fields in Romania on 1 August 1943. In the attack, 53 planes and 660 men were lost in the attack. Lambert's job was to help supply and ferry these planes (and B-17s, C-54s, C-47s, and DC-3s) and get them to the European Theater during the war. It was a big job. For instance, he recalled that "we've had as many as a hundred C-54s pop in on us overnight. We had to keep them, feed them, stock them up with food, brief them, tell them where they were going, this, that, and the other."[11] It was a very different job from the one he had in World War I, but he soon showed himself capable of acclimating himself to the new realities of flight and war.

After a brief period of time at Miami Beach, Florida, where he was busy studying, Lambert would be assigned to Rome, New York, and work for the Air Service Command, which was the predecessor designation for the Air Force Logistics Command. Rome, which controlled several sub-depots throughout the Northeast, was one of the biggest supply depots in the country during the war. Lambert was first assigned to Grenier Field in New Hampshire, then to Holton, Maine, and later and finally to Presque Isle, Maine. (Holton and Presque Isle are less than sixty miles from each other.) He steadily rose in authority, from Engineering Officer to Base Air Inspector to Executive Officer to Commanding Officer.

As was said before, Lambert sent letters home to Chloe Ann on a regular basis, and Chloe Ann saved them. Some of them may have been thrown out after Lambert's death, but there are still a good many. We do not always know when they were written. After Lambert's brief stay at Miami Beach, his letters were not dated, for security reasons, but only contained

Staff of officers who ran aircraft repair Sub Depot at Grenier Field, New Hampshire, during World War II. Lambert (standing, second from right) served as Base Air Inspector.

the day of the week and time they were written. The envelopes are not stamped but marked "Free," so we have no indication of the date for them, either. Lambert ended many of his letter by writing "Well see you tomorrow," which would indicate that he was writing on a daily basis.

These letters reveal a far different Lambert than the young man who took every opportunity for sex with any willing woman, to relieve his sense of stress. He is now a mature man, 48 years old, and one who wants only to be home with the wife whom he desperately missed. His only real complaint about his service in World War II is his enforced separation from Chloe Ann.

The letters are tender and loving ones, and he shows a sense of humor that is not common in *Combat Report* or *Barnstorming and Girls*. He is concerned about her well-being in his absence, and he genuinely misses her. In this correspondence, Lambert affectionately refers to Chloe Ann and himself as "Mom" and "Pop." This time of his life was his only lengthy separation from Chloe Ann in their lifetime together. At one point, their twenty-five-year anniversary, he writes that she has had "a lot of hardships during those years, but I hope that the next twenty five will bring you a lot of happiness, and I want to help see that you get all that, because you are the only person in this world that means anything at all to me."[12]

One of the letters, sent while he was still at Miami Beach and therefore not as bound to secrecy, does say something about what he is doing at the time. Lambert has just taken a final exam, one on Military Law, and he is somewhat concerned. "It is the only one that I am doubtful about. I had to guess the answers to most of the questions. I never did get a real chance to study the subject."[13] (Many college students, who have had to take required courses that they did not want to take and were not good in, can sympathize with Lambert.) They would finish the rest of their classes on Wednesday, 28 October, "then will wind up all the details." Naturally, he did not explain these details. He felt, however, that the last few days "will be years long, because I want so much to see you."[14] There is a sense of pride in these early letters, even though he misses Chloe Ann.

Besides his love and concern for Chloe Ann, Lambert also shows a good deal of love and concern for their dog Nickie. He tells Chloe Ann to "send me the pictures of the little girl. What has she been doing? If you keep her mind occupied I believe that she will be alright. Tell her I said hello. Is her tail still down?"[15] He refers to a letter Clyda sent to him, where he discovered that Paul Baker, Rita's future husband, is now taking Nickie on walks, so he writes and gives Chloe Ann instructions to give to Paul. "Above all things caution him not to let her play with other dogs and *not* to let her loose. I would rather you took her and then I know nothing will happen to her."[16] He then asked her what Nickie was doing and let Chloe Ann know he decided to keep Nickie's pictures with him.[17]

Rather tellingly, Lambert never asks Chloe Ann how his stepdaughter Clyda is doing. Clyda is not living at their home during this time. Lambert is also corresponding with Clyda, as already mentioned, although none of the wartime letters to or from her have been saved, and certainly he did not write letters to her every day. Still, he does seem to have some feeling for her, though not as much as for his dog.

After Miami Beach, Lambert moved to the main supply depot at Rome, New York. From a letter he sent to Chloe Ann from Rome, he was an Assistant Maintenance Officer with the responsibility of rebuilding airplanes, if he can get the necessary parts. Lack of parts was a major problem in 1942–1943. In a brochure published by the U.S. Army Air Forces on 1 September 1943, it was suggested that during this period where there was a lack of equipment, it was necessary to "cannibalize" planes and use them as a "source of spare parts for the tactical aircraft passing through or engaged in action."[18] With the exception of finding parts, Lambert believed his job "should be easy."[19] He ended his letter by letting her know it was ten o'clock and wondering "if you miss me as much as I miss you tonite…. Hope I can dream of you."[20]

Lambert stayed at Rome for only a short time. By Saturday, 7 November, Lambert sent a letter to let Chloe Ann know that he arrived at Manchester safe and sound. On the 8th, he informed her more precisely that he was now stationed at 333rd Sub Depot, Grenier Field Manchester, New Hampshire. His letter on Monday, the next day, tells her that he will stay at Grenier Field for thirty days as long as they did not change his job from Engineering Officer. He had to work seven days a week until he learned all the types of planes "from largest to the smallest and believe me the largest is plenty big."[21] He ended the letter by writing that it had been "one week ago today I left you, after our recent honey-moon. We are going to be that way all the time when I get home."[22] In a postscript, he lets her know that he now has a little Scottie dog by the name of Twiggs staying in his quarters.

Lambert had always liked dogs, at least from his time in the R.A.F. on. Twiggs becomes a regular feature in his letters. On top of one letter, he has drawn a picture of Twiggs' head so that Chloe Ann can get an idea of how she looks. In another letter written after he returned from Christmas leave, he told here that Twiggs' owner has not yet returned for him. From then on, Twiggs becomes a necessary companion. However, he still misses his dog Nickie, who he calls "his little girl." Her picture is in a prominent place in his room. He thanks Chloe Ann for sending him two new pictures of Nickie and hopes that she and Clyda could bring her with them when they meet him in Columbus.[23] A letter, which seems to be from Presque Isle in 1945, mentions the death of his dog Nickie in April 1945. He writes, "You can't feel any worse than I do. I had planned so much what I was going to do with the 'little girl' when this thing [the war] is all over. She is right here in front of me in that picture with you holding the leash."[24]

In another letter from Grenier Field, Lambert describes the bitter forty-miles per hour March winds on a day the sun finally came out and warmed the place up. The snow was melting, and the running water was filling up all the local streams. Lambert is spending his time "reading a manual about the duties of this new job. Looks to me like it is a full time job."[25] The job was created the previous November, and apparently it was a job he liked. He told Chloe Ann that it was a newly created position that was usually held by a Lieutenant Colonel. It was also the second job they have given to him since he had been there. He gives Chloe Ann a general description of his new responsibilities. "An Inspector goes around and finds what is wrong and makes recommendations to correct them, and that is as far as he can go."[26] He writes, "Now the Army has created this Compliance & Coordinating Officer, with duties to see that things are corrected. So ... he does have plenty of power if he wants to use it. He is supposed to take the bulk of the work off the CO's hands."[27] This position is apparently Lambert's new job. (His title will be referred to as Base Tactical Inspector in the local newspapers in 1944.) He tells Chloe Ann, "There is a devil of a lot of paper work involved in it. So looks like I will have to set up another office ... to handle the job."[28] Lambert is genuinely excited about the job, but is still concerned with rank, and that he wants to be promoted beyond the rank of captain. As previously mentioned, the Army would grant that wish; Lambert would have the rank of major by the end of the war.

Lambert's longing to be home with his wife is particularly strong just after he returns from leave. In a newspaper clipping from a Grenier area paper, for example, Lambert is mentioned for having recently returned from leave. He is quoted as saying, "Spiritually he was still in Ironton, O., his hometown, but bodily he was at Grenier Field." The article goes on to say that it was hoped his "frame of mind will change soon for the captain is very popular with the employees of the Sub-Depot."[29] In a letter, Lambert writes, "The thing we both have planned for the past three months has come and gone again and now we can look forward to the next leave. It seems like that each time I come home, I love you that much more and the parting is harder each time ... you and all the other things there have come to mean the whole universe to me and I want nothing else."[30] In another letter following his return from Christmas leave, he writes that he can still see her face looking up at him while he was on the train. "I hope for the time when we can be together again for good and not have to leave each other."[31] He remarks how pretty she looked on Christmas afternoon when she put on her new dress, and how she would make the other women in the Officers Club jealous. "Mom darling you are perfect."[32]

The newspaper comment in the last paragraph on how popular Lambert was in the Sub-Depot may be taken with a grain of salt. He may have been popular with many, but certainly not with all. We do not know if it was Lambert's personality, which could be abrasive, or his zeal as Base Tactical Inspector, that got him disliked by some. We do know that he made efforts to get transferred. But he was cautious about making a switch and in fact he stayed at Grenier Field.

We have only limited information on what jobs he did at Grenier Field. In one letter, he describes how he has arranged training classes from Rome that would run about fifty men through a course in three weeks, but he does not describe the type of work being done.[33] In two newspaper articles from a local Grenier newspaper, mentioned Lambert as Safety Officer in the course of praising the 333rd Sub-Depot for its safety record. The depot received prizes and awards for three successive months without a "lost-time accident" from September to November 1943.[34] Lambert evidently had many responsibilities at Grenier Field.

Lambert reflects on his work in one letter saying as much as he could, given the censorship. The letter first gives its setting: Lambert is sitting in a park in a "nice grassy plot with groves of pine trees ... [with] a small stream of water just over the knoll to my right."[35] He tells Chloe Ann that he and three fellow officers, ranging in ages from about thirty-eight to fifty-seven, sat on a bench in front of the main hanger from around 9:00 a.m. till noon and watched the planes leaving for the northeast. "They were all on their way, and we were just sitting. I suppose that the four of us have reached our landing field and made our landings."[36] He remarks that there is a B-25 overhead, so it may have been that an entire squadron was being sent overseas. Lambert writes that he had to run the machine shop throughout the night to get one of these planes away. He writes that he is "glad that bunch is on their way. They can do an awful lot of damage somewhere. This time tomorrow they will be there. A week from today some of them will be gone, and some of them will had done a lot of good."[37] He says his good-bye to Chloe Ann and heads to the shop for the second shift.

A newspaper article of 15 March 1945, in the Bangor papers, which was for some reason allowed to be far more specific than Lambert could be, stated that the North Atlantic Division of the Air Transport Command from May to December 1944 "crossed the Atlantic an average of once every 41 minutes. Counting tactical aircraft crossing ... planes are now crossing the Atlantic to the tune of once every 13 minutes—quite a change from ten years ago.... Dow Field and Presque Isle, Maine's biggest air bases, are extremely important cogs in this aerial highway to Europe and Asia. Ninety per cent of the soldiers at both bases are veterans of the various northern stations that are so vital in the maintenance of the North Atlantic route."[38] This article helps to put Lambert's role in the war into perspective. He was not a combatant, but he helped to keep the planes running and on time. It was not as glamorous as being a World War I ace, and he is not flying; but he is performing a vital service, and he knows it.

There are a number of comments in Lambert's letters that show how different he is from the hard-drinking, hard-loving young man he was in the First World War. In one particularly telling letter, probably sent in late 1944 or early 1945, he writes about the flight nurses and their behavior. "Most of them seem to be just kids. Some of them can't be more than 22 or 23 years old."[39] These nurses frequent the Officers Club and "from the way they dance & act, you would think that they had no cares in the world. And when they get a few drinks under their belts, they will start talking about some of the 'cares' that were on board. They try to drink to forget, but seems like it makes most of them talk more than ever and remember what they brought back."[40] These nurses were bringing home wounded soldiers from Paris. (Since Paris was liberated on 19 August 1944, these wounded soldiers were probably part of General

Thirteen. Lambert in World War II and Afterward

Omar Bradley's First U.S. Army fighting in France.) In fact, some of these nurses got on board with the wounded and traveled the entire distance with these soldiers. "Some of these patients are just about done, and they are brought over here just to be close to their homes and maybe see their parents a last time before they die."[41] When a ship had a medical officer on board, "most of the patients are just about hopeless." In a postscript he tells Chloe Ann, "Part of my job deals with loading and unloading of patients."[42] We can understand why these nurses drank so much. It was the same reason that Lambert and his mates did in the First World War: to relieve stress, to forget the dead and dying for a little while.

In this war, Lambert is abstemious. There is one humorous letter in which he tells Chloe Ann not to blame him for going out on the town and "coming home in this condition." He had gone with some buddies to Manchester for the evening, at the suggestion of Captain Peter L. Milliard. "One drink led to another and so on." But then he explains what the drinks had been: one round of chocolate milkshakes, followed by banana splits with strawberries, and that was followed by chocolate sundaes. Lambert writes, "You know how it is when you get with a bunch. Carousing around, drinking and keeping late hours. Boy was that stuff good. I don't know how it will go tonite, but it sure was good while we were eating it all."[43] This picture is a great contrast to the one he gave of himself and his companions in the First World War, of the hard-drinking, hard-loving young pilots.

In early 1944, the air war, like the ground war, took a decisive turn. A vivid example of the changes comes in a visit from James Doolittle, who had just taken over the Eighth Air Force on 5 January 1944, to Major General William E. Kepner's 8th Fighter Command. Doolittle saw a sign on the wall that read "THE FIRST DUTY OF THE EIGHTH AIR FORCE FIGHTERS IS TO BRING THE BOMBERS BACK ALIVE." Doolittle responded, "That statement is no longer in effect. Take that sign down. Put up another one that says: 'THE FIRST DUTY OF THE EIGHTH AIR FORCE FIGHTERS IS TO DESTROY GERMAN FIGHTERS.'"[44] From this point on, the pilots would be more aggressive, carrying the battle to the enemy. This new goal would inevitably mean more deaths, more destroyed planes, and more work for the supply depots such as Grenier Field and Presque Isle.

Lambert's life also sees a change during this period. He is transferred from Grenier Field, first—briefly—to Holton, and then to Presque Isle. Lambert is delighted by the change, particularly by the new attitude in the people at Presque Isle. He writes in one letter that "the people here are altogether different from those at Grenier. They are all so friendly and want to do something to help you out."[45] In another letter, he writes in the same vein: "It sure is a pleasure up here. Everyone seems a lot more friendly than they were at Grenier Field. They seem to want to put themselves out to do favors, and no one would do that down at the other place. So maybe you are right when you say that things will be different up here."[46] He even felt that he would be able to get more flying in than he did at Grenier. And his positive feelings about the place continue: speaking to a friend after the war, he described Presque Isle as "a paradise."[47]

The one problem with Presque Isle that he mentions is the weather. His letters to Chloe Ann speak of snow, fog, and rain. The deaths of the ten airmen who crashed near Grenier Field, which Lambert described in his letter of 26 April 1944, shows the hazards of fog in the region. The rain is the topic in a letter wrote after he landed in Presque Isle for the first time. Lambert describes how it started to rain ten minutes before he landed "and has been coming down ever since. I sure hope it lets up by noon tomorrow. I wouldn't want to get stuck up here."⁴⁸ ("Here" being the Northeastland Hotel where he was staying that first night.)

In a letter of June 1945, Lambert is letting Chloe Ann know that she was correct when she kept telling him "it will come through this time." (What had "come through" was Lambert's promotion to Major.) The rest of his letter, however, is the news that they will be moving the entire operation to the West Coast. "There is furniture, automobiles and a little of everything for sale here...." He tells Chloe Ann that he will not be affected by the move, "but we will probably close up shop here as there will be nothing to do."⁴⁹

Lambert does not say why the move will occur,

Lambert at Presque Isle, Maine.

but the reason seems fairly obvious. The war in Europe had ended on 8 May with the unconditional surrender of Germany. There was no further reason for a supply depot in the Northeast. It made sense to move the whole depot to the West Coast, closer to Japan, which would now be subjected to the same kind of aggressive air attack as Germany had been. The move, however, would probably be to an already extant base, now to be greatly expanded. However, such a place would already be staffed with senior officers, and there would probably be no place for someone like Lambert.

Lambert discusses the effects of the move with a touch of sadness in another letter. The place looks "really pitiful." The last plane has taken off to the southwest and he can "just barely hear the engines. They all hated to leave here so much as we hated to see them go."⁵⁰ The officers who were left closed four barracks and consolidated the remaining soldiers into the remaining barracks. He remarked with pride that "we had a real organization here and did a real job since Germany quit.... For the first time in the history of the field we were given an overall rating of Excellent" by the Division Inspectors.⁵¹ Lambert showed a great deal of respect for this new generation of pilots. He wrote that he hated to see them go. "All I have done this week is say so-long. Some of the first bunch are already in Manila."⁵² He gave a tribute: "We had a mighty good bunch of boys here. They drank hard and played hard when they were off duty, and they worked damned hard when they worked. A lot of them during

Thirteen. Lambert in World War II and Afterward

May, June & July flew as much as 150 hours a month, and that is a lot of flying."[53] It was apparent that to Lambert these pilots had a great deal in common with the men who flew in the Great War.

The war in the Pacific continued until August 1945. It was air power that brought it to an end: first the saturation bombing of Japanese cities, then the atomic bombs that fell on Hiroshima and Nagasaki. The Japanese signed the surrender document on 2 September 1945. Lambert was now 51 years old. The second great adventure of his life was over, and he was looking forward to returning to his life in Ironton with Chloe Ann. However, he was not finally mustered out of the Army until 23 May 1946, at Camp Atterbury, Indiana.

The immediate post-war world years would be quiet and rather uneventful ones for Lambert. He settled back into his former life in Ironton, again working as a designer for Henrite. The *Ironton City Directories* show him working for Henrite as a tool designer from 1947 to 1960. He told Robert Smith that he worked for eight months on one piece of machinery that was twenty-five feet in diameter. "We had to make every bit of machinery to build it."[54] Lambert had to design all those pieces of machinery.

However, in 1960, Henrite relocated, moving to Tennessee. Lambert did not movie with them. He told Robert Smith, "They wanted me to go with them. I didn't want to go."[55] By that time, Lambert was sixty-six years old and was not interested in moving.

It is not clear why Henrite relocated. It may have been simply that they were not making the profits they had been. There were a number of small industrial plants that did well during the Second World War and struggled thereafter without lucrative government contracts. If so, the movie to Tennessee did not improve their fortunes. A Henrite Products Corporation was located in Morristown, Tennessee, in 1960, but it had gone out of business by 1965.

At the same time that he was working for Henrite, Lambert was also a member of the U.S. Air Force Reserves. An article in the *Ashland Daily Independent* stated Lambert had entered the Reserves as a Captain and attended a training program at Wright Field in Dayton. He rose in both authority and rank in the following years. By the time he retired in 1954, Lambert was the commander of the Ashland-Ironton-Portsmouth-Wellston 9224 VARTU, and he received the rank of Lieutenant Colonel.[56] He continued to receive letters addressed from the Department of the Air Force and the Air Force Museum addressed to Lieutenant Colonel Lambert up to August 1981. It would be a consequence of his rank in the Reserves that people would respectfully refer to him as "Colonel Lambert."

From April 1955 to February 1959, Lambert was a member of the Ohio Defense Corps, established after World War II, now known as the Ohio Military Reserve. Its primary purpose was to "expand quickly to assist Ohioans in case of natural disaster or enemy attacks."[57] In this organization, also, Lambert had both high rank and an important office. Since the organization attempted to give its members the ranks they held in service, Lambert was referred to as a Lieutenant Colonel. He was the Commander of the 12th Battalion.

Lambert had a long-going and important role in Civil Defense in Ohio. Soon after World War II, the Soviet Union, which had been our great friend and ally during the War, became our great enemy and our great fear, as anyone old enough can remember. We were particularly afraid of an atomic attack. It was felt throughout the United States that in every state, there should be those who would plan what we could do in case of such an attack.

In 1961 and 1963, the *Ironton City Directories* list Lambert's primary profession as Director of Civil Defense, but he had been actively involved in Civil Defense at least from the

1950s on. For example, consider the minutes of the Tri-State Civil Defense Council Meetings of Thursday, 20 January 1955, which took place at the Woman's Club in Kenova, West Virginia. The meeting, attended by local Civil Defense leaders from Kentucky, Ohio, and West Virginia, shows that Lambert had an important role in and had a genuine understanding of local Civil Defense matters. Lambert informed the council that he had met with Ohio Governor Frank Lausche at a meeting of the Civil Defense Directors and City Managers on 20 December 1954. Lausche had just returned from a meeting with President Dwight Eisenhower and they discussed the need to expand Civil Defense. Lambert let the council know that an upcoming meeting on 26 January was designed to put into effect a county-wide communication system to help "standardize" police and sheriff cars along with the local taxi service. Plans had been formulated where Ashland and Ironton Ground Observation Corps Posts would be joined together and alternated every three or four days."[58] Mobility would make it more likely that the communications system would continue with no or limited interruptions in case of an emergency or an attack. Clearly Lambert was knowledgeable on Civil Defense affairs and took his job quite seriously, and others looked up to him.

Lambert holding his dog Nissie while standing next to the Lawrence County Civil Defense vehicle. Lambert ignored the advice of his friends and continued to use long chains when walking his dogs. It would have serious consequences later in his life.

In 1963, Lambert decided to go back to designing, but this time he opened his own design company, Industrial Machine Design, which he operated out of his home. But evidently he found too little work as a free-lance industrial designer, so he switched to another aspect of the field, designing structures. He is listed as a "structural designer" in the *Ironton City Directories* from 1965 to 1981, the year before he retired. But he kept the same name, Industrial Machine Design. We have copies of five blueprints that were used in building the Church of the Nazarene in Coal Grove, Ohio, a small village located in

Thirteen. Lambert in World War II and Afterward

Lawrence County, upriver from Ironton. The lower right had corner of each page states that the print was drawn by Industrial Machinery Design.

Lambert seems to have been at least modestly successful as a structural designer, and he was proud of the buildings he had designed. In several interviews over the years, Lambert described his designs and the buildings still in existence that utilized them. Bill Martin's article, "America's Forgotten Ace," published in *The Airman* magazine in 1980, stated that Lambert "designed at least 50 churches from Gallipolis to Chillicothe ... and all the new gas stations for the Rich Oil Company."[59] His most ambitious design was that for the Savings and Loan Building in Ironton. Residents were impressed by this building, particularly by Lambert's use of full columns.

Toward the end of this period of his life, Lambert was also working on the thing that would make him at least modestly famous and perhaps give him more personal satisfaction than anything else he ever did. He was writing a book about his experiences as a fighter pilot in the Great War, which would be called *Combat Report*. The creative impulse which had been behind his inventing, his designing, his pictures (of which more will be said later), and some of his letters, would now express itself in a new direction. But this book would almost certainly never have been written, and certainly never have been published, if it had not been for the support and encouragement he got from Royal Frey. Lambert's encounter with Frey was the most significant of his life.

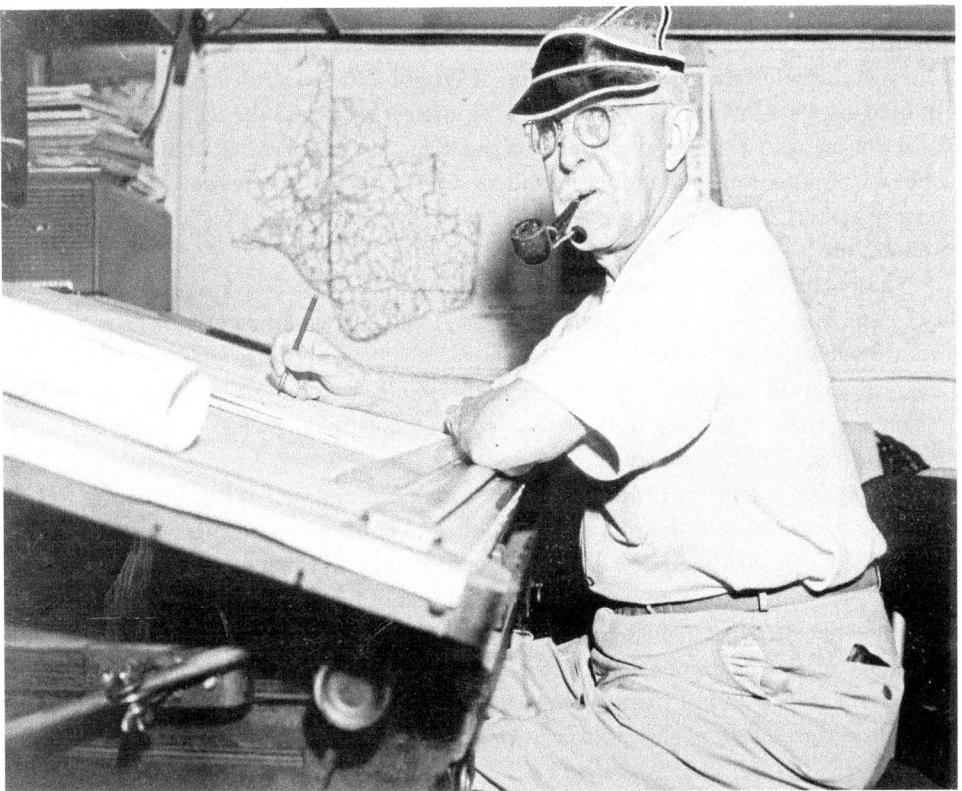

Late in life, Lambert worked for his own design company, Industrial Machine Design, which he operated out of his home.

Fourteen

Lambert and Friends
The Book Gets Published

On 2 August 1964, the *U.S.S Maddox* engaged three North Vietnamese torpedo boats in the Gulf of Tonkin off the coast of Vietnam. The Gulf of Tonkin Incident led to an escalation of the Vietnam War, especially the air war. Sixteen days after the Gulf of Tonkin Incident, Lambert turned seventy years old. That same month marked the golden anniversary of the beginning of the First World War. This anniversary generated new interest in the conflict as well as an interest in meeting those surviving veterans who fought in it. The bombing of North Vietnam and the space race continued to show the American public the importance of a strong and powerful air force and the need to control the skies in order to protect our interests at home and abroad.

In the next few years, Lambert would come to the attention of Lieutenant Colonel Royal D. Frey, the Chief of the Research Division at Wright-Patterson Air Force Base, who had a profound interest in World War I aviation. This interest led him to the second greatest American ace of the war, who was alive and well and living in Ohio. Frey was happy to learn that Lambert was in Ironton, only about three hours away from the base. He drove down to Ironton to meet Lambert. The meeting was the beginning of a new friendship and a new chapter in Lambert's life.

The first meeting of the two had come earlier, in 1961. Royal Frey had organized a World War I Reunion at the Air Force Museum in Dayton. This would be a reunion not only of those who flew for the United States in the Great War but also those who had flown for the Allies, especially France and England. One of the 399 in attendance was Lieutenant Colonel William C. Lambert of Ironton, Ohio. Looking at the list of attendees, it is not difficult to understand why Lambert believed that he was not special for what he had done in the war. He was with a large number of other men who had performed similar feats of daring and had survived the war. What he did not know and what no one recognized then, was that, next to Captain "Eddie" Rickenbacker, he had more victories than any other American at the reunion.

Since Royal Frey became such an important part of Lambert's career, we need to know more about him, to understand his interest in Lambert and his ability to provide what Lambert needed to complete and publish his book.

Royal Frey was not of Lambert's generation. His war was the next war, World War II. But he was also a flier, and an enthusiastic one. His enthusiasm for flying was apparent very early on, in first grade, when he would hold his hands together and make a strange sound as he ran around the room, puzzling his teacher. Frey graduated from high school, went on to The Ohio State University where he got a degree in engineering in 1941, and joined the Army Air Corps. He finished flight training in 1943 and was commissioned a Second Lieutenant.

During the Second World War, Frey flew the Lockheed P-38 Lightning. According to Dick Uppstrom, Frey's superior at the Air Force Museum, Frey was the youngest P-38 pilot in the war.[1] After flight training, Frey became a member of the 20th Fighter Group that was stationed at King's Cliffe, Northampton, in England, from 26 August 1943 to 11 October 1945. Almost immediately after joining the 20th, Frey found himself engaged in the major attack with the industrial areas of Frankfort, Germany as the target, on 29 January 1944. Around a dozen Fighter Groups, including Frey's 20th, accompanied the more than 700 bombers on this mission. Frey found himself engaged in combat with a Messerschmitt Me-110, a twin-engine monoplane. Frey shot down the enemy plane, but discovered that his plane too had extensive damage. However, he was able to "limp" back to King's Cliffe.

Frey "had been convinced he was destined to replace Eddie Rickenbacker as the top American ace."[2] However, during his brief time as a fighter pilot he had only two victories, both Me-110s. In less than two weeks, he was shot down by anti-aircraft fire.[3] One of the engines on his P-38 had quit while he was over Germany, so he aborted the mission and headed home at a reduced speed. Unfortunately, an antiaircraft battery had tracked him and proceeded to fire six shots at his plane. Frey saw five of them and felt the sixth. His P-38 "left a long black trail of smoke as it plunged toward the ground. It crashed two miles east of the village of Lüdinghausen about 25 kilometers south of Münster."[4] But Frey had, with great difficulty, bailed out of the plane before the crash.

Frey floated down to earth and landed in the front yard of a farm house. He then took off running through the fields until he was captured soon afterward by the Germans. He was escorted through the Frankfort railway station by an elderly soldier. "As my guard and I walked from one track over to the trolley line to get to Oberursel [location of the Luftwaffe Interrogation Center], the workers were still carrying out the mangled bodies of women and children. I really got scared at this point as I saw the crowd looking me over in a hostile manner. There was no mistaking that I was American.... However, no one bothered us as we stood waiting for the trolley."[5] After his interrogation, Frey was sent to Stalag Luft I in Barth, Germany where he would remain as a prisoner of war for almost fifteen months.

At Oberursel, he met Hanns Scharff, the German interrogator there. Frey developed a deep personal friendship with this man, which lasted long after the war. The friendship was a testimonial to the character of both men, no doubt, but it also shows us one important trait of Frey's: his ability to make friends with almost anyone, and to keep the friendship for a long time.

After the war in Europe ended, Frey was liberated by the Russians on 1 May. He spent two weeks in Russian hands before being returned to England, and he made friends with them as well. In England, he regained some weight that he had lost in captivity. (It was estimated that he had lost thirty pounds as a prisoner.) Frey finally arrived back in the United States on Thursday, 21 July.

Frey had received four Air Medals and a Purple Heart, so he was good copy for a human interest newspaper story. He told the reporter that after his sixty-days of leave, he would report to Miami, Florida, because he did not want to leave the service as a Second Lieutenant, and hoped for the opportunity to work on jet fighters. He also planned to attend Ohio State again, but was unsure of his major. He would eventually get Master's degrees in both History and Education from Ohio State.

By 1950, Frey was the historian for the Air Force Material Command. After receiving his M.A. in history, he became the civilian historian at Wright-Patterson Air Force Base and served in the Ohio Air National Guard. This position would be short-lived, however, for he was called back to active duty for the Korean War in 1951. He served with the Air Defense Command until 1953, flying Republic F-84 Thunderjets. The F-84 was a straight-wing fighter/bomber combination.[6]

After the Korean War, Frey would return to the Air Force Material Command in the position of Command Staff Editor until 1958. He would then transfer to the Air Force Museum as Chief of Research, and later became its Curator in 1972, a position he held until his retirement in 1981, with the exception of one year he spent in Europe in 1961–62.[7] In that year, Frey was put on active service and sent overseas, with the duty of logistics staff officer. He was stationed at Etain Air Base, about twelve miles east of Verdun. His daughters, Dana and Stacey remember how their father dragged them to all the World War I sites in France.[8] They were there as a consequence of the growing Cold War crisis in Berlin which resulted in the building of the Berlin Wall, but Frey used the time also to research on his passion: the air war in Europe during World War I. In May 1962, Frey's wife and children returned home, but Frey stayed behind to do some additional research.

According to his daughters, for Frey "working with World War I pilots was an act of love, not a job."[9] He would even bring these pilots home for dinner. Frey knew these pilots and how to deal with them. He understood their egos and their quirky behavior at times—and certainly Lambert had his own share of quirks. When Frey finally realized that Lambert was the second greatest American ace from the First World War (next to Rickenbacker), he did not wait for him to drop in at the Museum; he drove down to Ironton to talk with him.

Frey had a number of traits that would be advantageous in talking to Lambert, besides his gift of friendship and his love for World War I pilots. He admired great ability in anyone. That was his reason for his friendship with Scharff: he admired his gift for interrogation, even when that gift was used at his expense. Both Lambert and Frey had been combat pilots, although in different wars. Both had had very bad experiences in their wars: Lambert his PTSD, Frey his time in a prison camp. Nevertheless, both eagerly went back into the service—Frey immediately, Lambert after a while. Lambert could see that he and Frey were kindred spirits.

Frey's friendship would bear great benefits for Lambert. It was Frey's initiative that would put Lambert on the path to researching his combat records and writing *Combat Report*. He would have the opportunity to recall what he did in the Great War for a new generation of aviation enthusiasts. This opportunity came to him at a good time. He no longer had the demands of a full-time job to occupy him, and he needed something to do.

During the time he was writing his book, Chloe Ann died. She had been in fading health for some time, though Lambert's letters show that he neither recognized nor accepted her condition. Both she and Lambert had been heavy smokers, and the years of tobacco addiction had taken a heavy toll. She died at 2:25 p.m. on Tuesday, 9 February 1971. He had a hard time adjusting to life without her.[10] But writing *Combat Report* gave him something to do after her death. It may have kept him from falling into a deep depression.

During this period, there is a steady stream of letters between Frey and Lambert. In the

Fourteen. Lambert and Friends

April 1968 edition of *The Airman*, Frey published his first article on Lambert, "Forgotten Ace of World War I." The article shows that the familiarity between the two men had existed for some time, and that Lambert was already hard at work on the book. Frey wrote that Lambert "lives in Ohio, shuns publicity ... [and] few people, even in his hometown, had any idea of the significance of his achievements as a combat pilot. He never asked for, or expected, plaudits. He was modest about what he had done—even unimpressed."[11] Following the tradition of the R.A.F., Lambert spoke of the squadron and not the individual. Many knew he flew in the First World War as a pilot for the British, but they did not realize or appreciate his significance or what he had done in the war. Frey finished his article by stating, "Only in recent years have others finally convinced him that he did indeed score a remarkable record during World War I. In response to their urging, he has finally begun work on a book to describe in detail his days in the RFC and in particular, No. 24 RAF Squadron."[12]

The "others" here means not only Frey himself but also the aviation historian from London, E. Frank Cheesman. Cheesman, himself a former R.A.F. pilot, though his war was World War II, was on the staff of Harleyford Publications, Ltd. of Letchworth, Herts, England. It was Cheesman who brought Frey and Lambert together. While collecting information for "a contemplated volume dealing with the war aces of that conflict [i.e., World War I], Cheesman came [across] Col. Lambert's name."[13] (According to one source, Cheesman came across a sketch of "W. C. Lambert of Ironton" in a 1920s magazine.) Afterward, Cheesman contacted a friend, who was the Assistant Civil Air Attaché at the British Embassy in Washington, and asked him to track Lambert down. After finding him still living in Ironton, "voluminous correspondence followed," and then Cheesman arranged to come to the United Stated to visit Lambert. Before coming to see Lambert, however, he arranged to stop first at Wright-Patterson Air Force Base in Dayton for a week to do research and visit with Royal Frey. Finally, on Thursday, 23 February, Cheesman contacted Lambert, who drove up to Dayton to get him.[14]

Besides connecting Frey and Lambert with each other, Cheesman had one other important role to play in the production of *Combat Report*. He was the one who convinced Lambert to write the book.[15] One other time, Cheesman was staying with the Lamberts in Ironton for a few days. While there, he saw his collection of memorabilia. He then began to urge Lambert to use his collection to write his recollections of his aerial combat in the Great War. Perhaps Cheesman was a good persuader; perhaps Lambert had already been thinking of something like this. At any rate, Lambert did begin the book at the time that Cheesman visited him.

Cheesman was of great help to Lambert later on in his composition of the book, though more with his art than his writing. Lambert was painting and sketching pictures of aerial combat, and he wanted them to be exactly correct. Cheesman would often know the exact markings on, say, an S.E.5, or the sorts of colors that would be used in painting British aircraft. If he did not know, he would usually refer Lambert to someone who would know, often a fellow former R.A.F. pilot. Cheesman never complained about these queries. He was as much a stickler for accuracy as Lambert himself.[16]

One other person who was of great help to Lambert in this book and a friend of his later life was Bill Martin. While working for the Engineering Department at Armco Steel Company, Martin asked a co-worker, Donald Rist, who lived in Ironton, if he knew Lambert and could arrange a meeting between them. He could. On the day that Martin met Lambert and Chloe Ann, they were "sitting in their back yard. They welcomed me and served lemonade as we sat there, getting to know one another, on a beautiful summer evening."[17] In the course of

This photograph appeared in a newspaper article written by Don Mayne, editor of the *Ironton Tribune*. The article was featured in the "Talk of the Town" section of the paper, which Mayne devoted exclusively to Frank Cheesman's visit to Lambert's home. Left to right are Dr. Paul Penotte of Ironton, Cheesman, Ted Hayes of Ironton, Chloe Ann and Lambert. Permission given by the *Ironton Tribune*.

their conversation, Lambert discovered that in addition to being a pilot, Martin also was an experienced photographer. Lambert saw a way that Martin could be useful. Lambert was already working on *Combat Report* and "immediately enlisted [Martin's] help in getting his old pictures ready for reproduction. Clo, of course, was well aware of Bill's project and was supportive."[18]

What Frey, Cheesman, and Martin had in common was their admiration for the World War I pilots and a love for the machines they flew. Martin was initially "star-struck" when meeting Lambert. He was a living, tangible reminder of the world's first air war. Their desire to learn first-hand about the war and its aircraft was like a dream come true for Lambert. It would prove a renaissance for him in his old age.

Frey, particularly, had connections to people and information that would be vital to Lambert's work. The two of them would become colleagues, in a very real sense. However, as often with colleagues, there were often enough differences of opinion. For example, in a letter sent to Frey on 20 December 1967, Lambert is writing about some of his sketches that he has sent to Frey, particularly one entitled "Escorting the D.H. 9s." He tells Frey, "Remember all my sketches will be made from actual patrols; I do not think you have the time & date of that mission. The date was 20-5-18, time was 7:30-9:30 a.m. altitude 15,000 feet, all 3 Flights of 24 Squad. Did the job. I think this should be mentioned."[19] *Why* it needed to be mentioned is never explained, and in fact Frey's article on Lambert in *The Airman* does not mention any of these details.

In a sense, both men are right from their own points of view. Lambert is obsessed with the details, and for him this obsession paid off. It is the details that give the book its sense of reality; the reader feels that he is in the cockpit with Lambert, seeing what he sees and feeling what he feels. Frey's article is a general view of the man and his accomplishments. Of course, Frey will use some details, but he had neither the room nor the need for *all* of the details.

A letter that Frey sent to Lambert about three weeks later shows the kind of help that Frey was able to give. He supplies Lambert with the name and address of W. J. Taunton in the Air Historical Branch of the R.A.F., who would play an important role in investigating Lambert's record in the Great War. Any increase in the number of victories Lambert is credited with in that war would be a consequence of Frey's persistence and Taunton's research. Initially, Frey suggested that Lambert not contact Taunton directly before he had time to answer the USAF Museum's official request. He told Lambert, "We don't want to scare him off."[20]

On 9 January, the very next day, Frey sent Lambert a short letter letting him know that Taunton had replied to the museum's request and "was able to get to No. 24 Squadron records much earlier than he had previously indicated."[21] Frey enclosed a copy of Taunton's letter with his to Lambert. It would become a foundation statement, along with Lambert's log book, of Lambert's victories during the war. Frey responded that Taunton's "tally for you is 19½ planes and 2 balloons destroyed for 21½ victories, plus sharing in 3 balloons [for whatever that might be worth]."[22] This total would continue to change as people repeatedly focused on Lambert's record over the next several years while he was writing *Combat Report*. Frey pointed out that in 1918, "you men in the RAF were more interested in finishing the war as soon as possible than in claiming all you shot down. Unfortunately, it made it impossible to get confirmation after 50 years for victories not adequately recorded at the time."[23]

We need to look at the background of this request. The most famous American airman of the Great War was Captain "Eddie" Rickenbacker, "America's Ace of Aces." Lambert intensely disliked Rickenbacker (It is not certain that Rickenbacker ever knew that Lambert existed.) He thought that Rickenbacker was a boaster and a fraud. Lambert was imbued with the R.A.F. ethic, that if you boasted, you boasted of the squadron and not of yourself. The fighter pilot was a member of a team. It was the team, and not the individual, that was important. Rickenbacker's self-promotion of his individual victories did not set well with Lambert.

Moreover, Lambert recognized, as very few Americans probably did, that the title "America's Ace of Aces" was a hollow one. The fact was that a good many British fliers had substantially more victories than Rickenbacker, even if they did not boast of them. If the title had been "Leading Ace Flying for the British," Rickenbacker would not even been in the first ten.

Lambert's dislike, of course, was increased by his envy. Rickenbacker had parlayed his title of "America's Ace of Aces" into a career in commercial aviation. After being an executive in several airline companies, he became President and General Manager (1938–53) and Chairman of the Board (1954–63) of Eastern Airlines, which he built into a major passenger and transport system. Meanwhile, Lambert was unable to find any employment at all in commercial aviation.

Lambert became, at the time he was writing *Combat Report*, obsessed with showing that he had done better than Rickenbacker's record of twenty-six victories. Taunton's list was only the first of three such lists that he was able to get from official sources in England. Unfortunately, none of the three lists gave him more victories than Rickenbacker. However, each list had a few victories listed that the other two did not have. By the simple expedient of claiming all the victories listed on any of the three lists, Lambert was able in his own mind to claim to have surpassed Rickenbacker. But his friends persuaded him that no one else would accept this "proof." He had to be resigned to being No. Two, or after Rickenbacker's death, to being "America's Greatest Living Ace."

Around the same time, Lambert started another friendship which would prove very helpful to him. On 11 March 1966, Lambert had received a letter from Robert McGrath the owner of the World War I Aero Bookshop in West Roxbury, Massachusetts. In addition, McGrath also ran World War I Aero Publishers, which published such specialty books as *Japanese Code Names* and *Japanese Aircraft Insignia, Camouflage, and Markings*, both by Richard M. Bueschel. Clearly, McGrath was a man who would sympathize with Lambert's obsession with detail. The letter was to inform Lambert that he (McGrath) had been commissioned to write a book on Captain George H. E. McElroy, who flew with Lambert in No. 24 Squadron. This letter was the beginning of a friendship between McGrath and Lambert that would pay great dividends for both of them over the years. McGrath also told Lambert that he had had a recent phone call from Russ Manning, who was doing a book on No. 56 Squadron, and was able to give McGrath more information on No. 40 Squadron. (This material was important to McGrath because McElroy left No. 40 to command a Flight in No. 24.) McGrath called Manning a "gold-mine" of information.[24] (Later, Lambert would also receive materials from Manning that helped in his writing of *Combat Report*.) McGrath contacted Lambert to see if he "might have any personal recollection of McElroy" during his time with the squadron. He was also looking for "photos of 24 Sqdn. Members and 24 Sqdn. Aircraft and background material on personnel and personalities."[25] Members of McElroy's family had "graciously afforded" McGrath his combat diary, logbook, letters and other personal records, but McGrath needed to hear from the surviving members of his squadrons who knew him in combat.

From a postcard Lambert received from McGrath in 1967, it was apparent that McGrath now realized that Lambert was credited with twenty official victories. He intended to write a series of paperbacks on World War I aces and wanted to know if Lambert "would consider being the subject of one of these books?" Besides having knowledge of the war, Lambert had photographs from the period. McGrath asked Lambert to make copies of his pictures because he "would not want you to part with any of your pictures." McGrath had now realized that he had struck gold with Lambert as well.[26]

At the beginning of their friendship, McGrath was clearly the one receiving help from Lambert. But as Lambert was finishing his book and looking for a publisher, it would be important that he knew someone who was in the publishing field and knew how to find a publisher. McGrath would be a very useful friend to have.

We need to remember that, even before *Combat Report* was published, Lambert was gaining some publicity. Frey's article started this publicity. Lambert was then named in *Cross and Cockade International* and in stories in other aviation journals. Following these articles there began to appear stories in local, regional, and state newspapers and journals. These articles, such as Joe Gall's article "World War I Ace Flew 'Noisy Toy'" in *Ohio's Heritage* in

Fourteen. Lambert and Friends

1979, would continue to appear for the rest of Lambert's life. By 1980, the date of the publication of Bill Martin's article "America's Forgotten Ace" in *The Airman*, Lambert was no longer really "forgotten."

Combat Report was not always so titled. An article by Don Clancy, "Over Ohio," published in *The Columbus Dispatch* in 1971, promoted Lambert's upcoming book that was tentatively titled "The Called Us 'Haig's Heroes,'" a slight change from Lambert's initial proposal, "They Called Us 'Haig's Hawks.'" It was a good thing that the title was changed, for two reasons. First, the title "The Called Us 'Haig's Heroes' (or) 'Hawks'" sounds like the title of an article, not a book. Second, ironically, Field Marshal Douglas Haig was among those who at the beginning of the war discounted the value of having a military air force. In his personal draft for his final dispatch, Haig wrote, "Though aircraft and tanks proved of enormous value, their true value is as ancillaries of infantry, artillery, and cavalry."[27] However, this mention of the book with this title does show us that Lambert was well on his way with the writing and already considering titles.

Another man who proved to be a good friend of, and extremely helpful to, Lambert was the Great War Canadian ace Raymond Collishaw. Lambert had probably found out about Collishaw's through Cheesman. The former fighter pilot was now a military historian specializing in the Great War. Both his personal knowledge of the Great War, and his extensive library, were helpful to Lambert. And besides his personal help, Collishaw had published a directory of those former R.A.F. pilots who were still alive, the "Roster of War Birds." Lambert found this directory very helpful in getting addresses for the old comrades to whom he wrote.

The most important help that Collishaw gave Lambert, however, was that he wrote the Foreword to *Combat Report*. The foreword grew out of a disagreement between the two men as to what direction of the book should be. Collishaw, who was influenced by his service in the war and as an Air Historian, naturally thought that it should show the part that No. 24 Squadron had had in the overall war effort, and he told Lambert so. It is doubtful that Lambert could have written the book that way. What is certain is that he did not want to. In hindsight, it seems that Lambert was right and Collishaw wrong. The book gives the reader the experience of being a combat pilot in the Great War, and part of that experience is that the pilots did not ever know the big picture. All they knew from day to day was their target for that day.

Either Collishaw recognized this fact, or else (more probably) he realized that Lambert was not going to change his approach. So he wrote the preface to give that overall picture and show what No. 24 Squadron's place in that overall plan was. Both approaches are of value; having them together in the same book gives the reader a better picture than either could have been alone.

One of Lambert's old comrades that he was sending letters to during this time was Jack Southey in Colesburg, South Africa. Southey was assigned to A Flight from 30 March to 23 October 1918, so he and Lambert were in No. 24 Squadron at the same time. Of course, Lambert went to hospital in late August 1918, and Southey was still with the squadron for two more months. He left a little over two weeks before the Armistice.[28] At first, Lambert did not want Southey's help with the book itself; he wrote requesting photographs that would help him with his sketches. (All this time, in addition to writing the book, Lambert was doing sketches and drawings and paintings of aerial combat. Some of these he intended as illustrations for the book; with others, he was trying to sell copies or prints directly.) For example, Southey had a picture of Kurt Wusthoff's Fokker D. VII that was taken at Conteville. At

Lambert's request, Southey gave a great deal of attention to the details of the color of Wüsthoff's plane. He remembered "it was of printed fabric [diamond pattern] with green, brownish, and blue. I think the engine cowling was dark blue.... I examined the D. VII for bullet holes. There was a line of holes from the engine to the back of the cock-pit and I remember the fabric from the cock-pit towards the back was fairly light in color."[29]

In a later letter, from 16 February 1969, Southey describes an air battle that took place on 7 June 1918, which involved all three flights of the squadron. They left Conteville at 10:45 a.m. and engaged some Fokker Triplanes. It was on this day that Dawe was killed. Southey wrote, "I wondered if he had a presentiment because, the afternoon before, he was sitting in a deck chair watching two of us playing bumble puppy. I asked him to have a game. He refused and just sat brooding in his chair and was very quiet. He appeared to be under stress and seemed to bite his tongue as he sat there."[30] Lambert recognized a telling description when he saw one, and he used this letter almost verbatim in *Combat Report*.

Lambert was writing to Collishaw throughout this period, and an almost student/mentor relationship developed between the two. It is hard to choose among the many points that Collishaw made the ones that had the most effect on the book, but here are a few examples. Collishaw pointed out that from June 1918 onward, severe shortages, particularly in aviation gasoline and skilled pilots, began to plague the German Air Force, shortages such that Richthofen's Fighter Group was "unable to mount more than one Jasta on patrol."[31] In spite of this disadvantage, Collishaw pointed out that the American and R.A.F. casualties during the final two months of the war were among the heaviest for the entire conflict. He also reminded Lambert that No. 24 was the first fighter squadron ever sent to France. This information tended to support Lambert's claim that the quality and intensity of combat was greater during his period at the front than Rickenbacker.

On 30 May 1969, Collishaw sent Lambert a letter that contained several pages of information that were usable for *Combat Report*. This information included detailed material on the S.E.5a as a closed cockpit fighter, as well as an appreciation of the value of the plane as a fighter aircraft in 1918; notes on the use of the moveable Lewis gun in fighters; comments on No. 24 Squadron's victory on 17 June; and a lengthy appreciation for what Lambert's squadron did in 1918. Collishaw also helped Lambert with his paintings, which Lambert was doing along with his writing. For example, he gave Lambert help with the locations of markings on a Fokker Triplane.[32]

A letter of 29 October 1969 goes into details about a night attack that he made along with Captain Leonard "Tich" (or "Titch") Rochford, on a German aerodrome at Dorignies, 22 June 1918. He observes that "In fixed engines, the exhaust pipe becomes conspicuous in the dark; but with rotary engines, nothing can be seen at night. We used hand torches to keep in touch."[33] They were twenty-four miles over the German lines when they made their attack on the German hangers. Collishaw confessed that he could not recall all the details, because his entire "attention was concentrated on shooting up aircraft on the aerodrome and withdrawing."[34] His plane was hit with antiaircraft machine-gun fire and he got separated from Rochford, but they make it safely back to base.

Lambert intended to do a painting on the Dorignies attack, so Collishaw furnished Lambert with the number and color of his Bentley Camel, and described the difference between the colors on a Camel with a Bentley engine used for the Naval Fighter Squadrons and those used in the R.F.C. (Collishaw, who initially joined the Royal Naval Air Service), wrote that when painting this picture Lambert had to remember that the Naval Squadrons were recognized by their dark greenish chocolate khaki dope, while the R.F.C. Camels were colored a light sandy khaki.[35] Collishaw answered another of Lambert's questions as he described how "Rochford's Camel had no special markings, but their squadron differentiated between the various flights by using different colors. A Flight, commanded by Rochford, had red noses, B yellow, and C blue."[36] (How Lambert was going to show these colors, or indeed anything else, in a painting of a night attack, was never explained.)

Collishaw discussed the difficulty of finding a publisher for a book like Lambert's in a letter of 21 January 1970. He told of the difficulties of a friend and former pilot under his command, Marion Aten, who had written a book called *The Last Train Over the Rostov Bridge*. Eventually, Aten got in touch with a "creative writer," Arthur Orrmant, who introduced into Aten's factual story—a lot of spurious women and spurious love affairs."[37] After that, the book was "snapped up by a publisher ... and it has had an excellent sales history."[38] Collishaw told Lambert, "I am not at all suggesting that you should introduce some spurious women into your story; but that you should think in terms of your prospective reader, who knows nothing about the R.A.F. in France in 1918 ... a bare bones authentic account will be of interest only to the historian."[39] It is of interest whether Lambert's spurious accounts of his sexual exploits while on leave in London and at Jermyn Court, in *Combat Report*, were a consequence of Collishaw's letter, or if the overemphasis on sexual exploits in *Barnstorming and Girls* might also be a result of this letter.

In a later letter, Collishaw made more specific suggestions on finding a publisher. He suggested that Lambert consider publishing his book as a soft covered book with a company such as Ballantine Books of New York, including their address and instructing Lambert to write to Barrie Pitt, the Editor-in-Chief of Ballantine. He also included the address of Bantam Books, also of New York, and suggested that Lambert contact Thomas Funderbuck on Madison Avenue, letting Lambert know that he was currently in touch with Funderbunk. Collishaw emphasized the fact that both these publishers like to use "an abundance of photographs concerned with the story."[40] Undoubtedly, Collishaw knew this facet of their publication would appeal to Lambert.

It was in this letter that Collishaw informed Lambert that he intended to write, in the Foreword of Lambert's book, "a brief historical review concerning the period of your story," and mentioned his intent to emphasize "the important role played by the air at the time." Collishaw was going to write what he thought Lambert should have written all along. He also suggested that Lambert ask George Johnson, his former Flight Commander in No. 24 Squadron and later Air Marshal, Chief of Staff for the Royal Canadian Air Force, to write another Foreword for the book. (Johnson, however, declined the proposal, for two reasons: first, he would be too busy over the next two months to do it; second, he felt that Collishaw had already written a "very adequate Foreword.")[41]

In a letter of 15 February 1970, Collishaw gave more specific details of what his Foreword would be. He began by telling Lambert that he would "have liked to see more stress played on the three big operational phases of your story." These three phases were, first, the German Offensive; second, the opening of the British Final Offensive on the Roye-Amiens Road; and third, the final and victorious advance by the British, French, and American armies in conjunction.[42] Collishaw reminded Lambert that his squadron was in the "midst of these activities."

Besides asking for help with the factual details of the book from his friends, Lambert sought help from established writers on the literary side of the book, especially from Jesse Stuart of Greenup County, Kentucky, a well-known author in the Ohio-West Virginia-Kentucky area. It is not clear how Stuart influenced Lambert's prose. Lambert's writing does not sound much like Stuart's. What is clear, however, is that Stuart did what he could to get Lambert's book published with his own publisher, McGraw-Hill.

On 24 August 1967, Jesse Stuart sent a letter to Sam Stewart, Editor, at McGraw-Hill Publishers. By 1967, Stuart had published with McGraw-Hill a book of poetry, three collections of short stories, and a novel, *Mr. Gallion's School*. The two men, Stuart and Stewart, were familiar with each other; in fact, Jesse Stuart addresses him as "Dear Cousin Sam." Stuart begins his letter by describing how Lambert, a neighbor who lived across the Ohio River from him, had stopped by to show him his work on the history of the war. Stuart was impressed. Lambert needed a publisher and hoped his friend Jesse would use his connections and find him one. "I gave him your name and you can detail the synopsis, which he plans to send [as he doesn't have it finished yet] to you very soon. I told him I'd write to you for him."[43] Stuart gave Stewart a brief history of the Lamberts in the area and how "he's of the old stock American and served through both world wars."[44] It seems that Jesse was not above "spinning a yarn" on Lambert's behalf when he writes that this "delightful gentleman who was a good enough student to translate Virgil in high school, all on his own volition."[45] Stuart then plugs Lambert's book: "His book idea interests me, one of the pilots left, this close to me and I never knew it, who lives those days and remembers the men and talks of it if it were only yesterday. What he knows and remembers, I think should be preserved and I'm not a historian."[46] Stuart ends his letter with a postscript describing the correspondence Lambert had received from "all-over," the world. Unfortunately, even with Stuart's best efforts, McGraw-Hill elected not to publish Lambert's book.

By now, Lambert's primary focus was getting his book published. After McGraw-Hill, he contacted the organization Cross & Cockade about publishing it. However, Lonnie Raidor, Publication Director and Editor, pointed out to him that Cross & Cockade was a non-profit organization and so not in a position to publish his memoir, or any other book for that matter. Raidor did offer him one option; they could "have a private publication prepared by our people at [Lambert's] expense." In other words, they would prepare and publish Lambert's manuscript and he would pay for the expenses and "reap what financial gains there will be in your own sales."[47] Cross & Cockade would publicize the book through their own membership, but would not, of course, have any general advertising. Lambert understood that they had done all they could do for him, but he elected not to go that route. It was a risky proposition, in which he could spend a good deal and get little or nothing back, and at this time of his life, Lambert was not a gambler.

Somehow, Stanley Ulanoff, the aviation editor at Doubleday, was Lambert's literary agent for *Combat Report*. In the first letter we have from Ulanoff, 30 July 1970, to which is attached a letter to Ulanoff from Cornell Jaray of Kennikat Press dated 3 August, it is clear that Kennikat has agreed to publish the book, but that a serious issue has arisen. Jaray's letter stated that the manuscript had been returned from the copy letter with a note saying "a major rewrite job is in order before we can proceed."[48] Kennikat had not budgeted for a rewrite, so the additional cost, estimated at a minimum of $500, would have to be paid by "you [Ulanoff] and the Colonel."[49] Jaray was waiting on word from Ulanoff to proceed. Ulanoff suggested

Fourteen. Lambert and Friends

to Lambert that they accept Kennikat's revised offer. It would certainly mean an increase in cost, but not one that would need to be paid upfront, because the cost would be deducted from the royalties they would earn.[50]

Obviously this rewrite is a major stumbling block; but the tone of the rest of Ulanoff's letter is positive and suggests that the book is soon to be published. Ulanoff even knows what its dimensions will be; it will by six by nine inches.[51] It was too early for a brochure to be ready for mailing, but Ulanoff is already getting together a list of those to mail it to. He asked Lambert to send him a copy of the roster of Canadian World War I Flyers (probably Collishaw's "Roster of War Birds"), so he could send it to Kennikat's Publicity Department. And he promised that the list of those to be sent the brochure would include "all of the members of *Cross & Cockade* from all over the country."[52] Ulanoff thanked Lambert for following up with *The Airman* about the book, and told him that he (Ulanoff) would follow up with other air force publications including *Air Force Times* and *Air Force/Space Digest*. From this letter, it is easy to understand why Lambert assured so many friends that the book was about to be published.

On 10 August 1970, Lambert sent Jaray a letter acquiescing to the rewrite, but doing so in a characteristic way. He agreed, "providing you do not change the trend, or meaning of any of the narrative or the omission of any portion."[53] He did not object "to any re-phrasing as long as you maintain the intent of the facts as outlined. I have no objection to the charge as mentioned in your letter."[54] Again, we see Lambert's obsession with getting in all the details. If the intention of the re-write was to shorten the book by omitting some of these details, Lambert was going to nip that in the bud.

Jaray sent Lambert a letter on 17 November 1970 that seemed again to imply the book was about to be published. He informed Lambert that the manuscript had returned from the copy editor and was sent to be typeset. He expected galleys to be sent to him in three or four weeks, and assured Lambert he would be receiving a copy. He believed the publication date would be some time in the mid to late spring of 1971.[55]

The manuscript did not yet have a title. In response to Lambert's query about the title, Jaray suggested that they do not "yet have to commit ourselves firmly and perhaps when it is time, you and Colonel Ulanoff and I can have a three-way telephone conversation to discuss a title."[56] Answering another of Lambert's queries, this one about illustrations, Jaray said, "That is one of the last steps."[57]

Ulanoff, in a letter of 23 September 1971, acknowledges receiving the galleys Lambert sent him and promises to take them to the publishers shortly. He also told Lambert that he liked "your new idea for a title. Keep thinking them up. However, we'll leave the final decision to the publishers."[58]

But in spite of all these hopeful signs, Lambert's book deal with Kennikat unraveled in early 1971. Cheesman's letter of 16 March 1971 shows that Lambert was already having difficulties with Kennikat Press, and they were probably not going to publish the book. It seemed at the last moment, Kennikat was asking Lambert to pay for the publication, and we already know that Lambert was opposed to doing so. Cheesman was surprised and even shocked at this turn of events. He did not, of course, know the legalities of the publishing business in the United States, but he did tell him that in England he would have been entitled to compensation under the law of breach of contract. He believed that Lambert had no alternative but to find another publisher.[59]

In a later letter (4 July 1971), however, Cheesman had discouraging news for Lambert about finding another publisher. At least in England, he thought that there was a "downturn" in both the interest in and sales of books on aviation. The market had been saturated with aviation books, many of them "second rate hack efforts," and as a result publishers were becoming more cautious. In spite of these pessimistic opinions, however, Cheesman told Lambert that if he were making no progress with his book in the United States and would like to get it published in Britain, he (Cheesman) would help. And he urged Lambert to emphasize to possible publishers that the book was not so much an aviation book as a book about human beings involved in the struggle. If the publisher marketed the book in that way, Cheesman believed, it would be a "surefire success."[60]

At this crisis point, Robert McGrath reenters the picture. On 3 February 1971, McGrath sent Lambert a short note asking, "When will your new book be ready—let me know because I'm preparing a new catalog [#17] and I want to include your book—with a nice fat blurb and recommendation etc."[61] He also wanted to make sure Lambert remembered to send him an autographed copy, and he thought Lambert's personal paintings would assist the book's sales. The tone of the letter implies a certainty on McGrath's part that the book would soon be published.

However, he was disabused of that notion. McGrath's Sales Manager, B. Bneun, had sent a letter to Cornell Jaray at Kennikat on 5 May 1971. In the course of the letter, Bneun had casually mentioned "we have heard you are going to do a book by the famous World War I Ace—W. C. Lambert. If so, when?"[62] Jaray had scribbled a note by this question: "indefinite we may not at all."[63] McGrath sent this letter on to Lambert with a hand written note at the bottom, "just rec'd this. What is the story at present re: your book?"[64]

On 23 May 1971, McGrath sent another letter to Lambert in which he asked if Lambert had "decided to move out on Kennikat."[65] McGrath stated that he "knew them well and I won't even list their books—although I of course would have listed yours to boost its sales."[66] (This comment is in direct contradiction to the earlier letter of Bneun, which talks about one of Kennikat's books, Bill Rhode's *Bailing Wire, Chewing Gum, and Guts: The Story of the Gates Flying Circus*, which the World War I Aero Bookshop intended to list in their upcoming catalog.)[67] If things did not work out with Kennikat, McGrath offered to assist Lambert with his connections he had in the publishing business. He informed Lambert that he knew Stanley Ulanoff, who as we know was acting as Lambert's literary agent, and that he had a poor opinion of him; he says that he (McGrath) "was the person who suggested to Doubleday that WWI Aviation Classics be reprinted. Ulanoff was given the job as editor—he did a poor job of it so far."[68]

Lambert immediately responded to McGrath and let him know that his association with Kennikat was at an end. McGrath quickly responded, on 31 May, saying that I'm happy you are finished with them. On top of everything else poor book sales would have followed if they handled it."[69] McGrath then wanted to know if Lambert's agreement with Ulanoff was done saying that he did "not want [Ulanoff] jumping on my back if I was to seek assistance for you from some of my friends in this publishing game."[70] He writes, "Ulanoff is too busy to edit your book. They give the books off to others and then put their name in or on it as editor. If you get a release from Ulanoff I'll see what I can do for you."[71] In other words, McGrath was offering Lambert his services as literary agent, but only on the condition that Ulanoff was permanently out of the picture.

Fourteen. Lambert and Friends

During the rest of the year, Lambert was sending out his manuscript to a number of major American book publishers, what McGrath referred to as "quality publishers," but all of them rejected it. The first to do so was Doubleday. On 13 May 1971, Harold Kueber of Doubleday sent Lambert a letter that stated "at this moment we have an unusual number of manuscripts on hand in the field of aviation. As tempting as your memoir sounds, it is impossible for us to take on additional projects at this time."[72] Kuebler acknowledge that he had discussed Lambert's work with Ulanoff, but whatever Ulanoff had said had not been enough to persuade Kueber to publish the book.[73] On 15 June and again on 13 December 1971, he received letters a rejection letter from Virginia Hazirjian at Prentice-Hall. (There seems to be no clear explanation for the two different letters.) In the second one, Hazirjian said that she had appreciated the opportunity to "review and read your manuscript, *Combat Report*." (So we know that at this time Lambert had already given the book the title that would be the final one.) The consensus, however, "seems to be that it is doubtful we can achieve the market sales we would require to publish the book."[74] Evidently, the glut of aviation books on the market that Cheesman noticed in England seems to be there in America as well.

Lambert could not even get an article taken from his book published. On 9 July 1971, Jan Steenblik, Editorial Assistant for *Air Progress* magazine, sent Lambert a rejection letter for his manuscript "One Day's Combat." To add insult to injury, it was a form letter: Steenblik wrote, "It is the type of material that we prefer, but unfortunately it does not suit our current needs."[75]

McGrath, however, was not deterred. In a quick note to Lambert on 18 June 1971, McGrath said that he had "made a couple of direct approaches to publishers regarding your book—that is quality publishers." He promised to let Lambert know when he received a response, and wrote that he "told them I was your agent." He ended his note with a postscript that stated he "just wanted to let you know I was not sleeping on it."[76]

On 7 July 1971, McGrath happily reported, in a hand written note, that Lambert's book had been received by David Harris, Publication Editor of Houghton Mifflin, "a Class Publisher."[77] If Harris' response was not optimistic, McGrath was "already at work with Little-Brown—another first class publisher."[78] On 19 July 1971, McGrath had received a similar letter from Harris telling him that Lambert's book "would not be a viable one for our trade list ... we just don't think the market out there is large enough."[79] Two days later, Sandra Thomas from the Editorial Department of Little, Brown and Company sent a rejection letter to McGrath on his "proposed book on World War I aviation by America's 2nd ranking ace."[80] In both cases, as before, the publishers said nothing against the book, but they had doubts about their ability to make a profit from it.

McGrath, however, had another string to his bow. On 5 August, he informed Lambert about the rejection letters he had received and that he was pursuing a possible deal with Kimber in London. They were "very much interested. I am going to send your chapter to them to read [and slides]—if okay by you. Then if they like, we will have to send the whole manuscript."[81]

McGrath's optimism this time was warranted. In July, he received a letter from Amy Howlett, a Director for Kimber, saying, "The manuscript about W.C. Lambert sounds most interesting and if you would be kind enough to send it to us we should be delighted to consider it for our list."[82] McGrath forwarded Howlett's letter to Lambert with some hand written comments. Next to Howlett's name he wrote that he was "on friendly terms with her." He then wrote that he had sent "the chapter and slides to Kimber ... but haven't heard—maybe that is good. Will let you know pronto when I hear."[83] In a letter of 16 October to Lambert, he wrote, "I sent [Kimber] your material, plus my own build up etc.—looks like they will buy."[84]

McGrath's efforts were rewarded. On 16 October 1971, he sent Lambert another handwritten note on a purchase order with "Good News!" blazoned in large letters. He also included a copy of a letter he had received from Howlett showing that Kimber was interested in publishing his book. McGrath wrote that Lambert should tell the Kimber Company "I am your agent and they will take it from there."[85] He let Lambert know that he (Lambert) needed to make his own financial arrangements with Kimber, but since McGrath had been the one to contact them, Lambert was to tell them that McGrath was working on his (Lambert's) behalf.[86] McGrath had found Lambert a publisher in less than six months.

After receiving McGrath's letter of the 16th, Lambert immediately sent a letter to Howlett. He began it by stating, "My agent, Mr. Bob McGrath suggested that I write you."[87] He continued by letting Howlett know that he would be pleased to send her the complete manuscript "just as soon as I receive your reply to this letter."[88] He also informed her of his willingness to send pictures (he had about 130 official photographs and snapshots that were taken in France) and reminded her that she had the color slides of his sketches that were to be used in the book. He felt that "all these pictures will increase the sales potential of the book."[89] Lastly, he included Cheesman's address and let Howlett know that he was a "very good friend of mine. You might wish to talk to him."[90]

On 23 October, three days after sending his previous letter, Lambert sent a second one to Howlett which included his manuscript. This letter was in response to Howlett's letter to McGrath of 12 October, which informed McGrath that Kimber was "extremely interested in this [Lambert's book] and almost certainly would like to make an offer for it. Could you tell me where the rest of the manuscript is ... do you think you could arrange to send over the rest of it?"[91] Upon receiving a copy of Howlett's second letter from McGrath, Lambert immediately followed up with his second letter along with the galley sheets he had corrected (almost certainly from his dealings with Kennikat.) He wrote that he hoped to hear from Howlett soon, and finished by letting her know that the pictures and photos could be mailed to her at a later date.[92] His tone was guardedly optimistic, and Lambert shows he is excited at the prospects of finally getting his book published.

Of course, Lambert wrote Cheesman about the progress being made with Kimber and asked for his help. On 1 September 1971, Cheesman addressed Lambert's news. As it happened, he knew Kimber well, especially Francis de Salis, one of their Directors. In fact, Cheesman had just heard from Kimber the week before asking his opinion on "some potential works they had in view." He had also done some works for them on aviation books, including a McCudden biography and some volumes of *Communiqués*. He told Lambert that he "did not, of course, know [Lambert] had sent them the manuscript and as I have not read it cannot pass opinion on it in the way one should but I have written to [de Salis] and vouched for your good self as a great friend of mine."[93] He cautioned Lambert that Kimber would probably ask for someone else's opinion who might be more impartial: "I'm sure that if asked, and after reading it, I would get it a laudatory assessment!"[94] He did assure Lambert that he would give it as much support as he could.

Lambert now had a publisher, but he was not overjoyed as might have been expected.

He wanted to publish with a major American publisher, and he was not only publishing with an English firm but also with one that dealt only with military works. He wrote to McGrath seeking reassurance. McGrath replied on 20 December 1971, giving Lambert what he wanted. He assured Lambert that Kimber was a fine publisher of books on military topics. Unlike a textbook publisher like Prentice Hall, Kimber would approach Lambert's book as a "work of love." McGrath assured him that with a firm like Prentice Hall, he would have to get a firm publication date: "All publishers like to keep a stable full of manuscripts that they can fall back on from time to time."[95] McGrath insisted that Lambert should stick with Kimber; otherwise, "you would end up completely disgusted and there is a possibility that it never would be published."[96] Kimber would also give his work a "personal touch" that Prentice Hall would not.[97] McGrath offered to send a copy of a Kimber book on military aviation so Lambert could get a look at the finished product. In the end, Lambert evidently got the reassurance he needed and decided he would follow McGrath's advice and stick with Kimber.

Lambert was also nervous about the editing Kimber was doing on his book. He always wanted to be in control, and in this editing he had to rely on others. Again, McGrath assured him that he should "allow them to cut when they feel it is correct to do so."[98] Apparently, Kimber was eliminating material dealing with other squadrons besides No. 24. Lambert had taken Collishaw's advice (to a degree) and broadened his view of the air war on the Western Front. Kimber recognized that Collishaw's advice was bad; the focus of Lambert's book was on one man's—one fighter pilot's—experience in the Great War. When Lambert went beyond his own experience, the book was weakened.

One of Lambert's friends, John Mackenzie from Scotland, sent along with a letter of his own a copy of a letter he had received from Francis de Salis (who, as we know, was one of the Directors of Kimber), sent on 6 May 1972. The letter said, among other things that Kimber was "hoping to publish the book in October though this is going to be a bit of a rush and it may run over into the Spring of next year."[99] This letter seems to be the first indication Lambert had of the final publication date of the hardback edition of *Combat Report,* in the spring of 1973. The Corgi Books paperback edition would come out on 21 November 1975.[100]

With the publication of *Combat Report,* Lambert definitely left the status of "forgotten ace." He was a rarity, an accomplished ace of the Great War who could retell the story of that war to many Americans who did not know it. Many of the notable figures of early aviation were gone or would soon die. Rickenbacker would die in July 1973, and Lindbergh would follow him a year after in August 1974. At almost seventy-eight years of age, Lambert's achievements now gave him a certain celebrity status. The publicity he received from *Combat Report* would allow him to continue to live in the past and relive those moments from his glory days. Writers, reporters, and admirers would call on him; he would be in demand. The attention would change his life by giving him purpose and energy for the remaining nine years of his life. He was an ace, and one of the few still alive.

Fifteen

Lambert as Artist

Most of the different things that Lambert did, he did at specific times in his life. At one time he was a fighter pilot, at another a barnstormer, at another a salesman, and so on. But one thing he did throughout his life, and that was art-work—sketches, paintings, and drawings. One of his friends, Robert Smith, asked him when he knew he was a good painter. Lambert's self-deprecating comment was "I didn't know I was a good painter"; but he showed Smith a water painting of birds he did when he was ten years old.[1] The reader will remember that some of Lambert's letters home when he was at Grenier Field and Presque Isle were illustrated with sketches. The greatest number of his sketches, drawings, and paintings, however, are of planes and aerial combat, and most of them seem to have been done in his old age, his major creative period—at the time he was designing buildings and writing *Combat Report*.

Lambert was always an amateur; he never sought to take lessons or have professionals critique his work. But a number of people to whom he gave his paintings, particularly fellow veterans of the Great War, raved about them. A number of them also admired the sketches he did. For example, his former flight commander, C. O. Johnson, wrote of his sketches, "They are excellent. You have taken artistic license in compressing the action but by so doing you have made them more interesting and shown detail of aircraft very accurately by types. Your sketches are very good portrayal of the action in our aerial combat at that time."[2]

Not everyone, however, had a good opinion of Lambert's sketches. Lambert wanted to use his sketches as illustrations in *Combat Report,* and sent them to Frank Cheesman for his opinion. Cheesman took a good look at Lambert's sketches and put a good deal of thought into his comments before sending them to Lambert. His comments are devastating, particularly as Cheesman was a friend of Lambert's and did not want to hurt his feelings. He wrote that "unless illustrations other than photos are of a high artistic standard or technically very expert a publisher would be very hesitant about running to the expense of having these blocks made and especially in the large numbers you have in mind … it is an important economic factor controlling the price of the book…. If you had in mind color, of course, it would be that much more expensive."[3] He told Lambert that his sketches did not "come into that class [of "high artistic standard"] nor do they really constitute drawings of high grade technical expertise."[4] He thought that the real story was Lambert, so he should be true to the factual aspect of the book by using only photographs. "As you say, you are not an artist but a draughtsman. Somewhere between these two is the bare minimal requirement for a publisher. I believe that point has not been reached in these sketches." Cheesman particularly criticized Lambert for using the same background in his pictures. "Sameness must be avoided but cannot be if you insist on illustrating these scenes." He finally summed up his feeling by stating that he did "not feel that the present sketches, interesting as they are, have a sufficiently high artistic value; there is an unacceptable sameness about the scenes and, finally, it is very doubtful whether this form of illustration is as good as that of photos."[5]

Besides his sketches, Lambert did both drawings and paintings. The drawings are considerably worse than the paintings. As an engineer, Lambert thought of drawings as an engineer would: as something to reproduce the object from, not as something that appears to us as the object. He refused to use perspective in his drawings. As Bill Martin comments, "Lambert never had any artistic training. His drawings looked rather 'flat' as he made all the objects in the scene the same size. I tried to encourage him to make large foreground objects to give his drawings more depth, but I was never able to convince him."[6] The drawings are also generally static, with the object (usually an airplane) just being there. The paintings, on the other hand, did have perspective, so the objects appeared in them as they do to us. They were also full of movement, since they were usually scenes of airplanes attacking each other. For both these reasons, the paintings are artistically superior to the drawings.

The best statement of Lambert's intention in his paintings is one written by Jesse Stuart to give his "blessings" to Lambert's paintings. It was a general letter, addressed "To Whom It May Concern," that Lambert must have requested or Stuart offered to write for him. Evidently Lambert intended to include it with his paintings when he sent them to publishers in hopes of getting a book published of his World War I paintings. Stuart called Lambert's paintings

Lambert and his field uniform are both still the same size. He is showing guests one of his paintings that hangs in his home.

"pieces of art—art due to his experiences in World War I-which should be perpetuated."[7] He says that "what [Lambert] has done should be preserved in book form and in art galleries—Civilian and Military. Our future will have need of this—what he has done."[8] He points out that Lambert "was in the thick of World War I flying—when men went up in planes without much protection—and ... he has described this for you, for us, in pictures—which have turned out to be the best I have seen."[9] In other words, Lambert's pictures are both works of art and records of history. It is for this reason—that these paintings describe what actually happened—that Lambert is so obsessed with getting the details exactly right.

A good example of this need to get the exact details is the painting that Lambert did on a night attack that Collishaw and "Tich" Rochford on a German aerodrome at Dorignes, which was described in the previous chapter. Lambert was not there at the attack, so he wrote Collishaw to get the details right. In one letter, Collishaw sent an extensive description of the markings on his Sopwith Camel, and went into more detail on the attack on the aerodrome. He also remarked on how the "normal colored rondels acted as 'Bulls eyes' to hostile pilots."[10]

Those people to whom Lambert sent his paintings—friends and former comrades—were impressed by them. For example, Collishaw wrote about one of his "beautiful" paintings that "it shows what can be done properly and it is in strong contrast to the so called artistic license ... [in] many previous attempts to depict Air Scenes of the 1st War. I am having your painting mounted for my study."[11] Rochford, when he received a photograph of the picture that Lambert painted of the raid on Dorignes, was genuinely and pleasantly surprised by the gift. He wrote to Lambert "to thank you, an old comrade in arms, for presenting to me, via my friend Frank Cheesman, that delightful photograph of the picture you painted of Raymond Collishaw & myself attacking the aerodrome at Dorignies."[12] Rochford said that "the colouring was splendid & an excellent representation of the countryside, as I saw it at dawn break on that day so many years ago."[13] Rochford was impressed by Lambert's attention to detail and figured he must have "consulted a map of the area."[14]

Lambert's former squadron mate, J. H. Southey, was also excited by Lambert's paintings. He writes, "I am tremendously impressed by your pictures which show great artistic skill and which depict, with a wealth of detail, the actual air battles, dog-fights or duels which 24 Squadron fought in the air over 50 years ago. They vividly recall those stirring events which took place so long ago and, for me, the close comradeship which existed not only among pilots, but between pilots and ground crew, who did such a sterling job to keep us in the air. You have drawn each type of aircraft, whether German or Allied, with wonderful accuracy. Your pictures create a nostalgia ... [and] give me a lot of pleasure and, when framed and hung, will continue to do so."[15]

There are many examples of Lambert's concern with getting the details right. One concerns a painting Lambert was doing of Richthofen's final battle. He needed to get the markings on a Fokker triplane right, so he wrote to Collishaw. Collishaw replied, "German pilots were not permitted to interfere with German national markings and so, I am certain that Von R. did not, in respect to his Fokker Triplane.... The color of the rudder was white with a black Greek Cross on it. The same type of cross was on upper and lower surface of the wings."[16] Lambert had, no doubt, seen many Fokker triplanes during the war, but seeing them in the heat and excitement of combat, he did not trust his memory and checked with a friend.

Two letters of Cheesman's strike the reader as amusing. In one, Cheesman had recently received a letter from Lambert in which a picture of his plane had been included. Cheesman was scandalized by the markings on Lambert's plane. He does not actually shake his finger at Lambert and say, "This will never do!" but obviously that is what he means. He writes that such personal markings were "highly irregular and therefore [Lambert's marking] is unique as individual markings were not normally permitted by the Air Ministry—especially when it meant clashing with or eliminating the official symbols."[17] Cheesman even sends Lambert photos and booklets along with his letter so that Lambert could know the officially sanctioned colors and locations and styles of markings and letterings on specific British aircraft. In another letter, Lambert is again asking about markings, this time on German aircraft as well as British. Cheesman acknowledged that the Germans were probably given "more latitude in this matter" (he had to, since Lambert had seen the markings on German planes during his battles), but he insisted no proper British aircraft would be "painted up in Bizarre colors." He told Lambert that "nobody, I'm sure, had the time or inclination to go to the trouble to obtain paints outside those allotted for the usual purposes of a unit—even had they been available."[18] (Among the many shortages in Britain during World War I was a shortage of paint.)

Not only were Lambert's drawings and paintings welcomed by friends and old comrades-in-arms, but also by museums. These museums were not art museums, but historical museums, showing that at least one of Lambert's purposes was achieved: his paintings were seen as records of historical events.

The first museum to benefit from Lambert's art is, as we would expect, the Air Force Museum, where Royal Frey was. Early in 1968, Frey let Lambert know that his "drawings have been on display for three weeks" at the Museum. He also stated, "The caption [under his drawing] describes the scene, gives your name as the artist, and clearly shows you are one of the pilots on the mission."[19] Lambert is always, concerned about getting the details right; he is also concerned about getting recognition, not only for his role as artist, but also for his role as fighter in the conflict. Frey is reassuring him that all of these things he needs will be provided. Frey's care in this matter would bear great fruit for the Museum in the future. As Bill Martin said, "Lambert did tell me all along that the Air Force Museum would get first choice of his possessions when he died."[20]

The United States Air Force Museum was not the only one benefiting from Lambert's art. On 30 October 1970, Lambert had written to John Tanner, Director of the Royal Air Force Museum Foundation, offering the Museum his "paintings illustrating First World War combat action and relating to [his] time with No.24 Squadron."[21] The reply came from M. P. Sayer, keeper of General Collections at the R.A.F. Museum. Sayer was of course unfamiliar with Lambert's work, but was going to remedy that problem by viewing the copies "held by your friend, Mr. E. F. Cheesman."[22] The letter was an encouraging one: Sayer wrote that "the nature of the sources of recommendation for your pictures leave me in no doubt that copies of them would form a very welcome addition indeed to the collections which we are in the process of assembling."[23]

After a delay caused by various unforeseen circumstances (Sayer's heart attack at the beginning of December, a British postal strike), and after receiving a Christmas card from Lambert featuring one of his paintings, Sayer gratefully accepted Lambert's offer. The reproduced painting was "sufficient to show that we would be very pleased to accept your kind offer to present a set of photographic reproductions whenever it is convenient for you to do so."[24]

But after Lambert's pictures had been sent and received, there was still a delay. The Museum building was under construction and would not open for a year. Sayer let him know this fact, and Cheesman reiterated it, adding that the limited staff was busy doing research projects while also preparing exhibit plans for displays in the new building. Cheesman also made a pitch for himself, asking Lambert for the opportunity to purchase "one of the *original* paintings of this set to add to my collection of aeronautica."[25] This request shows the difference between Lambert's sketches and his finished paintings. Cheesman, as the reader may remember, was severely critical of Lambert's sketches, but he was impressed by the painting.

On 31 March, Sayer responded to Lambert's offer to send twenty-one prints as well as a "description of a single day's action by the pilots of No. 24 Squadron."[26] (This was a narrative of Lambert's air combat of 4 July 1918, when he crashed two Fokker D. VIIs and forced another one to land, taken from *Combat Report.*) Sayer expressed his gratitude for the gift and for his suggestions on the proper way to mount and frame the prints, but he informed Lambert that a "separate official" would be responsible for the method used in displaying exhibits; however, Sayer would pass along the advice to this individual.[27] As with the gift to the Air Force Museum, Lambert was concerned about how the exhibit would be displayed, as well as with receiving proper credit. It was yet another example of Lambert having to be in control.

When the package finally arrived, Sayer was in Normandy, but by 21 May, he had returned and responded to Lambert. Again he thanked Lambert for his gifts and for "the helpful notes on the back of the pictures and we will of course pay careful regard to all your suggestions regarding the mounting of the pictures."[28] However, he reminded Lambert that although they were all "deeply involved at this moment in establishing the broad layout of the galleries illustrating the history of the RAF," a Mr. Lee, the display officer of the museum, would be in charge of the actual display.[29] He also reminded Lambert that the museum was going through a building process and would not be opened until 1972, so it would be a short while before Lambert's exhibit was unveiled.

Lambert must have been impressed by the way the Museum treated him. On 29 May, he sent another letter, this time directly to Tanner, the museum director. Lambert asked them to return the narrative from the book he was writing after they had made a copy. Surprisingly, he also offered to make a financial donation to the Museum. The amount is not specified in Tanner's letter, but Tanner responded to Lambert's "very kind letter" by letting him know how to address "any bequest of money" to the museum in order that the funds will go to the museum's private fund and not the government, and "cannot in any way be diverted to any other use." Both Sayer and Tanner were struck by Lambert's continued generosity.[30] The financial offer seems to have caught them off-guard. Tanner wrote, "You have already been kind and generous to the Museum and anything else you do will greatly add to the debt of gratitude we already owe you."[31]

On 5 April 1971, Lambert received a letter from Paul E. Poberezny, President of the Experimental Aircraft Association Air Museum Foundation in Franklin, Wisconsin, in response to a letter of Lambert's offering to send him copies of his paintings. Poberezny told Lambert that the museum would be "very pleased to receive the paintings, and will display them."[32] He also let Lambert know that they were restoring an S.E.5 (as the reader will remember, Lambert's favorite fighter plane) and "look forward to your visit … we would like to have a picture of you with the SE5 for use in *Sport Aviation*" (which was EAA's magazine published

Fifteen. Lambert as Artist

for its members, and of which Paul Poberezny was Editor-in-Chief.)[33] On 20 April 1971, Lambert received a letter from Ronald Siwik, who sent him two issues of *Sports Aviation,* one of which—the March issue—featured the S.E.5. Siwik wrote, "As you can see they are doing a fine job there in Hales Corners and your contribution will be most appreciated."[34]

On 5 August, Lambert heard from Poberezny's secretary, Millie Reidenbach, informing him that the paintings had arrived. A little over a month later, on 7 September 1971, Bill Hodges, Assistant Director, wrote Lambert to acknowledge receiving his donation of 8 × 10 color reproductions of his paintings and to tell him that "the prints are framed and on display in the World War I photo section of our museum."[35] Hodges included a copy of the information page on Lambert, as "the second greatest American ace of World War I," which they posted with the pictures. However, they wanted Lambert to identify "Thorpe" for them.[36]

This request exposes the meanest side of Lambert. Lambert could be both irascible and controlling, but he was not usually mean. However, he was mean to Thorpe. The Reverend Thorpe had painted the details of these paintings for Lambert. Not only did Lambert pay him far too little for his time and skill, occasionally giving him $5, but he seldom gave him credit for his work. Lambert did in a way recognize Thorpe in the "Acknowledgments" in *Combat Report,* but his name is misspelled as "Thorne." This behavior can be explained by Lambert's dislike of admitting that he needed help on anything, especially his painting, but this explanation is no justification.

At least one other museum displayed Lambert's pictures. On 30 January 1973, James Smith of the Hebron Military Museum in Hebron, Ohio, sent Lambert a handwritten letter thanking him for his "wonderful" pictures.[37]

At the same time he was sending copies of his paintings to museums, Lambert was exploring the possibility of having his pictures reproduced for purchase by the general public, either individually or (preferably) collected in book form. However, he found even more difficulty in this search than in his search for a publisher for his book.

His first attempt was with Allbee and Sons, printers and lithographers from Waterloo, Iowa. Evidently Lambert had seen the prints of Charles R. d'Olive, another American ace, which were distributed by Albee and Sons. However, James Fox, President of Allbee and Son, let Lambert know that the company was "set up to distribute Mr. d'Olive's color prints" and was not equipped to make color prints of Lambert's paintings. He did offer Lambert the proposition that, if he was willing to "have these pictures convert to prints and then offer them to us for distribution I think we could include your prints with our current advertising."[38]

Lambert now looked for a company that could produce prints of his paintings and sketches. He contacted Flying Enterprises in Dallas, Texas. He probably got the idea of sending photographs of his paintings to this firm from an advertisement he saw in the Cross & Cockade publication. In the letter he received from Mitch Mayborn of Flying Enterprises, Mayborn admitted he did not know the procedure for reproducing paintings, so he had to send the photographs that Lambert had sent him to an acquaintance in order to get a proper estimate as well as suggestions on how they could be economically produced. He knew that usual price was around "$700 to $1000 at a minimum to adequately reproduce color work of quality and usually the payout is over several years."[39] He suggested that they issue a pair of limited edition books on Lambert's paintings that "should sell for, say $25.00 each [$45 for both] and be personally signed. This would provide a faster payout of the total cost with far fewer sales."[40] This option seemed to Mayborn the most feasible one, and he offered to design and produce the sets for a 40% commission. He believed that "there would be considerable pre-publication demand for paintings by the WWI ace."[41]

In a second letter, Mayborn discusses another idea, of selling limited edition posters of Lambert's paintings. He admitted that he had not had many orders for limited-edition posters, but he had sold "several hundred of the regular posters at $2.95 each or $2.50 for C & C members." He believed that "there would be considerable more interest in a painting by a WWI ace, especially when it contained your actual signature on each one sold."[42] He would be willing to do the promotion and marketing, with the initial mailings to Cross & Cockade members. He estimated that if they printed the maximum for a limited edition, which was 100 posters, they could expect an income of around $2,000 from the sale price of $20 per poster. But he also informed Lambert that he did not have "sufficient experience in this range to estimate the time required to sell the prints."[43]

Lambert did not pursue this matter with Mayborn. It may have been that there was too much that Mayborn did not seem to know. However, in the late 1970s, he was able to get Aeroprint, a company located in Boonton, New Jersey, to produce and sell a print of one of his paintings that they called "The Last Patrol." It was one of the most elaborate paintings that Lambert ever did, both in the number of planes involved and in the different actions that are going on at the same time. The painting showed fifteen S.E.5s escorting eight observation planes. At the top of the picture, eight Fokker D.VIIs are emerging from the clouds to attack three Sopwith Camels. When the Germans suddenly discover the large flight of S.E.5s below, they turn and run.[44]

"The Last Patrol," as was said, was the title given the print by Aeroprint. In fact, it was one of Lambert's earlier patrols. It displayed an engagement in which Lambert was involved on 9 May 1918.

The print was made from a painting that was to be used in *Combat Report*. Bill Martin, felt, rightly, that it was a mistake for Lambert to supply Aeroprint with only a copy from which to work. He tried to explain to Lambert the importance of supplying them with an original in which the resolution of his painting could be fully captured. But Lambert would not trust his originals being out of his possessions even if it was for just a short time.[45]

"The Last Patrol" sold fairly well, helped in part by people like George Gumbert, Jr., an Orthopedic Surgeon from Lexington, Kentucky, and member of an Aviation History group. Gumbert ordered fifty copies of "The Last Patrol" for himself and his group. Lambert was to visit Lexington and personally autograph the prints to increase their value and salability.[46]

Other people that we know of who bought a copy were historians, like the distinguished military historian Edward M. Coffman, a professor at the University of Wisconsin; friends, like Bill Martin who displayed an autographed copy in his home; and aviation enthusiasts, like Gumbert or Steve Sullivan, teacher of American History at Palatine High School in Palatine, Illinois, whose copy of "The Last Patrol" hung in his office at the high school. Evidently a number of people purchased the print after first buying a copy of *Combat Report*.[47]

It is difficult to give a balanced judgment of Lambert as artist. He was not a trained artist, and art was always a hobby with him, not a life work. There are serious problems, as we have seen, with both his sketches and his drawings. On the other hand, his paintings gave genuine pleasure to a number of people, among them those who had been active participants in the actions depicted and would be expected to be especially strict critics of those paintings. And museums vied to get copies of those paintings as records of important moments in aviation history. We can agree, at the least, that one of Lambert's goals—to record precisely the dog-fights of the First World War—he did achieve.

Sixteen

The Lambert They Knew

Almost all that we know about Lambert personally as a young man, as a fighter pilot and a barnstormer, comes from what he reveals to us in *Combat Report* and *Barnstorming and Girls*. About Lambert as a middle-aged man, when he was at Grenier Field and Presque Isle, we know something from his letters home to Chloe Ann. In these letters, Lambert is revealed as a devoted and caring husband, with a sense of humor and empathy, particularly with the young nurses and young men who are flying the planes. We would not necessarily assume from what Lambert tells us in his books that he would turn out to be that kind of person.

However, for Lambert's last years, we have the testimony of a good many people who knew him personally, so we can get a good idea of what he was like at that time. However, there is a caveat. We cannot assume "the Lambert they knew" is the same person as the young Lambert or even the middle-aged one. Obviously, there is a continuity in Lambert's life, as there is in any life. But there are also characteristics—and not admirable ones—that developed or intensified as Lambert aged. And there are some characteristics that are the opposite of the characteristics of the younger man.

To see this difference between the young Lambert and the old one, we might look at an account of a trip Lambert often took from Ironton to Wright-Paterson Air Force Base in Dayton, during which time the car was driven by Lambert's younger friend, Klaus Staerker. This fact—that Lambert was being chauffeured by another—is the first obvious difference from the younger Lambert. We saw the young Lambert as a daring fighter pilot and barnstormer, constantly flying on new routes, or as a Marmon salesman, driving customers all over to show off the car. But in his old age, though he did still drive around Ironton, he would not drive on longer trips out of town, so someone had to drive him.

Of course, one of the reasons for this decision on Lambert's part was that he was now a far worse driver than when he was younger. His sight was failing, especially his peripheral vision. He had trouble moving his head from side to side, so often he would back out of his driveway honking his horn to warn people he was coming.[1] He liked to drive with the windows open when it was winter and continued to light his pipe and talk with his hands as he drove. Ironton citizens have memories of Lambert driving through red lights as he went along the streets of the city.[2]

Bill Martin also saw Lambert's driving difficulties. On their way to a General Dynamics interview in 1980, he made Lambert pull off the road so that he could drive Lambert's car. He said that, even though it was early in the morning with very few cars on the road, he had to take over before Lambert killed them both. Lambert, who was then about eighty-five years old, was driving all over the road and not paying attention to what he was doing, so it was likely they would not make it to Dayton alive.[3]

While on the road with Lambert, Staerker initially used his own car; but because of the rising cost of gasoline in the 1970s and Lambert's failure to offer any financial assistance or even recompense him for his expenses, Staerker took to using Lambert's car for their excursions. From Lambert's own accounts, he was something of a spendthrift in his years as a fighter pilot and a barnstormer, but in his old age he was a miser. We have seen how badly he treated the Reverend Thorpe financially for helping to paint his pictures. In his old age, Lambert was infamous around Ironton for his dime tips.

Lambert needed to go to Wright-Patterson Air Force Base three or four times a year, and the route was always the same. According to Staerker, "Lambert would always stick to things and roads he knew and was unwilling to try new things or ways. He was afraid of the unknown, or those things outside of his control."[4] They would leave at the same time. Lambert would call Staerker the night before and tell him "we are going to the Daedalians Club tomorrow at 11:00 a.m." Staerker would then be told to be at Lambert's house at 9:00 a.m. for the trip. He would have Klaus fill up the gas tank at a station in Fairborn, a city near Dayton, so they would have enough gas to make it home. He would even put his finger into the gas tank to make sure it was indeed full.[5]

There were times, either because another route was quicker or simply for a change of scenery, that Staerker would take a different route home. When he discovered they were traveling on an unfamiliar road, Lambert would become unnerved. He would question Staerker about the road, if he had previously taken it and if it actually was a way back to Ironton. Even when Staerker showed him that the road was on a map, Lambert, formerly a pilot who navigated at times using a rolling map device he invented and proudly displayed in his home (and was later given to the Air Force Museum), would insist that they travel the same road they always traveled.[6]

Several times on the way from Ironton to Rio Grande, Lambert would point out to fields on the side of the road where he had once landed during his barnstorming days. That kind of comment was common with Lambert in his old age. Like many older people, but far more than most, he was living in the past by preference to the present. This time is when he was writing both *Combat Report* and *Barnstorming and Girls*, both books of reminiscence, and corresponding with old comrades-in-arms from not only the United States but also England and Canada and as far away as South Africa. His glory days in the past; he had more reason than most to want to live there.

Lambert's memory was still an excellent one, but at times he remembered—or invented—more than had happened. One good example was this inflation of the facts is Lambert's engagements with Richthofen. But in a 1970 interview with David Peyton for *Pathway Magazine*, Lambert stated that he did not recall ever meeting Richthofen in battle, but he was certain they had engaged in combat. In fact, Peyton stated, "Lambert recalls seeing the Red Baron lying dead."[7] (This statement is false. It was Daley, not Lambert, who saw Richthofen dead.) By the time he was interviewed at the Air Force Museum for General Dynamics in 1980, Lambert believed that he had engaged Richthofen three or four times. They had spent three weeks together on the front before Richthofen's death in April 1918, and, in fact, Lambert said that Richthofen was on his tail once, but he managed to get away.[8] He told Peyton that Richthofen "was bloodthirsty. He went after the cold turkeys, the slower aircraft. To us, he was just another pilot. We were never out to get him any more than any other German pilot. There were other German pilots we had more respect for."[9] A local newspaper article from 1978 stated that Lambert's "home is crowded with [his] pictures and a swatch of fabric from the plane of Germany's ace, Baron von Richthofen. 'We didn't think that much of him at the time,' he said."[10] If Richthofen was "just another pilot" to Lambert, it would be odd that Lambert kept that swatch of fabric from his plane as one of his proudest possessions (later willed them to the U.S. Air Force Museum), and that he spent so much time painting a picture of the Baron's final flight and getting the details right. Obviously he held Richthofen in far greater esteem than he admitted.

The views that those who knew him held of Lambert differ widely, depending largely on whether or not they shared his interest in World War I, aviation, and engineering, and on how he had treated them. The worst opinion of Lambert was that of the Reverend William C. Thorpe, who, as the reader will remember, had helped Lambert on coloring the illustrations for his book. Lambert had contacted Thorpe, who was an artist as well as a minister, to ask for his help. But Lambert not only never paid him anything like what he should have been paid, but also never even gave him a copy of the finished book; however, he did at times acknowledge Thorpe by including his name on certain paintings. Thorpe felt, with good reason, that Lambert had taken advantage of him. He also considered Lambert self-centered and opinionated, disregarding the feelings of others. He recalled one day when they drove to a gathering in Columbus in Lambert's car in the middle of winter with the windows down. Lambert continued to smoke his pipe, disregarding Thorpe's comfort. Thorpe felt that Lambert used people that he exploited them if they had something he wanted, and was otherwise indifferent to others. He felt that Lambert was a braggart and that he craved publicity while pretending not to care about it. He even questioned Lambert's exploits during the war, particularly his victories.[11]

We can sympathize with Thorpe's view of Lambert after his experiences with him, particularly with his feeling that Lambert used people. But when he questioned Lambert's victories, he let his dislike go too far. The victories are officially recognized ones. And Thorpe's mistake in his judgment makes us question his other ones.

Another person who disliked Lambert, for something like the same reason that Thorpe did, is Ms. Elizabeth Wilson, who worked for the City Manager from 1967 to 1992. She was given permission by the City Manager to do typing for people on the IBM typewriter in her office to earn extra income. She typed a considerable part of the manuscript that would become *Combat Report*. Lambert would bring her a few pages at a time, until she had typed about a hundred pages in all. However, he never paid her a cent for her services. Later on, when she would see Lambert walking his dog Nissie on the streets, she would cross the street to get away from him[12]

Another person who heartily disliked Lambert, but for other reasons, was his step-daughter Clyda M. Forson. As we have seen, Lambert was estranged from his step-daughter. Clyda had battled alcoholism all her life. Some of the neighbors thought that it was the alcoholism that alienated Lambert, but we do not know for sure. After Lambert's death, Bill Martin sent her a package with items that had belonged to her mother, Chloe Ann. Clyda appreciated Bill's thoughtfulness and wrote to thank him. In her letter, she remarked, "That part of my life I've tried very hard to forget, but being human it would be a lie to say I had truly forgiven Bill Lambert, then I would not be the one to sit in final judgment of him or anyone. Is almost impossible to think he ate up the role of 'Grandfather' but being an 'egomaniac' should really explain it."[13]

Even those who did not dislike Lambert often found it difficult to like him. Rita Baker, who with her husband Paul was Lambert's next-door neighbor in Ironton, found him "cranky" and "stern." She recalled that some of the neighborhood children thought Lambert was a "grouch." He used to walk the same path every evening with his dogs, and children would sometimes cross the street to get away from him. She felt you had to get know him to see his tender side. She knew he had a tender side, because he showed it to her husband Paul. Her husband and Lambert had similar interests, so Lambert was very fond of Paul and shared with him all sorts of things in which he was involved including drawings and planes. He was patient and encouraging with Paul. He would talk about his war exploits and his experiences as a pilot.[14]

Another person to whom Lambert showed his tender side was Kaye Clark, who was living down across the street and a few houses down from the Lamberts, and who was being raised by her grandparents. For Kaye, Lambert did not have a bad bone in his body. He would walk his dog a couple of times a day and she would accompany him with other children. There were times during the summer when he would have children over his house. They would be in the backyard around the pond, and Lambert would show *Heckle and Jeckle* cartoons on a makeshift screen using a 16mm projector. Lambert and Chloe Ann would serve popcorn and Kool-Aid to all the kids. Lambert, whom she called Cap, was like a second grandfather to her.[15]

Kaye's grandfather died of heart failure when she was nine. While her large extended family visited for the funeral, Kaye walked the streets aimlessly, trying not to cry. Lambert approached her on one of his walks. After she broke down and cried, Lambert took his dog home, then took Kaye home and proceeded to scold her grandmother for not looking after her granddaughter and her needs. As a consequence of "Cap's" intervention, the relationship between Kaye and her grandmother changed for the better. She was even surprised to see her grandmother cry at the funeral.[16]

Years later, after leaving Ironton with her husband, Kaye returned to visit and ran into Cap on the street. As usual, he was walking his dog. Excitedly she asked how Chloe Ann was doing and then discovered that she had recently died. Lovingly she told how Lambert's eyes swelled with tears as he spoke of his wife. It was not until after his death that she knew he had been a World War I aviator.[17]

Richard Baumgartner, a book editor from Huntington, West Virginia, knew a Lambert who was between the extremes of Thorpe and Kaye. He referred to Lambert as a "crusty old fart." He and his friend Larry Strayer developed a relationship with Lambert in the mid to late 1970s, but it took time to germinate. Lambert was cautious and reticent. But Baumgartner knew, as Paul Baker discovered, that if you shared Lambert's interest and showed that you were knowledgeable on the subject that interested him, he would open up to you. It was not until Baumgartner's specific questions on World War I aviation and planes showed that the he was not a novice that the ice began to thaw and trust was established. "Once you got to know Bill you were accepted.... If he liked you, you were in!"[18]

Baumgartner and Strayer discovered that there was at least one thing as important to Lambert as aviation, and that was the companionship of women. Whenever Larry brought his girlfriend with them, Lambert would perk up, strike a definitive pose, and describe his war experiences with great alacrity. "He would just light up when she entered the room."[19] Even at his advanced age, Lambert still liked the ladies and enjoyed impressing them. We can see from both *Combat Report* and *Barnstorming and Girls* that his amorous experiences in his early life, before his marriage, were still vivid memories to him.

Another thing Baumgartner found out about Lambert was that he sometimes liked "pulling your chain." It was part of him being hard to know and difficult to read. One incident Baumgartner recalled was that Lambert, who always owned dogs, as we know, told him that he had it arranged that his latest dog, Patrick, would be put to sleep if he, Lambert, passed away first. Lambert had led him to believe it was in his Will to have the poor beagle killed. Baumgartner was pleasantly surprised twenty-six years later to discover that Lambert had arranged to give Patrick to Rita Baker's daughter Bridget upon his death.[20]

Finally, we need to look at the moments of Lambert's two closest friends after his wife's death, Bill Martin and Klaus Staerker. We have already seen their comments on Lambert's driving; now we need to see what they have to say on his character generally. Both of them have a balanced view, recognizing Lambert's more unpleasant qualities as well as his good ones.

Bill Martin first knew Lambert, as we have seen, when he was preparing the pictures for *Combat Report*, before his wife's death. Later, he visited with or entertained Lambert during his years as a widower almost every Friday. He thought Lambert was articulate but "eccentric." He lived his life "like it was in the past." His house was a virtual museum to his years in the R.F.C. On its walls could be found pictures of the planes he had drawn, and mementos from the war: his R.F.C. wings, a German bullet, the timing chain and a piece of fabric taken from Richthofen's plane, and a watch from his own downed S.E.5a.[21]

Martin saw Lambert's parsimoniousness as part of his living in the past. He thought of prices as they had been many years before. When Bill and his wife Phyllis would take Lambert out to dinner, he never left more than a fifteen cent tip. Sometimes it was embarrassing. Once in 1972, Martin took Lambert across the Ohio to see a 1970 movie, *Darling Lili*. It was to be a special treat for Lambert since it featured SE5a planes in its action sequences—the planes, the reader will remember, that Lambert flew in combat during the war. After dinner, which was always "Dutch," Lambert agreed to pay for the movie tickets. Martin recalled a shocked look on Lambert's face as he approached him from the ticket booth. He asked, "Do you know what these tickets cost?" When Martin calmly suggested, "Eight dollars," Lambert was dumbfounded. He said, "The last picture show I attended, the tickets were only a quarter." Martin asked, "When was the last time you attended a theater?" And Lambert replied, "Around 1943."[22]

Initially, Bill Martin was in awe of Lambert for what he had done during the war. As a consequence, Martin and his wife Phyllis tolerated Lambert's idiosyncrasies, as well as his embarrassing behavior in public places. One of Lambert's favorite places to eat was Bailey's Cafeteria in Huntington. It was a place noted for its fried chicken, stuffed pork chops, and homemade pies—down-home fares. After their usual Friday night meal, Lambert had an annoying habit of lighting up a cigar. Martin saw that Lambert was oblivious to those around him and only thought of himself. If he wanted to light up and smoke, he simply did it without any consideration for those at his table or in the restaurant. On numerous occasions, Martin attempted to get Lambert to delay lighting his cigar until they were outside the restaurant, but Lambert simply ignored his request. "He simply did what he wanted to do."[23]

After Chloe Ann's death, Martin met Lambert for dinner every Friday evening after work. But after a while, he told Lambert that meeting him every Friday was becoming too taxing, that he wanted to spend more time with his family. Lambert was visibly hurt by the news, since he looked forward to these visits and dinner on the town.[24] Meanwhile, Martin introduced him to his friend Klaus Staerker, a co-worker from Armco's Engineering Department, who was anxious to meet the Great War ace. In many ways, Staerker later fulfilled the duties that Bill Martin used to perform. Along with his wife Mary Ruth, he took an active role in Lambert's life until Lambert's death eleven year later. Initially, Staerker's visits started with Friday nights at the Elks Club in Ironton. Lambert, who was a member, liked to go there Friday nights for the fish dinners they served. Later, Staerker visited Lambert two times a week, but that was changed even later to only Saturdays. At the end, Staerker estimated that he saw Lambert about twenty-five to thirty-five times a year.[25]

Staerker's view of Lambert was between that of Martin and Thorpe. "Friends had to be useful. Lambert was very stingy and did not give of himself—pure selfish." He felt that Lambert stuck to things he knew would work, and that he always had to be in control. "Lambert had a fear of the unknown.... He was extremely rigid.... He was afraid of change. It was his way and no way.... He would not admit failure ... and he would stick with anything that he knew would work and would not try new things."[26]

At First, Staerker was in awe of Lambert for what he had done during the Great War. After the glamour wore off, he continued to visit and take him places out of compassion for an old man who literally had no friends close by, however, he may have had at a distance. He realized that over time he had become a servant for Lambert, who used people and did not see such behavior as being wrong; however, there was a positive side to Staerker's association with Lambert.[27]

For example, one of the things that Staerker did for Lambert was to drive him to Wright-Patterson Air Force Base in Dayton for the monthly meetings of the Order of Daedaians. Lambert was a founding member of the Order, which initially included all World War I aviators commissioned before 11 November 1918. At these meetings, Lambert would introduce Staerker as his "German batman," making Staerker still more aware that Lambert saw him as a servant. However, Staerker did appreciate meeting famous aviators and astronauts during these trips. On one occasion, he met an Apollo astronaut and realized the uniqueness of the situation as it reflected the history of flight. He was in the presence of the distant past with Lambert and the future with a member of the Apollo space mission. What Staerker appreciated most about these trips were the conversations he had with Lambert about his years in the war. According to Staerker, "he never embellished stories. They remained the same ... he never bragged about his accomplishments."[28]

Staerker had the opportunity to reflect on his relationship with Lambert and the man himself, as well as talking Lambert over with his wife, who was a psychologist for the local school system. He concluded, "To put it straightforward, he was an O.C.D. [Obsessive Compulsive Disorder], stubborn, selfish, son-of-a-bitch." Staerker thought the reason Lambert was so little known was that he was "almost antisocial.... He would have been more famous had he been social."[29] Like Martin, Staerker saw Lambert as living in the past. "He adjusted and survived ... [but he] would not change." Staerker believed it was a lesson he had learned from the war. In the end, Staerker admitted that he "chose to hang out with him [Lambert]" out of a sense of compassion: He didn't have anyone."[30] Staerker, like Martin, continued to associate with Lambert out of a sense of duty and compassion. Upon reflection, Staerker poignantly summed up Lambert's life as that of one who "lived at the edge of greatness, but could never get there."[31]

Lambert, like all of us, was a flawed human being, with more and more obvious flaws than most of us. Some of the characteristics that made him virtually intolerable also made him a good fighter pilot. He was a self-made man, arrogant, courageous, extremely self-confident to the point of being obnoxious, obdurate, tenacious, and persevering. What many of his acquaintance felt was that, however offensive Lambert's personality could be, he was also part of a special breed. Even Thorpe admitted that he had to respect the man.[32] Lambert was someone who had performed feats on a world stage that would never be repeated and that were now legendary, and he knew it.

SEVENTEEN

The Rediscovered Ace

Ironically, from the time that Royal Frey's article on Lambert, "The Unknown Ace," was published, Lambert was no longer unknown. A few people now knew of him, and more heard of him and from him as he tried to get the facts accurate for his book, *Combat Report*. But the publication of that book made his name known to many more. It could now be said the Lambert had been rediscovered.

This period of his life was ushered in, not only by the publication of his book, but by the review of it in *Cross & Cockade Journal* in the summer of 1974. The review was anonymous, but the reviewer's name is now known. It was Norman Franks, one of the acknowledged scholars of the Great War, whose later (mid–1990s) book, *Above the Trenches*, became a necessary search for anyone who was researching the air portion of the war.[1]

The review was a laudatory one. It found *Combat Report* to be "one of the best-documented first-person narratives of World War I aviation history."[2] It was "highly recommended" to subscribers to the *Journal*. The reviewer believed its success was partly a consequence of the over fifty years Lambert took to write it. Prodded by friends to write his story, Lambert "had ample opportunity to mentally sift through his experiences and relate them with a somewhat more objective eye than if he had written about the experiences with the furious passion of air fighting still gripping him."[3] Franks believed that the great value of *Combat Report* was that Lambert "enhanced his personal recollections and flight log entries with material provided by a veritable 'Who's Who' of aviation history researchers—Frank Cheesman, Royal Frey, Russell Manning, and the late Kelly Wills." The review even mentioned Collishaw's role in the project and how Lambert "skillfully blended [Collishaw's account of No. 203 Squadron] into the general account." Consequently, as Collishaw hoped, "the reader is constantly kept aware of the 'big picture' of overall operations—not just those pertaining to Lambert's squadron."[4]

The only criticisms of his book was Lambert's "lack of listing of the research sources used; those would have been a helpful point of departure for other researchers engaged in a similar area of study."[5] He also said that the book could have used an index. But simply as a memoir, the book was a model.

On Lambert himself, the reviewer was astonished that the general public—and even scholars in the field—knew so little about him. Franks, wrote that "for some unknown reason, Lambert has been overlooked by the chronicler of aviation history—even though he is clearly an ace, having participated in an acknowledged twenty aerial combats ... he is one of the top ten American aces of World War I."[6] This comment echoed the view of Lambert in Frey's article. This myth would be repeated by journalists, interviewers, and others for the rest of Lambert's life. It was that Lambert had decided not to capitalize on his war record; he scorned public attention and the fame he so richly deserved for his accomplishments in the Great War. It was not until Frey wrote about him in *The Airman* that he began to be recognized for what he was, and his full fame did not come until after the publication of *Combat Report*.

Besides *Cross & Cockade Journal*, the main source that Lambert wanted praise from was Royal Frey, and he got it in heaping measure. On 21 September 1973, Frey wrote that he was halfway through *Combat Report* and that, though he was not one to "throw out plaudits where they are not deserved ... when it comes to realism, down-to-earth authenticity, factual non-glory type writing, and 'telling it' as it must have been, I have never read anything which approaches *Combat Report*."[7] He had thought the book would be interesting, but never "dreamed it would be so darn fascinating ... many times I felt I was at Conteville with you." He told Lambert that he should be proud of his work and what he had done for posterity, and he assured him that it was worth the time and effort he had put into it.[8] Almost immediately, Lambert forwarded Frey's letter to his publisher in England, Kimber.

The page on which Lambert's book was reviewed in *Cross & Cockade Journal* also contained the publication's "Bulletin Board." It reprinted two Resolutions from the Ohio House of Representatives. The first resolution, dated 27 July 1973, was "in Memory of Captain Eddie Rickenbacker." Rick had died four days earlier at the age of 82. The second resolution, dated 31 January 1974, saw the passing of Rickenbacker's baton to Lambert as the Ohio House of Representatives Resolution was passed "To Recognize Col. William C. Lambert of Ironton, America's Top Living World War I Air Ace." In this resolution, Lambert was recognized as "a modest man, whose enormous contributions have not been thoroughly recognized as he has shunned publicity."[9]

Several more such honors would follow in the next few years. On 11 July 1974, Congressman Clarence E. Miller paid tribute to Lambert in the American Congress and asked his colleagues to join him in "honoring men like William C. Lambert who helped preserve the principles on which this country was born."[10] Lambert's home city, Ironton, was not backward about joining this parade of honors. On 18 May 1977, the City of Ironton bestowed the honorary title of "Iron Master" on Lambert. On 14 December 1978, the Ironton City Council passed a resolution that designated "the area bounded by Second, Fourth, Railroad and Etna Streets as the Colonel William C. Lambert Development District."[11]

The state of Kentucky also bestowed multiple honors on Lambert. Kentucky, of course, was not Lambert's home state, but there was always a close connection between southern Ohio and the state directly across the Ohio River—sometimes a stronger connection than with central and northern Ohio. Twice Lambert was made a Kentucky Colonel, and on 28 September 1979, Kentucky Governor Julian M. Carroll bestowed on Lambert the title of "Kentucky's Ambassador of Good Will."

Publically, Lambert acted as if he did not care about all this publicity and praise. In an interview in 1975, for example, he is quoted as saying, "What good had it done ... a lot of publicity that I didn't care for."[12] In fact, Lambert was pleased at the honors, proud of his reputation, and not above trying to embellish it. During this time, he was trying to confirm that he had enough victories, officially, to surpass Rickenbacker. (See Appendix.) He failed in this endeavor, but that did not stop him from claiming more victories, anyway, than he was officially allowed. For example, in 1979, an article in *Ohio's Heritage* stated that he was "officially credited with

22 confirmed kills ... [but] he had several days when he shot down two aircraft. One time he shot down four, but wasn't credited for them."[13] As time went on, Lambert's stories and legend continued to grow, and so did his victories.

Lambert's pretended disinterest in publicity and honors extended to membership in organizations. For example, as previously stated, he was a member of the Order of Daedalians. In a letter to Frey, Lambert said that he finally consented to join even though he "never was much of a hand to join organizations."[14] In fact, Lambert was feigning disinterest to cover up his true feelings. He was pleased to join the organization, and was already a member of several other organizations. As the reader will remember, Bill Martin and later Klaus Staerker regularly took him to the Ironton Elks Club for dinner on Friday nights. Lambert did not want Royal Frey to swear him into the organization, evidently because he thought his reputation should get him in by itself. But the swearing-in was obligatory, and Lambert was duly sworn in at the meeting on Tuesday, 19 March. By June, Lambert was already leading "interesting discussions" at the Daedalian meetings at Wright-Patterson.[15] Klaus Staerker, as the reader may recall, regularly drove him to the meetings of the organization.

Lambert in his home reminiscing about the S.E.5. (On his pipe is the *Dry-Ez Pipe Rest* that Lambert patented in the 1930s.)

Newspapers picked up on Lambert's story, and articles about him appeared for the rest of his life. This is the time that local journalist Rich Baumgartner and his friend Larry Strayer became friends of Lambert. From 1971 to 1974, Lambert was being discovered by the general public. They now knew the "forgotten ace" living in their midst, and many of them wrote to him, requesting autographs. In January 1971, Harold Hoekstra wrote Lambert to tell him what a "pleasure it was to renew old friendships after 41 years."[16] Linda Miller of Amelia, Ohio, read an article on Lambert in the Sunday *Cincinnati Enquirer* and wrote him requesting an autographed photo.[17] Ray St. Germain, a postal worker in St. Paul, Minnesota, also requested an autographed photo. He was putting together a photo collection of World War I pilots. He wrote that he admired those "pilots or observers who flew on the Western Front back there in 1918. It sure took plenty of courage to go up in those wood and fabric planes of that time."[18] He thought it was a crime that so many of these pilots were "forgotten so soon." St. Germain wanted a picture of Lambert "from his flying days."[19] In a later letter thanking Lambert for the picture, St. Germain remarked, "The more I hear from some of you fellows the more I am amazed how patient you are with pest like me. After all, 54 years ago is a long time."[20]

These people wanted to know that what Lambert had done was actually real. It was as if they could not believe that they were communicating with a real World War I ace who was actually answering their letters. Lambert's behavior towards these correspondents showed a different side to Lambert than the curmudgeonly side he showed to so many. He answered their letters, granted their autograph request, and answered their questions.

Young people were also interested in Lambert and his stories. For example, he made an appearances at an eighth-grade class in the Fairland School District in Proctorville, Ohio, and invited "anyone" in attendance to visit his home. Sarah Ruth Levisay sent him a letter thanking him for "a wonderful experience ... [that] will be one of the most memorable occasions for those eighth graders to look back on for the rest of their lives."[21] School was over, but she was interested in arranging a visit to Lambert's home with her family in July. Michael Madden of San Pablo, California, met Lambert in his home while visiting the Ironton area. Upon returning to California, Madden wrote Lambert to thank him for showing him his pictures and the piece of Richthofen's plane. (Although no age is given, Madden's hand-written letter is indicative of a young adolescent boy.) Madden was so impressed by the encounter with Lambert that he was "starting a collection of World War I model airplanes."[22] Madden hoped to stop by and see Lambert again if they made the trip back to the area in 1974, but he wanted to know if they "could write back and forth, if you do have time could you tell me some more stories please!"[23] Kelly Lane's mother met Lambert at the annual R.A.F. Battle of Britain party at the Air Force Museum in 1973. She got Lambert's business card and gave it to her son, who promptly contacted him with a series of questions. Lane admitted he could go on forever, but astutely limited himself to four questions, which included how many planes Lambert shot down during the war, and the name and publisher of his book.[24]

It was not only people in the United States who wrote to Lambert. During a newspaper interview in November 1978, Lambert showed the journalist a letter he had received from Vanessa Julian-Otte, a teenager from London, England. She wanted an autograph and expressed her desire to someday fly open cockpit planes.[25]

In addition to letters from people wanting autographs and enquiring where they could purchase *Combat Report,* there were a number of people who were trying to get in touch with other World War I aces and requesting Lambert to supply their addresses. The most often asked for names were H. L. Bair, Johnson, Southey, and Collishaw. In one case, they wanted the addresses of "any English aces of W.W.I."[26] As with autographs, Lambert would almost always send back these addresses.

The 1970s even saw his appearance on television. The local paper carried a story that Mrs. Arlene J. Peterson of the Ohio Historical Center announced plans for the Ohio Historical Society's "The Seventeenth Star," about Lambert. It was a one-minute presentation displaying seven slides of Lambert, his plane, and some scenes of dogfights, trench strafing, and bombing, that were to be shown on WBNS-TV in Columbus.[27] In 1976, a far longer piece featuring Lambert was filmed in Kinston, New York, at the old Rhineback Air Drome Museum. Bill Martin vividly recalled the interview. Dominique Deviosse, a member of a television team from Pathé-Cinema Company of Paris, picked up "American's top World War One Ace" at the Albany Airport."[28] Lambert had the twenty-two paintings he wanted to use in his book with him. The film crew shot all his paintings in color. Apparently they had been in contact with Lambert for several months, arranging for him to be interviewed for their "History of Aviation" series. There would be seven one-half hour episodes that would appear on television in France, Great Britain, and Canada.

As he had during World War II, Lambert had the chance to fly during this period. Articles were written when Lambert flew a jet plane at the age of 84. He told one journalist, "The jets almost fly themselves."[29] Lambert flew a jet plane for the first time off a runway in Louisville, Kentucky, in December 1976. When interviewed about the flight, he told Art Ferguson of the *Ironton Tribune*, "I've always wanted to fly a jet since seeing my first one in 1945 at Orlando, Fla." He told Ferguson, who wrote many featured articles on Lambert, "He was especially thrilled by the take-off, which was a totally different experience than lifting a propellered craft off a runway.... They cruised to Worthington at altitudes of 8,000 to 13,000 feet, then he brought it down to 2,000 at the port...." The pilot then took over the controls and landed the aircraft. The entire flight was about a thirty-two-minute flight.[30]

Lambert also had two opportunities to fly in an open-cockpit airplane. A newspaper photo titled "Back in the Air" showed Lambert in a warm flying suit and hat holding a pair of gloves while standing next to David Smith and a newly-built, 1930 design, biplane. The caption under the photo stated that he took the controls of a plane for the first time in years.[31] On 7 September 1978, Lambert was featured in a photo with Mike Towler, an Ashland native in town to visit his parents. Towler was a pilot with Pacific Southwest Airlines, but in addition, he ran a one-plane (a biplane at that), one-man outfit called White Star Airline. He had taken Lambert for a ride and the local paper featured an article and photo on their flight together. The article described how "the 84-year-old Irontonian put down his characteristic pipe long enough to fly open-air around the towns."[32] Towler, an Air Force veteran, was impressed with Lambert, who "eased into his old role with confidence and surprising agility." Towler was surprised at Lambert's skills. "After we go aloft ... I watched him ahead, looking around. It seemed he was looking for Fokkers coming down from the clouds."[33]

On 10 November 1978, an article by Harry Franken, "Ace Pilot was Reluctant War Hero," appeared in the *Columbus Citizen-Journal*. The article centered on the war and Lambert's place in it; however, it explores several other angles of Lambert's life, particularly aging and the prospect of death. The octogenarian is beginning to come to grips with his advancing age.[34]

The article began with Lambert's showing the journalist a letter he received from an English girl requesting an autograph to the journalist. (This was the letter from Vanessa Julian-Otte, already mentioned.) Then the article quickly moved to the war. Lambert mentions some of the themes that he had previously written of in *Combat Report*—his dislike of strafing ground troops and his refusal to shoot at horses bogged down in the mud. He was not afraid to tell the reporter that he knew the meaning of fear. "I don't understand these pilots who say they were not afraid.... I was scared to death."[35]

The article then goes on to say that Lambert, although still "alert and vigorous," realizes "that one day he may not be able to care for his modest and comfortable home in Ironton."[36] The author says that although Lambert went to a nearby rest home for lunch, "he dreads the idea of being forced to move there."[37] He wanted to spend his remaining days "among mementos of past glories."[38] He had talked to Kenneth M. Mahan, Assistant Director of Ohio's Commission on Aging, to suggest that a program be enacted that would allow the elderly to be cared for in their homes.

Lambert was also not afraid to admit that he was now largely living in the past. In his mind, his squadron mate Daley would forever be the young man in his early twenties. On reminiscing, he said, "Today I can look back on those days and appreciate what they meant to me. Even now I relive the unforgettable days spent above the fields of France. What is life without memories?"[39]

On the prospects of dying, Lambert is ambivalent. He again describes, as he had before, how he planned to celebrate his 100th birthday. He invites people to his "wing ding" that was to be held at the Air Force Museum on New Year's Eve 1999. He was getting old, but he was not ready to die yet. Yet he realizes that "Father Time is the eventual winner in all battles."[40] And the article ends with a passage from the Book of Psalms 71:9: "Cast me not off in the time of old age; Forsake me not when my strength faileth." It is a curious choice for a professed agnostic, but it parallels Lambert's belief that "the Old Gentleman in the skies" was looking out for him over the fields of France.

The publication of *Barnstorming and Girls* harmed Lambert's reputation, particularly in Ironton. It was seen as sordid and offensive, as pornography. Wilma Bryant, Lambert's neighbor, described it as "filth."[41] After reading a few pages, Dick Uppstrom, Director of the Air Force Museum, had the book removed from the shelves of the Museum's gift shop and hidden, so that only adults who specifically requested to see it would be allowed to.[42] Because of this attitude, it was difficult to find anyone in Ironton who would admit to actually having read the book. The only person interviewed for this book who said he had read it was Robin Hingham, who had edited it. Neither Bill Martin nor Klaus Staerker, Lambert's two closest friends, had read it. (Martin, however, knew what its content was; he was the one who suggested that Lambert should write it.)

Those few friends of Lambert's who did read the book or at least a portion of it, like Bob Westervelt of Aeroprint, when they wrote to Lambert, often took refuge in uneasy humor. Westervelt wrote that he had only read a "bit" of the book. He then added that he had "naively thought barnstorming had something to do with flying aeroplanes. Although I do have an artist friend whose wife made him give up flying 'cause his wife was jealous of the plane. She thought of it as his surrogate mistress ... threatened to leave him. [He gave up the plane & kept his wife.]"[43]

Some others were considerably more balanced in their judgments. Jon Guttman of Cross & Cockade wrote to soften the blow after the *Journal* panned "the hell out of it," assuring Lambert that Jack Eder said "it's nowhere near that bad, although it could have been better-edited, and he's found racier stuff in New York."[44] Lambert's friend C. R. Glasebrook, known as Rick, who operated the non-profit Glasebrook Foundation for the Preservation of Military Aviation History in Carson City, Nevada, included in his foundation's newsletter a brief remark that *Barnstorming and Girls* was "a most candid and detailed account of Bill's flying and womanizing experiences.... [It] is a classic example of how an author can tell it all once he outlives all the participants." In an added handwritten note specific for Lambert, "Rick" added, "You had almost as much fun as I did in WWII!"[45]

Some people wrote Lambert that they had both read the book and liked it. Norman Gillman of Fareham, England, was one of those. He congratulated Lambert on the book and said that it was "a story of a time that will, I guess, never be repeated, and is unique in history."[46] John Nardine, a dentist from Canonsburg, Pennsylvania, was perhaps the greatest admirer of the book. He wrote to tell Lambert that after receiving the book on 24 April 1981, he stayed up nights reading it until he finished it on the 28th. He said that he "hated for the book to end for I enjoyed the people and the experiences contained therein. I took to your friends just like they were mine ... they seemed so sincere and most helpful and friendly— my type of people!!"[47] Nardine had liked the book and the people in it so much that he now wanted to know the fates of those individuals. Lambert, as the reader may remember, had changed the names of almost all the characters in the book. Nadine was not asking for names, he was genuinely interested in the rest of the story. He wanted to know the cause of Helen's death (never given in the book), if Lambert married Judie ("I took to her"), and what happened to Dave, Annie, Tom, Ginnie, and "Tiny." He was hoping that "they all had happy and pleasant futures, for I had a kinship with them as I read the book."[48]

Although Lambert's book would never sell well among the general public, he did have a niche audience—pilots and former pilots who had once themselves been barnstormers. Karl Voelter of the OX5 Aviation Pioneers and editor of the *OX5 News* wrote Lambert after receiving a photo-copy of an article about his new book in the *Ironton Tribune*. He wrote that most of the 4,500 members of the OX5 Aviation Pioneers were old barnstormers, and a short news article in the *OX5 News* would most assuredly attract interest among the membership. Voelter wanted Lambert to send him a "professional copy" along with the cost of the book, and the cost of any other particulars, such as autographed copies. He would convey this material on to his membership.[49]

With all of these other interests Lambert was pursuing, his correspondence with Great War experts lessened, but it was still there. James Dudgeon, a South African living in Edinburgh, Scotland, wrote him after reading *Combat Report*. He thought it was "an excellent book.... I rate it as the best autobiography that I have read, and also one of the most informative."[50] Dudgeon was making contact with the surviving pilots of the war in order to record their opinions and memories. He wrote, "Many of the small details have not been given suitable attention and will produce a gap in the information available to future historians."[51] He had three categories of questions for Lambert. He was asking about Lambert's own adventures in the war, the adventures of his squadron mates, and the machines they flew.

Dudgeon began with the specifics of the plane Lambert flew, C1084. He wanted all the details and markings. Did it have a Viper or Hispano engine and a full length exhaust? Dudgeon was making a $\frac{1}{6}$ scale flying model to fly in the United Kingdom national scale competition in 1980. He promised to send Lambert a photograph of the model, but warned there was "stiff competition in the scale combat section," and he could use Lambert at the control sticks.[52]

Dudgeon next addressed Lambert's comrades in No. 24 Squadron. He was especially interested in McElroy and Southey, and wondered if Redler of A Flight was the same person who also flew in No. 40 Squadron with Mannock. Being from South Africa, Dudgeon was especially interested in Southey and his whereabouts. He told Lambert, "Anything that you can remember about these men would be of value to me and greatly appreciated."[53] Dudgeon wanted the little things that did not always make its way into books.

Finally, Dudgeon wanted Lambert's help with a series of articles being written for *Cross & Cockade Journal* on the "description of aircraft; their construction, development, finish etc. Everything about them, right down to the last dial and switch."[54] Dudgeon felt that Lambert's memory of the types of airplanes he flew would be a valuable asset to this project. "Never before has anyone attempted a series which covers A/C in such detail."[55] In return, Dudgeon offered the resources of his collection to Lambert for the asking.

Another friendship that Lambert established was that with James Parks of Denver, Colorado, who had a passion for World War I aviation and even owned his own World War I museum. His love of World War I aviation was inspired by his father. He had started his collection of mementos from veterans as early as 1938. What Parks wanted from Lambert, as might be expected, was not so much information but artifacts. We know that Lambert's house was almost a museum to World War I aircraft and fliers. Many of his most treasured possessions had already been promised to the Air Force Museum, but there were still items that the Air Force Museum did not want, and others that they had no room to display.

Like Dudgeon, Parks had read and admired *Combat Report*. He was amazed at the detailed descriptions of aerial warfare and Lambert's ability to recall stories of individual combat. He wrote, "It is the best account of aerial combat that I have read in a long time. You must have a diary of your experiences of that time which helped you along."[56] Parks probably had an ulterior motive for that comment. He already was one of only three individuals who had received a portion of the wartime mementos of Josef Jacobs, leader of Jagdstaffel 7, an ace with 48 victories. "Most treasured by me is his diary and log book."[57] He would have loved to have added Lambert's log book to his collection. The only information he wanted from Lambert was an explanation of the game "bumble-puppy." Along with his first letter to Lambert, Parks included a copy of a newspaper article about the rebuilding of a Fokker D VII and some photographs from his museum.

In reply to Parks' letter, Lambert sent him a photo of one of his paintings. Parks had sent Lambert his copy of *Combat Report* to be autographed, and Lambert had done that. He answered the question on bumble-puppy. Most important to Parks, he was willing to donate certain objects to his museum, including a flying cap. Parks was happy to accept. He already had a British Army Captain's tunic; he saw the opportunity to make up a display "that would chronicle [Lambert's] part in the Great War."[58] In time, Parks had a picture taken of Lambert in a World War I uniform: Captain's tunic with D.F.C. ribbon, riding breeches, boots, Sam Browne belt, and R.F.C. cap. Not all of these, evidently, had been Lambert's; some of them Parks sent him to make the uniform authentic.[59] All of them would be part of the Lambert exhibit, along with an autographed copy of *Combat Report*.

Besides Lambert's appearing on television, there was for a time a chance that his work would appear in the movies. On 20 November 1980, Robin Higham, Lambert's publisher for *Barnstorming and Girls,* wrote Lambert that he was exploring the possibility of a movie script combining *Combat Report* and *Barnstorming and Girls*.[60] From his letter back to Higham, it seems that Lambert was excited about the possibility. Unfortunately, Claire Smith of Harold Ober Associates in New York City, Higham's "very good agent in New York," wrote Higham that unlike the late 1960s and early 1970s when movies on World War I aviation were popular, "People on the Coast simply don't feel that people are making movies in this area now." She did not think that anything could be done with the materials Higham had sent her, so she was returning them.[61] It was something of a repeat of what had happened when Lambert was trying to publish *Combat Report,* without a happy ending.

In June 1980, Lambert was featured with students from Rock Hill Junior High School in the *Ironton Tribune*. Four students—Kristy Murnahan, Paulette Barnhart, Tammy Thornton, and Deana Robinson—had placed third in the National History Day competition that was held in Washington, D.C. The theme of their project was "Individuals in History," and their subject was Lambert. Lambert had assisted them by giving them an interview, which they reduced to three minutes for their display. The article described how these girls became experts on World War I after working with Lambert on their project. Their display had a mobile with two Sopwith Camels and two S.E.5as, along with a German Albatros and a Fokker D VII. They included a replica of Lambert's dress uniform and reproduction of his painting "Morning Patrol," and it even included a relief map of the Somme River valley in France, where the students pinpointed in detail the towns and where Lambert's confirmed and unconfirmed victories occurred. The *Tribune* had a picture of Lambert in his home surrounded by the four girls and their advisor, proudly looking at their bronze third place medal.[62]

Lambert's old friend Bill Martin had one of the best articles on Lambert with "America's Forgotten Ace" in *Airpower* of May 1980. However, the title was now a misnomer. Lambert had been "forgotten" at one time, but he was so no longer. He was a recognized ace, and he continued to receive letters from all over the English-speaking world. Two good examples of these correspondents are Bill Cole, a pilot from Aurora, Ontario, and Sid Moore of Australia, who was training to be an amateur pilot.

Bill Cole was a romantic who idolized Lambert. He wished he "could have been at Conteville with you, Daley, and the others. I would have been proud to have been a part of such a great team."[63] About *Combat Report*, he said the book as "absolutely fascinating. It sure is one of the best descriptive reports on World War I flying, and combats with the Huns."[64] Besides writing Lambert letters, he phoned him and hoped to get to Ironton one day and meet him in person.[65] Sid Moore, likewise, hoped to get to meet Lambert in person so that they could have a "good old chat."[66] With his letter, he enclosed a picture of himself in an R.A.F uniform next to a restored de Havilland DH.82 Tiger Moth, a 1930s biplane. Moore had read both *Combat Report* and *Barnstorming and Girls*. On the second book, he wrote, "I settled down to enjoyable reading once I got over the initial shock of just how explicit the story is…. I commend you for your courage and openness."[67] In another letter, he wrote, "I am only twenty-three years old but I 'm sure I should have been born about 1895." He insisted, however, that he knew the Great War was not "the romantic, gay chivalrous days most young people think they were."[68] He signed his letters either "your Pal" or "your Mate."

The Lambert that these fans encountered was a considerably different person from the mean, abrasive, closed-in person that many in Ironton knew. He was open and generous, giving of his time, his knowledge and experience, his stories, and even sometimes his cherished mementos. By the second letter, most of Lambert's correspondents were on a first-name basis with him and considered him a friend. In reality, according to Klaus Staerker, these people did not know the real Lambert. They were "friends of the pilot as opposed to friends of the person."[69] Another way of seeing Lambert's personality would be that he had two sides, and his correspondents saw only the better one. It was the real Lambert they knew, but not the whole person.

Probably the last newspaper article on Lambert while he was still alive came out right after Memorial Day, in 1981. It featured a picture of the aged Lambert (he was now 86) smoking his pipe while sitting on the sun porch of his Ironton home and thinking "back to days of dogfights and deadlines of war, and the fame that has finally followed."[70] That is not a bad thumbnail description of this period of Lambert's life.

Eighteen

The Final Years

In his 80s, Lambert was not in the best of health. Age had caught up with him; even though he kept up with his correspondence, he was beginning to experience the difficulties that comes with aging. His habits changed. It used to be that he took a great deal of pride in his appearance. It used to be that, when Lambert went out for dinner with Bill Martin or Klaus Straeker, he would be clean and well-dressed. He would wear good shirts and slacks, with an occasional suit jacket as well. Now, after a trip to the hospital in 1981, the doctor told him they would not see him again unless he bathed and changed his clothes. Martin remembered him being noticeably embarrassed by the slight.[1]

Staerker recalls that during this time, Lambert did not go to bed, but slept in his chair in the living room of his home. He never changed his clothes or took a bath. His home also smelt terribly with thick scents of cigar and pipe smoke.[2]

A neighbor, Wilma Bryant, used to come over regularly to look in on Lambert. She helped to clean his home and take care of chores around the house which he could no longer perform. She was not paid for her services, but an agreement had been reached to reward her for her services after he died with his home and various appliances. But soon she got tired of Lambert's constant demands and abuse, and she quit. Afterward, of course, the state of his house suffered. Apparently, she continued to look in on Lambert from time to time, but she no longer worked for him.[3]

Lambert was now unable to take his dog Patrick for his usual walks, so he let the dog use the basement as a latrine.[4] Obviously, this added to the stench of unwashed clothes and thick tobacco smoke. The place was a terrible mess, but Lambert refused to leave his home for an assisted-living facility, even though he had already chosen the place he would go if he had to: the Jo-Lin Health Center, where his friend Jesse Stuart had stayed at the end of his life. But when it came to the crunch, he was unable to give up his home.

Lambert had been sick and was, briefly, in the hospital. He received a good many letters from friends concerned about his health, since he had not written them for a while. He sufficiently recovered to go home, and it seemed at first glance that life had returned to normal for him. He was still responding to the many letters he received for copies of his books and autographs. He was also actively pursuing another deal with Aeroprint to make more prints of his paintings. And he was trying to get *Combat Report* published in the United States. In August 1981, he even left his house to attend General Bryce Poe's retirement party. Poe, a fellow Daedalian, was deeply touched—for "so distinguished an airman to honor me in that way meant a great deal."[5]

Lambert even attempted to keep up his daily walks with Patrick. As it had been pointed out to him, the chain leash on that dog was much too long, but Lambert continued to do things his way. However, this over-long chain would be the cause of Lambert's final collapse.

It was late February 1982, and the remnants of winter—snow, gray skies, and cold breezy winds—were still part of the landscape. It was still flu season, and someone as old as Lambert was quite susceptible to the virus. Even though Lambert liked to walk his dog Patrick promptly at the same time and over the same route, the snow and weather forced him at times to take him into his backyard to get some exercise and answer the call of nature. On one particular walk, Patrick playfully circled Lambert several times and wrapped his long leash around Lambert's legs. The process resulted in Lambert's losing his balance and falling into the snow. Unfortunately, he could not extradite himself from his predicament. At his age, he did not have the strength or ability to turn over or sit upright so that he could remove the leash around his legs. Lambert used a cane when he walked, so it may have been that the cane was also encumbered in the chains around his legs. He laid there helpless for almost an hour in the cold, wet snow. According to Bill Martin, "His next-door neighbor happened to look out his upstairs window and spied Lambert lying in his backyard. He immediately went over there, helped Lambert up and carried him on his back into the house. He begged to take Lambert to the hospital then, but Lambert refused to go. A couple of days later, after pneumonia had set in, Lambert had to give in and go. I think the lady who lived a few doors up the street took him. She informed me of Lambert's condition, and I went to the hospital right after work to visit him. He wanted out of there and tried to talk me into helping him escape."[6]

Lambert ended up in Lawrence County General Hospital with a case of pneumonia. As his health deteriorated over the next three weeks, Lambert had regular visits from both Bill Martin and Klaus Staerker. Several times after getting off work from Armco, Klaus and his wife would make a courtesy call on Lambert. Klaus recalled that Lambert was responsive and in full control of his faculties, and could carry on a meaningful conversation with him, although a less lively one. The great difference from the usual Lambert is that he was no longer self-assured and self-confident. He had been stricken by something he could not control, and Klaus saw fear in his eyes. Even though he had prepared a Will and built the mausoleum for himself and his wife, he was not prepared to die. He was showing emotion, something he did not often show, and the emotion was fear, not what was expected of the courageous war hero. Lambert had admitted that in war there were times he was "scared to death," but this was the first time that Staerker had seen that side of him.[7]

At the end, Martin would recall, Lambert fading in and out of consciousness, finding himself back in the war, or thinking the rings on top of the privacy curtain were spiders webs. Martin wrote that Lambert "asked me to take his cane and wipe it across them [the spider webs]. He also asked that I hand him his old green plastic sun visor. He looked pretty funny, lying in that hospital bed with that sun visor on."[8]

Staerker is uncertain about the last time he visited Lambert in the hospital. He was not sure if he had visited him the day he died, but he was genuinely surprised when he received a phone call that Lambert had passed away. He had no idea that he was that close to dying.[9] Neither did Bill Martin. It was Friday, and the end of the work week at Armco. Martin was tired and decided to go home and enjoy the evening with his wife Phyllis. He planned to stop by to see Lambert sometime during the next day. However, much to both men's surprise, Lambert died that night. Martin received a phone call informing him of Lambert's passing.[10]

Lambert died on Friday, 19 March 1982, at 9:00 p.m. The coroner listed the causes as "cardiopulmonary arrest, Pulmonary Embolism Atrial Fibrillation, ASHD [Arteriosclerotic Heart Disease]." Lambert's body had finally shut down. The Great War Ace had finally gotten his last pair of wings.

Lambert had planned for his funeral and final resting place in the same manner as he tried to control his life. He had seen to all the details. He had decided to be buried in his blue U.S. Air Force uniform that was decorated with his Distinguished Flying Cross and several other campaign ribbons. Martin always remembered that it was the only time he ever saw Lambert in this uniform. He also had one of his favorite smoking pipes clasped in both his hands.

Friends came to view his body at James V. Hayes Funeral Home in Ironton. His death was front-page news in all the local papers along the Ohio River. His funeral was on Tuesday, 23 March with Monsignor John J. Yonk, pastor of St. Joseph's Church, officiating. (That seems like an odd choice for a professed agnostic, but after all, this was the same Lambert who had believed in the Great War that the "Old Gentleman up in the sky" was looking out for him.) In remembering Lambert, Yonk said that he "was perhaps the most outstanding citizen of our community. He was a character in every sense of the word. There was nothing phony or a sham about him. He said what he meant and you could count on it. He was indeed an asset to this community."[11] He saw Lambert's passing as "the end of an era."[12]

Royal Frey did not forget to honor his old friend. He was honored by both the Royal Air Force and the U.S. Air Force. Taking Lambert to his final resting place in the small mausoleum in Woodlawn Cemetery were military pallbearers from both England and the United States. They included three members of the R.A.F., including Squadron Leader J. P. Blackman, and three members of the U.S. Air Force, including Frey (who had recently retired), and all were above the rank of Lieutenant Colonel. Among the seventy-five people in attendance was his step-daughter Clyda, who drove in from Princeton, West Virginia, for the funeral. Since she was the only relative of Lambert at the funeral, the pallbearers presented the flag that was draped over his coffin to her. In attendance was a U.S. Air Force honor guard that fired the traditional twenty-one gun salute in Lambert's honor. "Taps" was played as the crowd respectfully stood and watched in silence while four A-7D jetfighters flew over the gravesite and formed the "missing man" formation in Lambert's honor. Lambert was laid next to Chloe Ann, his wife of 51 years. In all ways, the funeral was one that marked the passing of an American and English military hero.

In stark contrast to his dramatic and well-attended funeral, Lambert's Will marked how alone he was as a private person. His beloved wife, Chloe Ann, had died long before him. He was estranged from his step-daughter Clyda; all he left her in his Will was her mother's jewelry. He had almost no living relatives; only two cousins, one—Mrs. Beulah Foster—on his mother's side, and the other—Mrs. Doris Nazer—on his father's side. Both were left out of his Will; in fact, the Will stated that he had *no* living relatives.

Since Lambert had no person to leave his estate to, he left it to institutions. At first, he evidently considered leaving half of it to the R.A.F. Benevolent Fund. In fact, Bill Martin thought that he had done so. He stated that Lambert "had savings in the neighborhood of $200,000. He left one half to the R.A.F. Widows and Orphans Fund and the other half to the Air Force Museum...."[13] Lambert had contacted Cheesman about this bequest, and Cheesman had highly recommended the Fund, citing his own experience with it: how the Fund had tried to help his mother after his father died.[14]

Eighteen. The Final Years

But, although Lambert had led both Bill Martin and Frank Cheesman to believe that a large part of his estate was going to the R.A.F. Benevolent Fund, that was not in his Will. The estate was divided between the Royal Air Force Museum and the Air Force Museum Foundation at Wright-Patterson.

Besides the Will itself, Lambert made four Codicils, but only two of them applied after his death, the First and the Fourth. The First Codicil to his Will gave the Ohio Historical Society "all the balance of my non-military personal property of an antique or memorial nature."[15] The society received all Lambert's household furniture, which evidently had achieved antique stats by his death, and a baby grand piano.

The Second Codicil to Lambert's Will designated the Jo-Lin Health Center, a rest home in Ironton, to be the place he would go if he could no longer take care of himself.[16] It was the same place where his friend Jesse Stuart had been when he died, and Lambert had eaten at the restaurant there. But when push came to shove, Lambert could not bring himself to admit that he had to be taken somewhere other than his home because he was no longer capable of taking care of himself.

The Third Codicil, signed in June 1977, gave a neighbor, Wilma Bryant, his home and various appliances in return for taking care of Lambert. In that way, Lambert hoped, he could stay in his own home until he died. She used to come over regularly to look in on him and to clean his house and take care of chores that he could no longer perform. However, her patience wore thin with Lambert's continual demands and curses, so after a while she no longer was willing to work for Lambert, though she did continue to check in on him. On 20 February 1979, less than two years after sighing the Codicil, Lambert had it revoked.[17]

On 20 February 1979, the Fourth Codicil of his Will left money to the Foundation "to build and construct a full scale World War I SE-5 airplane."[18] This Codicil was carried out, although not as it was written. According to Bill Martin, "One evening Col. Dick Uppstrom called to tell me they had found a real S.E.5e, and asked if I thought Lambert would have approved purchasing that rather than building a replica. I answered that I felt most certainly he would. So, Uppstrom said they would proceed."[19]

We need to remember that most of Lambert's military memorabilia had already been given away in his lifetime, much of it to the Air Force Museum. Already in 1967, a letter of Frey's had told Lambert that his "drawings have been on display for over three weeks" and that the "von Richthofen tachometer cable donated to us through your efforts" was sitting right in front of the drawings.[20] In time, the Museum would receive the choicest of Lambert's aviation legacy, which included, besides the Richthofen items, Lambert's Webley revolver, uniforms, original log book, and selected correspondence. For instance, in a letter of 20 November 1973, Frey let Lambert know that how crowded the Museum was for space, so that there was "just no room" at present for them to exhibit Lambert's "map invention" that he used in his S.E.5 during the Great War.[21]

The other major recipient of Lambert's generosity was the R.A.F. Museum in London. In 1971, he donated twenty-one prints (copies of Lambert's paintings), and a "description of a single day's action by the pilots of No. 24 Squadron"[22] (a section from *Combat Report*). The day was 4 July 1918, when Lambert crashed two Fokker D. VIIs and forced another to land. Slightly later, he sent them a financial gift as well. On 2 May 1971, Southey wrote Lambert that he was "delighted that the R.A.F. Museum wants a complete set of your 21 paintings. It is indeed an honour and you will be remembered through them for all time."[23]

By the 1970s, most of Lambert's memorabilia was already given away. When he received a request for such items from the Doughboy Historical Society Memorial in Missoula, Montana, Lambert wrote back, "Sorry; all my material has been donated to the Air Force Museum at Wright-Patterson & the R.A.F. in London."[24] However, this statement was not strictly true. Even if the bulk of the items were already donated, Lambert still had a few left. In 1981, Lambert sent James Parks of Denver, Colorado, who was setting up his own World War I museum, a flying cap he had owned. (The name of the museum where he sent it was the World War Aviation Foundation and Museum; it has had a couple of name-changes since.) He also gave Parks permission to contact Dick Uppstrom about items, such as his "map invention," that were given to the Air Force Museum but were not being displayed.[25]

Even after Lambert's death, some of his military items were still being given away. In the early 1990s, Bill Martin loaned the Kentucky Aviation Museum several of Lambert's memorabilia that he had found in the house after Lambert's death. The museum officials greatly admired Lambert and the Museum still displays some of these artifacts today, although the exhibit on Lambert, according to Martin, "needs a lot of work ... to bring the exhibit up to the standard that I would like to see."[26]

Bill Martin also managed to rescue Chloe Ann's possessions and family photos after Lambert's death, and he sent them to Clyda, thinking that she deserved to have them, even though he knew that Lambert would have "turned over in his tomb had he known I sent all those things to her." Clyda was very grateful to Martin, but she still harbored resentment against Lambert.[27]

Lambert's habit of not throwing anything away meant that he had a great deal of personal documentation on hand when he wrote *Combat Report*. He had saved his log book and papers, magazines and newspaper clippings that helped to tell the story of his life as a war pilot. In the late 1970s, he met with Susan Smith, Aviation History Specialist for the Archives at Wright State University, about donations and preservation of documents and maps Lambert wanted to loan to the collection.[28] The rough-draft copy of *Combat Report* would be part of that collection.

Also, during the writing of *Combat Report* and afterward, in the period he was known as a celebrated ace, Lambert was carrying on an extensive and varied correspondence with former aces, aviation history specialists, and a great many ordinary people who were starstruck by a World War I ace. He kept these letters obsessively, but evidently he never realized their historical value. In September 1971, for example, he received a letter from the University of Wyoming Transportation History Foundation asking him to donate his papers, photographs, manuscripts, and other literary memorabilia to them. They were collecting and preserving as much as they could "pertaining to the history and development of twentieth century aviation and aeronautics."[29] They promised to index any collection they received with the Library of Congress, and they offered to restrict any items he wished restricted and to make copies of any manuscripts he wished returned.[30] Lambert did not even bother to reply to this letter.

And if Lambert did not see the value of his letters to anyone except himself, those who were cleaning out Lambert's house following his death saw even less importance in them. A few days after the funeral, on a whim, Bill Martin stopped by Lambert's old home after work and saw people shoveling pictures, letters, and papers into garbage bags for disposal. He asked if he could have what they were going to discard. Since he was saving them the trouble of throwing it away, they gave him permission to take what he wanted. As a consequence, much of Lambert's life story was saved. This writer is grateful to Bill Martin for his prompt action. Without those letters, much of this book could not have been written. On 15 March 2006, the letters that Martin had saved were donated to the Wright State University Library and added to the Lambert Papers.

However, some of Lambert's correspondence had already been thrown out by the time Bill Martin arrived. In almost every series of letters from a particular correspondent, there are gaps, letters that refer back to other letters that we do not have. Obviously, there is nothing to be done about this loss at this time. The researcher must work with what remains and be thankful that so much was saved.

After Lambert's funeral, Royal Frey was interviewed by WSAZ television (out of Huntington, West Virginia) on Lambert's life. As one of Lambert's oldest and dearest friends, he respectfully compared Lambert's accomplishments as a pilot to the present-day performances of our astronauts in space. To him, Lambert was a member of a daring and adventurous generation who disregarded their own safety, pushed the envelope, and helped to advance the future of aviation. His death was another indication that an era was coming to an end. Fewer and fewer Great War and barnstorming pilots were around to tell their stories. Lambert was one of the last representatives of a "rare breed."[31]

Epilogue

Klaus Staerker once poignantly summed up Lambert's life by saying that he "lived at the edge of greatness, but could never get there."[1] Staerker's explanation was that Lambert was "almost antisocial. He would have been more famous had he been social."[2] There was a great deal of truth to this judgment. Although Staerker was one of Lambert's few close friends, he referred to him as a "son-of-a-bitch." Richard Baumgartner, also a friend, called him a "crusty old fart." Bill Martin explained Lambert's meanness, but he never denied that he was often mean.

However, that does not fully explain why Lambert was not great. There have been a number of great individuals in history who have been personally unpleasant. Here are three more reasons to help explain why Lambert never achieved greatness.

First, during the period that would be central to his life, his time as a fighter pilot in the Great War, Lambert never thought of himself as a great man. He was exhilarated by flying in an open-cockpit airplane, excited by aerial combat, and secure in the knowledge that others in his flight had his back as he had theirs. He knew he was doing his part or more, but he did not consider himself special. He was imbued with the R.A.F. spirit, that if one boasted it would be of the achievements of the Squadron, not of one's own deeds. It is a variation of the old sport bromide "There is no *I* in team." He despised Rickenbacker's boasting about his record.

Therefore, whereas Rickenbacker parlayed his fame as "America's Greatest Ace" into a career in commercial aviation, Lambert, after a year spent barnstorming and flying for fun, married and settled down in his home town, Ironton, and effectively got out of aviation (except for the time during World War II when he managed a U.S. Army Air Corps supply depot). Since Lambert did not think of himself as a great man, no one else did.

Second, when Lambert, towards the end of his life, discovered that he was the second-greatest American ace of the Great War and started to be interested in gaining the recognition he deserved, he had a problem. People tend to remember the one who came in first and forget the second and third. Knowing this, Lambert made a concerted attempt to gain official recognition that he had more victories than Rickenbacker and *should* have been known as "America's Greatest Ace." (This attempt is chronicled in the Appendix.) However, the attempt failed.

Third, Lambert wanted *Combat Report* to be published by a major American book publisher, hoping that the book would gain enough publicity to become a bestseller. And his hopes might have come true—but no major American publisher would take a chance on the book. Instead, it was published by a small English publishing house. The book became well and favorably known in its niche market—former aces, people interested in the Great War, and young flying enthusiast—but not by the general public.

There is a further reason that Lambert was not seen as a great man, and one that rebounds to his credit. To his correspondents, he did not behave like an aloof and unapproachable Great Man. However he behaved in his daily life, to those who wrote him he was responsible, friendly, and helpful. Even someone like Sid Moore, who at first was a hero-worshiper of Lambert, in later letters signed himself either "your Pal" or "your Mate." Lambert did not let his irascible side show in his correspondence.

In the end, it probably does not matter whether Lambert was a great man or not. Certainly, it did not seem to matter to Lambert. He had gained recognition and honor in his home town. He had connected or reconnected with fellow aces from the

Lambert late in life.

Great War; he was known and respected among his peers. He was carrying on an extensive correspondence with younger fans who were excited to be actually writing to a Great War ace. In reflecting on his life, Lambert said that he was thankful for having had the opportunity to "do pretty near everything [he] wanted to do." After all, when everything is said and done, "nothing compares to the pleasures of flying in an open cock pit."[3]

More than anything else, Lambert had his memories. Reflecting on his war, that brief four-month period in 1918 out of a life that lasted eighty-seven years, he said, "Today I can look back on those days and appreciate what they meant to me. Even now I relive the unforgettable days spend above the fields of France. What is life without memories?"[4]

Appendix
The Numbers Game

As we have seen, Lambert both disliked and envied Rickenbacker. After *Combat Report* was published, Lambert began a concerted attempt to establish the number of his victories as greater than those of Rickenbacker, so that *he*, not Rickenbacker, would have the title of "America's Greatest Ace." But he could not do this by himself; he was forced to rely on the researches of others, especially in Great Britain. And to obtain the help of these others, he called on the help of his great friend, Royal Frey.

In Appendix I to *Combat Report*, we see Taunton's list of Lambert's victories. Taunton originally had given Lambert 21½ victories until he subtracted one victory because a Fokker was forced to land damaged, not destroyed. Lambert simply ignored this change. But 21½ victories would not be enough to challenge Rickenbacker, so Lambert set out to find more victories.

First, he wrote to Norman Franks. Franks was the person who had reviewed Lambert's book for *Cross & Cockade Journal*, a highly laudatory review. He was also a widely respected World War I scholar. His book *Above the Trenches*, published in the mid–1990s, would become the definitive book on the records of those pilots flying for Britain. In a letter of 18 October 1973 to Lambert, Franks included his own research on Lambert's record and listed his victories chronologically. He believed that Lambert had a total of 19¾ victories. (Strangely enough, in *Above the Trenches* he would list Lambert with 18 victories.) He concluded by saying that the discrepancy between the two lists was of no real consequence, because "in any event it is an impressive record and I am glad that is has been written down in *Combat Report* and written so well ... it has been a privilege to hear from you and have an opportunity to write to you."[1]

Unfortunately, "impressive" was not Lambert's objective. His goal was to find enough victories to become America's Ace of Aces in the Great War. He found an interesting way of at least getting closer to that goal. He simply put checks by those victories in Franks' list that were not in Taunton's list. Adding them together, he saw 3¼. He then added these newly discovered victories to Taunton's 21½ for a final total of 24¾.[2]

On 14 November 1973, Lambert sent Frey a letter that included a copy of Franks' letter and his comments. He informed Frey that Franks' total showed three victories on 4 May, 4 July, and 10 August 1918, that were not listed in Taunton's letter of 3 January 1968; however, "these 3 definitely are in my Log Book & also in the Squadron History."[3] Cheesman was the only person to report that Lambert downed a Fokker D. VII on 19 August 1918. Lambert argued that all three men had researched the official records and had come away with three different figures. They were all renowned scholars of World War I aviation and their credibility could not be questioned; however, each scholar missed victories that the others had found. Lambert used balloons as an example. "Each of them missed the number of balloons, but the sum total of the 3 of them is right: 3½ balloons."[4] Lambert then explained how the totals of the three scholars equaled the total found in his log book "as to dates, types of machine & the facts of the machines [EA]."[5] He told Frey, "My thinking at the end of the war was 17½ E.A. credits confirmed. Evidently others have been confirmed since I left & I was not informed. Therefore: 21½ Taunton + 3¼ Franks + Cheesman 1½ = 26¼."[6] Lambert is trying to show that his claim is based, not on his own calculations, but on the work of three independent authorities. He proceeds to put all of this information on Frey's shoulders. "You have the findings of each of the three men. Should we try to have the above confirmed or should we just accept what Taunton shows in his letter?"[7]

Frey responded to Lambert with a letter sent on 20 November. He enthusiastically agreed with the first of Lambert's choices: "if you are credited with 26¼ [victories], we want to know it."[8] As the Air Force historian, Frey saw the chance of a lifetime. Such a finding would rewrite the history of American aces in the war. He let Lambert know that the individual in charge of the Historical Branch of the Air Ministry, Group Captain E. B. Haslam, was an acquaintance, and he was going to turn the entire investigation over to him. He needed, however, for Lambert's file to be returned to him, because it contained Taunton's letter of which he needed a copy. Afterward he would send the findings to London to discover the final truth of Lambert's victory total. He would let Lambert know as soon as he heard from London.[9]

The implications of Lambert's findings are interesting to contemplate. If correct, Lambert would reap immediate gains, which would include major media attention and probably book deals. *Combat Report* might even become a bestseller. Lambert would also benefit financially, but even more in publicity and reputation. Guest appearances and requests for interviews from both sides of the Atlantic would be forthcoming. The city of Ironton would also prosper from the attention Lambert would receive. Cities and towns in the Ohio River basin often sponsor yearly festivals and celebrations. It would not be out of the ordinary to think that a Lambert Museum would have been established in honor and a festival in his name.

Of course, there would be skeptics and detractors about Lambert's claim. The resulting demotion of Rickenbacker's status would result is a wave of supporters defending Rick's place in history. An icon who had won the Medal of Honor, started Eastern Air Lines, and survived on a raft in the Pacific Ocean for three weeks during World War II, would not have his place in history easy supplanted. You do not replace a hero and a legend overnight. After all, supporters would point out that Rickenbacker fought for the Americans and not the British, so he is *still* the "American Ace of Aces." The controversy might result in a reconfiguring of how victories are tabulated and aces are determined. For example, should a balloon count as much as an airplane, or not? The debate, reevaluation, and reinterpretation would continue up to the present and beyond. Could a reevaluation into Rickenbacker's record reveal more victories? If the exact details of Richothofen's death are still an issue, certainly the case supporting Lambert would not have been accepted without a fight. Whichever way it was finally decided, Lambert, not Rickenbacker, would become a legend.

On 23 November 1973, Frey sent Haslam a lengthy letter on Lambert's findings. Frey began by reminding Haslam that he had offered his services to him if he ever needed the assistance. Frey realized the time would eventually arrive, just not so soon. He then laid down Lambert's argument for him in precise detail. He stated that Lambert was "somewhat curious as to how many [victories] he might actually have to his credit, although he does not particularly wish to press the matter. However, we of the AF Museum certainly wish to press it and learn how many he actually has so our display will be correct for future generations."[10] (Obviously, Frey was stretching the truth about his "close personal friend" not being concerned about his victories!) Frey asked if it was possible for Taunton, Cheesman, and Franks to get together and come to a final conclusion. As he pointed out in support of Lambert's thesis, "all three had access to the same official historical records, although they came up with different answers."[11] He included copies of the various letters for Haslam to examine. He concluded by thanking Haslam for his assistance and stressing that "it is very important to us, and to history, to get this matter resolved, particularly before Lambert passes on."[12]

Frey sent Lambert a copy of his letter to Haslam, and Lambert replied the next day. From his letter, it was obvious that Lambert was more than "somewhat curious" about his victory total. He addressed Taunton's decision on the Fokker D. VII on 19 August 1918, which he had changed from being shot down to inconclusive, thereby lowering Lambert's victory total. Lambert stated that "Two Dolphins witnessed the combat & could not have failed to see it crash and burn."[13]

Lambert may have been impatient waiting for a reply from the Air Ministry. So he wrote to Frank Cheesman, who responded to Lambert the day after receiving Lambert's letter on 4 December 1973. Lambert had also had a number of questions and concerns about his book, and Cheesman addresses these first. Then he takes up Lambert's claim of additional victories and the possibility of being America's Ace of Aces. He began by giving Lambert a "word of warning about becoming involved in disputatious matters which may arise"—in particular, combat scores![14] He hoped that his comments would help Lambert to keep "clear of unwanted involvements on this subject." He told Lambert that he had written Appendix I in *Combat Report* "deliberately to explain the book title but primarily to put across to the reader your 'score' as you *estimated* it likely to be after reflecting upon your log book entries and other relevant documents."[15] Chessman also stated that he also explained that while the "*official* [i.e., Communiqués] figure was undoubtedly acceptable to the RAF, HQ *for their purposes* [i.e., assessing enemy loss] there was equally justification for pilots and units to regard their *own* claim figures as being true if the facts were honestly reported."[16] He stated that both of these approaches were allowed to flourish. He suggested Lambert should stay true to what he had originally stated and not change "if people should try to put words in your mouth or distort what I suggest here."[17] Evidently Cheesman believed—or acted as if he believed—that others, especially Franks, were suggesting to Lambert that he had more victories. They were the ones trying to corrupt the official process and record.

Undoubtedly, Cheesman continued, almost every pilot who had success in air combat probably had successes that went unrecorded. It was impossible to keep track of these scores. With the exception of where enemy aircraft were seen to "burn, blow-up or crash," it was impossible to "exactly estimate the correct 'score' of a pilot."[18] In combat, staying alive, achieving the squadron objectives, and winning the war were far more important objectives. Protecting an artillery spotter whose efforts could save the lives of hundreds in the trenches was significantly more important than any enemy aircraft listed as "out of control." Cheesman used Lambert's friend Callender as an example of someone who "*was not seen by his adversary to have been hit during the fight.*"[19] For Cheesman, Lambert's record is the one recorded in Appendix I of his book, and Lambert should "in all honesty," adhere to this source "which correspond with the entries in the text." This listing "carries the bare essentials enough for the thinking reader to see that there are two sides to this question."[20] The victories recorded in Appendix I were "what you saw and experienced at the time."[21] In essence, Cheesman was telling Lambert to leave well enough alone.

Cheesman then went after both Franks and Taunton, since he thought of them as the ones who had disturbed Lambert's mind. He took the issue as a personal matter. He was a former R.A.F. pilot, an expert in the field of the Great War, a friend of Lambert's, and assisted Lambert with *Combat Report:* he did not like having his findings called into question. Of Franks himself, he said he was "one of the recent generation to become interested in WWI aviation and, perhaps, still somewhat spellbound and absorbed by the sparkle of the 'ace' aspects of the subject."[22] Of Franks' conclusion and methodology, he remarked, "It is unlikely that [Franks'] so-called *confirmations* break any new ground as we have been going over the only available documents for the past 30 years. The fact that [Franks] does not agree with the victory list which Royal Frey obtained from the Air Ministry means nothing, as I threw that out soon after starting to compile that list in Appendix I. There were things in there which did not belong and others which should have been included so I started from the beginning!"[23]

Cheesman defended his own methodology by defining the terms used to determine victories. He stated that the "term 'confirmed' should be confined to the final assessments of the RAF, HQ staff only.... Anything lower down the scale [i.e., squadron, Wing or Brigade] does not count. Only HQ could confirm [or throw out] a claim."[24] Cheesman insisted that only the decisions of R.A.F. Head Quarters were "*officially* recognized.... Only these are entitled to be called *officially* conceded victories."[25] Cheesman conceded that a pilot's or squadron's claim may have been correct, but it was "unofficial" without the approval or confirmation of R.A.F. HQ as the final arbiter.

Next, Cheesman went after Taunton, if not by name. Cheesman was acquainted with Taunton, so he did not attack the man himself, but his methodology. He thought that whoever "put the Frey list together did not understand the subject well enough to choose either one or the other method and it resulted in a mixture of both which was well-nigh useless."[26] Taunton, he believed, had used results that were both "official" and unofficial; therefore, he had committed a serious error. Cheesman stated that "the RAF *under no circumstances* are allowed to quote totals for pilots or even units ... had his superior known of this he would have certainly been told off about this breach of rules."[27] Taunton's list, then, was not only incorrect; it was illegal. Cheesman allowed that he "was doubtless acting in the best of good faith and trying to be helpful" but insisted that he "should have never issued that list and added it up and made a signed statement to Frey."[28] In fact, he told Lambert that he should "keep it [Taunton's list] out of sight—at least of anyone on this side of the Atlantic."[29]

As with Franks, Cheesman found Lambert's record to be "sufficiently splendid to stand up on its own to any sort of scrutiny and you clearly won about 20 victories [I have no doubt this is a conservative judgment on my part!]"[30] The ones that Cheesman had allowed were those recorded by R.A.F. Headquarters; however, Cheesman admitted that "there were no doubt several others for which you were just unlucky in being unable to obtain their OK to but which, in your own mind, you know damned well that you destroyed."[31] The implication is that other aces were in the same situation, and that the only proper behavior was to be satisfied with the "official" judgment.

When Lambert received this letter, so different from what he was hoping for, he took refuge in pretended incomprehension. He wrote Frey that he could not "fathom what [Cheesman] means in part of it."[32] He hoped that Frey could make sense out of it. But in the end, he told Frey that if the quest caused any more difficulties, he would suggest that they "drop it & take what Taunton has to say in his list. I am too old to take up any more problems."[33]

Tactfully, Frey responded to Lambert by letting him know that Cheesman's letter had also puzzled him. "I've read the letter three times and simply do not get his point. There are almost two pages of rambling."[34] Frey had already asked the Air Ministry to reinvestigate Lambert's record. He suggested that they wait until they hear from the Air Ministry before making any decisions.

It took about two months for Frey to receive the Ministry's response. On 5 February 1974, "Teddy" Haslam responded to Frey's request for a reinvestigation into Lambert's record. He had turned the investigation over to F. W. Coles, Taunton's successor, who went over the original documents to determine the number of victories Lambert had achieved in the Great War. What could be found in Coles' enclosed letter was the "fruit of several weeks' careful study." Haslam enforced the point that the documents Coles used "are not complete and the evidence is not always complementary"; in fact, they could be contradictory at times. Consequently, the conclusions regarding Lambert's record "cannot have the fiat of official say-so." The findings could be used, however, to give Lambert "the satisfaction of having the evidence in his possession."[35] The ending of Haslam's letter is rather pathetic. He says that Frey would appreciate the time involved on behalf of his limited staff to research Lambert's record, but he hoped Frey would not "come back with another such request for some time." He suggest it would be better if Frey simply came to London to research the records himself.[36]

Coles' accompanying letter reinforced Haslam's warning that the accuracy of the research would always be in question because of "conflicting evidence so often found in documents of this era and the fact that the documents are frequently incomplete."[37] He was sending Frey his assessment of Lambert's record, but conceded that it was "open to all researchers to place their own interpretation upon the evidence of research."[38] Coles then gave the results of his research. He accepted all of Taunton's findings and added "a further $1 + \frac{1}{2} + \frac{1}{3} + \frac{1}{4}$." (If two or more pilots shared in a victory they were given a percentage.) For example, Coles discovered that Lambert had destroyed a balloon with another pilot on 21 April, so he shared that victory and received ½ point credit. His list also contained victories mentioned in Franks' letter to Lambert. Coles' calculations would place Lambert's final total at twenty-two victories, the same as Franks. The only place Coles differs from Franks is that Franks gave Lambert three victories on 4 July and one on 4 August, and Coles gave him two victories on each of these days. Coles then addressed a flight that occurred on 19 August 1918, where Cheesman had found an additional victory for Lambert. Coles' investigation showed that No. 24 Squadron's records listed an encounter with a Fokker Biplane, but it was only listed as Lambert engaging the plane and not as a victory or the plane sent down out of control; consequently, Lambert could not add this plane to his total.[39] (This conclusion is somewhat ironic, given Cheesman's emphasis that only officially recorded victories should be counted.) Coles concluded his letter by hoping that Frey would be satisfied with his conclusions. If not, he suggested, as Haslam did, that Frey go to the Public Record Office and consult for himself the documents that had been returned.[40]

Coles created the concise six-page document that listed thirty-two incidents and included a "key of Reference" to indicate the sources used to validate Lambert's record. He had conducted a thorough and exhaustive study beyond what anyone else had attempted. It was definitive and was used extensively in this work.

Frey clearly recognized, as he evidently had not before, the effort involved in this report. His wish to help Lambert had caused him to push the envelope farther than was ordinarily necessary. Moreover, Frey's request had had the unintended consequences of seeming to call into question the work of Taunton, Haslam's and Cole's former colleague. Therefore, Frey's thank-you letter goes far beyond the norm as well. He excessively flatters both Haslam and Coles for the "tremendous amount of research effort that [Coles] put forth." He let them know that he realized the amount of work necessary to complete his request, "I would have happily withdrawn it."[41] He said Coles was "a real professional in the strictest sense of the word and we request that you pass to him our expressions of appreciation." He insisted that these were not "simply idle words on my part—I fully comprehend the great volume of work he put forth to produce the listing which you sent to us and we are truly indebted to him." He also made it clear that he had no intention of pursuing the issue further. Frey ended his letter by asking, "Now, are we still friends?"[42]

Frey immediately sent the report to Lambert, who immediately wrote back. Like Frey, he was appreciative that "those boys dug into a lot of corners." He also observed, "Like Franks and Taunton, they included some not recorded by the other two and omitted a few recorded by Franks and Taunton."[43] (This statement is, in fact, incorrect; they accepted all of Taunton's findings and added a few.) Finally, he told Frey that for the past few years they had been using the Taunton report, and he felt that this "report by Taunton comes closer to my log book than any I have seen. So, why not do as I requested once before, just accept Taunton as final."[44] One thing that Lambert did not say, but that probably weighted heavily with him, is that Taunton's list was presented as authoritative, whereas Coles' list was emphatically not authoritative and at best probable.

Taunton's list, of course, does not put Lambert ahead of Rickenbacker as to victories. It seemed as if Lambert had finally accepted that he would have to be contented with the title of "Greatest Living American Ace" of World War I. Rickenbacker would remain the "Ace of Aces." Frey's letter back to Lambert concurred with Lambert's conclusion that they should "stick to Taunton's score of 21½ air-to-air victories. Besides, that is the figure we are already using in your display."[45]

However, though Lambert accepted the official investigations into his record were at an end, he still did not accept their findings. In fact, we have written evidence that he did not. In 1978, a newspaper article, "Colonel Lambert still Flying Legend," appeared in one of the local papers. Under a photo of Lambert sitting in a chair is a caption that states, "Lambert claims to have shot down 30 enemy planes, more than the famous Eddie Rickenbacker."[46] No doubt, Lambert had by this time convinced himself that he had shot down thirty enemy planes. And perhaps he may have been right, and simply not have been given official credit for some of the planes he shot down. One thing is certain: he never again tried to get official recognition for more victories than he was given by Taunton.

Chapter Notes

Introduction

1. Michael Korda, *Hero: The Life and Legend of Lawrence of Arabia* (New York: HarperCollins, 2010), p. xvi.
2. Peter Kilduff, *The Red Baron: Beyond the Legend* (London: Cassell Military Paperbacks, 1994), p. 117.
3. Manfred von Richthofen, cited in Kilduff, *The Red Baron: Beyond the Legend*, p. 155.
4. Herbert A. Johnson, *Wingless Eagle: U.S. Army Aviation through World War I* (Chapel Hill: University of North Carolina Press, 2001), p. 29.
5. Manfred von Richthofen, cited in Kilduff, *The Red Baron: Beyond the Legend*, p. 31.
6. Erwin Böhme, *Briefe eines deutschen Kampffiegers an ein junges Mächen* (1930), p. 112, cited in Kilduff, *The Red Baron: Beyond the Legend*, p. 7.
7. Kilduff, *The Red Baron: Beyond the Legend*, p. 8.
8. Manfred von Richthofen, cited in Kilduff, *The Red Baron: Beyond the Legend*, p. 9.
9. *Ibid.*, p. 47.
10. Kilduff, *The Red Baron: Beyond the Legend*, p. 18.
11. Walter Raleigh, *The War in the Air*, Vol. I (Uckfield: East Sussex: The Naval and Military Press, Ltd., n.d.), p. 12.
12. "William Pitsenbarger [1944–1966]," *Ohio's Aviation Heritage: Teacher Resource Guide* (National Museum of the United States Air Force Education Division), pp. 9–11, http://www.nationalmuseum.af.mil/shared/media/document/AFD-070702-079.pdf.
13. *Ibid.*, p. 6.
14. Klaus Staerker, Interview with Author, 14 September 2013.
15. *Ibid.*

Chapter One

1. James Tobin, *To Conquer the Air: The Wright Brothers and the Great Race for Flight* (New York: Free Press, 2008), pp. 44–45.
2. "Wilbur Wright to the Smithsonian Institute, Dayton, Ohio, 30 May 1899," printed in Fred C. Kelly, ed., *Miracle at Kitty Hawk: The Letters of Wilbur and Orville Wright* (New York: Da Capo Press, 2002), p. 15.
3. *Ibid.*, pp. 15–16.
4. Crouch, *The Bishop's Boys: A Life of Wilber and Orville Wright*, p. 161.
5. Richard P. Hallion, *Taking Flight: Inventing the Aerial Age from Antiquity Through the First World War* (New York: Oxford University Press, 2003), p. 181.
6. *Ibid.* The Wright Brothers would develop a close friendship with Chanute that would last until Chanute's death in 1910. Their correspondence sheds light on the progress in developing the airplane and the problems inherent in getting a patent for it.
7. *Ibid.*, pp. 15–16, 174–175, 221.
8. Hallion, *Taking Flight*, p. 179.
9. *Ibid.*, p. 185.
10. Crouch, *The Bishop's Boys: A Life of Wilber and Orville Wright*, p. 166.
11. Wilbur Wright, "Some Aeronautical Experiments," 18 September 1901, Wright Papers, I, p. 100, cited in Tobin, *To Conquer the Air*, pp. 164–165.
12. Hallion, *Taking Flight*, p. 186.
13. Octave Chanute to Wilbur Wright, Chicago, Illinois, 19 December 1901, and Wilbur Wright to Octave Chanute, Dayton, Ohio, 23 December 1901, printed in Kelly, ed., *Miracle at Kitty Hawk: The Letters of Wilbur and Orville Wright*, pp. 55–56. On 13 May 1900, Wilbur wrote Chanute for the first time. It was the beginning of a friendship between Chanute and the bothers that would last until Chanute's death a decade later.
14. Crouch, *The Bishop's Boys: A Life of Wilber and Orville Wright*, p. 201.
15. *Ibid.*, p. 182.
16. Orville Wright to Katharine Wright, Kitty Hawk, North Carolina, 14 October 1900, printed in Kelly, ed., *Miracle at Kitty Hawk: The Letters of Wilbur and Orville Wright*, p. 33.
17. Crouch, *The Bishop's Boys: A Life of Wilber and Orville Wright*, pp. 196–197.
18. Hallion, *Taking Flight*, p. 186.
19. *Ibid.*, p.190.
20. *Ibid.*
21. Crouch, *The Bishop's Boys: A Life of Wilber and Orville Wright*, p. 203.
22. Wilbur Wright's Diary, 30 July 1901, printed in Kelly, ed., *Miracle at Kitty Hawk: The Letters of Wilbur and Orville Wright*, p. 41.
23. Hallion, *Taking Flight*, p. 192.

24. *Ibid.*
25. *Ibid.*; Crouch, *The Bishop's Boys: A Life of Wilbur and Orville Wright*, p. 213.
26. *Ibid.*, pp. 221–222; Hallion, *Taking Flight*, p. 193.
27. Crouch, *The Bishop's Boys: A Life of Wilbur and Orville Wright*, p. 222.
28. *Ibid.*, p. 226.
29. Hallion, *Taking Flight*, p. 193.
30. *Ibid.*, p. 196; Crouch, *The Bishop's Boys: A Life of Wilbur and Orville Wright*, p. 239.
31. Hallion, *Taking Flight*, p. 196.
32. Wilbur Wright to Milton Wright, 2 October 1902, cited in Hallion, *Taking Flight*, p. 195.
33. Hallion, *Taking Flight*, p. 200.
34. *Ibid.*, p. 202.
35. Crouch, *The Bishop's Boys: A Life of Wilbur and Orville Wright*, p. 242.
36. *Ibid.*, p. 243; Hallion, *Taking Flight*, pp. 200–201.
37. James Tobin, *To Conquer the Air: The Wright Brothers and the Great Race for Flight* (New York: Free Press, 2003), pp. 4–6, 30–31, 44–45.
38. Hallion, *Taking Flight*, p. 204; Crouch, *The Bishop's Boys: A Life of Wilbur and Orville Wright*, pp. 264–269.
39. Cited in Tobin, *To Conquer the Air*, p. 223.
40. Orville Wright to C. H. Hitchcock, Washington, D.C., 21 June 1917, cited in Fred C. Kelly, ed., *Miracle at Kitty Hawk: The Letters of Wilbur and Orville Wright* (New York: Da Capo Press, 2002), pp. 405–406.
41. Herbert George Wells, *Tono Bungay*, 10 March 2012: http://www.gutenberg.org/files/718/718-h/718-h.htm.
42. Vachel Lindsay, "Abraham Lincoln Walks at Midnight," *Poetry Foundation* (Chicago: 2014), assessed on 30 September 2014: http://www.poetryfoundation.org/poem/176810.
43. Michael Paris, "The First Air Wars—North Africa and the Balkans, 1911–13," *Journal of Contemporary History*, Vol. 26, No. 1 (Jan. 1991), pp. 97–98. Military tensions boosted aircraft sales. In 1912, Italy order 14 Bristol monoplanes and the Romanian government, facing a conflict in the Balkans with Bulgaria, ordered ten. Hugh Driver, *The Birth of Military Aviation: Britain 1903–1914* (London: Boyden Press, 1997), p. 116.
44. *Ibid.*, pp. 51–52.
45. Edward V. Rickenbacker, *Rickenbacker: An Autobiography* (Englewood Cliffs, NJ: Prentice-Hall, 1967), p. 356.

Chapter Two

1. *Ironton, Ohio: Its Industries, Resources, and Facilities* (Ironton, OH: Ironton Register Print, 1881), p. 12.
2. Melissa Girardot, "The Furnaces," *The Lawrence Register*, http://lawrencecountyohio.com/furnaces/stories/stats1888.htm.
3. Payne, "Modernity Lost," p. 36.
4. *Ibid.*, pp. 99–100.
5. Harry Franken, "Reluctant Hero of World War I Cherishes Memories," *Citizen-Journal*, n.d., p. 9, Lambert File, USAF Museum.
6. Howell and Abel, *Ironton City Directories, 1914–1915* (Ironton, OH: Howell and Abel), p. 104; ———, "W.G. Lambert," *The Ironton Tribune*, 6 November 1957, n.p.
7. William C. Lambert, *Barnstorming and Girls* (Manhattan, KS: Sunflower University Press, 1980), p. 56.
8. Robert J. Smith, *Air Force Logistics Command Oral History Interview #18*, transcript, Lt. Col. William C. Lambert (Office of History Headquarters, Air Force Logistics Command, Dayton, OH, September 1980), pp. 1–2. Hereafter, Smith, *Interview #18*.
9. *Ibid.*; Smith, *Interview #18*, p. 2.
10. Lambert, *Combat Report*, p. 13.
11. *Ibid.*, p. 14; Smith, *Interview #18*, pp. 1–2.
12. Lambert, *Combat Report*, p. 14.
13. Smith, *Interview #18*, p. vii.
14. Lambert, *Combat Report*, p.15.
15. *Ibid.*, pp. 15–16.
16. Lambert, "*Combat Report—Typed Manuscript,*" p. 5.
17. Smith, *Interview #18*, p. 4.
18. Herbert A. Johnson, *Wingless Eagle: U.S. Army Aviation through World War I*, (Chapel Hill, NC: North Carolina Press, 2001), p. 30.
19. *Ibid.*, pp. 30–31.
20. *Ibid.*, pp. 31–32.
21. *Ibid.*, p. 33.
22. George P. Scriven, *Report to the Secretary of War, 1913*, p. 57, cited in Johnson, *Wingless Eagle*, p. 63.
23. Harry Franken, "Reluctant Hero of World War I Cherishes Memories," *Citizen-Journal*, n.d., p. 9, Lambert File: United States Air Force Museum, Dayton, OH. Hereafter, Lambert File, USAF Museum.
24. *Ibid.*, p. 459.
25. Smith, *Interview #18*, p. 5.
26. Martin, *America's Forgotten Ace*, p. 2. (This story is repeated in many articles on Lambert.) *Ironton City Directories, 1914–1915*, p. 105.
27. Franken, "Reluctant Hero of World War I Cherishes Memories," p. 9.
28. Frey, "Forgotten Ace of World War I," p. 20.
29. Smith, *Interview #18*, pp. 7–8.
30. Smith, *Interview #18*, p. 8.
31. *Ibid.*
32. Lambert's files in the Directorate of History and Heritage, National Defence Headquarters, Ottawa, Canada K1A 0K2, were sent to me via email by Major Mathias Joost, War Diaries Team, on 2 September 2011.
33. Lambert, "A Very Strange Story," pp. 4–5.
34. http://www.thefreedictionary.com/nitrocellulose.
35. These identification papers were given to the author as part of a collection of personal effects and correspondence that belonged to William C. Lambert and are still in the author's possession. They will be donated to the Briggs Lawrence County Library in Ironton, Ohio, after the completion of this project. Yancey is also referred to in an article retyped at the

end of Lambert's manuscript, "A Very Strange Story." Lambert apparently kept the article, "Explosions at Nobel Destroy 5 Buildings," that was printed in a Toronto paper on 22 November 1917. He retyped the article and placed it in the back of his story as verification of the events described in the article.
  36. Jacob White, Ph.D. to Samuel J. Wilson, "Email: Canadian Explosives, LTD," 27 September 2011.
  37. William C. Lambert, "Notebook," n.p. This book was given to the author as part of a collection of personal effects and correspondence that belonged to William C. Lambert and is still in the author's possession but will be donated to either the U.S. Air Force Museum in Dayton, Ohio, or the Briggs Lawrence County Library in Ironton, Ohio, after the completion of this project.
  38. Sullivan, *Aviation in Canada 1917–1918*, p. 18.
  39. Lambert, *Combat Report*, p. 18.
  40. Smith, *Interview #18*, p. 9.
  41. Lambert, "Combat Report—Typed Manuscript, Chapter I," Box 3, File 16, MS-221, p. 2. Lambert numbered the pages in each chapter of his rough draft, beginning with page 1 for each chapter.
  42. Lambert, *Combat Report*, p. 18.
  43. Lambert, *Combat Report*, pp. 18, 20; Lambert, "Combat Report—Typed Manuscript, Chapter I," pp. 4–5.
  44. Lambert, "Combat Report—Typed Manuscript, Chapter I," pp. 6–7.
  45. *Ibid.*, pp. 3–4.
  46. Lambert, "Combat Report—Typed Manuscript, Chapter I," p. 8.
  47. Lambert, *Combat Report*, p. 22.
  48. Smith, *Interview #18*, p. 11.
  49. Lambert, *Combat Report*, p. 22.

Chapter Three

  1. Lambert, *Combat Report*, p. 18.
  2. *Ibid.*
  3. Lambert, "A Very Strange Story," p. 33.
  4. William C. Lambert, "Combat Report—Typed Manuscript, Chapter 3, Box 3, File 18 MS-221," p. 13.
  5. *Ibid.*, p. 20. In addition to his books, Lambert also kept his RFC *Pilot's Flying Log Book*. The original was given to the Air Force Museum in Dayton, Ohio; however, Bill Martin made copies of the book and included a copy in the effects he gave to me for my research.
  6. *Ibid.*, p. 22.
  7. William C. Lambert, "Combat Report—Typed Manuscript, Chapter 2, Box 3, File 17 MS-221," p. 1. Hereafter: Lambert, "Combat Report—Typed Manuscript, Chapter 2."
  8. William C. Lambert, *Pilot's Flying Log Book*, p. 3; Lambert, *Combat Report*, p. 24.
  9. Lambert, *Combat Report*, p. 24.
  10. Lambert, *Pilot's Flying Log Book*, p. 3; Lambert, *Combat Report*, pp. 25–26.
  11. Lambert, "Combat Report—Typed Manuscript, Chapter 2," p. 3.
  12. Lambert, *Combat Report*, p. 26.
  13. *Ibid.*, Lambert, "Combat Report—Typed Manuscript, Chapter 2," p. 4.
  14. Lambert, *Pilot's Flying Log Book*, p. 3.
  15. *Ibid.*, p. 4.
  16. *Ibid.*; Lambert, *Combat Report*, p. 26.
  17. Lambert, "Combat Report—Typed Manuscript, Chapter 2," p. 4.
  18. *Ibid.*, p. 5.
  19. Lambert, *Pilot's Flying Log Book*, pp. 5, 8.
  20. Lambert, *Combat Report*, p. 28.
  21. Lambert, *Pilot's Flying Log Book*, p. 7.
  22. *Ibid.*, p. 10; Lambert, "Combat Report—Typed Manuscript, Chapter 2," p. 8; Lambert, *Combat Report*, p. 28.
  23. Andrew A. Callender to Majorie, Borden, Canada, September 1917, cited in Callender, *War in an Open Cockpit*, p. 22.
  24. Lambert, "Combat Report—Typed Manuscript, Chapter 2," p. 8; Lambert, *Combat Report*, p. 28.
  25. Peter Hart, *Aces Falling: War Above the Trenches, 1918* (London: Weidenfeld and Nicolson, 2007), p. 47.
  26. *Ibid.*
  27. Lambert, "Combat Report—Typed Manuscript, Chapter 2," p. 8.
  28. *Ibid.*
  29. Lambert, "Combat Report—Typed Manuscript, Chapter 2," pp. 8–9; Lambert, *Combat Report*, pp. 28–29.
  30. *Ibid.*, p. 9; Lambert, *Combat Report*, p. 29.
  31. Lambert, *Combat Report*, p. 30.
  32. Lambert, *Pilot's Flying Log Book*, p. 10.
  33. *Ibid.*; Lambert, *Combat Report*, p. 30.
  34. _____, "25 Years Ago," The Ironton News, 13 September 1942, n.p. Lambert Collection, Lawrence County Museum, Ironton, OH.
  35. Smith, *Interview #18*, p. 19.
  36. Lambert, *Pilot's Flying Log Book*, p. 12.
  37. Lambert, *Combat Report*, p. 30.
  38. Callender, *War in an Open Cockpit*, p. 32.
  39. Lambert, "Combat Report—Typed Manuscript, Chapter 2," p. 12.
  40. *Ibid.*, p. 13
  41. Lambert, *Combat Report*, p. 32.
  42. Lambert, "Combat Report—Typed Manuscript, Chapter 2," p. 14.
  43. Lambert, "Combat Report—Typed Manuscript, Chapter 3," pp. 1–2.
  44. Lambert, *Pilot's Flying Log Book*, p. 16.
  45. Lambert, "Combat Report—Typed Manuscript, Chapter 3," p. 2.
  46. *Ibid.*, p. 3.
  47. *Ibid.*
  48. William C. Lambert, "What Were They Like To Fly," p. 1, Lambert Collection.
  49. *Ibid.*
  50. Hart, *Aces Falling*, p. 38.
  51. V. M. Yeates, *Winged Victory* (London: Grub Street Publishing, 2004), p. 25.
  52. William C. Lambert, "What Were They Like To Fly," p. 2, Lambert Collection.
  53. *Ibid.* p. 4.
  54. William C. Lambert, *Out of the Sun*, Interviewed by Robert J. Smith, Video, General Dynamics,

Ft. Worth Division, 1980. Hereafter: Lambert, *Out of the Sun*.
   55. Lambert, "Combat Report—Typed Manuscript, Chapter 3," p. 4; William C. Lambert to N. W. Gillman, Manuscript: Chattis Hill, Stockbridge, Hants, December 1917, p. 3, Lambert Collection.
   56. Lambert, *Out of the Sun*.
   57. Lambert, "Combat Report—Typed Manuscript, Chapter 3," p. 14.
   58. Lambert, *Combat Report*, pp. 37–38.
   59. Lambert, *Pilot's Flying Log Book*, pp. 16, 26.
   60. *Ibid.*, p. 21.
   61. Lambert, *Combat Report*, pp. 38–39.
   62. Lambert, "Combat Report—Typed Manuscript, Chapter 4," p. 1.
   63. *Ibid.*

Chapter Four

   1. *Ibid.*, pp. xiv–xvii.
   2. Lambert, *Combat Report*, p. 39.
   3. Lambert, "Combat Report—Typed Manuscript, Chapter 4, Box 3, File 19 MS-221," p. 1. Hereafter: Lambert, "Combat Report—Typed Manuscript, Chapter 4."
   4. *Ibid.*, pp. 1–2.
   5. *Ibid.*, p. 2; Lambert, *Pilot's Flying Log Book*, p. 27.
   6. Lambert, "Combat Report—Typed Manuscript, Chapter 4," p. 5.
   7. *Ibid.*
   8. *Ibid.*
   9. Lambert, *Combat Report*, pp. 39–42.
   10. Lambert, "Combat Report—Typed Manuscript, Chapter 4," p. 6.
   11. Lambert, "Combat Report—Typed Manuscript, Chapter V," Box 3, File 20, MS-221, p. 2.
   12. *Ibid.*, p. 3.
   13. Rickenbacker, cited in Lewis, *Eddie Rickenbacker: An American Hero in the Twentieth Century*, p. 131.
   14. Lambert, *Combat Report*, p. 47.
   15. *Ibid.*, pp. 47–48; Lambert, "Combat Report—Typed Manuscript, Chapter V," pp. 6–7.
   16. Lambert, "Combat Report—Typed Manuscript, Chapter V," p. 7.
   17. *Ibid.*, p. 8; Lambert, *Combat Report*, p. 48.
   18. Lambert, "Combat Report—Typed Manuscript, Chapter V," p. 8.
   19. Lambert, *Combat Report*, p. 50.
   20. *Ibid.*
   21. *Ibid.*
   22. *Ibid.*
   23. *Ibid.*
   24. Lambert, "Combat Report—Typed Manuscript, Chapter V," p. 8.
   25. Lambert, *Combat Report*, p. 50
   26. Lambert, "Combat Report—Typed Manuscript, Chapter V," p. 11.
   27. *Ibid.*, p. 14.
   28. *Ibid.*
   29. *Ibid.*, pp. 11–12.
   30. *Ibid.*, p. 12. Lambert originally spelled his name as "Hammersly," but later on in the manuscript the correct spelling is used.
   31. Lambert, *Pilot's Flying Log Book*, p. 27.
   32. Lambert, "Combat Report—Typed Manuscript, Chapter V," p. 12.
   33. *Ibid.*
   34. *Ibid.*
   35. *Ibid.*, pp. 12–13.
   36. *Ibid.*, p. 13.
   37. *Ibid.*, p. 13.
   38. *Ibid.*
   39. Lambert, *Pilot's Flying Log Book*, p. 27.
   40. Christopher Cole, ed., *Royal Air Force 1918* (London: William Kimber, 1968), p. 34.
   41. Lambert, "Combat Report—Typed Manuscript, Chapter V," p. 14; Shores, Franks, and Guest, *Above the Trenches*, p. 213.
   42. Illingworth, *A History of 24 Squadron*, p. 88.
   43. Lambert, "Combat Report—Typed Manuscript, Chapter V," p. 17; Illingworth, *A History of 24 Squadron*, p. 40; Lambert, *Combat Report*, pp. 63, 80, 112.
   44. Lambert, *Pilot's Flying Log Book*, p. 27; Lambert, "Combat Report—Typed Manuscript, Chapter V," p. 17.
   45. Lambert, "Combat Report—Typed Manuscript, Chapter V," p. 17.
   46. Lambert, *Combat Report*, p. 54; Lambert, *Pilot's Flying Log Book*, p. 27.
   47. Lambert, "Combat Report—Typed Manuscript, Chapter V," pp. 18–19.
   48. Lambert, *Out of the Sun*.
   49. Lambert, "Combat Report—Typed Manuscript, Chapter V," p. 19; Lambert, *Combat Report*, p. 55.
   50. Illingworth, *A History of 24 Squadron*, p. 40.
   51. Lambert, "Combat Report—Typed Manuscript, Chapter V," p. 19.
   52. Lambert, *Out of the Sun*.
   53. Shores, Franks, and Guest, *Above the Trenches*, p. 270.
   54. Lambert, "Combat Report—Typed Manuscript, Chapter VI," Box 3, File 21, MS-221, p. 3.
   55. Wilson, *The Anatomy of Courage*, pp. 10, 35, 37.
   56. Lamberton, *Fighter Aircraft of the 1914–1918 War*, p. 154.
   57. Lambert, "Combat Report—Typed Manuscript, Chapter V," p. 20.
   58. Lambert, *Combat Report*, p. 56.
   59. Illingworth, *A History of 24 Squadron*, p. 41.
   60. Lambert, *Pilot's Flying Log Book*, p. 27; Lambert, *Combat Report*, p. 57.
   61. Lambert, *Combat Report*, p. 57.
   62. Lambert, "Combat Report—Typed Manuscript, Chapter V," p. 24.
   63. Illingworth, *A History of 24 Squadron*, p. 41.
   64. Lambert, "Combat Report—Typed Manuscript, Chapter V," p. 23.
   65. *Ibid.*, p. 22.
   66. *Ibid.*
   67. *Ibid.*

68. *Ibid.*
69. Wilson, *The Anatomy of Courage*, pp. 38–39.
70. *Ibid.*, p. 39.
71. *Ibid.*

Chapter Five

1. Lambert, "Combat Report—Typed Manuscript, Chapter VI," p. 2.
2. *Ibid.*, p. 3; Lambert, *Pilot's Flying Log Book*, p. 27.
3. Lambert, "Combat Report—Typed Manuscript, Chapter VI," p. 4.
4. *Ibid.*
5. Shores, Franks, and Guest, *Above the Trenches*, p. 230; Lambert, *Pilot's Flying Log Book*, p. 27.
6. Lambert, *Out of the Sun*.
7. Shores, Franks, and Guest, *Above the Trenches*, p. 213.
8. Lambert, "Combat Report—Typed Manuscript, Chapter VI," p. 4.
9. London, The National Archives, William Carpenter Lambert, File C40499, AIR/76/285.
10. Lambert, "Combat Report—Typed Manuscript, Chapter VI," pp. 4–5.
11. Lambert, *Pilot's Flying Log Book*, p. 27; Lambert, "Combat Report—Typed Manuscript, Chapter VI," p. 5.
12. Lambert, *Pilot's Flying Log Book*, p. 28; Lambert, "Combat Report—Typed Manuscript, Chapter VI," pp 5–6.
13. Lambert, "Combat Report—Typed Manuscript, Chapter VI," p. 6.
14. *Ibid.*
15. Shores, Franks, and Guest, *Above the Trenches*, p. 244.
16. *Ibid.*
17. Shores, Franks, and Guest, *Above the Trenches*, pp. 230–231; Lambert, *Pilot's Flying Log Book*, p. 28; W. J. Taunton to Royal D. Frey, Letter, 3 January 1968.
18. Cole, ed., *Royal Air Force 1918*, p. 69.
19. Lambert, "Combat Report—Typed Manuscript, Chapter VI," p. 7.
20. *Ibid.*
21. *Ibid.*, pp. 7–8.
22. *Ibid.*, p. 8.
23. *Ibid.*, pp. 8–9.
24. Lambert, *Pilot's Flying Log Book*, p. 28.
25. Lambert, "Combat Report—Typed Manuscript, Chapter VI," p. 9.
26. John H. Murrow Jr., *The Great War in the Air: Military Aviation from 1909 to 1921* (Washington, D.C.: Smithsonian Institute Press, 1993), 171.
27. Lambert, "Combat Report—Typed Manuscript, Chapter VI," p. 9.
28. *Ibid.*, pp. 9–10.
29. *Ibid.*; Lambert, *Pilot's Flying Log Book*, p. 28.
30. Lambert, "Combat Report—Typed Manuscript, Chapter VI," p. 11.
31. *Ibid.*, p. 12; Lambert, *Pilot's Flying Log Book*, p. 28.
32. Lambert, "Combat Report—Typed Manuscript, Chapter VI," p. 12.
33. *Ibid.*
34. *Ibid.*, p. 13.
35. Captain Horace D. Barton was an ace with nineteen victories from South Africa who would be awarded the Distinguished Flying Cross and Bar. Captain Conway M. G. Farrell was an ace from Regina Saskachewan who would be awarded the Distinguished Flying Cross, gazette in November, and would later be transferred to McCudden's old unit No. 56 Squadron in late August 1918 to become a flight commander. Lieutenant E. Harrison would be killed in action later in the war.
36. Lambert, *Combat Report*, p. 67.
37. Lambert, "Combat Report—Typed Manuscript, Chapter VI," p. 14.
38. Lambert, *Pilot's Flying Log Book*, p. 28.
39. Lambert, "Combat Report—Typed Manuscript, Chapter VI," p. 15.
40. *Ibid.*, p. 13.
41. *Ibid.*, pp. 15–16.
42. *Ibid.*, pp. 16–17.
43. *Ibid.*, pp. 17–18.
44. *Ibid.*, p. 18; Lambert, *Out of the Sun*.
45. Lambert, "Combat Report—Typed Manuscript, Chapter VI," pp. 19–20; Lambert, *Pilot's Flying Log Book*, p. 28.
46. Lambert, "Combat Report—Typed Manuscript, Chapter VI," pp. 19–20.
47. *Ibid.*, p. 20.
48. *Ibid.*, p. 21.
49. *Ibid.*; Shores, Franks, and Guest, *Above the Trenches*, p. 260. Lieutenant Ronald T. Mark was an ace with fourteen victories, eight of them shared, who was awarded the Military Cross and Bar.
50. Martin Van Creveld, *The Art of War: War and Military Thought* (New York: HarperCollins, 2005), p. 169.
51. Jones, *The War in the Air*, Vol. VI, pp. 137, 141.
52. Jones, *The War in the Air*, Vol. IV, p. 278.
53. Lambert, "Combat Report—Typed Manuscript, Chapter VI," p. 21.
54. *Ibid.*, pp. 21–22.
55. *Ibid.*, pp. 22–23.
56. *Ibid.*, p. 23.
57. Lambert, *Combat Report*, p. 71.
58. Lambert, "Combat Report—Typed Manuscript, Chapter VI," p. 23.
59. *Ibid.*
60. *Ibid.*, p. 24.
61. *Ibid.*
62. *Ibid.*
63. Shores, Franks, and Guest, *Above the Trenches*, p. 230.
64. Lambert, "Combat Report—Typed Manuscript, Chapter VI," p. 24.
65. Lambert, *Combat Report*, pp. 72–73.
66. *Ibid.*, p. 73.
67. Lambert, "Combat Report—Typed Manuscript, Chapter VI," p. 26.
68. *Ibid.*

69. *Ibid.*
70. *Ibid.*
71. Shores, Franks, and Guest, *Above the Trenches*, p. 256.
72. Lambert, "Combat Report—Typed Manuscript, Chapter VI," p. 27.
73. Lieutenant James Dawe was an ace from Rickmansworth, Hertforshire.
74. Lambert, "Combat Report—Typed Manuscript, Chapter VI," pp. 27–28.
75. *Ibid.*, p. 28.
76. *Ibid.*
77. *Ibid.*, pp. 28–29.
78. *Ibid.*, p. 29.
79. Lambert, *Pilot's Flying Log Book*, p. 29.
80. Lambert, "Combat Report—Typed Manuscript, Chapter VI," p. 30.
81. *Ibid.*, p. 31
82. *Ibid.*
83. *Ibid.*, p. 34.
84. Farwell, *Over There: The United States in the Great War, 1917–1918*, pp. 165–166.
85. Hochschild, *To End All Wars*, pp. 320–321.
86. Farwell, *Over There: The United States in the Great War, 1917–1918*, p. 166.
87. Lambert, "Combat Report—Typed Manuscript, Chapter VI," p. 32
88. *Ibid.*, pp. 32–33.
89. *Ibid.*, p. 33.
90. *Ibid.*
91. *Ibid.*
92. *Ibid.*
93. *Ibid.*, pp. 33–34.
94. Lambert, *Pilot's Flying Log Book*, p. 29.
95. W. J. Taunton to Royal D. Frey, Letter, 3 January 1968.
96. Lambert, "Combat Report—Typed Manuscript, Chapter VI," p. 35
97. *Ibid.*
98. Lambert, *"Combat Report—Typed Manuscript, Chapter VII,"* Box 3, File 22, MS-221, p. 22.
99. *Ibid.*, pp. 34–35.
100. Shores, Franks, and Guest, *Above the Trenches*, p. 260.
101. Lambert, "Combat Report—Typed Manuscript, Chapter VI," p. 35.
102. *Ibid.*
103. Farwell, *Over There: The United States in the Great War, 1917–1918*, p. 166.
104. Lambert, "Combat Report—Typed Manuscript, Chapter VI," p. 36.
105. *Ibid.*
106. W. J. Taunton to Royal D. Frey, Letter, 3 January 1968.
107. Lambert, "Combat Report—Typed Manuscript, Chapter VI," p. 37.
108. *Ibid.*
109. *Ibid.*
110. Lambert, *Pilot's Flying Log Book*, p. 29; Lambert, "Combat Report—Typed Manuscript, Chapter VI," pp. 39–40.
111. Lambert, "Combat Report—Typed Manuscript, Chapter VI," pp. 39–40.
112. Shores, Franks, and Guest, *Above the Trenches*, p. 136.
113. Lambert, "Combat Report—Typed Manuscript, Chapter VI," p. 40.
114. V. M. Yeates, *Winged Victory* (London: Grub Street, 2004), p. 174.
115. *Ibid.*
116. Wilson, *The Anatomy of Courage*, p. 38.

Chapter Six

1. Farwell, *The United States in The Great War, 1917–1918*, pp. 167–168.
2. Hochschild, *To End All Wars*, p. 327.
3. Lambert, *Pilot's Flying Log Book*, p. 29; Lambert, "Combat Report—Typed Manuscript, Chapter VII," p. 1.
4. Lambert, "Combat Report—Typed Manuscript, Chapter VII," p. 1.
5. *Ibid.*
6. Lambert, *Combat Report*, p. 82.
7. Lambert, "Combat Report—Typed Manuscript, Chapter VII," p. 2.
8. Guttman, *SE5a VS Albatros D V: Western Front 1917–18*, p. 61.
9. Lambert, *Combat Report*, p. 83.
10. *Ibid.*, p. 84.
11. Lambert, "Combat Report—Typed Manuscript, Chapter VII," p. 6.
12. *Ibid.*, p. 7.
13. *Ibid.*; Lambert, *Combat Report*, p. 85.
14. Lambert, "Combat Report—Typed Manuscript, Chapter VII," p. 8.
15. *Ibid.*
16. *Ibid.*, pp. 8–9.
17. *Ibid.*, p. 9.
18. *Ibid.*
19. Lambert, *Combat Report*, p. 88.
20. W. J. Taunton to Royal D. Frey, Letter, 3 January 1968.
21. Lambert, "Combat Report—Typed Manuscript, Chapter VII," pp. 9–10.
22. *Ibid.*, p. 10.
23. *Ibid.*, p. 11.
24. *Ibid.*, p. 12.
25. Farwell, *The United States in The Great War, 1917–1918*, p. 168.
26. Lambert, "Combat Report—Typed Manuscript, Chapter VII," pp. 12–13.
27. *Ibid.*, p. 13
28. *Ibid.*
29. *Ibid.*, pp. 14–15.
30. *Ibid.*, p. 15.
31. *Ibid.*
32. *Ibid.*
33. *Ibid.*, pp. 15–16.
34. *Ibid.*, p. 16.
35. *Ibid.*
36. Lambert, *Combat Report*, p. 91.
37. Lambert, "Combat Report—Typed Manuscript, Chapter VII," p. 16.
38. *Ibid.*

39. Lambert, *Out of the Sun.*
40. Lambert, "Combat Report—Typed Manuscript, Chapter VII," pp. 16–17.
41. *Ibid.*, p. 17; Lambert, *Pilot's Flying Log Book,* p. 29.
42. Lambert, "Combat Report—Typed Manuscript, Chapter VII," p. 18.
43. *Ibid.*
44. *Ibid.*, p. 18.
45. *Ibid.*, pp. 18–19.
46. Martin Gilbert, *The First World War: A Complete History* (New York: Henry Holt, 1994), p. 429.
47. Lambert, "Combat Report—Typed Manuscript, Chapter VII," p. 19.
48. *Ibid.*, pp. 19–20.
49. *Ibid.*, p. 20.
50. *Ibid.*, p. 23.
51. *Ibid.*, p. 24
52. *Ibid.*, p. 23.
53. *Ibid.*, p. 23
54. *Ibid.*, pp. 25–26.
55. *Ibid.*, p. 26.
56. *Ibid.*, p. 28.
57. *Ibid.*, pp. 29–31.
58. Foch, *The Memoirs of Ferdinand Foch,* translated by T. Bentley Mott (New York: Doubleday, Doran & Co., 1931), pp. 326–327.
59. Keegan, *The First World War,* p. 408; Gilbert, *The First World War: A Complete History,* p. 431.
60. Cole, ed., *Royal Air Force 1918,* p. 108.
61. Lambert, "Combat Report—Typed Manuscript, Chapter VII," p. 31.
62. *Ibid.*; Lambert, *Pilot's Flying Log Book,* p. 30.
63. Lambert, "Combat Report—Typed Manuscript, Chapter VII," p. 31.
64. *Ibid.*, p. 32.
65. *Ibid.*
66. Shores, Franks, and Guest, *Above the Trenches,* p. 136.
67. Lambert, "Combat Report—Typed Manuscript, Chapter VII," pp. 32–33.
68. *Ibid.*, p. 34; J. H. Southey to William C. Lambert, Letter, 16 February 1969, Lambert Papers MS-221. Lambert described Bumble Puppy in his interview with Robert Smith in 1980: "You have a tennis ball—they call it a tennis tether in this country.... And that's on a string. You had a bat ... with a handle.... Whoever could wind it (the tennis tether) up at the very tip end of the top of the pole and got it where you couldn't touch it, then that fellow won." Smith, *Interview #18,* pp. 68–69. McCudden gives a similar explanation on page 176 in his book *Flying Fury.*
69. Wilson, *The Anatomy of Courage,* p. 108.
70. Lambert, "Combat Report—Typed Manuscript, Chapter VII," p. 34.
71. *Ibid.*, p. 35.
72. Foch, *The Memoirs of Ferdinand Foch,* p. 327.
73. Lambert, "Combat Report—Typed Manuscript, Chapter VII," p. 35.
74. *Ibid.*, pp. 36–37.
75. *Ibid.*, pp. 37–38.
76. *Ibid.*, p. 39.
77. *Ibid.*, p. 40.
78. *Ibid.*
79. Cole, ed., *Royal Air Force 1918,* p. 111.
80. Spencer C. Tucker and Priscilla Roberts, *The Encyclopedia of World War I: A Political, Social, and Military History,* Vol. I (Santa Barbara, CA: ABC-CLIO, 2005), p. 750.
81. Lambert, "Combat Report—Typed Manuscript, Chapter VII," pp. 40–41.
82. *Ibid.*, pp. 41–42; Lambert, *Pilot's Flying Log Book,* p. 30.
83. Lambert, "Combat Report—Typed Manuscript, Chapter VII," p. 44.
84. *Ibid.*, pp. 45–46; Lambert, *Pilot's Flying Log Book,* p. 30.
85. Lambert, "Combat Report—Typed Manuscript, Chapter VII," pp 45–46.
86. Fry, *Air of Battle,* p. 165.
87. Lambert, "Combat Report—Typed Manuscript, Chapter VII," p. 46; Shores, Franks, and Guest, *Above the Trenches,* p. 214.
88. Lambert, "Combat Report—Typed Manuscript, Chapter VII," p. 46.
89. *Ibid.*, p. 47.
90. *Ibid.*, p. 48.
91. *Ibid.*, p. 49.
92. *Ibid.*
93. *Ibid.*, p. 51.
94. Lambert, *Out of the Sun.*
95. Lambert, "Combat Report—Typed Manuscript, Chapter VII," p. 51.
96. *Ibid.*
97. *Ibid.*, p. 52.
98. *Ibid.*, p. 53.
99. *Ibid.*
100. *Ibid.*
101. *Ibid.*, pp. 53–54.
102. *Ibid.*, p. 54.
103. *Ibid.*
104. *Ibid.*, p. 55.
105. *Ibid.*
106. J. H. Southey to William C. Lambert, 17 December 1967, reprinted in Lambert, "Combat Report—Typed Manuscript, Chapter VII," p. 56.
107. Lambert, *Pilot's Flying Log Book,* p. 30.
108. Lambert, "Combat Report—Typed Manuscript, Chapter VII," p. 57.
109. *Ibid*, pp. 57–58; Lambert, *Combat Report,* p. 117; Illingworth, *A History of 24 Squadron,* pp. 86, 88.
110. Lambert, "Combat Report—Typed Manuscript, Chapter VII," p. 59.
111. *Ibid.*
112. *Ibid.*, pp. 59–60.
113. Hynes, *The Soldiers' Tale: Bearing Witness to Modern War,* p. 24.
114. Lambert, "Combat Report—Typed Manuscript, Chapter VII," p. 60.
115. *Ibid.*
116. *Ibid.*, p. 61.
117. Smith, *Interview #18,* p. 45.
118. Lambert, "Combat Report—Typed Manuscript, Chapter VII," p. 61.
119. *Ibid.*, p. 60.
120. *Ibid.*; Lambert, *Pilot's Flying Log Book,* p. 30.

121. Lambert, "Combat Report—Typed Manuscript, Chapter VII," p. 61.
122. *Ibid.*, p. 62.
123. *Ibid.*, p. 63.
124. *Ibid.*
125. Lambert, *Out of the Sun.*
126. *Ibid.*
127. Lambert, "Combat Report—Typed Manuscript, Chapter VII," p. 63.
128. *Ibid.*
129. *Ibid.*, pp. 63–64.
130. *Ibid.*, p. 64.
131. *Ibid.*
132. *Ibid.*
133. *Ibid.*, p. 65.
134. *Ibid.*; Lambert, *Pilot's Flying Log Book*, pp. 30–31.
135. Lambert, *Combat Report*, pp. 120–121; Lambert, *Pilot's Flying Log Book*, p. 31.
136. Lambert, "Combat Report—Typed Manuscript, Chapter VII," p. 66.
137. *Ibid.*
138. *Ibid.*, p. 67.
139. *Ibid.*
140. *Ibid.*, p. 68
141. *Ibid.*, p. 69.

Chapter Seven

1. Lambert, "Combat Report—Typed Manuscript, Chapter VIII," Box 3, File 23, MS-221, p. 1; Michael Duffy, "On This Day-1 July 1918," *firstworldwar.com* (22 August 2009), accessed on 9 May 2013: http://www.firstworldwar.com/onthisday/1918_07_01.htm.
2. Henri Pètain cited in Cruttwell, *A History of the Great War 1914–1918*, p. 532.
3. Wilson, *The Anatomy of Courage*, p. 38.
4. Lambert, "Combat Report—Typed Manuscript, Chapter VIII," pp. 1–2.
5. *Ibid.*, p. 2.
6. *Ibid.*
7. Lambert, *Out of the Sun.*
8. Lambert, "Combat Report—Typed Manuscript, Chapter VIII," p. 2.
9. *Ibid.*, p. 3.
10. *Ibid.*
11. *Ibid.*
12. *Ibid.*, pp. 3–4.
13. *Ibid.*, p. 5.
14. Lambert, "Combat Report—Typed Manuscript, Chapter VIII," p. 5.
15. Shores, Franks, and Guest, *Above the Trenches*, p. 185; Illingworth, *A History of 24 Squadron*, p. 89.
16. Lambert, "Combat Report—Typed Manuscript, Chapter VIII," p. 6.
17. *Ibid.*, p. 7.
18. *Ibid.*
19. *Ibid.*, p. 20; Lambert, *Out of the Sun*; Smith, *Interview #18*, pp. 58–59
20. Lambert, "Combat Report—Typed Manuscript, Chapter VIII," p. 8.
21. *Ibid.*
22. *Ibid.*, pp. 8–9.
23. Edward Mannock, Diary, 20 July 1917, cited in Jones, *King of the Airfighters*, p. 137.
24. Lambert, "Combat Report—Typed Manuscript, Chapter VIII," pp. 8–9.
25. *Ibid.*, p. 9.
26. *Ibid.*, p. 12.
27. *Ibid.*, p. 13.
28. *Ibid.*
29. Smith, *Interview #18*, p. 60.
30. Lambert, "Combat Report—Typed Manuscript, Chapter VIII," p. 14.
31. Smith, *Interview #18*, p. 35.
32. Lambert, "Combat Report—Typed Manuscript, Chapter VIII," p. 14.
33. *Ibid.*, p. 15.
34. *Ibid.*
35. *Ibid.*, pp. 16–17.
36. *Ibid.*, p. 17.
37. *Ibid.*
38. *Ibid.*, p. 64.
39. *Ibid.*, p. 17.
40. *Ibid.*, pp. 17–18.
41. *Ibid.*, p. 19.
42. *Ibid.*, p. 20.
43. *Ibid.*; Lambert, *Pilot's Flying Log Book*, p. 31.
44. Lambert, "Combat Report—Typed Manuscript, Chapter VIII," p. 21.
45. *Ibid.*
46. *Ibid.*, p. 22.
47. *Ibid.*, pp. 22–23.
48. *Ibid.*, p. 23.
49. *Ibid.*
50. *Ibid.*
51. *Ibid.*, p. 24.
52. *Ibid.*
53. *Ibid.*, p. 28.
54. Shores, Franks, and Guest, *Above the Trenches: A Complete Record of the Fighter Aces and Units of the British Empire Air Forces, 1915–1920* (London: Grub Street, 1996), p. 230.
55. Lambert, "Combat Report—Typed Manuscript, Chapter VIII," p. 24.
56. *Ibid.*, p. 25.
57. Cole, ed., *Royal Air Force 1918*, p. 126.
58. Lambert, "Combat Report—Typed Manuscript, Chapter VIII," p. 26.
59. *Ibid.*
60. Hynes, *The Soldiers' Tale: Bearing Witness to Modern War*, pp. 85–86.
61. Lambert, "Combat Report—Typed Manuscript, Chapter VIII," p. 27.
62. *Ibid.*
63. *Ibid.*, p. 28.
64. *Ibid.*, pp. 28–29.
65. *Ibid.*, p. 30.
66. *Ibid.*, p. 30.
67. *Ibid.*
68. *Ibid.*, p. 31.
69. *Ibid.*, p. 32.
70. Michael Duffy, "On This Day-2 July 1918," *firstworldwar.com* (22 August 2009), accessed on 24

May 2013: http://www.firstworldwar.com/onthisday/1918_07_05.htm.
71. Lambert, "Combat Report—Typed Manuscript, Chapter VIII," p. 32.
72. *Ibid.*, p. 33.
73. *Ibid.*, p. 34.
74. *Ibid.*
75. *Ibid.*
76. *Ibid.*
77. *Ibid.*, p. 36, 41.
78. *Ibid.*, p. 37.
79. *Ibid.*, p. 38.
80. Smith, *Interview #18*, p. 83.
81. Lambert, "Combat Report—Typed Manuscript, Chapter VIII," p. 33.
82. *Ibid.*, p. 40.
83. *Ibid.*
84. *Ibid.*, p. 41.
85. *Ibid.*, p. 42.
86. *Ibid.*, p. 42.
87. *Ibid.*, pp. 44–46.

Chapter Eight

1. Lambert, "Combat Report—Typed Manuscript, Chapter VIII," pp. 47–49.
2. *Ibid.*, pp. 48–49.
3. *Ibid.*, p. 49.
4. *Ibid.*, p. 46.
5. *Ibid.*
6. *Ibid.*, pp. 50–51.
7. *Ibid.*, p. 50; Gordon, "Paul and August Thayer Iaccaci: American Aces of No. 20 Squadron RFC/RAF," *Over the Hill*, Vol. 17, No. 1 (Spring 2002), p. 27.
8. Lambert, "Combat Report—Typed Manuscript, Chapter VIII," p. 52.
9. *Ibid.*, p. 54
10. *Ibid.*, pp. 53–54.
11. *Ibid.*, p. 54.
12. *Ibid.*, pp. 55–56.
13. Virginia Woolf, cited in John V. H. Dippel, *War and Sex: A Brief History of Men's Urge for Battle* (Amherst, NY: Prometheus Book, 2010), p. 108.
14. Clare Makepeace, "Sex and the Somme: The officially sanctioned brothels on the front line laid bare for the first time," *MailOnline* (28 October 2011), accessed on 7 June 2013: http://www.dailymail.co.uk/news/article-2054914/Sex-Somme-Officially-sanctioned-WWI-brothels-line.html#ixzz2VYVtfozZ.
15. Makepeace, "Sex and the Somme: The officially sanctioned brothels on the front line laid bare for the first time," *op. cit.*
16. Allen, "The Forgotten Ace," p. 12; Smith, *Interview #18*, pp. 53–55.
17. Smith, *Interview #18*, pp. 53–55.
18. Dippel, *War and Sex: A Brief History of Men's Urge for Battle*, pp. 138–139, 142–143.
19. Modris Eksteins, *Rites of Spring* (New York: First Mariners Books, 2000), p. 225.
20. *Ibid.*, p. 150.
21. Paul Fussell, *The Great War and Modern Memory* (New York: Oxford University Press), p. 271.
22. Eksteins, *Rites of Spring*, pp. 33–34, 224.
23. Lambert, "Combat Report—Typed Manuscript, Chapter VIII," p. 70.
24. *Ibid.*, p. 56.
25. *Ibid.*
26. *Ibid.*, p. 57.
27. *Ibid.*, p. 61.
28. *Ibid.*, p. 58.
29. *Ibid.*
30. Smith, *Interview #18*, pp. 93–94.
31. Lambert, "Combat Report—Typed Manuscript, Chapter VIII," p. 66.
32. *Ibid.*, p. 58.
33. *Ibid.*, p. 59.
34. *Ibid.*
35. *Ibid.*, p. 64.
36. Smith, *Interview #18*, p. 95.
37. Lambert, "Combat Report—Typed Manuscript, Chapter VIII," p. 69.
38. Wilson, *The Anatomy of Courage*, p. 77.
39. Lambert, "Combat Report—Typed Manuscript, Chapter VIII," pp. 76–77.
40. *Ibid.*, p. 81.
41. *Ibid.*
42. *Ibid.*, pp. 87–88.
43. *Ibid.*, p. 93.
44. *Ibid.*
45. Gilbert, *The First World War: A Complete History*, p. 439.
46. Foch, *The Memoirs of Marshal Foch*, p. 352; Neiberg, *Fighting the Great War*, p. 330.
47. Jones, *The War in the Air*, Vol. VI, pp. 413–414; Farwell, *Over There: The United States in The Great War, 1917–1918*, p. 178; Duffy, "On This Day-15 and 18 July 1918," firstworldwar.com (22 August 2009), accessed on 12 June 2013: http://www.firstworldwar.com/onthisday/1918_07_18.htm.
48. Lambert, "Combat Report—Typed Manuscript, Chapter VIII," p. 94.
49. *Ibid.*; Shores, Franks, and Guest state that "Daley was fatally injured in a flying accident on 3 July 1918 in B8261, dying five days later"; Shores, Franks, and Guest, *Above the Trenches*, p. 131.
50. Lambert, "Combat Report—Typed Manuscript, Chapter VIII," p. 95.
51. *Ibid.*, p. 94.
52. *Ibid.*, pp. 94–95.

Chapter Nine

1. Wilson, *The Anatomy of Courage*, p. 105.
2. Lambert, "Combat Report—Typed Manuscript, Chapter VIII," p. 96.
3. Cole, ed., *Royal Air Force 1918*, p. 139.
4. Lambert, "Combat Report—Typed Manuscript, Chapter VIII," pp. 96–97.
5. *Ibid.*, pp. 97–98.
6. *Ibid.*, p. 99.
7. Lambert, *Pilot's Flying Log Book*, p. 31.
8. Lambert, "Combat Report—Typed Manuscript, Chapter VIII," p. 101.
9. *Ibid.*

10. *Ibid.*, p. 102.
11. Cole, ed., *Royal Air Force 1918*, p. 140.
12. Lambert, "Combat Report—Typed Manuscript, Chapter VIII," pp. 101–102.
13. *Ibid.*, p. 102; Lambert, *Pilot's Flying Log Book*, p. 31.
14. Smith, *Mick Mannock, Fighter Pilot: Myth, Life and Politics*, p. 138.
15. Lambert, "Combat Report—Typed Manuscript, Chapter VIII," p. 102.
16. *Ibid.*, p. 103.
17. Cole, ed., *Royal Air Force 1918*, p. 142.
18. Lambert, "Combat Report—Typed Manuscript, Chapter VIII," pp. 103–104.
19. Cole, ed., *Royal Air Force 1918*, p. 145.
20. *Ibid.*
21. Shores, Franks, and Guest, *Above the Trenches*, pp. 271–272.
22. Lambert, "Combat Report—Typed Manuscript, Chapter VIII," p. 106.
23. Cole, ed., *Royal Air Force 1918*, pp. 145–146; Lambert, "Combat Report—Typed Manuscript, Chapter IX," p. 1
24. Lambert, "Combat Report—Typed Manuscript, Chapter IX," p. 1.
25. *Ibid.*
26. *Ibid.*
27. *Ibid.*, p. 2.
28. *Ibid.*; Lambert, *Pilot's Flying Log Book*, p. 32.
29. Cole, ed., *Royal Air Force 1918*, p. 149.
30. Lambert, "Combat Report—Typed Manuscript, Chapter IX," pp. 3–4.
31. *Ibid.*, p. 4.
32. Smith, *Interview #18*, p. 75.
33. Lambert, "Combat Report—Typed Manuscript, Chapter IX," p. 4.
34. *Ibid.*
35. *Ibid.*, pp. 4–5.
36. *Ibid.*, p. 5.
37. *Ibid.*
38. *Ibid.*; Shores, Franks, and Guest, *Above the Trenches*, pp. 230–231; W. J. Taunton to Royal D. Frey, Letter, 3 January 1968; Lambert-WWI Combat Successes, USAF Museum, p. 5; Lambert, *Pilot's Flying Log Book*, p. 32.
39. Lambert, "Combat Report—Typed Manuscript, Chapter IX," p. 5.
40. *Ibid.*, p. 6.
41. *Ibid.*; Cole, ed., *Royal Air Force 1918*, p. 152.
42. Hochschild, *To End All Wars*, p. 332.
43. Lambert, "Combat Report—Typed Manuscript, Chapter IX," pp. 6–7.
44. *Ibid.*, p. 7.
45. *Ibid.*, p. 7–8.
46. *Ibid.*, p. 8.
47. Lambert, *Pilot's Flying Log Book*, p. 32.
48. Lambert, "Combat Report—Typed Manuscript, Chapter IX," p. 8.
49. Mertz von Quirnheim, cited in Gilbert, *The First World War: A Complete History*, p. 448.
50. Ludendorff, cited in Cruttwell, *A History of the Great War 1914–1918*, p. 547.
51. Keegan, *The First World War*, p. 410; Foch, *The Memoirs of Marshal Foch*, p. 379; Hochschild, *To End All Wars*, p. 332; Cruttwell, *A History of the Great War 1914–1918*, pp. 548–549.
52. Cruttwell, *A History of the Great War 1914–1918*, p. 550.
53. Ludendorff cited in Cruttwell, *A History of the Great War 1914–1918*, p. 550.
54. Lambert, "Combat Report—Typed Manuscript, Chapter IX," p. 14; Illingworth, *A History of 24 Squadron*, p. 45.
55. J. H. Southey, letter to William C. Lambert, 27 December 1967, reprinted in Lambert, "Combat Report—Typed Manuscript, Chapter IX," pp. 14–15.
56. Lambert, "Combat Report—Typed Manuscript, Chapter IX," p. 15.
57. *Ibid.*, p. 16.
58. *Ibid.*
59. *Ibid.*, pp. 16–18.
60. *Ibid.*, p. 19.
61. *Ibid.*
62. *Ibid.*, p. 20.
63. Smith, *Interview #18*, pp. 73–74.
64. Werner, *Knights of Germany: Oswald Boelcke German Ace*, p. 224.
65. Lambert, "Combat Report—Typed Manuscript, Chapter IX," p. 26.
66. Illingworth, *A History of 24 Squadron*, p. 45.
67. Smith, *Interview #18*, p. 74.
68. Lambert, "Combat Report—Typed Manuscript, Chapter IX," p. 20.
69. *Ibid.*; Illingworth, *A History of 24 Squadron*, p. 46.
70. Lambert, "Combat Report—Typed Manuscript, Chapter IX," p. 20.
71. *Ibid.*, pp. 20–21; Smith, *Interview #18*, p. 74.
72. Lambert, "Combat Report—Typed Manuscript, Chapter IX," p. 21.
73. *Ibid.*; Smith, *Interview #18*, p. 74.
74. Lambert, "Combat Report—Typed Manuscript, Chapter IX," p. 21.
75. Smith, *Interview #18*, p. 74.
76. Lambert, "Combat Report—Typed Manuscript, Chapter IX," pp. 22–24; Illingworth, *A History of 24 Squadron*, p. 46.
77. Lambert, "Combat Report—Typed Manuscript, Chapter IX," p. 22.
78. *Ibid.*, p. 23.
79. *Ibid.*, p. 25.
80. *Ibid.*, pp. 24–25.
81. *Ibid.*, pp. 26–29.
82. Cole, ed., *Royal Air Force 1918*, p. 152.
83. Jones, *The War in the Air*, Vol. VI, p. 442.
84. Lambert, "Combat Report—Typed Manuscript, Chapter IX," p. 35; "Erich Löwenhardt, 'Aces,'" *The Aerodrome* (1997–2013), accessed on 5 July 2013: http://www.theaerodrome.com/aces/germany/lowenhardt.php.
85. Jones, *The War in the Air*, Vol. VI, pp. 445–446.
86. Lambert, "Combat Report—Typed Manuscript, Chapter IX," pp. 29–30.
87. *Ibid.*, p. 32.
88. Foch, *The Memoirs of Marshal Foch*, p. 380.
89. Jones, *The War in the Air*, Vol. VI, p. 451.

90. Lambert, "Combat Report—Typed Manuscript, Chapter IX," p. 31.
91. *Ibid.*
92. *Ibid.*
93. Wilson, *The Anatomy of Courage,* p. 109.
94. Lambert, "Combat Report—Typed Manuscript, Chapter IX," pp. 31–32.
95. *Ibid.,* p. 33.
96. *Ibid.,* pp. 33–34.
97. *Ibid.,* p. 35.
98. *Ibid.,* p. 36.
99. *Ibid.*
100. W. J. Taunton to Royal D. Frey, Letter, 3 January 1968.
101. Lambert, "Combat Report—Typed Manuscript, Chapter IX," p. 37.
102. Ibid., pp. 37–38; Shores, Franks, and Guest, *Above the Trenches,* p. 230.
103. Lambert, "Combat Report—Typed Manuscript, Chapter IX," p. 38.
104. *Ibid.*
105. *Ibid.,* p. 39.
106. *Ibid.*
107. *Ibid.,* pp. 39–40.
108. *Ibid.,* p. 40–41.
109. Shores, Franks, and Guest, *Above the Trenches,* p. 230.
110. Lambert, "Combat Report—Typed Manuscript, Chapter IX," p. 41.
111. *Ibid.,* pp. 41–42; Lambert, *Pilot's Flying Log Book,* p. 32.
112. Jones, *The War in the Air,* Vol. VI, pp. 454–455.
113. Cole, ed., *Royal Air Force 1918,* p. 156.
114. Jones, *The War in the Air,* Vol. VI, p. 456.
115. Lambert, "Combat Report—Typed Manuscript, Chapter IX," p. 54; Illingworth, *A History of 24 Squadron,* p. 87.
116. Lambert, "Combat Report—Typed Manuscript, Chapter IX," pp. 43–44.
117. Cole, ed., *Royal Air Force 1918,* p. 159.
118. Lambert, "Combat Report—Typed Manuscript, Chapter IX," p. 45.
119. *Ibid.,* p. 44.
120. *Ibid.*
121. *Ibid.,* p. 46.
122. *Ibid.*
123. Lambert, *Pilot's Flying Log Book,* p. 32.
124. Lambert, "Combat Report—Typed Manuscript, Chapter IX," p. 47.
125. *Ibid.*
126. *Ibid.*
127. Cole, ed., *Royal Air Force 1918,* p. 161.
128. Foch, *the Memoirs of Marshal Foch,* pp. 384–386.
129. Cruttwell, *A History of the Great War 1914–1918,* p. 552.
130. Lambert, "Combat Report—Typed Manuscript, Chapter IX," p. 48.
131. *Ibid.,* p. 49.
132. *Ibid.*
133. *Ibid.*
134. *Ibid.,* p. 50.
135. *Ibid.,* pp. 50–51.
136. *Ibid.,* p. 51.
137. Lambert, *Pilot's Flying Log Book,* p. 32.
138. Lambert, "Combat Report—Typed Manuscript, Chapter IX," p. 52.
139. Cole, ed., *Royal Air Force 1918,* p. 161.
140. Lambert, "Combat Report—Typed Manuscript, Chapter IX," p. 53; Lambert, *Pilot's Flying Log Book,* p. 33.
141. Lambert, "Combat Report—Typed Manuscript, Chapter IX," p. 53.
142. *Ibid.*
143. *Ibid.,* p. 54.
144. Gilbert, *The First World War: A Complete History,* p. 452.
145. Cole, ed., *Royal Air Force 1918,* p. 162.
146. *Ibid.*; Lambert, "Combat Report—Typed Manuscript, Chapter IX," pp. 54–55; Lambert, *Pilot's Flying Log Book,* p. 33.
147. Cole, ed., *Royal Air Force 1918,* p. 164; Lambert, "Combat Report—Typed Manuscript, Chapter IX," pp. 55–56.
148. Lambert, "Combat Report—Typed Manuscript, Chapter IX," p. 56; Lambert, *Pilot's Flying Log Book,* p. 33.
149. Lambert, "Combat Report—Typed Manuscript, Chapter IX," p. 56; Cole, ed., *Royal Air Force 1918,* p. 164.
150. Lambert, "Combat Report—Typed Manuscript, Chapter IX," p. 56.
151. Cole, ed., *Royal Air Force 1918,* p. 167.
152. Lambert, "Combat Report—Typed Manuscript, Chapter IX," p. 57.
153. *Ibid.,* pp. 58–59.
154. *Ibid.*; Shores, Franks, and Guest, *Above the Trenches,* pp. 230–231; Lambert, *Pilot's Flying Log Book,* p. 33.
155. Lambert, "Combat Report—Typed Manuscript, Chapter IX," pp. 59–60.
156. Lambert, *Pilot's Flying Log Book,* p. 33.
157. Lambert, "Combat Report—Typed Manuscript, Chapter IX," pp. 60–61.

Chapter Ten

1. London, *The National Archives,* "William Carpenter Lambert," AIR/76/285.
2. Lambert, "Combat Report—Typed Manuscript, Chapter IX," pp. 61, 63; Illingworth, *A History of 24 Squadron,* p. 89.
3. Lambert, "Combat Report—Typed Manuscript, Chapter IX," pp. 61–62.
4. *Ibid.,* p. 63.
5. Peter Leese, *Shell Shock: Traumatic Neurosis and the British Soldiers of the First World War* (New York: Palgrave Macmillan, 2002), pp. 46–47.
6. *Ibid.,* pp. 33–34.
7. *Ibid.,* p. 69.
8. Lambert, "Combat Report—Typed Manuscript, Chapter IX," p. 62.
9. *Ibid.*
10. *Ibid.*
11. *Ibid.,* pp. 62–63.

12. Lewis, *Eddie Rickenbacker: An American hero in the Twentieth Century*, p. ix.
13. "Ruptured Eardrum (Perforated Tympanic Membrane)," *Core Physicians: The Art of Wellness* (2010), accessed on 22 July 2013: http://www.corephysicians.org/news-and-health-library/health-library/otorhinolaryngology/otla3957/.
14. Kenneth Baillie, "Altitude air pressure calculator," *Altitude.org* (April 2010), accessed on 22 July 2013: http://www.altitude.org/air_pressure.php.
15. Smith, *Interview #18*, p. 76.
16. Dave Peyton, "Ironton Man's Record: 21½ German Planes," *The Herald-Advertiser* (Huntington, WV, 19 May 1968), p. 3.
17. *Ibid.*
18. Associated Press, "Colonel Lambert Still Flying Legend," *The Ironton Tribune* (Ironton, OH, 4 November 1980), n.p.
19. Leese, *Shell Shock: Traumatic Neurosis and the British Soldiers of the First World War*, p. 123.
20. *Ibid.*; Smith and Pear, *Shell Shock and its Lessons*, p. 1.
21. Leese, *Shell Shock: Traumatic Neurosis and the British Soldiers of the First World War*, p. 98.
22. Leese, *Shell Shock: Traumatic Neurosis and the British Soldiers of the First World War*, p. 160.
23. *Ibid.*, p. 3.
24. "Melita," *Bonsor's North Atlantic Seaway: Haws' Merchant Fleets*, accessed on 6 August 2013: http://www.greatships.net/melita.html; 'S/S Melita, Canadian Pacific Line," *Norway Heritage: Hands Across the Sea*, accessed on 6 August 2013: http://www.norwayheritage.com/p_ship.asp?sh=melit.
25. Lambert, *Barnstorming and Girls*, p. 3.
26. *Ibid.*
27. *Ibid.*

Chapter Eleven

1. Lambert, *Barnstorming and Girls*, p. 1.
2. *Ibid.*, pp. 14–15; Smith, *Interview #18*, pp. 106–108.
3. "Trespassing on Pasture Land Caused Warrant," *Ironton Register* (24 May 1920), n.p.
4. *Ibid.*
5. *Ibid.*
6. *Ibid.*
7. "New Airplane Arrives Here," *Ironton Register* (1 June 1920), n.p.
8. *Ibid.*
9. *Ibid.*
10. Lambert, *Barnstorming and Girls*, p. 12.
11. *Ibid.*
12. *Ibid.*
13. *Ibid.*, pp. 17–18.
14. Carroll V. Glines, *Roscoe Turner: Aviation's Master Showman* (Washington, DC: Smithsonian Institution Press, 1995), p. 27.
15. Smith, *Interview #18*, p. 97.
16. *Ibid.*, p. 98. Smith noted that Lambert "refused to give their (Tom's and Dave's) true identity."
17. Lambert, *Barnstorming and Girls*, pp. 203, 205.
18. *Ibid.*, p. 211.
19. *Ibid.*, pp. 265, 267–268.
20. *Ibid.*, p. 266.
21. Smith, *Interview #18*, pp. 100–101.
22. Lambert, *Barnstorming and Girls*, p. 289.
23. *Ibid.*, pp. 7, 19.
24. *Ibid.*, p. 90.
25. *Ibid.*, pp. 78, 112, 130.
26. *Ibid.*, p.1
27. *Ibid.*
28. Klaus Staerker, interview with author, 14 September 2013; William Martin, interview with author, 16 September 2013. (It is important to point out that neither Staerker nor Martin ever read *Barnstorming and Girls*.)
29. Higham, "Publisher's Forward"; Lambert, *Barnstorming and Girls*, n.p.
30. Higham, "Publisher's Forward"; Lambert, *Barnstorming and Girls*, n.p.
31. "New Books," *Aviation News*, Vol. 9, No. 26, p. 13.
32. Martin Caidin, *Barnstorming* (New York: Duell, Sloan and Pearce, 1965), p. 4.
33. Lambert, *Barnstorming and Girls*, p. 95.
34. *Ibid.*, p. 285.
35. Clyda F. Marion to William C. Lambert, Letter, 30 November 1981, Lambert Collection.
36. Clyda F. Marion to William Martin, Letter, 15 December 1984, Lambert Collection.
37. Lambert, *Barnstorming and Girls*, p. 160.
38. Caidin, *Barnstorming*, p. 95.
39. Lambert, *Barnstorming and Girls*, pp. 98, 164.
40. *Ibid.*
41. *Ibid.*, p. 97.
42. *Ibid.*, p. 165.

Chapter Twelve

1. *Ironton City Directories*, 1922–23, pp. 214–215.
2. *Ironton City Directories*, 1924–25, p. 157.
3. "Plane Falls Injuring Two," *Morning Irontonian*, 26 October 1920. A copy of this news article was given to the author by William Martin, along with copies of pictures from the accident. There is no date or page number on the clipping. Martin supplied the date of the crash. These articles will become part of the donated collection given to the U.S. Air Force Museum after the completion of this work.
4. *Ibid.*
5. *Ibid.*
6. *Ibid.*
7. "Anson's Chances for Recovery Grow Brighter," *Morning Irontonian*, 27 October 1920.
8. "May Remove Anson To Home Next Tuesday," *Morning Irontonian*, n.d.
9. "Plane Falls Injuring Two."
10. *Ibid.*
11. Martin, Interview with Author, 5 October 2013.
12. Smith, *Interview #18*, p. 109.
13. The Marmon Club, "Welcome to the Marmon Club," *marmonclub.com*, accessed on 23 September 2013: http://www.marmonclub.com/index.html; The Marmon Group, "The Marmon Wasp," *marmon.com*

(2013), accessed on 23 September 2013: http://www.marmon.com/MarmonWasp.asp.
14. Smith, *Interview #18*, p. 110.
15. *Ibid.*, pp. 110–111. A two-seat Marmon roadster was more likely to go for around $5,000, and a seven-passenger limousine would sell for less than $6,500. Clymer, *Treasury of Early American Automobiles, 1877–1925* (New York: Bonanza Books, 1950), p. 63.
16. Smith, *Interview #18*, pp. 114–115.
17. Martin, Interview, 24 August 2013.
18. Allen, *The Overlooked Ace*, p. 39.
19. Glines, *Roscoe Turner: Aviation's Master Showman*, pp. 93–94.
20. *Ironton City Directories*, 1930, p. 165
21. Smith, *Interview #18*, p. 115.
22. Baker, Interview with Author, 3 July 2007.
23. Smith, *Interview #18*, pp. 115–116.
24. Gillenwater, "Ironton, Ohio—The rise and fall of 'Little Chicago,'" *Yahoo Voices* (6 September 2007), accessed on 14 October 2013: http://voices.yahoo.com/ironton-ohio-rise-fall-little-chicago-522880.html?cat=16.
25. Smith, *Interview #18*, p. 115.
26. Smith, *Interview #18*, pp. 130–131.
27. Elmer Stewart to William C. Lambert, Letter, 28 January 1931, p. 1, Lambert Collection; Elmer Stewart to William C. Lambert, Letter, 27 August 1931, p. 1, Lambert Collection.
28. "Pat" White to William C. Lambert, Letter, 27 January 1932, Lambert Papers MS-221.
29. Dr. Armitage Whitman to William C. Lambert, 19 September 1940, Lambert Papers MS-221.
30. *Ibid.*
31. *Ibid.*
32. Dr. Armitage Whitman to William C. Lambert, Letter, 24 September 1940, Lambert Papers MS-221.
33. Elmer Stewart to William C. Lambert, Letter, 11 September 1939, p. 1, Lambert Collection.
34. Elmer Stewart to William C. Lambert, Letter, 20 October 1939, Lambert Collection.
35. Brooks Marshall to William C. Lambert, Letter, 14 November 1940, Lambert Papers MS-221.
36. "Lambert Company Quitting Business" (newspaper article), n.d., Lambert Papers MS-221.
37. *Ibid.*
38. "Henrites Have Expanded Since Spring of 1927," *Ironton Evening Tribune*, 8 October 1949, n.p.; *Ironton Sunday Tribune*, 9 October 1949, *Lawrence County Register*, accessed on 15 November 2013: http://lawrencecountyohio.com/business/stories/Henritesstore.htm.
39. "Henrites Have Expanded Since Spring of 1927," *Ironton Evening Tribune*, 8 October 1949, n.p.
40. Smith, *Interview #18*, p. 128.

Chapter Thirteen

1. R.A. Dellaye, Headquarter Commander for W.A. Curtis, Group Captain, for Chief of the Air Staff to William C. Lambert, Letter, 7 February 1941, File No. 745-L-72, Lambert Papers MS-221.
2. Smith, *Interview #18*, p. 120.
3. Captain F. W. Patten, Infantry Reserve and Acting Assistant Adjutant General to the Adjutant General, Washington, D.C., Memo, 30 August 1940, Lambert Papers MS-221.
4. The Adjutant General, War Department to William C. Lambert, Letter, 2 September 1942, Lambert Collection.
5. The U.S. National Archives and Records Administration, "The 1973 Fire, National Personal Records Center," *National Archives at St. Louis*, accessed on 19 December 2013: http://www.archives.gov/st-louis/military-personnel/fire-1973.html.
6. Marnita R. Fair to Author, Letter, 16 December 2013. Included with the letter was NA From 13164.
7. *Ibid.*, p. 123.
8. Smith, *Interview #18*, pp. 124–125.
9. *Ibid.*, p. 126.
10. Tony Holmes, *Jane's Vintage Aircraft Recognition Guide* (HarperCollins: 2005), p. 141.
11. *Ibid.*, p. 122.
12. William C. Lambert to Chloe Ann Lambert, Letter, Wednesday, 7:30 p.m. (November-December 1945), pp. 1–2, Lambert Papers, MS-221.
13. *Ibid.*, pp. 2–3.
14. *Ibid.*, p. 3.
15. William C. Lambert to Chloe Ann Lambert, Letter, 20 September 1942, pp. 1–2.
16. William C. Lambert to Chloe Ann Lambert, Letter, Saturday, 8:00 p.m., 24 October 1942, p. 5, Lambert Papers MS-221.
17. *Ibid.*
18. U.S. Army Air Forces, *The Air Transport Command*, 1 September 1943, p. 6, Lambert Collection.
19. W. C. Lambert to Chloe Ann Lambert, Letter, 4 November 1942, pp. 1–2.
20. W. C. Lambert to Chloe Ann Lambert, Letter, 4 November 1942, p. 2.
21. *Ibid.*
22. W. C. Lambert to Chloe Ann Lambert, Letter, 8 November 1942, p. 2.
23. William. C. Lambert to Chloe Ann Lambert, Letter, Thursday, 6:30 p.m. (probably in May 1945), pp. 1–2, Lambert Papers, MS-221.
24. William C. Lambert to Chloe Ann Lambert, Letter, 23 April 1945, Lambert Papers, MS-221.
25. William C. Lambert to Chloe Ann Lambert, Letter, Sunday, 6:15 p.m., p. 1, Lambert Papers, MS-221.
26. *Ibid.*
27. *Ibid.*, p. 2.
28. *Ibid.*
29. "Officers of Sub-Depot Recently Returned from Leave" (newspaper article), n.p., n.d., Lambert Collection.
30. William C. Lambert to Chloe Ann Lambert, Letter, Monday, 8:00 p.m., p. 1, Lambert Papers, MS-221.
31. William C. Lambert to Chloe Ann Lambert, Letter, Sunday, 8:00 p.m., p. 1, Lambert Papers, MS-221.
32. *Ibid.*
33. William C. Lambert to Chloe Ann Lambert, Letter, Wednesday, 9:00 p.m., pp. 1–2, Lambert Papers, MS-221.

34. "Safety Record," 1943, (newspaper article), n.p., n.d., Lambert Collection.
35. William C. Lambert to Chloe Ann Lambert, Letter, Sunday, 3:30 p.m., p. 1, Lambert Papers, MS-221.
36. Ibid., pp. 1–2.
37. Ibid., p. 2.
38. "N.A.D. Planes Make Ocean Crossing Every 41 Minutes" (newspaper article), n.p., 15 March 1945, p. 2, Lambert Collection.
39. William C. Lambert to Chloe Ann Lambert, Letter, Tuesday, 6:50 p.m., p. 1, Lambert Papers, MS-221.
40. Ibid., p. 2.
41. Ibid.
42. Ibid.
43. William C. Lambert to Chloe Ann Lambert, Letter, Thursday, 10:40, n.d., Lambert Papers, MS-221.
44. Doolittle, *I Could Never Be So Lucky Again*, p. 352.
45. William C. Lambert to Chloe Ann Lambert, Letter, Wednesday, 7:00 p.m., p. 2, Lambert Papers, MS-221.
46. William C. Lambert to Chloe Ann Lambert, Letter, Friday, 6:50 p.m., p. 2, Lambert Papers, MS-221.
47. Smith, *Interview #18*, p. 122.
48. William C. Lambert to Chloe Ann Lambert, Letter, Presque Isle, Maine, Monday, 9:20 p.m. p. 1, Lambert Collection.
49. Ibid., pp. 5–6.
50. W. C. Lambert to Chloe Ann Lambert, Letter, Tuesday, 6:30 p.m. (August 1945), pp. 2–3.
51. Ibid., pp. 1–2.
52. Ibid., p. 3.
53. Ibid.
54. Smith, *Interview #18*, p. 128.
55. Smith, *Interview #18*, p. 128.
56. "Lambert's Book to be Published in October," *Ashland Daily Independent* (12 August 1973), p. 11.
57. "Ohio Defense Corps," *Ohio History Central* (20 May 2013), accessed on 3 January 2014: http://www.ohiohistorycentral.org/w/Ohio_Defense_Corps?rec=2403.
58. Tri-State Civil Defense Council, *Meeting*, (Kenova, WV: Woman's Club, WV, 20 January 1955), pp. 1–2, Lambert Papers, MS-221.
59. Martin, "America's Forgotten Ace," p. 38.

Chapter Fourteen

1. Richard Uppstrom, Interview with Author, 2 August 2007.
2. Raymond F. Toliver, *The Interrogator: The Story of Hanns Joachim Scharff Master Interrogator of the Luftwarffe* (Atglen, PA: Schiffer Military History, 1997), p. 135.
3. Stacy and Dana Frey, Interview with Author, 17 May 2008; Royal D. Frey, "The Luftwaffe's Master Interrogator," *The Air Force Magazine* (June 1976), p. 68; "WWII AAF Combat Chronology: January 1944 through June 1944, Saturday, 29 January 1944," *Eighth Air Force Historical Society* (n.d.), accessed on 14 January 2014: http://www.8thafhs.org/combat1944a.htm.
4. Toliver, *The Interrogator*, p. 135.
5. Ibid., pp. 135–136.
6. Holmes, *Vintage Aircraft Recognition Guide*, p. 408.
7. Don Baird, "Aviation Makes Memories," *The Columbus Dispatch* (Sunday, 16 February 1986), n.p.; Ann Davis, "Royal Desmond Frey," findagrave.com (3 August 2009), accessed on 16 January 2014: http://www.findagrave.com/cgi-bin/fg.cgi?page=gr&GRid=40240675.
8. Stacy and Dana Frey, Interview with Author, 17 May 2008.
9. Stacy and Dana Frey, Interview with Author, 17 May 2008.
10. William Martin, email message to Author, 17 January 2014.
11. Royal D. Frey, "Forgotten Ace of World War I," *The Airman* (April 1968), pp. 22–23.
12. Ibid., p. 23.
13. Ibid.
14. Ibid.
15. Lambert, "Combat Report—Typed Manuscript, Preface," p. 1.
16. Frank Cheesman to William C. Lambert, Letter, 2 March 1970, p. 1, Lambert Papers MS-221.
17. William Martin, email message to Author, 17 January 2014.
18. Ibid.
19. William C. Lambert to Royal D. Frey, Letter 20 December 1967, Lambert Papers MS-221.
20. Ibid.
21. Royal D. Frey to William C. Lambert, Letter, 9 January 1968, Lambert File, USAF Museum.
22. Ibid.
23. Ibid.
24. Robert D. McGrath to William C. Lambert, Letter, 5 December 1970, Lambert Papers MS-221.
25. Robert D. McGrath to William C. Lambert, Letter, 11 March 1966, Lambert Papers MS-221.
26. Robert D. McGrath to William C. Lambert, Letter, 1927, Lambert Papers MS-221.
27. Douglass Haig quoted in Denis Winter, *The First of The Few: Fighter Pilots of the First World War* (Athens, GA: University of Georgia Press, 1983), p. 11.
28. Illingworth, *A History of 24 Squadron*, pp. 86–89.
29. J. H. Southey to William C. Lambert, Letter, 6 November 1968, Lambert Papers MS-221.
30. J. H. Southey to William C. Lambert, Letter, 16 February 1969, Lambert Papers MS-221.
31. Raymond Collishaw to William C. Lambert, Letter, 28 October 1968, p. 2.
32. Raymond Collishaw to William C. Lambert, Letter, 29 June 1969.
33. Raymond Collishaw to William C. Lambert, Letter, 29 October 1969, p. 1.
34. Ibid., pp. 1–2.
35. Ibid., p. 2.
36. Ibid.

37. Raymond Collishaw to William C. Lambert, Letter, 21 January 1970, p. 1.
38. *Ibid.*
39. *Ibid.*, pp. 1–2.
40. Raymond Collishaw to William C. Lambert, Letter, 3 February 1970, p. 1, Lambert Papers MS-221.
41. George O. Johnson to William C. Lambert, Letter, 22 February 1970, Lambert Papers MS-221.
42. Raymond Collishaw to William C. Lambert, Letter, 15 February 1970, p. 1, Lambert Papers MS-221.
43. Jesse Stuart to Samuel Stewart, Letter, 24 August 1967, Lambert Papers MS-221.
44. *Ibid.*
45. *Ibid.*
46. *Ibid.*
47. Lonnie Raidor to William C. Lambert, Letter, 26 January 1970, p. 2, Lambert Collection.
48. Cornell Jaray to Stanley M. Ulanoff, Letter, 3 August 1970, Lambert Papers MS-221.
49. *Ibid.*
50. *Ibid.*, p. 2.
51. Stanley M. Ulanoff to William C. Lambert, Letter, 30 July 1970, pp. 1–2, Lambert Papers MS-221.
52. *Ibid.*
53. William C. Lambert to Cornell Jaray, Letter, 10 August 1970, Lambert Papers MS-221.
54. *Ibid.*
55. Cornell Jaray to William C. Lambert, Letter, 17 November 1970, p. 1, Lambert Papers MS-221.
56. *Ibid.*, p. 2.
57. *Ibid.*
58. Stanley M. Ulanoff to William C. Lambert, Letter, 23 September 1971, Lambert Papers MS-221.
59. Frank Cheesman to William C. Lambert, Letter, 16 March 1971, pp. 1–2.
60. Frank Cheesman to William C. Lambert, Letter, 4 July 1971, p. 1.
61. Robert D. McGrath to William C. Lambert, Letter, 3 February 1971, Lambert Papers MS-221.
62. Robert D. McGrath to William C. Lambert, Letter, 5 May 1971, Lambert Papers MS-221.
63. *Ibid.*
64. *Ibid.*
65. Robert D. McGrath to William C. Lambert, Letter, 23 May 1971, Lambert Papers MS-221.
66. *Ibid.*
67. McGrath to Lambert, Letter, 5 May 1971.
68. McGrath to Lambert, Letter, 23 May 1971.
69. Robert D. McGrath to William C. Lambert, Letter, 31 May 1971, Lambert Papers MS-221.
70. *Ibid.*
71. *Ibid.*
72. Harold Kuebler to William C. Lambert, 13 May 1971, Lambert Papers MS-221.
73. *Ibid.*
74. Virginia Hazirjian to William C. Lambert, 13 December 1971, Lambert Papers MS-221.
75. Jan W. Steenblik to William C. Lambert, 9 July 1971, Lambert Papers MS-221.
76. Robert D. McGrath to William C. Lambert, 18 June 1971, Lambert Papers MS-221.
77. Robert D. McGrath to William C. Lambert, Letter, 7 July 1971, Lambert Papers MS-221.
78. *Ibid.*
79. David Harris to Robert D. McGrath, Letter, 19 July 1971, Lambert Papers MS-221.
80. Sandra Thomas to Robert D. McGrath, Letter, 21 July 1971, Lambert Papers MS-221.
81. Robert D. McGrath to William C. Lambert, Letter, 5 August 1971, Lambert Papers MS-221.
82. Amy Howlett to Robert D. McGrath, Letter, 14 July 1971, Lambert Papers MS-221.
83. *Ibid.*
84. Robert D. McGrath to William C. Lambert, Letter, 16 October 1971, Lambert Papers MS-221.
85. *Ibid.*
86. *Ibid.*
87. William C. Lambert to Amy Howlett, Letter, 20 October 1971, Lambert Papers MS-221.
88. *Ibid.*
89. *Ibid.*
90. *Ibid.*
91. Amy Howlett to Robert D. McGrath, Letter, 12 October 1971, p. 1, Lambert Papers MS-221.
92. William C. Lambert to Amy Howlett, Letter, 23 October 1971, Lambert Papers MS-221
93. Frank Cheesman to William C. Lambert, Letter, 1 September 1971, Lambert Papers MS-221.
94. *Ibid.*
95. Robert D. McGrath to William C. Lambert, Letter, 16 October 1971, pp. 1–2, Lambert Papers MS-221.
96. *Ibid.*, p. 2.
97. *Ibid.*
98. *Ibid.*, p. 1.
99. John Mackenzie to William C. Lambert, Letter, n.d., May 1972, Lambert Papers MS-221.
100. Sarah Shaw to William C. Lambert, Letter, 12 November 1974, Lambert Collection.

Chapter Fifteen

1. Smith, *Interview #18*, pp. 43–44.
2. C. O. Johnson to William C. Lambert, Letter, 14 November 1968, Lambert Papers MS-221.
3. Frank Cheesman to William C. Lambert, Letter, 11 September 1968, p. 1, Lambert Papers MS-221.
4. *Ibid.*
5. *Ibid.*
6. William Martin, email message to Author, 28 October 2013.
7. Jesse Stuart, Letter of Recommendation, 24 June 1969, p. 2, Lambert Papers MS-221.
8. *Ibid.*, p. 2.
9. *Ibid.*
10. Raymond Collishaw to William C. Lambert, Letter, 21 January 1970, p. 6.
11. Raymond Collishaw to William C. Lambert, Letter, 29 October 1969, Lambert Papers MS-221.
12. Leonard H. Rochford to William C. Lambert, Letter, 3 May 1970, p. 1, Lambert Papers MS-221.
13. *Ibid.* pp. 1–2.
14. *Ibid.*, p. 2.

15. J. H. Southey to William C. Lambert, Letter, 13 December 1968, Lambert Papers MS-221.
16. Raymond Collishaw to William C. Lambert, Letter, 29 June 1969, Lambert Papers MS-221.
17. Frank Cheesman to William C. Lambert, Letter, 2 March 1970, p. 1, Lambert Papers MS-221.
18. *Ibid.*
19. Royal D. Frey to William C. Lambert, Letter, 8 January 1968, Lambert File, USAF Museum.
20. William Martin, email message to Author, 28 January 2014.
21. M. P. Sayer to William C. Lambert, Letter, 4 November 1970, Lambert Papers MS-221.
22. *Ibid.*
23. *Ibid.*
24. M. P. Sayer to William C. Lambert, Letter, 10 February 1971.
25. Frank Cheesman to William C. Lambert, Letter, 16 March 1971, p. 1.
26. M. P. Sayer to William C. Lambert, Letter, 31 March 1971, Lambert Papers MS-221.
27. *Ibid.*
28. M. P. Sayer to William C. Lambert, Letter, 21 May 1971, Lambert Papers MS-221.
29. *Ibid.*
30. John Tanner to William C. Lambert, Letter, 7 June 1971, Lambert Papers MS-221; M. P. Sayer to William C. Lambert, Letter, 7 June 1971, Lambert Papers MS-221.
31. John Tanner to William C. Lambert, Letter, 7 June 1971.
32. Paul H. Poberezny to William C. Lambert, Letter, 5 April 1971, Lambert Paper, MS-221.
33. *Ibid.*
34. Ronald Siwik to William C. Lambert, Letter, 20 April 1971, Lambert Papers MS-221.
35. Millie Reidenbach to William C. Lambert, Letter, 5 August 1971, Lambert Papers MS-221; Bill Hodges to William C. Lambert, Letter, 7 September 1973, Lambert Papers MS-221.
36. *Ibid.*
37. James E. Smith Jr., to William C. Lambert, Letter, 30 January 1973, p. 1, Lambert Papers MS-221.
38. James Fox to William C. Lambert, Letter, 29 December 1970, Lambert Papers MS-221.
39. Mitch Mayborn to William C. Lambert, Letter, 22 May 1971, Lambert Papers MS-221.
40. *Ibid.*
41. *Ibid.*
42. Mitch Mayborn to William C. Lambert, Letter, 4 June 1971, p. 1, Lambert Papers MS-221.
43. *Ibid.*
44. William Martin, email to Author, 6 April 2014.
45. William E. Martin to Author, Letter, 11 May 2014, p. 2.
46. George M. Gumbert Jr., to William C. Lambert, Letter, 31 August 1979, Lambert Papers MS-221.
47. Edward M. Coffman to William C. Lambert, Letter, 28 October 1980. Lambert Papers MS-221; Steve Sullivan to William C. Lambert, Letter, 9 February 1981, Lambert Papers MS-221.

Chapter Sixteen

1. Staerker, Interview, 14 September 2013.
2. *Ibid.*; Martin, interview with Author, 24 August 2013.
3. Martin, interview with Author, 24 August 2013.
4. Staerker, Interview, 14 September 2013.
5. *Ibid.*
6. *Ibid.*
7. Peyton, "The Forgotten Ace of WWI," pp. 30–31.
8. Lambert, *Out of the Sun.*
9. Peyton, "The Forgotten Ace of WWI," p. 30.
10. "Colonel Lambert Still Flying Legend" (1978), n.p., Lambert Collection.
11. Thorpe, Interview, 23 June 2007.
12. Elizabeth French (Wilson), Interview with Author, 20 July 2007.
13. Clyda Forson to Bill Martin, Letter, 15 December 1984, Lambert Papers, MS-221.
14. Rita Baker, Interview with Author, 3 July 2007.
15. Kaye Welch (Clark), Interview with Author, 3 January 2008.
16. *Ibid.*
17. *Ibid.*
18. Richard A. Baumgartner, Interview with Author, 14 August 1997.
19. *Ibid.*
20. *Ibid.*
21. Martin, Interview with Author, 16 September 1997.
22. *Ibid.*
23. Martin, Interview with Author, 16 September 2013.
24. Martin, Interview with Author, 20 July 2007.
25. Staerker, Interview, 14 September 2013.
26. *Ibid.*
27. *Ibid.*
28. *Ibid.*
29. *Ibid.*
30. *Ibid.*
31. *Ibid.*
32. Thorpe, Interview, 23 June 2007.

Chapter Seventeen

1. Review of *Combat Report* by William C. Lambert, *Cross & Cockade Journal,* Vol. 15, No. 2, Summer 1974, p. 191.
2. *Ibid.*
3. *Ibid.*
4. *Ibid.*
5. *Ibid.*
6. *Ibid.*
7. Royal D. Frey to William C. Lambert, 21 September 1973, Lambert File, USAF Museum.
8. *Ibid.*
9. H. R., "Resolution To Recognize Col. William C. Lambert of Ironton, America's Top Living World War I Air Ace," *Ohio House of Representatives,* No. 277,

31 January 1975, reprinted in "Cross and Cockade Bulletin Board," *Cross & Cockade Journal*, Vo. 15, No. 2, Summer 1974, p. 191.

10. Clarence E. Miller, "Congressman Miller Pays Tribute to Top World War I Ace," *Congressional Record—House* (11 July 1974), H 6459.

11. Resolution No. 78–74, Ironton City Council, 14 December 1974, Lambert Papers MS-221.

12. Al Allen, "The Overlooked Ace, William Lambert of Ironton was No. 2," *The Columbus Dispatch Magazine*, 9 November 1975, p. 36.

13. Joe Gall, "World War I Ace Flew 'Noisy Toys,'" *Ohio Heritage*, Vol. 11, No. 1 (January-February 1979), p. 6.

14. William C. Lambert to Royal D. Frey, Letter, 23 February 1974, Lambert File, USAF Museum.

15. Dan McGrath to William C. Lambert, Letter, 26 June 1974, Lambert Papers MS-221.

16. Harold D. Hoekstra to William C. Lambert, Letter 10 January 1971, p. 1, Lambert Papers MS-221.

17. Linda Miller to William C. Lambert, Letter, 6 November 1971, Lambert Papers MS-221.

18. Ray St. Germain to William C. Lambert, Letter, 3 May 1973, Lambert Papers MS-221.

19. *Ibid.*

20. Ray St. Germain to William C. Lambert, Letter, 5 June 1973, Lambert Papers MS-221.

21. Sarah Ruth Levisay to William C. Lambert, Letter, 29 June 1972, p. 1, Lambert Papers MS-221.

22. Michael J. Madden to William C. Lambert, Letter, 23 August 1973, Lambert Papers MS-221.

23. *Ibid.*

24. Kelly Lane to William C. Lambert, Letter, 22 September 1973, pp. 1–2, Lambert Papers MS-221.

25. Harry Franken, "Ace Pilot was Reluctant War Hero," *Columbus Citizen-Journal* (10 November 1978), p. 1.

26. Richard Sohow (sic.) to William C. Lambert, Letter, 2 December 1973, Lambert Papers MS-221.

27. "Historical Society Honors Lambert on Telecast 'Spot,'" Lambert Collection.

28. Art Ferguson, "Colonel Lambert to Appear in International Aviation Film," *Ironton Tribune* (1976), n.p., Lambert Collection.

29. Staff, "From Ace to Author: A Biographical Sketch of Colonel Wm. C. Lambert," p. 11.

30. Arthur S. Ferguson, "Col. Lambert Flies Jet for First Time," *Ironton Tribune* (December 1976), n.p., Lambert Collection.

31. "Back in the Air," photo by Johnny Workman (9 March 1976), n.p, Lambert Collection.

32. George Wolfford, "WWI Ace, 'Youngster' Recall Past," *Ashland Daily Independent* (7 September 1978), p. 24.

33. *Ibid.*

34. Harry Franken, "Ace Pilot was Reluctant War Hero," p. 3.

35. *Ibid.*
36. *Ibid.*
37. *Ibid.*
38. *Ibid.*
39. *Ibid.*

40. Harry Franken, "Ace Pilot was Reluctant War Hero," p. 3.

41. Klaus Staerker, Interview with Author, 16 April 2014.

42. Richard Uppstrom, Interview with Author, 2 August 2007.

43. Robert L. Westervelt to William C. Lambert, Letter 30 November 1981.

44. Jon Guttman to William C. Lambert, Letter, 24 October 1981, p. 1, Lambert Papers MS-221.

45. C. R. Glasebrook to William C. Lambert, 26 October 1980, p. 2, Lambert Papers MS-221.

46. Norman W. Gillman to William C. Lambert, Letter, 12 December 1981, Lambert Papers MS-221.

47. John V. Nardine to William C. Lambert, Letter, 30 April 1981, Lambert Papers MS-221.

48. *Ibid.*

49. Karl E. Voelter to William C. Lambert, Letter, 27 October 1980, Lambert Papers MS-221.

50. James M. Dudgeon to William C. Lambert, Letter, 14 May 1979, Lambert Papers MS-221.

51. *Ibid.*

52. James M. Dudgeon to William C. Lambert, Letter, 4 July 1979, p. 2, Lambert Papers MS-221.

53. *Ibid.*
54. *Ibid.*
55. *Ibid.*

56. James J. Parks to William C. Lambert, Letter, 4 July 1979, p. 2, Lambert Papers MS-221.

57. *Ibid.*, p. 1.

58. James J. Parks to William C. Lambert, Letter 7 August 1979, Lambert Papers MS-221.

59. James J. Parks to William C. Lambert, Letter, 25 June 1981, Lambert Papers MS-221.

60. Robin Higham to William C. Lambert, 20 November 1980, Lambert Papers MS-221.

61. Claire M. Smith to Robin Higham, Letter, 28 May 1981, Lambert Papers MS-221; Robin Higham to William C. Lambert, Letter, 22 June 1981, Lambert Papers MS-221.

62. Carol Kitts, "RHJH Students Capture 3rd Place in History Award," *The Ironton Tribune* (8 June 1980), n.p.

63. William H. Cole to William C. Lambert, Letter, 1 February 1980, Lambert Papers MS-221.

64. *Ibid.*

65. William H. Cole to William C. Lambert, Letter, 19 February 1980, Lambert Papers MS-221.

66. Sid Moore to William C. Lambert, Letter, n.d., 1981, p. 1, Lambert Papers MS-221.

67. Sid Moore to William C. Lambert, Letter 20 July 1981, p. 3, Lambert Papers MS-221. (This letter was the last one Lambert received from Moore. Consequently, the other two that Moore sent which were not dated were probably sent in the late spring or early summer 1981.)

68. Sid Moore to William C. Lambert, Letter, n.d., 1981, p. 2, Lambert Papers MS-221.

69. Klaus Staerker, Interview with Author, 16 April 2014.

70. Beverly Childers, "William Lambert, World War I Flying Ace, is Now No. 1," *Ashland Daily Independent* (25 May 1981), p. 1.

Chapter Eighteen

1. William Martin, email to Author, 15 April 2014.
2. Klaus Staerker, Interview with Author, 16 April 2014.
3. *Ibid.*
4. Rita Baker, Interview with Author, 3 July 2007.
5. Bryce Poe II to William C. Lambert, Letter, 14 August 1981, Lambert Papers MS-221.
6. William Martin, email to Author, 16 April 2014.
7. Klaus Staerker, Interview with Author, 16 April 2014.
8. William Martin, email to Author, 16 April 2014.
9. Klaus Staerker, Interview with Author, 16 April 2014.
10. William Martin, email to Author, 16 April 2014.
11. Richard Baumgartner, "A Final Salute is Given: World War I Ace, Bill Lambert Buried Overlooking the Ohio," *The Herald Dispatch* (24 March 1982), p. 2.
12. Sam Piatt, "Col. Lambert, WWI Ace, Buried in Ironton," *The Daily Independent* (24 March 1982), p. 16.
13. William Martin, email message to Author, 30 January 2014.
14. Frank Cheesman to William C. Lambert, Letter, 12 April 1971, pp. 1–2, Lambert Papers MS-221.
15. William C. Lambert, Last Will and Testament of William C. Lambert, 31 March 1982, Available at Briggs Lawrence County Library, microfilm: 82–55.
16. *Ibid.*
17. *Ibid.*
18. *Ibid.*
19. William Martin, email message to Author, 30 January 2014.
20. Royal D. Frey to William C. Lambert, Letter, 8 January 1968.
21. Royal D. Frey to William C. Lambert, Letter, 10 November 1973, Lambert File, USAF Museum.
22. M. P. Sayer to William C. Lambert, Letter, 31 March 1971, Lambert Papers MS-221.
23. J. H. Southey to William C. Lambert, Letter, 2 May 1971, Lambert Papers MS-221.
24. Dennis Gordon to William C. Lambert, Letter, 11 August 1979, Lambert Papers MS-221.
25. James J. Parks to William C. Lambert, Letter, 25 June 1981, Lambert Papers MS-221.
26. William E. Martin to Author, Letter, 11 May 2014, p. 2.
27. William Martin, email message to Author, 28 January 2014.
28. Susan Smith to William C. Lambert, Letter, 29 September 1979, Lambert Papers MS-221.
29. Gene M. Gressley to William C. Lambert, Letter, 24 September 1981, p. 1, Lambert Papers MS-221.
30. *Ibid.*
31. "Col. William C. Lambert, DFC (Funeral)," *WSAZ Evening News* (Huntington, WV), Tuesday, 23 March 1982.

Epilogue

1. Klaus Staerker, Interview with Author, 14 September 2014.
2. *Ibid.*
3. Franken, "Reluctant Hero of World War I Cherishes Memories," p. 11.
4. *Ibid.*, p. 3.

Appendix

1. Norman L. R. Franks to William C. Lambert, Letter, 18 October 1973, Lambert File, USAF Museum.
2. *Ibid.*
3. William C. Lambert to Royal D. Frey, Letter, 14 November 1973, p. 1, Lambert File, USAF Museum.
4. *Ibid.*, pp. 1–2.
5. *Ibid.*, p. 2.
6. *Ibid.*
7. *Ibid.*
8. *Ibid.*
9. *Ibid.*
10. Royal D. Frey to E. B. Haslam, Letter, 23 November 1973, p. 1, Lambert File, USAF Museum.
11. *Ibid.*, p. 2.
12. *Ibid.*
13. William C. Lambert to Royal D. Frey, Letter, 24 November 1973, Lambert File, USAF Museum.
14. *Ibid.*
15. Frank Cheesman to William C. Lambert, Letter, 4 December 1973, p. 2.
16. *Ibid.*
17. *Ibid.*
18. *Ibid.*
19. *Ibid.*
20. *Ibid.*
21. *Ibid.*
22. *Ibid.*
23. *Ibid.*
24. *Ibid.*, p. 3.
25. *Ibid.*
26. *Ibid.*
27. *Ibid.*
28. *Ibid.*
29. *Ibid.*
30. *Ibid.*
31. *Ibid.*
32. William C. Lambert to Royal D. Frey, Letter, 11 December 1973, p. 1, Lambert File, USAF Museum.
33. *Ibid.*, p. 2.
34. Royal D. Frey to William C. Lambert, Letter, 17 December 1973, Lambert File, USAF Museum.
35. E. B. Haslam to Royal D. Frey, Letter, 5 February 1974, Lambert File, USAF Museum.
36. *Ibid.*
37. F. W. Coles to Royal D. Frey, Letter, 5 February 1974, Lambert File, USAF Museum.
38. *Ibid.*
39. *Ibid.*
40. *Ibid.*

41. Royal D. Frey to E. B. Haslam, Letter, 22 February 1974, Lambert File, USAF Museum.
42. *Ibid.*
43. William C. Lambert to Royal D. Frey, Letter, 23 February 1974.
44. *Ibid.*
45. Royal D. Frey to William C. Lambert, Letter, 3 March 1974.
46. "Colonel Lambert Still Flying Legend" (1978), n.p., Lambert Collection. (Clipping from paper without any identification.)

Bibliography

Unpublished Sources and Document Collection

I am grateful to William E. Martin for allowing me to use William C. Lambert's personal papers, effects, and correspondence in the writing of this book. Some of these sources have already been donated to the Wright State University Special Collections and Archives at Wright State University in Dayton, Ohio. The remaining materials will be donated to the U.S. Air Force Museum Research Division in Dayton, Ohio. Copies will also be given to the Wright State University Special Collections and Archives and the Briggs Lawrence County Public Library in Ironton, Ohio.

Archives

Directorate of History and Heritage, National Defence Headquarters, Ottawa, Canada K1A 0K2.
Kentucky Highland Museum, Ashland, KY.
Lambert Collection, Lawrence County Museum, Ironton, OH.
Lambert File, Briggs Lawrence County Public Library, Ironton, OH.
Lambert File: United States Air Force Museum Research Division, Wright-Patterson Air Force Base, Dayton, OH.
Lambert, William C. "Lambert Papers." Wright State University Special Collections and Archives, Wright State University, Dayton, OH. MS-221.
The U.S. National and Archives and Records Administration, St. Louis, MO.
William Carpenter Lambert, File C40499, AIR/76/285. The National Archives, Kew.

Interviews

Baker, Rita. 3 July 2007.
Baumgartner, Richard A. 14 August 1997; 7 April 2008.
(Clark), Kaye Welch. 3 January 2008.
Frey, Dana. 17 May 2008.
Frey, Elizabeth J. 18 August 1997.
Frey, Stacey. 17 May 2008.
(Gossett), Janenne Bruce. 19 July 2007.
Martin, William E. 16 September 1997; 20 July 2007; 16 September 2013.

Morton, Paul R. 10 January 2008.
Robinson, Doris. 20 July 2007.
Staerker, Klaus. 14 September 2013.
Thorpe, William C. 23 June 2007.
Uppstrom, Richard. 2 August 2007.
White, Vivian. 28 August 2008.
(Wilson), Elizabeth French. 20 July 2007.

Video

Lambert, William C. *Out of the Sun.* Interviewed by Robert J. Smith, Video, General Dynamics, Ft. Worth Division, 1980.
"Col. William C. Lambert, DFC Funeral." *WSAZ Evening News.* Huntington, WV. Tuesday, 23 March 1982.

Primary Sources

Baring, Maurice. *Flying Corps Headquarters 1914–1918* (London: William Blackwood and Sons, 1968).
Bodenschatz, Karl. *Hunting With Richthofen—The Bodenschatz Diaries: Sixteen Months of Battle with JG Freiherr von Richthofen No. 1*. Translated By Jan Hayzlett (London: Grubb Street, 1996).
Brittain, Vera. *Testament of Youth* (New York: Penguin Books, 1994).
Callender, Alvin Andrew. *War in an Open Cockpit: The Wartime Letters of Captain Alvin Andrew Callender*. Edited by Gordon W. Callender, Jr., and Gordon W. Callender, Sr. (West Roxbury, MA: World War I Aero Publishers, 1978).
Collishaw, Raymond. *Air Command: A Fighter Pilot's Story* (London: William Kimber, 1973).
Doolittle, James H. with Glines, Carroll V. *I Could Never Be So Lucky Again* (New York: Bantam Books, 1992).
Douglas, Sholto. *Years of Combat* (London: Collins, 1963).
Earhart, Amelia. *The Fun of It* (Chicago: Academy Chicago Publishers, 1977).
Foch, Ferdinand. *The Memoirs of Ferdinand Foch*. Translated by T. Bentley Mott (New York: Doubleday, Doran and Co., 1931).
Graves, Robert. *Goodbye To All That* (New York: Anchor Books, 1985).
Gray, Thomas. *The Poems of Thomas Gray with a Selection of Letters and Essays* (New York: E. P. Dutton, 1922).
Grider, John MacGavock. *War Birds: Diary of an Unknown Aviator*. Edited by Elliot White Springs (College Station: Texas A&M University Press, 1988).
Immelmann, Franz. *Immelmann: 'The Eagle of Lille'* (London: Greenhill Books, 1990).
Kelly, Fred C., ed. *Miracle at Kitty Hawk: the Letters of Wilbur and Orville Wright* (New York: Da Capo Press, 2002).
Kinney, Curtis. "I fought the Red Baron," *The American Legion Magazine*. December 1968.
_____, with Titler, Dale M. *I Flew a Camel* (Philadelphia: Dorrance, 1972).
Lambert, William C. "A Very Strange Story" (Ironton, OH: n.p., 1972).
_____. *Combat Report* (London: William Kimber, 1973).
_____. *Barnstorming and Girls* (Manhattan, KS: Sunflower University Press, 1980).
Lewis, Cecil. *Sagittarius Rising* (New York: Harcourt, Brace and Co., 1936).
Lindbergh, Charles A. *The Spirit of St. Louis* (St. Paul, MN: Minnesota Historical Society Press, 1993).
McCudden, James. *Flying Fury: Five Years in the Royal Flying Corps* (London: Greenhill Books, 2000).
Miller, Clarence E. "Congressman Miller Pays Tribute to Top World War I Ace." *Congressional Record—House*. 11 July 1974. H 6459.
Nagel, Fritz. *Fritz: The World War I Memoirs of a German Lieutenant*. Edited by Richard A. Baumgartner (Huntington, WV: Blue Acorn Press, 1995).
Reece, Robert H. *Night Bombing with the Bedouins: By One of the Squadrons* (Boston and New York: Houghton Mifflin Company, 1919).
Richthofen, Manfred von. *The Red Air Fighter* (London: Greenhill Books, 1990).
Rickenbacker, Edward V. *Fighting the Flying Circus* (New York: Frederick A. Stokes, 1919).
_____. *Rickenbacker: An Autobiography* (Englewood Cliffs, NJ: Prentice-Hall, 1967).
Rochford, Leonard. *I Chose the Sky* (London: William Kimber, 1977).
Smith, Robert J. *Air Force Logistics Command Oral History Interview #18, Transcript, Lt. Col. William C. Lambert*. Office of History Headquarters, Air Force Logistics Command, Dayton, OH, September 1980.
Stuart, Jesse. *Clearing the Sky and Other Stories* (Lexington: University of Kentucky Press, 1984).
Thwaites, Reuben Gold. *Afloat on the Ohio: An Historical Pilgrimage of a Thousand Miles in a Skiff, from Redstone to Cairo* (Chicago: Way and Williams, 1897).
Thwaites, Reuben Gold. *Pilgrims on the Ohio: The River Journey and Photographs of Reuben Gold Thwaites, 1894*. Essays by Robert L. Reid and Dan Hughes Fuller (Indianapolis: Indiana Historical Society, 1997).
Udet, Ernst. *Ace of the Iron Cross*. Edited by Stanley M. Ulanoff. Translated by Richard K. Riehn (New York: Doubleday, 1970).
Washington, George. *Writings* (New York: Library of America, 1997).
_____. *Ironton City Directories*. From 1893–1894 to 1982.
_____. U.S. Census Bureau.

Secondary Sources

Adams, R.J.Q., ed. *The Great War, 1914–1918; Essays on the Military, Political and Social History of the First World War* (College Station: Texas A&M University Press, 1990).

Bibliography

Archibald, Norman. *Heaven High Hell Deep 1917–1918* (New York: Albert and Charles Boni, 1935).
Ballard, Jack Stokes. *War Bird Ace: The Great War Exploits of Capt. Field E. Kindley* (College Station: Texas A&M University Press, 2007).
Barlett, Donald L. and Steele, James B. *Howard Hughes: His Life and Madness* (New York: W.W. Norton, 1979).
Becker, Carl M. *Home and Away: The Rise and Fall of Professional Football on the Banks of the Ohio, 1919–1934* (Athens: Ohio University Press, 1998).
Bennett, David J. *He Almost Changed the World: The Life and Times of Thomas Riley Marshall* (Bloomington, IN: Author House, 2007).
Bloom, Philipp. *The Vertigo Years: Europe, 1900–1914* (New York: Basic Books, 2008).
Bourget, Charles L. *Royal Aircraft Factory S.E.5a*. Vol. I, No. 6 (West Roxbury, MA: WWI Aero Publishers, 1966).
Bowen, Ezra and the Editors of Time-Life Books. *Knights of the Air* (Alexandria, VA: Time-Life Books, 1980).
Bowyer, Chaz. *For Valour: The Air VCs* (London: Caxton Editions, 2002).
Caine, Geoffrey and Caine, Renate N. *Making Connections: Teaching and the Human Brain* (Menlo Park, CA: Addison-Wesley, 1994).
Charlton, James, Editor. *The Military Quotation Book* (New York: St. Martin's Press, 1990).
Childers, Thomas. *Soldiers from the War Returning: The Greatest Generation's Troubled Homecoming from World War II* (New York: Mariner Books, 2009).
Clymer, Floyd. *Treasury of Early American Automobiles, 1877–1925* (New York: Bonanza Books, 1950).
Cobb, Ivo Geikie. *A Manual of Neurasthenia* (London: Bailliere, Tindall and Cox, 1920).
Cole, Christopher, ed. *Royal Air Force 1918* (London: William Kimber, 1968).
Coffman, Edward M. *The War to End All Wars: The American Military Experience in World War I* (New York: Oxford University Press, 1968).
Creveld, Martin van. *The Art of War: War and Military Thought* (New York: HarperCollins, 2005).
Crouch, Tom D. *The Bishop's Boys: The Life of Wilbur and Orville Wright* (New York: W.W. Norton, 1989).
Dick, David. *Jesse Stuart: The Heritage* (North Middletown, KY: Plum Lick, 2005).
Diggens, Barry. *September Evening: The Life and Final Combat of the German World War One Ace Werner Voss* (London: Grub Street, 2003).
Dippel, John V. H. *War and Sex: A Brief History of Men's Urge for Battle* (Amherst, NY: Prometheus, 2010).
Driver, Hugh. *The Birth of Military Aviation: Britain 1903–1914* (London: The Boyden Press, 1997).
Eksteins, Modris. *Rites of Spring* (New York: First Mariners, 2000).
Farwell, Bryon. *Over There: The United States in the Great War, 1917–1917* (New York: W.W. Norton, 1999)
Ferguson, Niall. *The War of the World: Twentieth-Century Conflict and the Descent of the West* (New York: Penguin, 2006).
Franks, Norman L. R., Frank W. Bailey, and Russell Guest. *Above the Lines: A Complete Record of the Fighter Aces of the German Air Service, Naval Air Service and Flanders Marine Corps, 1914–1918* (London: Grubb Street, 1993).
_____. *Blood April ... Black September* (London: Grubb Street, 1995).
_____, Frank Bailey, and Rich Duiven. *Casualties of the German Air Service 1914–1920* (London: Grubb Street, 1999).
Fussell, Paul. *The Great War and Modern Memory* (New York: Oxford University Press, 2000).
Gilbert, Martin. *The First World War: A Complete History* (New York: Henry Holt, 1996).
Glines, Carroll V. *Roscoe Turner: Aviation's Master Showman* (Washington, D.C.: Smithsonian Institution Press, 1995).
Guttman, Jon. *SE5a Vs Albatros DV: Western Front 1917–18* (Oxford, UK: Osprey, 2009).
Hack, Richard. *Hughes: The Private Diaries, Memos and Letters* (Beverly Hills: New Millennium Press, 2001).
Hale, Jr., Nathan G. *The Rise and Crisis of Psychoanalysis in the United States: Freud and the Americans, 1917–1985* (New York: Oxford University Press, 1995).
Harries, Meirion and Susie. *The Last Days of Innocence: America at War, 1917–1918* (New York: Vintage Books, 1997).
Harrison, Tom. *Bion, Rickman, Foulkes and the Northfield Experiments: Advancing on a Different Front* (London: Jessica Kingsley, 2000).
Hart, Peter. *Aces Falling: War Above the Trenches, 1918* (London: Weidenfeld and Nicolson, 2007).
_____. *Bloody April: Slaughter in the Skies Over Arras, 1917* (London: Cassell Military Paperbacks, 2005).
Hawker, Tyrrel Mann. *Hawker, V.C.* (London: The Mitre Press, 1965).
Herwig, Holger H. *The First World War: Germany and Austria Hungary, 1914–1918* (New York: St. Martin's Press, 1997).
Hinderaker, Eric. *Elusive Empires: Constructing Colonialism in the Ohio Valley, 1673–1800* (New York: Cambridge University Press, 1997).

Bibliography

Hobsbawm, Eric. *The Age of Capital, 1848–1875* (London: Abacus, 2006).
Hochschild, Adam. *To End All Wars* (New York: Mariner Books, 2012).
Holmes, Tony. *Jane's Vintage Aircraft Recognition Guide* (New York: HarperCollins, 2005).
Hoover, Robert A. and Shaw, Mark. *Forever Flying: Fifty Years of High-Flying Adventures, from Barnstorming in Prop Planes to Dogfighting Germans to Testing Supersonic Jets* (New York: Pocket Books, 1996).
Hudson, James J. *In Clouds of Glory: American Airmen Who Flew with the British During The Great War* (Fayetteville: University of Arkansas Press, 1990).
Hynes, Samuel. *The Soldiers' Tale: Bearing Witness to Modern War* (New York: Penguin Books, 1998).
Illingworth, A. E. *A History of 24 Squadron* (London: Naval and Military Press and the Imperial War Museum, 2004).
Johnson, Herbert A. *Wingless Eagle: U.S. Army Aviation through World War I* (Chapel Hill: University of North Carolina Press, 2001).
Johnson, Robert S. *Thunderbolt* (New York: Ballantine Books, 1959).
Jones, H. A. *The War in the Air: Being the Story of the part played in the Great War by the Royal Air Force.* Vol. II (London: Naval and Military Press, 2002).
_____. *The War in the Air: Being the Story of the part played in the Great War by the Royal Air Force.* Vol. III (London: Naval and Military Press, 2002).
_____. *The War in the Air: Being the Story of the part played in the Great War by the Royal Air Force.* Vol. IV (London: Naval and Military Press, 2002).
_____. *The War in the Air: Being the Story of the part played in the Great War by the Royal Air Force.* Vol. V (London: Naval and Military Press, 2002).
_____. *The War in the Air: Being the Story of the part played in the Great War by the Royal Air Force.* Vol VI (London: Naval and Military Press, 2002).
_____. *The War in the Air: Being the Story of the part played in the Great War by the Royal Air Force.* Appendix (London: Naval and Military Press, 2002).
Jones, Loyal. *Appalachian Values* (Ashland, KY: Jessie Stuart Foundation, 1994).
Keegan, John. *A History of Warfare* (New York: Knopf, 1993).
Kilduff, Peter. *The Red Baron: Beyond the Legend* (London: Cassell Military Paperbacks, 1994).
_____. *Hermann Goring, Fighter Ace: The World War I Career of Germany's Most Infamous Airman* (London: Grubb Street, 2010).
Kipling, Rudyard. *War Stories and Poems* (New York: Oxford University Press, 1992).
Knepper, George W. *Ohio and its People* (Kent, OH: Kent State University Press, 1997).
Korda, Michael. *Hero: The Life and Legend of Lawrence of Arabia* (New York: HarperCollins, 2010).
Lamberton, W. M. *Fighter Aircraft of the 1914–1918 War.* Edited by E.F. Cheesman (Letchworth, England: Harleyford, 1961).
Lawson, Eric and Jane. *The First Air Campaign: August 1914–November 1918* (Conshohocken, PA: Combined Books, 1996).
Leese, Peter. *Shell Shock: Traumatic Neurosis and the British Soldiers of the First World War* (New York: Palgrave Macmillan, 2002).
Lewis, Bruce. *A Few of The First: The True Stories of the Men who Flew in and before the First World War* (London: Leo Cooper, 1997).
Lewis, Jon E., ed. *Fighter Pilots: Eyewitness Accounts of Air Combat from the Red Baron to Today's Top Guns* (New York: MJF Books, 2002).
Lewis, Peter. *Squadron Histories R.F.C., R.N.A.S., and R.A.F. 1912–1959* (London: Putnam, 1959).
Longstreet, Stephen. *The Canvas Falcons: The Men and the Planes of World War I* (New York: Barnes & Noble, 1995).
McCaffery, Dan. *Billy Bishop Canadian Hero,* 2nd Ed (Toronto: James Lorimer, 2002).
Maltby, Marc S. "The Origins and Early Development of Professional Football, 1890–1920." Ph.D. Dissertation (Athens: Ohio University, 1987).
Marshal, S. L. A. *World War I* (New York: First Mariner Books, 2001).
Morrow, Jr., John H. *The Great War in the Air Military Aviation from 1909 to 1921* (Washington, D.C.: Smithsonian Institution Press, 1993).
_____. *The Great War: An Imperial History* (London and New York: Routledge, 2005).
O'Connor, Mike. *Airfields & Airmen: Somme* (South Yorkshire: Pen and Sword, 2002).
O'Shea, Stephen. *Back to the Front* (New York: Avon, 1996).
Neilberg, Michael, S. *Fighting the Great War: A Global History* (Cambridge, MA: Harvard University Press, 2007).
Neumann, Georg Paul. *The German Air Force in the Great War* (London: Hodder and Stoughton, 1921).

Payne, Philip G. *"Modernity Lost: Ironton, Ohio, In Industrial and Post-Industrial America,"* Dissertation (Ohio State University, 1994).
Pengelly, Colin. *Albert Ball V.C.: The Fighter Pilot Hero of World War I* (South Yorkshire, England: Pen and Sword, 2010).
Philip, Jordan D. *Ohio Comes of Age, 1873–1900: The History of the State of Ohio.* Vol. V, Carl Wittke, ed. (Columbus: Ohio State Archaeological and Historical Society, 1943).
Raleigh, Walter. *The War in the Air.* Vol. I (Uckfield, East Sussex: Naval and Military Press, 2002).
Remarque, Erich Maria. *The Road Back* (New York: Ballantine, 1998).
Revell, Alex. *Brief Glory: The Life of Arthur Rhys Davids DSO MC* (South Yorkshire, England: Pen and Sword, 2010).
_____. *High in the Empty Blue: The History of 56 Squadron, RFC/RAF 1916 to 1920* (Mountain View, CA: Flying Machines, 1995).
Sassoon, Siegfried. *The Complete Memoirs of George Sherston: Memoirs of an Infantry Officer* (London: World Books, 1940).
Shores, Christopher, Franks, Norman, and Guest, Russell. *Above the Trenches: A Complete Record of the Fighter Aces and Units of the British Empire Air Forces, 1915–1920* (London: Grub Street, 1996).
_____. *Above the Trenches: Supplement* (London: Grubb Street, 1996).
Skinner, Stephen. *The Stand: The Final Flight of Lt. Frank Luke, Jr.* (Atglen, PA: Schifffer Military History, 2008).
Smith, Adrian. *Mick Mannock, Fighter Pilot: Myth, Life and Politics* (London: Palgrave, 2001).
Smith, Grafton E. and Pear, Ton Hatherly. *Shell Shock and its Lessons* (Manchester: Manchester University Press, 1917).
Steel, Nigel and Hart, Peter. *Tumult in the Clouds: The British Experience of the War in the Air, 1914–1918* (London: Hodden and Stoughton, 1997).
Strachan, Hew, ed. *The Oxford Illustrated History of the First World War* (New York: Oxford University Press, 1998).
Sullivan, Alan. *Aviation in Canada 1917–1918* (Toronto: Rous and Mann, 1919).
Taylor, A. J. P. *The First World War* (New York: A Perigee Book, 1972).
Tobin, James. *To Conquer the Air: The Wright Brothers and the Great Race for Flight* (New York: Free Press, 2003).
Toliver, Raymond F. *The Interrogator: The Story of Hanns Joachim Scharff Master Interrogator of the Luftwarffe* (Atglen, PA: Schiffer Military History, 1997).
Treadwell, Terry C. and Wood, Alan C. *German Knights of the Air 1914–1918: The Holders of the Orden Pour Le Mérite* (New York: Barnes & Noble, 1997).
Tucker, Spencer C. and Roberts, Priscilla. *The Encyclopedia of World War I: A Political, Social, and Military History.* Volume I (Santa Barbara, CA: ABC-CLIO, 2005).
van Wart, Montgomery, and Suino, Paul. *Leadership in Public Organizations: An Introduction.* 2nd ed. (Armonk, NY: M.E. Sharp, 2012).
Werner, Johannes. *Knight of Germany: Oswald Boelcke German Ace.* Translated by Claud W. Sykes (London: John Hamilton, 1973).
Weyl, A.R. *Fokker: The Creative Years* (London: Putnam Publications, 1965).
Wilson, Charles McMoran. *The Anatomy of Courage: The Classic WWI Account of the Psychological Effects of War* (London: Constable and Robinson, 2007).
Wilson, Jean Moorcroft. *Siegfried Sassoon: The Making of a War Poet* (New York: Routledge, 1998).
Winter, Denis. *The First of the Few: Fighter Pilots of the First World War* (Athens: University of Georgia Press, 1983).
Winters, Jay, and Baggett, Blaine. *The Great War and the Shaping of the 20th Century* (New York: Penguin Studio, 1996).
Wortman, Marc. *The Millionaires' Unit* (New York: Public Affairs, 2006).
Ziegler, Philip. *King Edward VIII* (New York: Alfred A. Knopf, 1991).
_____. *Directory of Iron and Steel Works in the United States and Canada.* 18th ed. (New York: American Iron and Steel Institute, 1916).
_____. *Jane's Fighting Aircraft of World War I* (London: Random House, 2001).
_____. *Roger Lambert and His Descendants.* Compiled by Ira C. Lambert (Toms River, New Jersey: n.p., 1933).
_____. *Russell High School. Croaker Yearbook Class of 1938* (Russell, KY: 1938).

Articles

Allen, Al. "The Overlooked Ace: William Lambert of Ironton was No. 2." *The Columbus Dispatch Magazine.* 9 November 1975.

Babington, Anthony. *Shell-Shock: A History of the Changing Attitudes to War Neurosis* (London: Lee Cooper, 1997).

Baillie, Kenneth. "Altitude air pressure calculator." *Altitude.org* (April 2010). http://www.altitude.org/air_pressure.php.

Baird, Don. "Aviation Makes Memories." *The Columbus Dispatch*. Sunday, 16 February 1986.

Beard and General Electrization." Presented to the American Association of the History of Medicine, Boston (1980). http://med.brown.edu/HistoryofPsychiatry/Beard.html.

Boucher, William Ira. "German Two-Seaters," *An Illustrated History of World War I*. 3 December 2011. http://www.wwiaviation.com/German_2seaters.html.

Brown, Edward M. "An American Treatment for the 'American Nervousness': George Miller

Browne, Malcolm W. "100 Years of Maxim's Killing Machine." *New York Times*. 26 November 1985.

Browne, O'Brien. "Edward Mick Mannock: World War I RAF Ace Pilot." *Aviation Magazine*. 17 May 2007. http://www.historynet.com/edward-mick-mannock-world-war-i-raf-ace-pilot.htm.

Bryce, Lord James. "Presidency: Why Great Men are Not Chosen President?" *The American Commonwealth*. http://hnn.us/articles/448.html.

Childers, Beverly. "William Lambert, World War I flying ace, is now No.1." *Ashland Daily Independent*. 25 May 1981.

Clancy, Daniel F., ed. "Ex-ODC Man is Top Living Ace of World War I." *Ohio Defense Corps News*. No. 46 (December 1973).

Coffman, Edward M. "Why We are Not Interested in World War I and Should Be." *Cantigny at Seventy-Five: A Professional Discussion* (Wheaton, IL: The Cantigny First Division Foundation, 1994).

Corns, John B. "Industrial, Invincible Ironton." *The Ohio Magazine*. Vol. 3 (1907).

De Angelo, Joseph, P.E. *The Link Flight Trainer: A Historic Mechanical Engineering Landmark*. Edited by St. George, Laura and Moody, James. Roberson Museum and Science Center, Binghamton, New York. 10 June 2000. http://files.asme.org/asmeorg/Communities/History/Landmarks/5585.pdf.

Finck, William. "Classical Records and German Origins," Part Six. 2008. http://christogenea.org/wrf_essays/Classical%20Records/Classical%20Records%20And%20German%20Origins6.pdf.

Franks, Norman. "Review of *Combat Report* by William C. Lambert." *Cross & Cockade Journal*, Vol. 15. No. 2 (Summer 1974).

Frey, Royal D. "Forgotten Ace of World War I." *The Airman*. Vol. XII. No. 4 (April 1968).

_____. "A.E.F. Combat Airfields and Monuments in France-WWI." *Journal of The American Aviation Historical Society*. Vol. 17. No. 3 (1972).

_____. "The Luftwaffe's Master Interrogator." *The Air Force Magazine* (June 1976).

Gall, Joe. "World War I Ace Flew 'Noisy Toys.'" *Ohio Heritage*. Vol. 11. No. 1 (January–February 1979).

Garber, Steve. "Sputnik and the Dawn of the Space Age." *NASA*. 10 October 2007. http://history.nasa.gov/sputnik/.

Gillenwater, Ginger. "Ironton Ohio— The rise and fall of "Little Chicago." *Yahoo Voices*. 6 September 2007. http://voices.yahoo.com/ironton-ohio-rise-fall-little-chicago-522880.html?cat=16.

Girardot, Melissa. "The Furnaces." (*The Lawrence Register*.) http://lawrencecountyohio.com/furnaces/stories/stats1888.htm.

Henry, Patrick. "Our Old Citizens: A Reminiscence by (Rev.) Patrick Henry." Ironton, OH (1912). http://www.lawrencecountyohio.com/stories/misc/stories/henrypatrick.htm.

Huddleston, Eugene L. "Place Names in the Writings of Jesse Stuart." *Western Folklore*. Vol. 31. No. 3. July (1972).

Huffman, Dale. "Seeds of Friendship Planted in War Grew." *Dayton Daily News* (n.d.).

Jain, Bob. "World War I Pilots Share Memories." *The Denver Post* (22 April 1981).

Jakab, Peter L. "Wood to Metal: The Structural Origins of the Modern Airplane." *Journal of Aircraft*. Vol. 36. No. 6. American Institute of Aeronautics and Astronautics Inc. (November–December 1999).

Jakle, John A. "The Ohio Valley Revisited: Images from Nicholas Cresswell and Reuben Gold Thwaites." *Always a River: The Ohio River and the American Experience*. Edited by Reid, Robert L. (Bloomington: Indiana University Press, 1991).

Janus, Allan. "Lion Cubs? Yeah, We've Got Lion Cubs, Too." *Air Space: Smithsonian National Air and Space Museum*. 27 December 2010. http://blog.nasm.si.edu/tag/wwi/.

Jones, Edgar. "Post-combat Disorders: The Boer War to the Gulf War." Edited by Harry Lee and Edgar Jones. *War and Health: Lessons from the Gulf War* (West Sussex, England: John Wiley and Sons, 2007).

Kouns, Sharon M. "Furnaces of the Hanging Rock Iron Region. Lawrence County, Ohio." *The Lawrence Register*. http://lawrencecountyohio.com/furnaces/index/indexlawohfurnaces.htm.

Lewis, W. David. "A Man Born Out of Season: Eddie Rickenbacker, Eastern Airlines, and the Civil Aeronautics Board." *Business and Economic History*. Vol. 25. No. 1 (Fall 1996).

Mack, Rachel. "Unger's Celebrates 60th Anniversary." National Shoe Retail Association. http://www.nsra.org/get_srt_art.php?aid=17.

Makepeace, Clare. "Sex and the Somme: The officially sanctioned brothels on the front line laid bare for the first time." *MailOnline*. 28 October 2011. http://www.dailymail.co.uk/news/article-2054914/Sex-Somme-Officially-sanctioned-WWI-brothels-line.html#ixzz2VYVtfozZ.

Mallory, David. "Sky Pilot… Ironton Resident 'Top Air Ace in WWI." *The Herald-Dispatch*. 30 May 1977.

Martin, William E. "America's Forgotten Ace." *The Airman* (May 1980).

Mayo Clinic. *Post-Traumatic Stress Disorder (PTSD)*. 6 April 2011. http://www.mayoclinic.com/health/post-traumatic-stress-disorder/ds00246/dsection=symptoms.

Miller, James F. "Eight Minutes Near Bapaume: An Aeronautical Analysis of Richthofen vs. Hawker, 23 November 1916." *Over the Front*. Vol. 21. No. 2 (2006).

National Institute of Mental Health (NIMH). *Post-Traumatic Stress Disorder*. 29 March 2013. http://report.nih.gov/nihfactsheets/ViewFactSheet.aspx?csid=58&key=P.

Parks, Andy. "Vintage Aero Flying Museum." *Discover Weld County Colorado*. Weld County, CO (2013). http://www.discoverweld.com/vintageaeroflyingmuseum.html.

Payton, Dave. "Ironton Man's Record: 21½ German Planes." *The Herald-Advertiser*. Huntington, WV. 19 May 1968.

_____. "Shultz Paid Tribute to Great Flying Ace." *The Herald-Dispatch*. 19 December 1999.

Piatt, Sam. "Col. Lambert, WWI Ace, Buried in Ironton." *The Daily Independent*. 24 March 1982.

Pollard, Dave. "P-38, Lightning Pilot Returns Home After Many Experiences in Europe." *The Columbus Dispatch*. 25 June 1945.

Richard, J. "Battle of the Lys, 9–29 April 1918." *Military History Encyclopedia on the Web*. 27 August 2007. http://www.historyofwar.org/articles/battles_lys.html.

Schumm, Jeremiah A. and Chard, Kathleen M. "Alcohol and Stress in the Military." *National Institute on Alcohol Abuse and Alcoholism*: Alcohol Research: *Current Reviews*. Vol. 34. No. 4. http://pubs.niaaa.nih.gov/publications/arcr344/401–407.htm.

Shaw, James A. "Officers and Gentlemen: Gentlemanly Mystique and Military Effectiveness in the Nineteen Century British Army." *Military History Online*. http://www.militaryhistoryonline.com/general/articles/officersandgentlemen.aspx.

Sherman, Stephen. "Consolidated B-24 Liberator." *AcePilots.com*. 21 January 2012. http://acepilots.com/planes/b24.html.

Taylor, Roland E., ed. "Former Air Force Museum Curator Royal Frey Dies." *Moonlight Serenader*. 2nd ed. Vol. 37. No. 242 (Berkshire, UK: Pica Litho, 1993).

Vincent, George H. "A Retarded Frontier." *American Journal of Sociology*, 4 (July 1898).

Wilhelm, Hubert G. H. "Settlement and Selected Landscape Imprints in the Ohio Valley." *Always a River: the Ohio River and the American Experience*. Robert L. Reid, ed. (Bloomington: Indiana University Press, 1991).

Wilson, E. S. "Early Days of Ironton." *The Ohio Magazine*. Vol. 3 (1907).

Wilson, Trevor. "The Significance of the First World War in Modern History." R.J.Q. Adams, ed. *The Great War, 1914–1918: Essays on the Military, Political and Social History of the First World War* (College Station, TX: Texas A &M University Press, 1990).

_____. "EMIGH—Trojan A2 1946." *Aerofiles*. 5 February 2009. http://aerofiles.com/_e.html.

_____. "Eugene W. Kettering Model Aircraft Collection." *National Museum of the US Air Force*. 29 September 2009. http://www.nationalmuseum.af.mil/factsheets/factsheet.asp?id=15609.

_____. *Ironton, Ohio: Its Industries, Resources, Facilities* (Ironton, OH: Ironton Register Print, 1881).

_____. "Lightweight Trio." *Flight*. 4 May 1950. http://www.flightglobal.com/pdfarchive/view/1950/1950%20%200853.html.

_____. The Marmon Club. "Welcome to the Marmon Club." marmonclub.com. http://www.marmonclub.com/index.html.

_____. The Marmon Group. "The Marmon Wasp." marmon.com. (2013). http://www.marmon.com/MarmonWasp.asp.

_____. "Melita." *Bonsor's North Atlantic Seaway: Haws' Merchant Fleets*. http://www.greatships.net/melita.html.

_____. "S/S Melita, Canadian Pacific Line." *Norway Heritage: Hands Across the Sea*. http://www.norwayheritage.com/p_ship.asp?sh=melit.

_____. "New Books." *Aviation News*. Vol. 9. No. 26 (22 May–4 June 1981).

_____. Ohio Defense Corps. *Ohio History Central*. 20 May 2013. http://www.ohiohistorycentral.org/w/Ohio_Defense_Corps?rec=2403.

_____. Order of Daedalians. "Order of Daedalians and Daedalian Foundation." Daedalian.org. (2012.) http://www.daedalians.org/.
_____. "Paul Howard Poberezny EAA Founder and Aviation Legend, 1921–2013." *EAA The Spirit of Aviation* (2014). http://www.eaa.org/paul/.
_____. Research and Innovative Technology Administration. "The First U.S. Federal Pilot License." *The United States Department of Transportation* (2013). http://ntl.bts.gov/lib/47000/47700/47707/first_pilots_license.pdf.
_____. *Rubber World*. Vol. 66 (Bill Brothers Publishing Corporation, 1922).
_____. "Ruptured Eardrum (Perforated Tympanic Membrane)." *Core Physicians: The Art of Wellness* (2010). http://www.corephysicians.org/news-and-health-library/health-library/otorhinolaryngology/otla3957/.
_____. Siemens Schuckert DIII. *The Old Rhinebeck Aerodrome*. http://www.oldrhinebeck.org/index.php?option=com_k2&view=item&id=146:siemens-schuckert-diii&Itemid=87.
_____. Veteran Tributes. "Jesse O. Creech." *Veterantributes.org*. http://veterantributes.org/TributeDetail.php?recordID=918.
_____. *Warplane, Military Innovation: Key Innovations*. "Wright Brothers Biplane." http://www.pbs.org/wnet/warplane/topicfeature.html.
_____. "William Pitsenbarger [1944–1966]." *Ohio's Aviation Heritage: Teacher Resource Guide*. National Museum of the United States Air Force Education Division. http://www.nationalmuseum.af.mil/shared/media/document/AFD-070702-079.pdf.
_____. "WWI Collector to Speak during Nat'l Library Week. *Lowery Airman* (27 March 1981).
_____. "WWII AAF Combat Chronology: January 1944 through June 1944, Saturday, 29 January 1944." *Eighth Air Force Historical Society* (n.d.). http://www.8thafhs.org/combat1944a.htm.

Magazines and Journals

The Air Force Magazine.
The Airman.
Airpower.
The American Legion.
Aviation News.
Buckeye Hill Country.

Cross & Cockade Journal.
Hearthstone.
Journal of The American Aviation Historical Society.
Ohio Heritage.
The Ohio Magazine.

Newspapers

Ashland Daily Independent, Ashland, KY.
The Beacon, Union-Leader Publishing Company, Manchester, NH.
The Columbus Dispatch, Columbus, OH.
The Daily Independent, Ashland, KY.
Dayton Daily News, Dayton, OH.
The Denver Post, Denver, CO.
The Herald-Advertiser, Huntington, WV.
The Herald-Dispatch, Huntington, WV.

Huntington Advisor, Huntington, WV.
Ironton Evening Tribune.
Ironton News.
Ironton Register.
Ironton Sunday Tribune.
Ironton Tribune.
Morning Irontonian.
The New York Times.

Index

A-7D jetfighters 218
Aaron, Henry (Hank) 3
Abbeville 32, 55, 68, 71, 73, 89–90, 99–100, 103, 108
Achilles 3
Aeronautics Branch of the Commerce Department 159
Aeroprint 198, 212
Ailette River 53
Air Commerce Act of 1926 159
Air Force Logistics Command 166; *see also* Air Service Command
Air Force Logistics Command Oral History project 16
Air Force Material Command 178
Air Force/Space Digest 187
Air Force Times 187
Air Historical Branch, R.A.F. 181
Air Ministry 143
Air Power 215
Air Progress 189
Air Service Command 166; *see also* Air Force Logistics Command
Aircraft Production Board 13
The Airman 175, 179–181, 183, 187, 208
Aisne River 53, 58, 66
Ajax 3
Albany Airport 211
Albatros D. III 33, 35, 42–44, 55; Albatros C.III (two-seater) 46, 64, 135
Albatros D. V 43, 46–47, 51, 53–54, 56, 60–62, 66, 68, 73–74, 79–84, 91–93, 113, 122, 128–129, 132–133, 215
Albert 36–37, 39, 43, 48–50, 86, 118
Alexander the Great 89
Allbee and Sons 197
Alpha Portland Cement Company 15
Amelia, Ohio 209
American Civil War 15, 142
American 42nd Division 109
American Revolution 90
American 2nd Division 58, 61

American 3rd Division 61
Amiens 31, 55, 58, 66, 84, 90, 95, 112, 119, 134
Amiens-Roye-Noyon road 69
Amiens-Roye road 59
Andre 132
Anson, Howard 156–158
Apollo astronaut 205
"Archie" 66, 94, 116
Armco Steel Company 179, 205, 217
Armentières 143
Armistice 1, 143–144, 183
Armstrong, Neil A. 5
Armstrong Whitworths 34
Arnold, Gen. Henry H. "Hap" 164
Arteriosclerotic Heart Disease (ASHD) 218; *see also* Pulmonary Embolism Atrial Fibrillation
Ashland, Kentucky 148, 152, 173–174, 211
Ashland Daily Independent 173
Ashland-Ironton-Portsmouth-Wellston 9224 VARTU 173
Assistant Civil Air Attaché 179
Assistant Maintenance Officer 168
Aten, Marion: *The Last Train Over the Rostov Bridge* 185
Athens, Tennessee 148–149
Atlanta, Georgia 148–149, **150**
Aurora, Ontario 215
Australian Flying Corps 135
Auxi Le Château 59, 65, 73, 89
Aviation News 151
Avre River 55
Avro 22, 27–28
Ayencourt 68

B-17 Flying Fortress 165–166
B-24 Liberator 165–166
B-25 Mitchell 170
Bailey's Cafeteria 204
Bair, Lt. Hilbert L. 76, 98–99, 110, 113, 125–126, 136–137, 210
Baker, Bridget 204
Baker, Paul 168, 203

Baker, Rita 160, 168, 203–204
Ball, Albert 1–2
Ballantine Books 185
Bangor, Maine 170
Bantam Books 185
Barger field 146
Barnhart, Paulette 214–215
Barnstorming and Girls 2, 7, 15, 26, 89, 143, 145–146, 148–149, **150**, 151, 154, 167, 185, 200–201, 204, 212, 214–215
Barrie, Ontario, Canada 23
Barth, Germany 177
Barton, Capt. Horace D. 46, 50, 53–54, 65, 76, 79, 120, 124
Base Air Inspector 166, **167**, 168
Base Tactical Inspector 169–170
La Bassée Canal 143
"battle fatigue" 139; *see also* combat fatigue
Battle of Lys 35
Baumgartner, Richard 203–204, 209, 220
Bayonvillers 92
Beauchamp, Lt. F.E. 120
Beaverton, Ontario, Canada 23
Becquigny 56
Beechwood Park 17, 146
Bell, Alexander Graham 12
Berlin Wall 178
Bertangles 31–32, 49, 51, 66, 97, 113, 127, 130–139
Birks 23
Birley, James 40
Birmingham, Alabama 89
Bishop, William A. (Billy) 4, 6, 65
Black Friday 159
Blenheim Castle 70
Blériot monoplane 14
Blücher-Yorck Offensive 51, 64, 66; *see also* Third Battle of the Aisne
Bneun, B. 188
Boelcke, Oswald 3, 5, 91, 121–122
Boer War 99, 107
Böhme, Erwin 4–5
Book of Psalms 212
Boonton, New Jersey 198

Bootlegging 153–154
Boston, Massachusetts 148
Boulogne 100–102, 108, 140
Bradley, Gen. Omar N. 170–171
Bray 41, 47, 79, 87
Brecht, Bertolt: "Questions from a Worker Who Reads" 5
Briggs Lawrence County Public Library 2
Bristol F. 2 Fighter 20, 33–34, 51, 100–101, 118, 128, 131
British Base Hospital 140
British Embassy 179
British Medium Mark A Whippet tank 120–121
British Third Army 132
Brown, Capt. R.A. 1
Brubaker, James Gordon 152
Bruno, Harry 101
Bryant, Wilma 212, 216, 219
"Buckingham Palace" 70, **70**, 83, 108, 113, 129, 131, 133–134
Bueschel, Richard M.: *Japanese Code Names* and *Japanese Aircraft Insignia, Camouflage, and Markings* 182
Buffalo, New York 18
Buffington, Lt. F.J. 146, 157; *see also* "Dave"
Bumble-Puppy 46, 68, 72, 87, 111, 184, 214
Burwash Hall 20; *see also* University of Toronto

C-47 166
C-54 166
Cabrera, Miguel 3
Cachy 76
Cadet Course No. 8 20, 82, 101
Café Royale 27, 29, 100, 102
Caidin, Martin 151
Caix 64, 83, 95, 115, 120
Callahan, Lawrence 65
Callender, Alvin A. 24, 65, 101
Cambrai 119
Cambridge, Ohio 5
Camp Atterbury, Indiana 173
Camp Borden, Ontario, Canada 23–24, 26, 101
Camp Mohawk, Deseronto, Canada 26, 101, 104
Camp Rathburn, Ontario, Canada 22–23, 101, 104
Campbell, Fred 163
Canadian Expeditionary Force 19–20, 23
Canadian Explosives, Ltd. 19–20, 100
Canadian Pacific Line 143
Canche River 31
Candas 31
Canonsburg, Pennsylvania 213
Cappy 85, 135
Carnegie, Andrew 10

Carr, William 107
Carroll, Gov. Julian M. 208
Carson City, Nevada 212
Century Magazine 18
Cerisy 90
Chanute, Octave 10–11; *Progress in Flying Machines* 9
Charles S. Grey Deaconess Hospital 157
Château-Thierry 55, 64, 109–110
Chattis Hill, England 22, 27–28, 112
Chaulnes 49–50, 74, 83, 119–120, 124, 127, 130, 134
Cheesman, E. Frank 179–180, **180**, 187–190, 192, 194–196, 207, 218–219, 225–229
Chemin des Dames Ridge 52–53
Chillicothe, Ohio 175
Chippily 79, 90
Chips 36, 61, 71, 73
Chrysler Motor Company 162
Church of the Nazarene 174
Cincinnati, Ohio 15, 146–147, 151
Cincinnati Butcher's Supplies 160
Cincinnati Enquirer 209
Civil Defense 173–174
Clancy, Donald (Don) 183; "Over Ohio" 183
Clarke, Kaye 203
Claxton, William Gordon 65, 82, 100–101, 104–105, 108
Clemenceau, Georges 58
Coal Grove, Ohio 174–175
Coblenz 48, 83
Coffman, Edward M. 198
Cold War 178
Cole, Bill 215
Coles, F.W. 229–230
Colesburg, South Africa 183
Collier's: The National Weekly 18
Collins, José 104
Collishaw, Raymond 4, 6, 183–185, 191, 194, 207, 210
"Colonel Lambert Still Flying Legend" 230
Colonel William C. Lambert Development District 208
Columbia Club 162
Columbus, Ohio 1, 5, 169, 202, 210
Columbus Citizen-Journal 211
The Columbus Dispatch 183
"combat fatigue" 30, 68, 139, 141; *see also* (PTSD)
Combat Report 2, 7, 17, 22–24, 26, 27, 32, 34, 38–39, 45, 54, 56, 62, 67, 71, 89, 114, 119, 122, 124, 131, 136, 140–141, 146, 150–151, 156, 167, 175, 178–180, 182–185, 189, 191–192, 196, 198, 200–202, 204, 207–208, 210–211, 213–216, 220, 225–226, 228

"Combat Report" (rough-draft) 36, 62, 73
Combined Chin Rests and Pipe Supports patent 161; *see also* "Dry Ez Adjustable Pipe Rest"
Commanding Officer 166
Compiegne 55, 70
Compliance & Coordinating Officer 168
Compton, Lt. H. Neville 22
Conestoga wagons 48
Consolidated Aircraft Supply and Maintenance Company 154
Conteville 31–34, 47, 49, 51–52, 54–56, 58, 60–61, 63–66, **66**, 68–69, **70**, 71–72, 74, 76, 78–79, 81–82, 84–87, 89, 93, 95–97, 104, 108, 110, 112–113, **115**, 116, 119, 124, 126–127, 129, 131–133, 183–184
Coolidge, Calvin 159
Copper Hill, Tennessee **148**
Corbie 44, 112
Crimea 64
Cross & Cockade 186, 197–198, 212
Cross & Cockade Journal 207–208, 212–213, 225
Crossen, Lt. E.P. 46, 53–54, 64–65, 67–68
Crouch, Tim 10
Curtiss, Glenn 18–19
Curtiss Flying School 21
Curtiss J.N. 4 (Jenny) 22–24, 27, 145, 147–149, 151, 157

Daedalians Club (Order of Daedaians) 201, 205, 209, 216
Daley, Lt. John E.A.R. 34, 36–37, 41–42, 44, 50–51, 53–54, 56, 58–67, 73–75, 78–79, 81–82, 84–91, 93–97, 99, 110–112, 114, 121, 127, 136, 212
Daley's Theatre 104, 106
Dallas, Texas 197
Daniels, John T. 13
"Danny" 152
Darling Lili 204
"Dave" 145–147, 148, 151, 153–154; *see also* Buffington, Lt. F.J.
Dawe, Lt. James J. 37, 50–51, 56, 64, 67–68, 73, 85, 183
Dawn Patrol 45
Dayton, Ohio 2, 5, 9–11, **109**, 131, 136, 147, 149, 151, 153–155, 173, 179, 200–201
DC-3 166
Degoutte, Gen. Jean 109
de Havilland DH. 82 Tiger Moth 215
Denver, Colorado 220
Department of Aeronautics at the National Air and Space Museum

Index

10th *see also* Smithsonian Institution
de Salis, Francis 190–191
Deviosse, Dominique 210–211
D.F.W. **115**, 116–117
D.H. 4 (Airco) 46, 49, 71–72
D.H. 9 (Airco) 47–49, 180
DiMaggio, Joseph D. (Joe) 3
Dippel, John 104
Directorate of History and Heritage 2, 19; *see also* National Defence Headquarters, Ottawa
Distinguished Flying Cross (DFC) 3, 104–105, 108–109, **109**, 110, 151, 214, 218
Ditchingham Hall 107
d'Olive, Charles R. 197
Dompierre 41
Doolittle, Gen. James H. 171
Dorignies 184, 194
Doubleday 186, 189
Doughboy Historical Society Memorial 220
Dow Field 170
Drake, Sir Francis 14
"Dry Ez Adjustable Pipe Rest" 161–162
Dudgeon, James 213

Eastern Airlines 6, 181, 226
Eaton, George T. 164
Eder, Jack 212
Edinburgh, Scotland 213
8th Fighter Command 171
Eisenhower, Dwight D. 4, 174
Elks Club 205, 209
Engineering Officer 166, 168
Estrees 126, 132
Etain Air Base 178
Experimental Aircraft Association Air Museum Foundation 196

Fairborn, Ohio 201
Fairland School District 210
Falkland Island War 143
Fareham, England 212
Farrell, Capt. Conway M.G. 46, 49, 54, 61, 67, 79
Ferdinand, Franz 13
Ferguson, Art 211
First U.S. Army 171
Fisher, Elizabeth 15
Flanders front 52
Flood of 1937 160
Flying Enterprises 197
Foch, Ferdinand 66, 110, 119, 132
Fokker D VII 37, 48–50, 62–63, 66–67, 71–72, 75–76, 77, 78–84, 91–93, 107, 113, 116–117, 122, 125–126, 128–129, 132, 136–138, 141, 183–184, 196, 198, 211, 214–215, 219, 225, 227, 228
Fokker Dr. 1 (Fokker triplane) 5, 33, 35, 45, 47, 49, 66–67, 78–82

Folkstone, England 102
Ford, Henry 158
Forson, Clyda 152, 168, 202–203, 218, 220
Forson, Clyde Miller 152
Fort Hayes Exchange 164
Foster, Beulah 218
Foster, Lt. George B. 65, 67–68, 72, 82
Foucacourt 132
Founder's Day parade 18
Fouquescourt 129
14th Division 67
Fourth of July 16–17, 90, 93, 97; *see also* Independence Day
Fox, James 197
Foxx, James E. (Jimmy) 3
Franken, Harry: "Ace Pilot was Reluctant War Hero" 211
Frankfort, Germany 177
Franklin, Wisconsin 196
Franks, Norman 207, 225–230; *Fokker Dr I Aces of World War 1*; *Above the Trenches* 207, 225
Fresnoy 136
Frey, Dana 2, 178
Frey, Royal D. 2, 18, 175–180, 195, 207–209, 218–219, 221, 225–228, 230; "The Unknown Ace" 207
Frey, Stacey 2, 178
Frigidaire 160
Fromelles 51
Funderbuck, Thomas 185

Gall, Joseph (Joe): "World War I Ace Flew 'Noisy Toy'" 182–183
Gallipolis, Ohio 175
General Dynamics 63, 162, 200, 202
General Electric Company 160
General Motors Corporation 6, 162
Gentile, Dominic S. (Don) 5–6
George, Lloyd 135
George III, King of England 90
George V, King of England 20, 26, 79, 90, 105
Geraghty, Lt. W.G.C. 139
German 18th Army 68
Gilfillan, Dean 161
Gillman, Norman 212–213
"Ginnie" 213
Gladstone, Manitoba 105
Glasebrook, C.R. (Rick) 212
Glasebrook Foundation 212
Glenn, John H. 5
Göring, Herman 1
Gotha GV 48, 51
Grant, Ulysses S. 4
Great Depression 159–160, 162
Greenup, Kentucky 16, 87, 186
Grenier Field, New Hampshire 7, 166, **167**, 168–171, 192, 200

Grider, John McGavock 65
Ground Control Approach landing system (GCA) 165–166
Gulf of Tonkin 176
Gulf of Tonkin Incident 176
Gumbert, George, Jr. 198
Guttman, Jon 212

Haggard, H. Rider 107
Haig, Sir Douglas 119, 132, 183
Haigh, Lt. J.S. 130, 135
Halberstadt 56, 66, 72, 118–119, 126–128
Halifax, Nova Scotia 26, 144
Hall, Henry 146
Hamel 46, 52, 90–91, 95
Hammersley, Lt. Reuben 34–35, 48–51
Hampshire, England 27
Hangard 34, 45, 59
Hangard Wood 43
Hangest 72, 81
Hanging Rock 145–146
Hanging Rock Iron Company 18, 20
Hannover C 51, 128–129
Harding, Warren G. 154–155
Harleyford Publications, Ltd 179
Harold Ober Associates 214
Harries, Lt. Thomas M. 76, 85, 88, 93, 113, 125–126, 136–137
Harrison, Lt. E. 46
Harrison, William Henry 4
The Harvard Club 162
Haslam, Capt. E.B. (Teddy) 226–227, 229–230
Haubourdin Aerodrome 135
Le Havre 103
Hayes, Theodore (Ted) **180**
Hazell, Maj. Tom Falcon 77, 87, 90–91, 93, 97, 110, 120, 129, 132, 136
Hazirjian, Virginia 189
Hebron, Ohio 197
Hebron Military Museum 197
"Hellen" 147, 151–152, 213
Hellett, Lt. T.T.B. 36–37, 44, 49–50, 56, 58, 61, 70–71, 74–76, 83–86, 90, 110, 113, 125–126, 136
Hell's Angels 45, 160
Henrite Products Corporation 173
Henrites Products Company 163, 173; *see also* Henrite Products Corporation
HH-43 Huskie 6
Higham, Robin 151, 212, 214
Hiroshima, Japan 173
Histon, Arthur 162
"History of Aviation" 211
Hodges, Bill 197
Hoekstra, Harold 209
Hollebeke 51
Holton, Maine 7, 166, 171
Home Establishment 143, 154

Horace Le Gris Cigar Stand 162
Horatio 4
Hornoy 38
Howlett, Amy 189–190
Huffaker, E.C.: *On Soaring Flight* 10
Hughes, Howard 160
Huntington, West Virginia 203–204, 221

Iaccaci, Capt. August Thayer 65, 101
Iaccaci, Lt. Paul Thayer 65, 101
Ignaucourt 50, 95
Immelmann turn 63
Independence Day 16, 97; *see also* Fourth of July
Indianapolis, Indiana 159
Indianapolis 500 Race 158
Industrial Machine Design 174–175, **175**
Ironton, Ohio 1–2, 4, 6, 14, 15–21, 23, 26, 98, 145, 147, 153, **159**, 169, 173–176, 179, **180**, 203, 205, 208–209, 215, 218, 226
Ironton City Directories 156, 158, 160, 173–174
The Ironton News 26, **180**
Ironton Register 146
Ironton Tribune 211, 213–215

Jacobs, Josef 214
Jagdstaffel (*Staffel*) 5, 56
Jagdstaffel 7 214
James V. Hayes Funeral Home 218
Jaray, Cornell 186–188
Jasta 4 124
Jasta 10 124
Jasta 11 124
Jenkins, Kentucky 148
Jermyn Court 102, 105–106, 108, 185
Jim 36, 61, 71, 73
Jo-Lin Health Center 216, 219
Johnson, Capt. George, O. 1, 36–37, 39, 41, 43, 45–46, 53, 56, 58, 61–65, 67, 70–72, 74–77, 185, 192, 210
"Judie" 152, 213
Julian-Otte, Vanessa 210–211
Junkers J-I 72–73

Kelvinator 160
Kemmel 119
Kennikat Press 186–188, 190
Kenova, West Virginia 174
Kentucky Aviation Museum 220
Kentucky Colonel 208
"Kentucky's Ambassador of Good Will" 208
Kepner, Gen. William E. 171
Keystone Kops 149
Kilduff, Peter: *Herman Göring Fighter Ace: The World War I Career of Germany's Most Infamous Airman* 1
Kimber *see* William Kimber and Company, Ltd
King's Cliffe, Northampton 177
"King's Shilling" 79
Kingston, Jamaica 87
Kinston, New York 210
Kitty Hawk, North Carolina 10–13, 16
Korda, Michael: *Hero: The Life and Legend of Lawrence of Arabia* 3
Korean War 178
Kueber, Harold 188–189

Lackawanna Steel Company 18, 20
Lahm, Frank P. 5–6
Lake Simcoe 23
Lambert, Carl (brother to William C. Lambert) 16, 54, 65, 156
Lambert, Chloe Ann (Forson, Brubaker) 152, 154, 156, 158, 162, 164–173, 178–179, **180**, 200, 202–203, 205, 218
Lambert, Reuben (uncle to William C. Lambert) 15
Lambert, William (father to William C. Lambert) 15
Lambert, William (grandfather to William C. Lambert 15
Lambert Brothers and Company 15
Lambert Cadet 70442 20
Lambert Electric Company 160, 163
LaMotte 36, 46, 52, 61, 85–86, 88, 90, 93
Lane, Kelly (mother) 210
Langley, Samuel Pierpont 9, 12; *Story of Experiments in Mechanical Flight and Experiments in Aerodynamics* 9–10
La Rhone rotary engine 27
"The Last Patrol" 198
Lausche, Gov. Frank 174
Lawrence County Civil Defense **174**
Lawrence County General Hospital 217
Lawrence County Museum 2
Lawson, Capt. E.A.C. 98, 138
LeMay, Curtiss E. 5
Letchworth, Herts, England 179
Levisay, Sarah Ruth 210
Lewisburg, West Virginia 136
Lexington, Kentucky 149, 198
Liberty engine 158
Library of Congress 220
Liege 51
Lilienthal, Otto 9–11: *The Problem of Flying* and *Practical Experiments in Soaring* 10
Lindbergh, Charles A. 6

Lindeburg, Lt. E.W. 34–35, 49, 67
Lindsay, Vachel: "Abraham Lincoln Walks at Midnight" 14
Little, Brown and Company 189
Liverpool, England 26, 143
Lomme Aerodrome 135
London 29, 48, 52, 74–75, 89, 95, 100, 103–109, 112, 141, 143, 179, 210, 220
Long Branch, Ontario, Canada 21–22
Louisville, Kentucky 211
Louisville and Nashville (L & N) Railroad 147, 149
Lowe, Capt. Cyril N. 43, 46, 49, 53–54, 67–68, 78
Löwenhardt, Erich 38, 124
Lucas estate 146
Luce River 39, 95–97, 115, 117–118, 120, 123
Ludendorff, Gen. Erich 51–53, 61, 64, 66, 83, 87, 109, 119
Luftwaffe Interrogation Center 177
Luke, Frank Jr. 1–2
L.V.G. C 58, 64, 72, 125–126, 128–129

MacCracken, William P. 159
MacDonald, Capt. I.D.R. 38–39, 46, 49–50, 53–54, 56, 61–65, 67–68, 72, 76–77
Mack Sennett Bathing Beauties 149
Mackenzie, John 191
Madden, Michael 210
U.S.S. *Maddox* 176
Mahan, Kenneth M. 212
Maid of the Mountains 104, 106–107
Main de Massiges 109
Manchester, New Hampshire 168, 171
Manila, Philippines 172
Mannheim 51, 83
Manning, Russell 182, 207
Mannock, Edward C. (Mick) 4, 6, 48, 51, 54, 113–115, 213
Marcelcave 33, 50, 56, 58, 64, 97
Maricourt 79, 85
Mark, Lt. Ronald T. 48–49, 54–55, 59
Marmon (automobile) 158–159, 200
Marmon, Harold 158
Marmon, Howard 158
Marmon, Walter 158
Marmon Wasp 158
Marne River 55, 64, 110
Martin, Phyllis 204, 217
Martin, William (Bill) 2, 16, 22, 151–152, 157, 175, 179–180, 183, 193, 195, 198, 200, 204–206, 209–212, 215–222; "America's Forgotten Ace" 183, 215
Marting Hospital 157

Matigny 31
Matthews, Alec 136
Matz River 70
Mayborn, Mitch 197–198
Mayne, Donald (Don) **180**
McCook Field 131
McCudden, Maj. James T.B. 113, 190; *Communiqués* 190
McDougall, Lt. P.A. 51, 56
McElroy, Capt. George E. 31–34, 81, 114–115, 182, 213
McGrath, Robert 182, 188–191
McGraw-Hill Publishers 186
McKinley, William 12
McMurtrie, Lt. E.G. 46, 54, 58
Means, James: *Aeronautical Annuals* for 1895, 1896, and 1897 9
Medal of Honor 6
S.S. *Megantic* 26
S.S. *Melita (Meleta)* 143–144
Memorial Day 215
Menzies, Lt. J.T. 139
Mericourt 126
Messerschmitt Me-110 177
Metz 51, 54
Mézières 43
Miami Beach, Florida (Miami) 166, 168, 177
Michael Spring Offensive 5, 31, 131
Military Cross 49
Miller, Rep. Clarence E. 208
Miller, Lt. J.A. 71
Miller, Linda 209
Milliard, Capt. Peter L. 171
Ministry of Defence, Great Britain 143
Missoula, Montana 220
Mitchell, Silas Weir 142
Model T 158
Montdidier 38, 52, 55–56, 69, 119, 124
Monthly Weather Review 10
Montigny 32
Montreal, Canada 26
Montreuil 31
Moore, Sid 215, 220
Moreuil 31, 34, 41, 46, 51, 55–56, 58, 66, 71, 75, 118
Morlancourt 119
Morning Irontonian 156
"Morning Patrol" (print) 215
Morristown, Tennessee 173
Morrow, Capt. Ernest T. 100
Moselle River 83
Mother-Sill Sea Sick Remedy 27
Mouillard Louis-Pierre: *Empire of the Air* 10
Mt. Kilimanjaro 141
Murnahan, Kristy 214–215

Nagasaki, Japan 173
Nardine, John 213
National Air and Space Museum 10; *see also* Smithsonian Institution
National Archives, Kew 2
National Defence Headquarters, Ottawa 2, 19
National History Day 215
National Personnel Records Center 165
Nazer, Doris 218
Neal, Squire W.H. 146
Nelson, Horatio 1st Viscount Nelson 5
Nesle 136–137
Neurasthenia 142
New York City 144, 162, 212, 214
The New York Times 17
Nickie (Lambert's dog) 168–169
Nieuports 69
1911 Bennett trophy 18
Ninth Air Force 166
Nissie (Lambert's dog) **174**
No. 2 Auxiliary School of Aerial Gunnery 29
No. 3 Squadron 131
No. 4 Squadron Royal Australian Air Force 80–81
"No. 20 Bristol" (person) 102, 105–108
No. 20 Squadron 65, 100, 102, 113
No. 22 Squadron 51
No. 23 Squadron 31, 137
"No. 24 cavalry" 71
No. 24 Squadron 1, 4, 24, 28, 30–31, 33, 36, 39, 41–43, 46, 48–56, 59, 61–62, 64–65, 68–69, 71, 73, 75, **77**, 78–79, 81–82, 94–95, 98, 104, 106, 108, 110, 113, **115**, 116–118, 123–125, 130–132, -134–136, 140, 179, 181–184, 194–196, 213, 229
No. 32 Squadron 101
No. 40 Squadron 81, 114, 182
No. 41 Squadron 65, 85, 100
No. 42 Aero Squadron 16
No. 46 Squadron 139
No. 48 Squadron 131, 139
No. 49 Squadron 47
No. 56 Squadron 112, 182
No. 62 Squadron 100
No. 74 Squadron 51
No. 78 Squadron 26
No. 80 C.R.S. 22
No. 85 Squadron 65, 133
No. 133 Eagle Squadron 6
No. 203 Squadron 207
No. 205 Squadron 46, 49, 71
No. 209 Squadron 1, 45, 47–48, 131
Nobel, Canada 19, 22, 100, 123
Normandy 196
North Atlantic Division of the Air Transport Command 170
Northeastland Hotel 172

Norwich, England 107
Noyon 58, 69, 71

Oberursel, Germany 177; *see also* Luftwaffe Interrogation Center
Obsessive Compulsive Disorder (O.C.D.) 205
Ohio Air National Guard 178
Ohio Defense Corps (ODC) 173
Ohio Historical Center 210
Ohio Historical Society's "The Seventeenth Star" 210, 219
Ohio House of Representatives 208
Ohio Military Reserve 173
Ohio River 15, 23, 26, 87, 160, 186, 204, 208, 218, 226
The Ohio State University 177–178
Ohio's Commission on Aging 212
Ohio's Heritage 182–183, 208–209
Oise River 58, 68
Olive Foundry and Machine Shops 15
Olympia, Washington 164
Operation Gneisenau 66–67, 70
Orlando, Florida 106, 211
Orrmant, Arthur 185
Ottawa, Canada 19
Ottoman Empire 14
OX 5 Aviation Pioneers 213
OX-5 engine 145
OX 5 News 213

P-38 Lightning 177
P-47 Thunderbolts 6
P-51 Mustangs 6, 158
Pacific Southwest Airlines 211
Packard Motor Company 162
Palentine, Illinois 198
Palentine High School 198
Palmer, Lt. John 49, 53, 58–60, 67, 69, 71, 110–111
Panneau signals 26
Pardoe, Blaine: *Terror of the Autumn Skies: The True Story of Frank Luke, America's Rogue Ace of World War I* 1
Paris 51–53, 58, 61, 66, 70, 79, 89, 170, 211
"Paris Guns" 53
Parks, James 214, 220
Parry Sound 20
Parvillers 129
Passmore, Lt. F.S. 59, 79
Pathé-Cinema Company 148, 211
Pathway Magazine 201
Patrick (Lambert's dog) 204, 216–217
Pearl Harbor, Hawaii 6
Pengelly, Colin: *Albert Ball V.C.: The Fighter Pilot Hero of World War I* 1
Penotte, Dr. Paul **180**

Index

Peronne 41
Perry Sound, Canada 100
Pershing, Gen. John J. (Black Jack) 4
Pétain, Gen. Henri P. 67, 83
Peterson, Arlene J. 210
Peyton, David 201
Pfalz D-III 33, 35, 38–39, 41, 46–51, 53, 60–61, 91–92, 128
The Philadelphia Inquirer 17
Piazza, Capt. Carlos 14
Pierce-Arrow 158–159
Pilot Certificate No. 9367 26
Pilot's Flying Log Book (Lambert's Log book) 2, 22–23, 32, 35, 37–38, 54, 56, 67, 71, 138, 214, 220, 225
Piqua, Ohio 5–6
Pitsenbarger, William H. 5–6
Pitt, Barrie 185
Pittsburgh, Pennsylvania 15
Ploesti Oil Fields 166
Poberezny, Paul E. 196–197
Poe, Gen. Bryce 216
Portsmouth, Ohio 159, 173
Post, August 18
Post-Traumatic Stress Disorder (PTSD) 30, 139, 141–143, 145, 149, 154, 178
Pour le Mérite 76
Pratt, David 20
Pratt & Whitney R-1830-65 Twin Wasps engines 166
Prentice-Hall 189, 191
Preservation of Military Aviation History 212
Presque Isle, Maine 7, 166, 169–171, **172**, 192, 200
Princeton, West Virginia 218
Princeton Club 162
Privy Council 42
Proctorville, Ohio 210
Prohibition 146
Proust, Marcel: *Remembrance of Things Past* 59
Proyard 46, 119–120
Public Record Office 230
Pujols, Albert 3
Pulmonary Embolism Atrial Fibrillation 218; *see also* Arteriosclerotic Heart Disease (ASHD)
Purple Heart 177

Queen Alexandra's Hospital 140
Le Quesnal 82
Quirnheim, Col. Mertz von 119

The Radio Shop 160
R.A.F. Battle of Britain party 210
R.A.F. Benevolent Fund 218–219
R.A.F. Widows and Orphans Fund 218
Rafusa Fliers 146–147
Raidor, Lonnie 186
Raleigh, Sir Walter 14
Rathbun, Richard 9
Red Cross 100
Redler, Lt. Herbert Bolton 35, 213
Reidenbach, Millie 197
Republic F-84 Thunderjets 178
Research Division at Wright-Patterson Air Force Base 176
Revell, Alex: *Brief Glory: The Life of Arthur Rhys Davids, DSO, MC and Bar* 1
Rheims 41, 53, 55, 109
Rhineback Air Drome Museum 210
Rhode, Bill: *Bailing Wire, Chewing Gum, and Guts: The Story of the Gates Flying Circus* 188
Rhys Davids, Arthur 1–2
Rich Oil Company 175
Richards, Gen. George 164
Richthofen, Lothar Von 124
Richthofen, Manfred Von 1, 3–5, 24, 37–38, 88, 91, 194, 201–202, 204, 210, 219, 226
"Richthofen's crowd" 34; Richthofen's hunting ground 37; Richthofen's territory 36
Richthofen's Fighter Group (Jasta) 184
Rickenbacker, Edward V. (Eddie) 1, 3, 5–6, 14, 28, 32, 176–178, 181–182, 191, 208, 220, 225–226, 230
Rio Grande, Ohio 201
Rist, Donald 179
Rist, Edward 162
Riverview Park 156–157
Robeson, Maj. V.A.H. 55, 73, 76, 79, 85, 89, 99, 104, 108–110, 119, 131, 134, 139
Robinson, Deana 214–215
Rochford, Capt. Leonard ("Tich" or "Titch") 184–185, 194
Rock Hill Junior High School 214
Rogers, Floyd "Slats" 153
Rollot 68
Rome, New York 166, 168, 170
Roosevelt, Theodore 12
Roosevelt Hospital 157
Rorison, Lt. J.A. 133
Roscoe, Turner 147–148
Rosiéres 34, 43, 56, 58, 64, 67, 74, 81, 86–87, 94–96, 116, 125, 130, 134
"Roster of War Birds" 183, 187
Royal Air Force (R.A.F.) 1, 2, 3, 6, 42, 48, 51, 65, 67, 85, 89, 100, 104, 106, 110, 112–116, 124, 130, 143, 146, 148, 168, 179, 181, 184–185, 218, 220, 227–228; *see* Royal Flying Corps, Royal Naval Air Service
Royal Air Force Museum 195–196, 218–220
Royal Air Force Museum Foundation 195
Royal Aircraft Factory R.E. 8 34, 112, 123
Royal Automobile Club 100–102, 104, 106–108
Royal Canadian Air Force (R.C.A.F.) 7, 164
Royal Flying Corps (R.F.C.) 6, 14, 18–20, 23–26, 29, 30, 94, 100, 143, 146, 166, 179, 184–185, 204, 214–215
Royal Naval Air Service (R.N.A.S.) 6, 143, 184
Royal Scottish Automobile Club 42
Roye 38, 69, 78, 120, 136
Roye-Amiens Road 185
Ruhl, Arthur: "The Aeroplane: The Annals of Aviation in the Attempt to Fly Lengthwise Rather Than Downward" 18
Rumey, Lt. Fritz 56
Ruth, George H. (Babe) 3
The Ryan and Gilfillan Company 158–160

Safety Officer 170
Saigon, South Vietnam 6
St. Germain, Ray 209–210
St. John, New Brunswick 143–144
St. Joseph's Church 218
St. Lawrence valley 26
St. Louis, Missouri 20, 165
St. Omer 65, 82
St. Paul, Minnesota 209
St. Quentin 143
Salmond, Gen. Sir John Maitland 43
San Pablo, California 210
Savoy Hotel 102
Sayer, M.P. 195–196
Scharff, Hanns 177–178
Schmutzler, Sgt. 46
School of Aeronautics 21
Scientific American 18
Scout Experimental 5 (S.E.5) 27–28, 30–32, 36–37, 44–48, 50–51, 55, 58, 60–61, 67, 72, 74–76, 79–80, 82–85, 88, 91–93, 95–96, 98, 110, 118–119, 125, 127–130, 196–198, 215, 219
Scout Experimental 5a (S.E.5a) 5, 30, 32, 45–46, 204
Scriven, Gen. George P. 18
Second Battle of Aisne 52
Second Battle of Amiens 119, 130
Second Battle of the Marne 109
Selwyn, Capt. W. 33–34, 36–37, 41–42, 58, 61, 67, 70–72, 74–76, 78–79, 81–86, 88, 90, 91, 93–95, 97–99, 110–111, 113, 116–121, 124–126, 130–132, 136–137, 139

Index

Sennett, Mack 149, **150**
Shakespeare, William 4
shell shock 6, 30, 139, 141–142; *see also* (PTSD)
Sherwin-Williams 149
Siwik, Ronald 197
Smeaton's coefficient 11
Smith, Adrian 113
Smith, Claire 214
Smith, David 211
Smith, James 197
Smith, Robert 16, 19, 78–79, 98, 148–149, 160, 173, 192
Smith, Susan 220
Smithsonian Annual Report 9
Smithsonian Institution 9, 10
Soissons 41, 52, 55, 110
Somme battlefield 125
Somme bridges 124
Somme Offensive 40
Somme River 36, 47, 51–52, 55, 74, 76, 78–79, 87, 90, 106, 112, 132, 215; Somme bridges 124
Sopwith Camel 5, 27–28, 36–37, 46–48, 51, 80–81, 95, 118, 121–122, 131, 133, 185, 194, 198, 215
Sopwith Dolphin 32, 116, 118, 122, 131, 137, 227
Sopwith F.I Camel with Bentley 184
Sopwith Scout (Pup) 27, 29
Souain 109
South, Lt. H.R. 70, 131, 134
Southey, Lt. John H. (Jack) 38, 50, 56, 64–65, 67–68, 70, 72, 76, **77**, 78, 83, 99, 110, 120, 183–184, 194, 210, 213, 219
Spa 118
Spads 27–28, 31–32, 55, 69, 118, 131, 137
Sport Aviation 196–197
Springs, Elliott White 65
Staerker, Klaus 6–7, 151, 154, 200–201, 204–206, 209, 212, 215–217, 222
Stalag Luft I 177
Station Hospital at Fort Hayes 164
Steenblik, Jan 189
Stewart, Elmer 161–162
Stewart, Samuel (Sam) 186
Stinson, Edward "Eddie" 145–146
Stinson Aircraft Company 145
Stirling, Lt. W.C. 135
Stockbridge, England 27–29, 32
Strand Palace 102, 108
Strayer, Larry 203–204, 209
Stuart, Jesse 186, 193–194, 216, 219
Stutz Bearcat 158
Sullivan, Steve 198
Sunflower Press 151
Supermarine Spitfire 6
Sykes, Maj. Gen. Sir Frederick Hugh 43

"Talk of the Town" **180**
Tanner, John 195–196
Tarbutt, Lt. 112
Taunton, W.J. 181, 225–230
Taylor 23
Taylor, Charlie 12
Taylor, Zachary 4
Ternoise River 31
Text Book on Aerial Gunnery 24
Thames 13
Thiescourt 68
Thionville 55, 83
Third Battle of the Aisne 40, 51–52, 58, 61, 64, 66; *see also* Blücher-Yorck Offensive
Thomas, Sandra 189
Thornton, Tammy 214–215
Thorpe, Rev. William 197, 201–203, 205–206
333rd Sub-Depot 168–170
"Tiny" 213
"Tom Blue Berry" 148, 154, 213
Tomb of the Unknown Soldier 4
Toronto, Canada 19–20, 22, 100, 153
Towler, Mike 211
Trafalgar 5
Trenchard, Hugh 48
Trenchard's Independent Air Force 48
Trèves 83
Turnberry Scotland 29
20th Fighter Group 177
"25 Years Ago" 26
Twiggs (dog) 168–169

Udet, Ernst 124
Ulanoff, Stanley 186–189
Ulysses 3
U.S. Air Force 173, 218
U.S. Air Force Museum 2, 5, 103, **109**, 136, 173, 176, 177–178, 181, 195, 201–202, 210, 212, 214, 219–220, 227
U.S Air Force Museum Foundation 219
U.S. Air Force Museum Research Division 2
U.S. Air Force Reserve 7, 173
U.S. Army 18
U.S. Army Air Corps 7, 106, 165, 177
U.S. Army Air Service (Forces) 16, 26, 145, 168
U.S. Army Board of Ordnance and Fortifications 9
U.S. Congress 144
U.S. Marine Corps 7, 164
U.S. National Archives and Records 2
U.S. Weather Bureau 10
University of Toronto 20–21
University of Wisconsin 198
University of Wyoming Transportation History Foundation 220
Uppstrom, Richard (Dick) 177, 212, 219–220

Vaire Wood 90
Verdun, France 178
Versailles Treaty 154
"A Very Strange Story" 19, 22
Vesle River 53
HMS *Victory* 5
Vietnam War 143, 176
Villers-Bretonneux 32–33, 36, 39, 41, 43, 52, 61, 74–75, 86, 94–95, 112, 115, 126
Vladivostok 135
Voelter, Karl 213
Volstead Act (18th Amendment, Prohibition) 153–154
Voss, Werner 38

Wapakoneta, Ohio 4
Warfusée 32, 49, 64, 90, 92
Washington, George 4
Washington, D.C. 9, 10, 144, 179, 215
Waterloo, Iowa 197
Watkins, Lt. J.R. 120, 124
WBNS-TV 210
Weir, William Douglas, 1st Viscount 42–43
Wells, H.G.: *Tono-Bungay* 13; *The War in the Air* 17
Wellston, Ohio 173
Wenz, Alfred 124
West Roxbury, Massachusetts 182
West Seneca, New York 18
Westervelt, Bob 212
White House 70
White Star Airline 211
Whitman, Dr. Armitage 162
Wiencourt 61, 64, 115, 123
Wilhelm II, Kaiser of Germany 119
William Kimber and Company, Ltd. 189–191, 208
Wills, Kelly 207
Wilson, Lt. E.B. 32, 34, 37, 42, 48, 51, 56, 58, 61, 66–67, 70–72, 74, 78, 88
Wilson, Elizabeth 202
Wimereux 140
Windsor Castle 70
"Wing Structures for Airplanes" (patent) 161
Wings 45
Wolff, Lt. 46
Woodstock, Ontario, Canada 36
Woolf, Virginia 102
World War I Aero Bookshop 182
World War I Reunion 176
Wren, Lt. A. 83–86, 88, 90, 110, 113, 118, 125–126, 136
Wright, Orville 9–13
Wright, Wilbur 9–13

Wright Brothers (Wrights) 5, 9–13, 17–18
Wright Brothers-built Model B 17
Wright Cycle Company 9
Wright Field, Dayton, Ohio 173
Wright Flyer 13
Wright-Patterson Air Force Base 176, 178–179, 200–201, 205, 209, 219–220
Wright State University Special Collections and Archives 2, 220–221
WSAZ-TV 221
Wüsthoff, Lt. Kurt 76, 77, 183–184

Yale Club 162
Yeates, Victor M.: "Winged Victory" 27–28
Yonk, Mon. John J. 218
Yonkers, New York 162

www.ingramcontent.com/pod-product-compliance
Ingram Content Group UK Ltd.
Pitfield, Milton Keynes, MK11 3LW, UK
UKHW050538150426
5217IPUK00026B/1989